ALLAH'S ANGELS

ALLAH'S ANGELS

Chechen Women in War

Paul J. Murphy

Naval Institute Press
Annapolis, Maryland

Naval Institute Press
291 Wood Road
Annapolis, MD 21402

Library of Congress Cataloging-in-Publication Data

Murphy, Paul J.
    Allah's angels : Chechen women in war / Paul J. Murphy.
        p. cm.
    Includes bibliographical references and index.
    ISBN 978-1-59114-542-4 (hardcover : alk. paper) 1. Chechnia (Russia)—History—Civil War, 1994—Women. 2. Women—Russia (Federation)—Chechnia. 3. Women and war—Russia (Federation)—Chechnia. I. Title.
    DK511.C37M87 2010
    947.086--dc22

                                                                                    2010037896

Printed in the United States of America on acid-free paper

14 13 12 11 10   9 8 7 6 5 4 3 2
First printing

Time in its irresistible and ceaseless flow carries along on its flood all created things and drowns them in the depths of obscurity. . . . But the tale of history forms a very strong bulwark against the stream of time, and checks to some extent its irresistible flow and, of all things done it, as many as history has taken over, it secures and binds together, and does not allow them to slip away into the abyss of oblivion.

Anna Comnena, the *Alexiad*

Contents

Preface ix
Prologue 1

ONE
Mat Ogni: The Traditional Chechen Woman 7

TWO
Welcome to Hell! 27

THREE
The Pain Continues 67

FOUR
Baking Bread 102

FIVE
The Sisterhood 136

SIX
Mountains of Bodies 166

SEVEN
I'm Not Who You Think I Am   197

EIGHT
Rising from the Ashes   220

NINE
Saving Pompeii   256

Notes   273
Index   279

Preface

I BEGAN COLLECTING material for *Allah's Angels* while still living in Russia and shortly before my earlier book *The Wolves of Islam: Russia and the Faces of Chechen Terror* was published in 2004. It has been a challenging task.

There's a wealth of information in the Russian-language realm on the recent Chechen wars and terrorism, particularly if you live in Moscow. Just pick up any Russian newspaper; the television is replete with video footage and daily reportage; so are the law enforcement, court, media, and separatist websites, as is my own (translated from the Russian) *Russia-Eurasia Terror Watch* (www.retwa.com). But comparatively little is found on the ordinary Chechen woman and her wartime roles.

I needed to go to Chechnya, but it wasn't a matter of just hopping on a plane and flying to Grozny to interview women on the street. That became particularly problematic after the Chechen Jihadist website www.Kavkazcenter.com, angered by something I had said in a 2005 interview, branded me a CIA "special agent" in the pay of the "monstrous [Putin] regime." Despite official travel restrictions and what happened to *Forbes* magazine journalist Paul Klebnikov, I quietly lobbied to go anyway. There was a fleeting opportunity in 2007, but it wasn't until the spring of 2009 that I was finally told I could make the trip, the ten-year designation of Chechnya as a KTO

(Counterterror Operations) zone having been lifted. By then the manuscript was just about complete anyway.

The respected Moscow-based Human Rights Center "Memorial" provided the best single source of written information. Still, "Memorial" reports on only about 30 percent of the territory of Chechnya—which, for the reader who doesn't know, consists of roughly six thousand square miles situated on the northern slopes of the Greater Caucasus, in the Chechen plain, and the Terek-Kuma lowlands of southern Russia. The wartime interviews of Chechen refugees conducted by Human Rights Watch provided other valuable information, and the nongovernmental organization (NGO) Union Women of the Don has produced some valuable research on Chechen women, which I cite in the book.

Except for Yulia Yuzik's 2003 work on female suicide bombers—*Nevestiy Allakha* (Allah's Brides)—there are no books on Chechen women. I have cited Yuzik's and other works on the Chechen wars and terrorism where they are used. I have also drawn on information in such important English-language books as Dr. Khassan Baiev's *The Oath* (2003); Asne Seierstad's *The Angel of Grozny: Orphans of a Forgotten War* (2008); Anna Politkovskaya's *A Russian Diary* (2007) and *A Small Corner of Hell: Dispatches from Chechnya* (2003); and Anne Nivat's *Chienne de Guerre: A Woman Reporter behind the Lines of the War in Chechnya* (2001).

The human factor has been critical for this book. *Allah's Angels,* like my earlier book, would not have been possible without the many hours of conversation, discussions, debates, arguments; the thoughtful contributions of countless people over the course of a decade living in Russia; and my work in Congress on a counterterrorism cooperation project with the Russian State Duma. Each person I spoke with had something unique to say. Most were generous in sharing information. Some told me their personal stories; others contributed firsthand knowledge of places and events; while still others offered strong opinions, guidance, and suggestions, read portions of the manuscript, and even corrected factual errors. It's not necessary or even desirable to mention all of them here, but they include former Chechen students of mine, professors and political analysts, Russian policemen and soldiers, journalists, Russian politicians and a longtime friend in Russia's diplomatic corps, Chechen human rights activists, and Chechen friends and acquaintances in Russia and elsewhere I have come to know over the years.

I am especially indebted to Elza P——, a Chechen teacher of Russian, and to Said S——, a former translator for Djokhar Dudayev, the first Chechen president, who graciously tolerated my endless questions over the course of several years and tried to guide me through the intricacies of Chechen culture. If I have made mistakes here, it is because I didn't listen carefully enough or missed a nuance along the way.

I would also like to thank Gistam Sakayeva, a former Chechen war refugee and today a board member of the Grozny-based NGO Reliance, which provides assistance to victims of gender-based violence and helps single and widowed women build self-sufficient lives. She was kind enough to share with me some of her insights into today's women's rights issues and the problem of gender-based violence in Chechnya.

I am also grateful to Senator Aleksandr Torshin, the deputy speaker of the Federation Council, Russia's upper house of parliament, and its foremost expert on the North Caucasus, for sharing his unique insights and perspectives with me in the spring of 2009.

I also had valuable conversations with Ousam Baysayev, a Radio Free Europe/Radio Liberty reporter; and Milana Bakaeva, a vibrant twenty-seven-year-old Chechen woman I met in Washington, D.C., in June 2007, when she was promoting her wonderful new book *Danser sur les ruines. Une jeunesse tchétchène* (Dancing on the Ruins: A Chechen Youth). She is now with the Human Rights Center "Memorial." I refer to Milana in my book by her pen name, "Terloeva."

Thanks must also go out to the website www.KavkazWeb.net for facilitating a valuable two-hour "live chat" session with people from the North Caucasus in 2007. Also, I have learned many new things from anonymous people all over the world who have contacted me over the years at www.retwa.com.

I regret that I wasn't able to meet with Ilyas Akhmadov, President Maskhadov's foreign minister, who is now living in political asylum in the United States. Understandably, he is a difficult person to contact, and despite the intercession of his American handler, he declined to meet with me.

This has been an ambitious and difficult book. I intended to write about women and children but quickly understood that that cannot be done in one book. I had also hoped to complete a manuscript in a couple of years after *Wolves of Islam*. It's taken five, but I believe *Allah's Angels* is better for it, because I have had more time to reflect and rethink events and history. Moreover, time has confirmed the central theme of the book: that death constantly haunts the Chechen woman and, despite the tremendous rebuilding that is going on in Chechnya today, peace and sanity remain elusive for her.

It has also been an emotionally trying book to write. I'm deeply saddened by the enormous pain and suffering of the Chechen people, on the one hand, and by the killing of innocent Russian civilians in senseless suicide attacks, on the other. I loathe the shameful looting, raping, and killing of innocent Chechens by some Russian soldiers, but I am equally horrified by the images of severed heads of Russian soldiers pounded onto stakes and soldiers' castrated and bullet-riddled bodies hanging from wooden crosses.

No matter whom you speak to, emotions run high on all sides on the subject of the recent Chechen wars. I believe I have presented a fair and balanced account here. At the same time, I understand that there will be those who will be displeased, offended, and even angered by some of the things I have to say. I hasten to add that the conclusions drawn in this book are mine alone and should not be attributed to the people I have mentioned unless that is specifically stated.

For my critics, I acknowledge that *Allah's Angels: Chechen Women in War* is necessarily incomplete and flawed. Not everything that needs to be said can be put into a single book, so some subjects and personages do not get as much attention as they should, while others may be left out altogether. Moreover, the story is dynamic, and "new chapters" are being written every day.

Finally, I am reminded of what the great historian Bertram D. Wolfe wrote in his *Three Who Made a Revolution:* "One's book begins to seem unfinished as soon as it is completed. Things said in closing chapters suggest changes in earlier ones. . . .While the book is on press, the writer is already making changes in proof. When he looks at the first bound copy, his satisfaction diminishes as 'typos' leap out of its pages, and fresh questions arise in his mind about things which yesterday seemed so certain."

Prologue

"FOR THE FIRST TIME in many years I'm full of hope. Things are getting better. Life is returning to normal. I'm almost scared to say so, but I'm starting to think that I've made it out [of these wars] alive," Natasha confided to her close friend in the early spring.

She didn't.

Her lifeless, handcuffed body with two small, perfectly round bullet holes in the back of her head and three more in her chest lay crumpled up in the tall grass of a ditch, barely visible from the busy road above on that hot mid-July afternoon in 2009.

The fifty-year-old woman had been missing since early morning. Meticulously punctual, she had been absent for an important ten o'clock appointment. Colleagues had been frantically calling her cell phone all day, and Lana, her fifteen-year-old daughter, stood impatiently waiting to be picked up from school.

Neighbors saw and heard everything—the four masked men who snatched her off the street a block from her house at half past eight that morning; her cries for help; the brutes punching her in the face; even the blood splattering from her mouth as her kidnappers threw her into the back of the white Zhiguli car and sped away. They knew why she had been taken.

Natasha was a despised critic of "Little Stalin," as she secretly called the ruler of her tiny corner of the earth. Her embarrassing exposé about the summer execution of Rizvan in his underwear in the village square for helping Islamic Jihadists had particularly angered Little Stalin; so had her refusal to wear a headscarf. Natasha's endless investigations into the kidnappings, secret arrests, and midnight house burnings were "only confusing the people," "actually helping the militant scum."

Friends had told her there were powerful people out to get her. She even fled to England once because of it. "People warned her—I warned her that if she came back, someday she would die," her close friend Fatima Tlisova reflects. "Why? Why, did she do what she did? Because she was a Chechen. Because these were her people."

Natasha's story is not thriller fiction. Natalya Estimirova—Natasha, as her friends called her—was a living human being with a soul, and she didn't deserve to die this way. A former history teacher and tireless human rights activist for the respected Moscow-based Human Rights Center "Memorial" since 2000, she was slain because of her high-profile, probing investigations into human rights abuses in President Ramzan Kadyrov's (Little Stalin's) Chechnya.

"She spoke the truth. She openly, sometimes even harshly, assessed some processes which happen in our country," Russia's president, Dimitry Medvedev, told his public. In the United States she was eulogized as "devoted to shining a light on human rights abuses," as "uncompromising in her willingness to reveal the truth wherever that might lead," and as "speaking out on behalf of people whose suffering was ignored."

In 2004, Natasha received the Swedish Parliament's "Right to Existence" Prize for her courage and dedication to human dignity. The European Parliament's Robert Schumann Medal followed in 2005, and the Anna Politkovskaya RAW-in-War award in 2007.

"Last night I was thinking how much she took with her; how much information; how many people will be left like orphans," Tlisova laments. "I don't think someone can replace her. It is an invaluable loss for Chechnya." Natasha will be missed.

ON THE FRONT LINES OF BATTLE

In life, Natasha Estimirova shone as a beacon of truth. In passing, she exposed yet another, final shameful truth—that death constantly stalks the Chechen woman, that peace and sanity remain elusive for her in Ramzan Kadyrov's Chechnya.

Natasha's tragedy is the story of every Chechen woman who over the past decade and a half has had to endure incomprehensible pain and suffering caused by two apocalyptic wars with Russia and by the present conflict with Islamic Jihadists bent on carving out a new Taliban-like Islamic state in Chechnya and the North Caucasus.

In 1991 the former Soviet Air Forces general and rebel Chechen president Dzokhar Dudayev unilaterally declared Chechnya independent of the Soviet Union. Chechen military forces, powerful warlords with private armies and hired foreign Islamic mercenaries, independence fighters, Islamic extremists, criminals, and terrorists—and ordinary Chechens, too—have been fighting Russia ever since.

Chechnya won the first war (1994–96). The second began when Chechen warlord Shamil Basayev crossed into neighboring Dagestan (Russia's sovereign territory) to establish a new Islamic state—a "pure Islamic land" that would be wiped clean of Russian "infidels." This physical act of war, accompanied by a declaration of holy war (Jihad) against Russia and the 1999 terrorist bombings of apartment buildings in Moscow, started the second war.[1] Russian military forces soon completed the destruction of Chechnya begun five years earlier, leaving a decimated population.

Chechnya is physically very different today. A shiny new "European city" is rising from the ashes of Grozny, the republic's once desolate capital where dogs gnawed on rotting corpses. Mothers are pushing their babies in strollers in newly built parks decorated with fountains, and kids are back in school. Even a new world-class mosque, the largest in Europe, capable of accommodating up to ten thousand people, has been built.

Gudermes, Chechnya's second-largest city, is simply beautiful now. With its sixteen-story apartment complexes and a Disneyland-style aquapark with large separate pools for men and women, with its cafés and restaurants, it has nothing physically left to remind the visitor that there was ever a war here.

Rebuilding is going on everywhere, but behind this modern-day Potemkin's village façade of peace and tranquility, a vicious terror and counterterror war is raging. I once had real hope for Chechnya. Shamil Basayev was killed by a truckload of his own explosives in July 2006. The next year, kidnappings were down, and attacks on Russian forces and the Chechen government were fewer. Senator Aleksandr Torshin, the deputy speaker of the Federation Council, was very upbeat when I spoke with him in Washington, D.C., in the spring of 2009. Chechnya was quickly being rebuilt, there were fewer than a hundred fighters (he said) left in the mountains, and the decade-old KTO (Counterterror Operations) regime had come to an end. I was told that I could finally go for a visit.

But within a month suicide bombers were back at work in the heart of Grozny. Twelve would blow themselves up by year's end, and no one dared go near a park trash can, because there might be a bomb in it. Kidnappings had reached epidemic proportions by the summer (twice as many as in 2008). Murders like that of Natasha and Rizvan soared. Little Stalin began holding families directly responsible for their Jihadist relatives' actions; more and more homes were burned, and Kadyrov swore he would kill anyone with the slightest "stench of Wahhabism." Violence again spiraled out of control.

The Chechen woman has been on the front lines of battle since 1994. Each has experienced her own kind of pain, but all are the true casualties and principal victims of these bloody wars. Years of daily violence, mother's grief, and the fight for the survival of her family has changed how the traditional Chechen woman lives and left her exhausted, with deep physical and mental scars. A reluctant participant, she has ventured far beyond her traditional roles in Chechnya's strongly patriarchal society to become a stronger, more courageous, and self-reliant human being.

But today her wartime contributions are underappreciated. Men are resentful of the woman's new roles, and the rights she has earned are being taken away in the name of traditional Islam. Violence against women is accepted, even encouraged in certain instances, and is definitely on the rise. She is again being gunned down, blown up by Jihadists' bombs, kidnapped, snatched off the street for interrogation about her "terrorist" relatives, her house burned because she is suspected of aiding and abetting Wolves (Jihadist fighters).[2] She is again forced to marry somebody she doesn't even know, killed if she behaves "immorally" or dares to speak the truth about human rights abuses, and told that she is the "property" of her husband and that her proper place is in the kitchen.

HER INCREDIBLE JOURNEY

The pages that follow tell the story of the Chechen woman's incredible journey from Grozny's pits of hell in 1994—dodging bombs and bullets, hiding her daughters from rapists, and scavenging for food—through the years of killing, the moral decay, insanity, searching for her men, and dealing with the greed, deceit, depression, thoughts of suicide, and the multitude of human beings turned into beasts in the second war—to her present dilemma.

The story would be incomplete without also the women who fight on the side of the Chechen Jihad, the wives who accompany their husbands into the mountains, cook, clean, and engage in combat; the snipers who hide in wait for young Russian officers to appear on the battlefields; the "Black Widows," who perpetrate unimaginable violence, killing with their insidious suicide bombs; and the women who collect intelligence, hide arms, provide safe houses and food to fighters, act as couriers with money, and play a host of other vital noncombatant roles without which today's Jihad could not function.

Anyone who has read *The Wolves of Islam: Russia and the Faces of Chechen Terror* knows that I have no sympathy for those who seize theater-goers and schoolchildren as hostages, take the lives of innocent young people at rock concerts, or blow up Russian passenger planes full of people. I was asked in a 2005 interview with *Russian Profile* magazine why Chechen women do these horrible things—"Are they all desperate housewives widowed by Russian soldiers killing for personal revenge?" The reader will see that the answer is infinitely more complex, that it has as much to do with why Wolves adopted suicide terror to fight Russia in the first place as it does with why women carry it out.

Extreme violence is at the core of the Chechen woman's story. The graphic descriptions in this book of war, rage, ethnic hatred, moral decay, blood revenge, barbaric human cruelty, and disregard for human and women's rights will shock, repulse, and even anger the reader.

It's not my intention to leave the reader with a sense of utter hopelessness for Chechnya; I do not believe that extreme violence is endemic to Chechen society. But this endless Jihad and the circle of violence in which Natasha became trapped is perpetuating it. The Jihadists must be stopped, but Ramzan Kadyrov's vile mockery of human dignity and his self-invented system of "mountain justice" have gone too far. I believe that people have become more terrified of Little Stalin and his secret police than they are of the Jihadists.

The Chechens are a warm and wonderful people, with rich traditions. They prize freedom, work hard, and have strong blood and family ties. I'm confident Chechnya will recover physically, but I am afraid that society's wounds will not; they will take generations to heal. But that process can be hastened if the Chechen woman is allowed to play her rightful role.

ONE

Mat Ogni: The Traditional
Chechen Woman

I ONCE SAW AN AD in the English-language newspaper the *Moscow Times* that read, "American man seeks Chechen girl for marriage." The advertiser was surely dreaming of the beautiful, kind-hearted, tender, affectionate, caring, and unselfish bride so romantically described in Chechen literature and tradition. I doubt that he ever found his girl. If he had, she would have been considerably more complex than he could have ever imagined.

It's true, young Chechen girls possess all the ideal outer and inner qualities of beauty, but what the American probably didn't know is that their identities are solidly grounded in centuries-old tradition; in Islam; in adherence to strict social, ethical, and moral codes that define right and wrong as well as how they must behave in any situation; a hierarchy of values; strong Chechen family orientation; and the very real conviction that marriage to a foreigner is the best way of ruining any chance of having a happy family life.

THE COOK, THE CLEANER, THE PEACEKEEPER

The woman's traditional role in Chechnya's family-oriented, patriarchal society centers on the household. She is the *mat ogni,* "keeper of the home fires," "guardian of the hearth," while her husband is the traditional breadwinner and head of the family.

The kitchen is her chief domain. "My husband doesn't even know where the cups are," Elza P—— tells me. "Cooking is the woman's business and the man has no business in the kitchen," she adds. It is forbidden turf; I begin to feel uncomfortable even standing there talking to her about it.

Regardless of the woman's education, her job outside the home, the increased independence she has gained because of the recent wars, even her contemporary role as the breadwinner in many households, she is supposed to understand that her "highest duty," her real purpose in life, is to be a good wife and mother—to cook, clean house and make it comfortable for her husband, carry water (real men don't do that), have babies (four to five are ideal), and raise and educate the children in traditional family and societal values. This includes shielding the children from their father's bad side and always portraying him as the ideal husband and father, even if he beats her. Women are, in the words of one woman, not exactly happy with their role as "the serving soldiers" of Chechnya's patriarchal society.

She is also the traditional guardian of peace. Tradition says that the Chechen woman has a remarkable power to prevent bloodshed between two Chechen men by simply removing her shawl from her shoulders or throwing her handkerchief to the ground. Teenage girls have stopped fights between romantic suitors this way, just as a Chechen woman is supposed to have the power to stop a blood feud.

Tradition also says that blood vengeance, punishment, and murder are prohibited in her presence, that if the enemy of a Chechen man touches the hem of a woman's dress, the Chechen man must lay down his weapon because his enemy is protected by that woman. Military combatants are also supposed to stop fighting if a woman appears on the battlefield. It's too bad nobody respects these peacekeeping traditions anymore.

The woman's authority and value in traditional Chechen society is supposed to derive from these roles, making her life twice as valuable as that of a man's. "We believe that women are more valuable than men, as reflected in the proverb that the life of a woman is worth two men," Dr. Khassan Baiev, a Chechen surgeon, writes in his book *The Oath: A Chechen Surgeon under Fire*.[1] This value is reflected in another Chechen tradition, that if a man takes the life of a Chechen woman or rapes her, male members of her family have the right to extract "blood vengeance" by taking the lives of two males of the offender's family.

As long as she conforms to her expected roles, the Chechen woman commands respect and honor in traditional Chechen society. Zalpa Bersanova, a

Chechen ethnographer, in 2004 described respect for women as the second-most "sacred Chechen value." The moral behavior of both men and women is the first. This book challenges some of Bersanova's assumptions.

Men traditionally rise to their feet to greet a woman; shaking hands, though, is taboo. They will offer her a seat but may themselves remain standing, as many Chechen men are nervous in female company. This is particularly true in the company of in-laws, out of fear of doing something that might be interpreted as a sign of disrespect. "My grandfather couldn't sit down in the presence of a woman," Said S—— tells me.

Respect toward a mother-in-law and a wife's relatives will earn the man a special place in "paradise" (heaven). Disrespect will bring him disgrace.

Tradition also says that Chechen men are bound to protect the honor of a woman. This is illustrated by an old tale about a man who asks a woman for overnight shelter without realizing that she is home alone. Tradition prohibits her from refusing, so she serves him dinner and makes a bed for him. In the morning, the man realizes that the woman is alone and has stayed awake all night. As he's washing up and preparing to leave, he accidentally brushes his little finger against the woman's hand. To protect her honor, the man cuts off his finger before leaving.

In 2000 Khava Barayeva, Chechnya's first female suicide bomber, appealed to the tradition of protecting a woman's honor to inspire Chechen men to go to Jihad against Russia. She told a video camera before driving her explosives-laden truck into a Russian police enclave in Alkhan-Kala, "Our forefathers would have killed anyone who tried to touch their women, but today Muslim women are getting attacked and raped in front of those who claim to be men—they have no sense of jealously for the honor of their Muslim sisters to the extent that they sit [at home] and drink tea while listening to this appalling news. Do you consider yourselves men?"

Women still don't participate in the decision making of the governing *teipes* (communities of several clans sharing common territory and equal social status) to which they belong, and they have traditionally not held public office, but that's changing. President Djokhar Dudayev's general procurator, Elza Shapirova, was one exception. But even in her case, Chechnya's history books say that "she never forgot her higher duty." The four women who were elected to the Chechen parliament on 27 November 2005 are also exceptions. Surely they haven't forgotten their "higher duty" either.

A little Chechen girl is taught at an early age ethical norms, customs, and etiquette regarding her proper role in the family and society. She grows up knowing that she must be the weaker of the sexes, to be subordinate to the male, to know that her husband will be the head of the household and the most important person in the family, and that her wishes and ambitions must always come second. This helps explain why so many Chechen men are reluctant to marry girls who come from fatherless families, especially in this day and time. They're afraid she won't know her proper place, will misbehave, disobey, and treat her husband disrespectfully.

There was even a time when a young bride wasn't allowed to speak with members of her husband's family or even sit at the same dinner table, but strict adherence to that tradition faded in the cities during the Soviet era. The tradition still prevails in some high mountain regions, where neither the woman nor the children are allowed to sit down and eat at the same table with the man. He eats first, the children second, and the mother last.

If the husband has male friends over, his wife will usually not sit down with them, even if politely invited to do so. "We're not interested in hearing gossip between two men about another man's wife," Elza P—— pipes up as I talk with her husband about these things. The woman is obliged instead to bring finely prepared dishes of food from the kitchen and attend to the guests.

If men are talking in public and the topic turns to "male conversation" or politics, the Chechen woman will likely excuse herself. During Soviet times it was dangerous for a woman to overhear a conversation about politics. It still is.

It's taboo to discuss family affairs and problems outside the home. Even today, many women are reluctant to consult a male doctor about female health problems. Nor do men and women who are not married to one another talk about such taboo subjects as sex and childbirth.

The Chechen woman is bound by tradition to be a proper lady at all times, and inappropriate behavior can make her subject to severe and even violent sanctions. She mustn't cut her hair short or ever be seen in a pair of jeans or pants. She traditionally dresses in bright colors and wears a head scarf, though she doesn't hide her face in public.

The practice of veiling and wearing the long, head-to-toe, black, Arab-style robe is not traditional in Chechnya. Despite the immense pressure that Wahhabis put on Chechen women in the 1990s to wear the traditional Muslim dress, few complied. "Their dress was unacceptable for our society," Aza, a middle aged Chechen woman, says. "They were demanding that women wear very strict *hijab* outfits. For centuries our women didn't wear the hijab, and we didn't have such strict rules."

"I never saw more than probably a hundred women wearing that kind of dress," Said S—— adds. Said does remember a friend who studied in Saudi Arabia and insisted that his wife wear the traditional custom when he came home. She refused. "Of course, women don't like to be commanded around!" Elza P—— retorts.

A young girl shouldn't go wandering about on her own. For one thing, she risks being kidnapped for marriage or ransom, or worse still, forced into becoming a suicide bomber. If she goes out, she's obliged at least to tell her brother where she's going and what time she'll be home. In earlier times, she would never go anywhere alone; she was always accompanied by a male member of the household.

In public the Chechen woman walks behind the man, because once upon a time Chechnya's narrow mountain paths were rife with wild beasts, highway robbers, and deadly enemies, and it was the man's job to protect the woman. There are fewer wild beasts now, but otherwise things haven't changed much.

MARRIAGE FOR LOVE

Chechen men marry girls who are healthy, attractive, and have untarnished reputations, who will be obedient and hard workers. Marriage comes early, usually in a girl's sixteenth year, although marrying much earlier isn't unusual nowadays. Fourteen- and fifteen-year-olds marrying has become more common; many never finish school. A twelve-year-old girl married in 2008.

Salina was only thirteen when she married Khasan, a man of forty who had never been married. Her parents had been killed by a Russian missile, and her grandmother, having fallen ill and no longer able to take care of her, had decided Salina should be taken out of school and married off to somebody who could.

Khasan was a kind and loving husband. Salina gave birth to her first son a year after their marriage and her second at age fifteen. Now she lives with her husband's family, because Khasan went missing—simply disappeared without a trace—just before her sixteenth birthday.[2]

"Age doesn't matter. Once a girl has had her period she is ready for marriage. Even if she is twelve years old, she is a woman," says Khozh-Akhmed

Kadyrov, head of Chechnya's Council of Muftis and cousin of the late Chechen president Akhmad Kadyrov.

What's more important than age is that the girl be "pure, physically and religiously."

Girls are required to marry outside their own clan, and marriage between blood relatives as far as seven generations back is strictly prohibited.

Like everything else, the courtship and wedding are steeped in strict rules and rich tradition, with lots of ritual and chivalry. A "date" constitutes a meeting in a public place to talk, but physical contact of any kind, even holding hands, is strictly forbidden. Public affection is taboo anytime. Boys and girls, even husbands and wives, don't hold hands, hug, or kiss outside the home.

Marriage is one of four critical events in a Chechen woman's life. As in being born, dying, and giving birth, second chances are rare, so she has to get it right the first time. That's why she's very selective in her choice of a man. There was a time when a girl wouldn't marry a man unless he had killed at least one Russian soldier. Today, she's more concerned about his being from an "intelligent family" and having a job. She usually knows who his parents are and everything else there is to know about him. Her brothers are very protective and will learn all about her suitor if they don't already know him.

If she has multiple suitors—which is rare nowadays, because of the shortage of men caused by the wars—she will politely inform each that she will soon make her choice (that is, if she isn't kidnapped for marriage first or the suitors don't kill one another). The unlucky men are obliged to accept her rejection with dignity and show no emotion, as any such display would be shameful and unmanly.

The lucky man, for his part, now has the impossible task of convincing the bride's family that he is worthy of her, and he must obtain from her father (or eldest brother, if the father is deceased) a blessing and her hand in marriage. If her father approves, the wedding usually takes place on a Sunday, beginning at noon. Wedding vows are taken separately. The process begins when the bride is taken to the home of the groom's friend or relative—"neutral territory"—never to the bridegroom's house.

A mullah conducts the ceremonies in front of "two reliable witnesses." He goes to the bride first and determines whether she is marrying of her own free will and if she will take the man to be her husband. He also asks the bride's father if he consents to the marriage. If he objects, the mullah will try to persuade him otherwise. Elza P—— told me of one case in which the mullah spent three days with the family, but the stubborn father wouldn't budge. The mullah has the right to act in the name of the father in such cases. Once this matter is settled, he advises the bride of her duties as a wife and blesses the wedding. The wedding is now half-complete.

The mullah next goes to the groom, who has been in seclusion and contemplation for three days, and asks him if he will take the woman to be his bride. He too is advised of his marital duties. The couple is now officially married.

Now, the real festivities begin, but only the groom's family celebrates. The bride is whisked from her temporary quarters by motorcade to the husband's family home, escorted by her husband's best friend or relative and her female escort. The bride sits in the back seat of the lavishly decorated car.

It's a crazy journey. Baiev describes his wife's own experience: "On the hood of the Lincoln, tied down by yellow ribbons, was a red and yellow prayer rug, and a propped-up baby doll dressed in a miniature white wedding dress—a symbol of fertility and happiness. The cars slowly wound through the potholed streets of Alkhan-Kala, honking their horns, young men fired off Kalashnikov rifles, and boys strung ropes across the road, stopping the cars until passengers coughed up coins."[3]

A transparent fabric is fancily draped in a special corner of the groom's house where the bride in all her glowing beauty receives guests. "I looked like a New Year's [Christmas] tree," Lisa Mekhidova recalls about her wedding day in the Chechen-produced Masha Novikova documentary *Three Comrades*. The bride welcomes the children first, hugs them, and slips a few rubles into their pockets or purses to bring her luck in bearing children.

The exchange of money is an important ritual in any Chechen wedding. The male escort gives money to the bride's female escort. And the groom's family gives money to the parents of the bride to buy her things—clothing, a ring, etc.—for the wedding. It may be only a ceremonial gift if the bride's family has plenty of money. What is important is that the gesture be made.

The wedding reception is exhausting for the bride. A feast awaits her guests. Male friends and relatives of the groom arrive at the house with bouquets of flowers in hand and ask the bride's "permission" to eat and drink.

Of course, she says yes, but she herself must remain standing and otherwise silent, despite their taunting and joking attempts to "untie her tongue." The men toast to her health and happiness and leave money in a vase or plate, her father-in-law making the biggest contribution.

The bride's family is absent from the big event—they're at home "mourning" the loss of their daughter. Nor does the groom attend. He has his own celebration with his friends. These parties are raucous and often get out of hand. On Sunday, 26 November 2006, drunken friends of the groom firing a Kalashnikov rifle from an apartment balcony in the Leninsky District of Grozny killed twelve-year-old Seda Albiyeva playing in the yard below.

As long as she's single, the daughter is under the guardianship of her family. But once she marries, she becomes the total responsibility and the "property" of her husband. She isn't allowed to visit her family unless he gives his approval. She addresses her husband's parents simply as "Mama" and "Papa," or "Nana" and "Dyada," never by their first or last names.

SHE WILL BE MY WIFE!

The age-old "beautiful Caucasian custom" of "bride stealing" might be unpopular with modern-day women, but it's a tradition as old as the North Caucasus itself and is alive and well with young men as an alternative way of finding a bride. Men swear that "stronger marriages" come out of it than from "marriages for love." Such "theft" brought jail sentences in Soviet times, and sometimes it still does.

The way this kind of marriage proposal works is that the boy abducts, with his friends, the girl of his dreams at a time when she is most vulnerable—coming home from school, going to work, shopping, etc. They grab her and hustle her into a waiting car, then shuttle her from one hideout to another so the police or her relatives can't find her.

The kidnapper will try very hard to cajole his prized catch into marrying him, while his parents or other relatives pay a cordial visit to her parents with an offer of money for her hand in marriage. If her parents reject the offer, she will ideally be returned home with her "honor" intact. But more often than not, economic circumstances compel them to accept whatever her kidnapper has to offer.

"She will be my wife! I will steal her, as I've helped steal five brides for my friends. . . . Madina will come to love me when she knows me better," twenty-eight-year-old Aslan told Asiyat Vazayeva, a Chechen reporter who did a story on bride-stealing for the Institute of War and Peace Reporting in the summer of 2003.

Nineteen-year-old Aina, a pretty flower shop woman working in Nazran, Ingushetia, was kidnapped too. "As I was choosing the flowers, one of them [the kidnapper's friends] seized me by the waist and dragged me out of the shop to a car. At first I didn't understand what was going on. My sisters tried to rescue me, but two of the guys held them back. I tried to resist, but what could I do against two strong men? They threw me in the car and took me away. . . . They took me to the old people. I said I didn't agree and they took me home. . . . That was the worst night of my life."

A twenty-one-year-old jobless man grabbed Tamila, also twenty-one, a student at Nazran university, while she was attending classes:

> I hoped that when I mentioned my boyfriend, he [the kidnapper] would calm down, but he got even more angry. He began to threaten that he would deprive me of my honor and I would be forced to stay with him anyway. I said I would rather die than live with a beast like him. A fight broke out in the courtyard and they [his friends] were going to take me somewhere else. But luckily the boy's father turned out to be a decent man and when he heard I didn't agree, he put me in his car and took me home.

Another man, Kh. A. Dzagiyev, by now has served out his prison sentence for his 2006 bout with lovesickness. In September of that year he and his friends were near the bus station in Malgobek, Ingushetia, when he saw a pretty woman he just had to have. He grabbed her in front a large crowd, including a traffic policeman, who promptly arrested him for attempted kidnapping.

Salambek Shikhabov and Said-Emi Raduyev, both from the settlement of Komsomolskoye, Chechnya, will be spending the next few years behind bars for their failed attempt to steal a bride. On 28 August 2008 a drunken Shikhabov persuaded his friend to help him kidnap a woman who did not even know Shikhabov. She was with her mother on their way home when

Shikhabov and his friend grabbed her and tried to push her into their car. But she was strong and fought back. Shikhabov smacked her around, but with the help of her mother she broke free. "I have no intention of marrying the uncivilized brute," she told the court.

Nineteen-year-old Diana (not her real name) was not so lucky. Diana's abductor snatched her from a small village in Chechnya and persuaded her to marry him, but that was only the beginning of her nightmare. Her husband abused her and repeatedly beat her. She finally divorced him and returned home to live with her parents, but then her mother died, and her father raped her.[4]

Despite protests and even court convictions, many woman do end up marrying their abductors. Elza P—— tells me that a woman who is kidnapped knows very well that the man is risking his life for her. After all, he could be sent to jail or even killed by her relatives. For that reason, "he must be very much in love with her." Mariyat Muskeyeva, a Chechen government cultural official, agrees: "It's a sign that a man really loves her. If a woman can tell her children that their father kidnapped her, it's a great love story."

During Soviet times, a kidnapped woman would often marry her kidnapper because she didn't want to ruin his future. A woman might also agree because an unmarried woman has no status in society. She may also feel pressured to marry her kidnapper, especially if his family is a good one. And of course, some women even dream of being kidnapped by a handsome, wealthy stranger.

Others feel sorry for their abductors. Fifteen-year-old Shumist Kadyrova ran barefoot across a mountain meadow to escape from her forty-five-year-old abductor, but his friends caught up with her. They married days later and lived happily ever after. "He was a nice man, a good soul. He had a good heart," she says. She pitied him because he couldn't find a wife his own age.

Still other women succumb to suitors who persist, even after prison. Fatima's family had her young kidnapper arrested, prosecuted, and imprisoned for three years. But after he got out of prison, he pursued her so aggressively that Fatima married him after all.

There are consensual abductions too. Ruslan Chamchayev carried out a "friendly abduction" of his bride Aminat in the mid-1990s. Both star in the *Three Comrades* film. They dated for months, then he asked her to marry him. "I wanted to say yes, but just couldn't bring myself to do it for three and a half years," Aminat says. She finally consented when he abducted her.

Things can go horribly wrong in these kidnappings. The culprit may even pay with his life. On 4 June 2008 Shamil Dachayev, the brother of eighth-grader Dachayeva, caught up with a speeding car hauling his sister away and broke out the back window with his pistol. The gun discharged, killing the kidnapper, nineteen-year-old Ilyas Umarov.

Risks are worse for the woman. If the abductor's family fails to contact her parents and she is not returned home within three days, she may be considered "soiled" and a shame to the family, and be forced to spend the rest of her life with her captor. Her parents may never let her come home.

She might also be raped, a fate worse than death itself in Chechen culture. If she is raped, she has a choice of either staying with her abductor in a forced marriage, reporting it to police and becoming a social outcast, or keeping her mouth shut. Most victims take the third option. That's why the crime is seldom reported; the shame, social stigma, and patriarchal repercussions are simply too great for most women to bear. It's as Sergei Kovalyev, President Yeltsin's human rights ombudsman, says: "You have to understand the Caucasus. It's easier for a woman to kill herself than to say 'I've been raped!'"

Some women believe the victim should kill herself: "If they [the raped women] come home, they would be better off shooting themselves. If anyone laid a hand on them they would be written off for good here in Chechnya. It's a kind of law. A sullied daughter is worse than a dead one to her father. It's a terrible disgrace. She'll never get married and no one will say a kind word to her, even though it was not her own fault she was dishonored."[5]

If a woman doesn't immediately report the rape to her mother, she will be seen as complicit (as having "encouraged" or "accepted" the rape) and therefore deserving of punishment, possibly even death.

Rape victims have even been persuaded by the religious gurus of those fighting Russia that Allah will absolve them of their "sin" if they become suicide bombers.

The easiest solution is to marry the man, solving the problem for everybody.

PRESERVING THE HONOR OF THE FAMILY

Above all, the Chechen woman is expected to preserve her family's honor. Disregard of the rules of moral behavior, bad behavior, even rape, brings shame on the entire family and can become a death sentence. There's a long tradition in Chechnya of fathers killing daughters, husbands killing wives, brothers killing sisters, and of the lives of women who shame and disgrace their families being snuffed out in "honor killings."

"The honor of the family lies in the daughter's behavior—namely, that she is virtuous, respectful, a good housekeeper, a good mother, and does not break traditions or do anything immoral," Khozh-Akhmed Kadyrov teaches.

At the very least, a man will divorce his unfaithful wife. He may also publicly humiliate and beat her or have his friends do it.

Twenty-three-year-old Malika disappeared from home in March 2006 and was reported missing. But almost a month later, when she did return home, her husband accused her of infidelity (with a Russian soldier, no less) and kicked her out of their apartment. She took refuge with her aunt, but her plight turned into horror when Argun city police showed up to "question" her. They whisked her away to a secret location, shaved her head and eyebrows, painted her scalp green (the color of Islam), smeared a black cross over her forehead, and made her confess to an affair with a Russian soldier. The fact that she was pregnant didn't matter; they stripped her and beat her with fists, sticks, and hoses until she was battered and bloody. Malika's assailants then made her dress and drove her back to her husband's apartment building, where she was forced to dance in the courtyard in front of the neighbors. "Look how ugly you are," her tormentors chanted. When she finally staggered away she was kicked a final time. She miscarried two days later.

Malika's in-laws insist that she had had an affair with a Russian serviceman—a Christian—whom she had met at the store where she worked as a cashier. She claims she was faithful to her husband, even though he beat her, and that she was kidnapped by masked men. Police say she left Chechnya voluntarily to live with her Russian lover and returned home only when things didn't work out.

The video of Malika's torture was sent by cell phone all over Argun. Other girls could learn from her transgressions.

President Kadyrov promised to punish those responsible. Natasha Estimirova reported that Malika's tormentors were formally dismissed from the police force but got new jobs in the Russian Defense Ministry's Yug and Sever battalions in Chechnya, fighting terrorists. No charges were ever brought.

Malika is lucky to be alive. Any association with a Russian soldier is strictly taboo, contrary to the mores of Chechen society, and it is likely to result in a death sentence by the woman's own family or Wahhabi militants. Elza P—— tells me that a woman who sleeps with a Russian soldier and so disgraces the family deserves to die, that her parents would welcome militants killing their daughter, saving them the trouble.

That was the fate of several Chechen women in March 2003 who were caught fraternizing with Russian soldiers in a Grozny café. They were shot in the backs of their heads.

Police suspect honor killing in the 2005 murders of seventeen-year-old Dzhanet Arsemikova and her sister Liana Bakayeva, fifteen, from Stariye Atagi. On 19 December, the bodies of both girls were found on the side of the road near the village of Shiskin Les, in the Podolsky District of the Moscow region, with gunshot wounds to the backs of their heads.

Dzhanet, a first-year university student, was the daughter of Musa Arsemikov, an official killed in the December 2002 terror attack on the Chechen government's administrative complex in Grozny. The family had moved to the Podolsky District after his death. Liana was still in high school. Both girls had accompanied their aunt, who had been visiting, to the Podolsky train station the night before.

Investigators rule out robbery as a motive for the killings, because one girl had three hundred dollars in cash and a mobile telephone in her purse, which had not been taken. Condoms were also found (but why would good Chechen girls need condoms?), and both girls were wearing short skirts, much too revealing for respectable Chechen girls.

Some believe honor killing was also responsible for the deaths of six women in Grozny in November 2008. The victims, ranging in age from twenty-five to thirty-six, were found at multiple locations around the city and its surroundings on 25–26 November, with gunshot wounds to their heads and chests. A seventh body, that of an eighteen-year-old Alkhan-Yurt girl, was found two days later. Two of the murdered women were the wives of two brothers from the village of Kurchaloi, Kurchaloyevsky District. Another victim, age twenty-nine, was a divorced woman from the Achkoi-Martanovsky District. The remaining women were from Grozny, the Groznensky District, and Dagestan.

Six bodies with similar wounds had been found in a forest near Tsentroi, Chechnya, a year earlier.

On 3 February 2009 another body, that of twenty-two-year-old Mestoyeva from the village of Komsomolskoye, Groznensky District, was found with six bullet wounds in a shallow grave in a forest three to four kilometers from the *stanitsa* (large village) of Grebenskaya, Shelkovsky District. Her older brother had shot her with a pistol on 7 January in the Leninsky District of Grozny for "immoral behavior." The Chechen court gave him only six years behind bars.

In June 2009 another older brother killed his sister in their parents' house for "immoral behavior."

Honor killings like these are numerous. "Unfortunately, we have such women who forget the rules of proper behavior [the code of conduct of women from mountain tribes]. . . . With regards to these women, their relatives, men who have been shamed by such behavior, take matters into their own hands," Chechnya's ombudsman for human rights Nurdi Nukhazhiyev told the press in his commentary on the 2008 murders.

President Kadyrov publicly condemned the murders and again called for the victims' killers to be brought to justice, but they haven't been and probably won't be. "In our tradition, if a woman leads a loose lifestyle, if she sleeps with a man, then they [her relatives] will kill them both," Kadyrov says of the murders. According to him, the seven women killed in 2008 were going abroad to work in a brothel. "It's necessary to teach sisters and daughters from childhood, so this doesn't happen to them; mothers must bring their children up properly!" he reminds families.

NEVER MARRY A FOREIGNER

Elza P—— tells me there are four things that any respectable Chechen girl knows she must never do if she wants to have a happy life: drink alcohol, smoke, cheat on her husband, and marry a foreigner (and a Russian is a foreigner).

Chechen girls rarely marry outside their ethnic group. "Such marriages usually end in disaster," Elza says. "Why?" I ask. "Because she will have a miserable life," Elza retorts, looking at me as if I should already know this.

The foreign spouse will corrupt traditional Chechen values and family traditions, making life especially miserable for the children. Moreover, the man's family may be geographically too far away, making it difficult or impossible to support the extended Chechen family in time of need. Relatives are very important in Chechen culture—the more the better, because they provide the needed social, security, and financial net.

"They [the Chechens] taught us to sleep alongside them, but not with them. We live in peace, but we each knew we were a different species. They forbade their children to marry Russians," Yevgeniya Morozova, an ethnic Russian born in Chechnya, told Czech journalist Petra Prochazkova in 2000.

President Ramzan Kadyrov is flatly against marriages to foreigners. "No! A Chechen man can marry a Russian woman, but a *Chechenka* [Chechen woman]—I am categorically against her marrying others," he told the newspaper *Komsomolskaya pravda* in January 2006.

"We don't have such a custom [of marrying a foreigner]," the mother of Amnat Nagayeva, the suicide bomber who blew up a Russian airliner in August 2004, admonishes. Amnat secretly married an Abkhazian man when her family lived in the Rostovskaya Oblast of Russia in the early 1990s, but when her father found out about it, he promptly took her away from her husband and sent her home to Chechnya.

Fatima and Sergei

Twenty-eight-year-old Fatima from Grozny forgot to follow the rules, too.

Fatima lived with her common-law Russian husband Sergei in Saint Petersburg for two and a half years before he deserted her, leaving her alone with two small children, jobless, and with only six months' rent money to live on. When I heard of Fatima's story I felt sorry for her, but I'm more sorry for the children.

Fatima had come to Saint Petersburg to study and met Sergei at the university. They dated for two years. She told her parents about the man of her dreams on one of her trips home; naturally, they were shocked and forbade her from returning to Saint Petersburg. So Fatima ran away. She and Sergei moved in together, and they had a child out of wedlock.

Both finished the university. Sergei pursued his career, while Fatima sat at home raising their son. They lived together another six months after their second boy, Artem, was born. Then one day Sergei left, leaving a little bit of money and a note behind saying he had found "true love." The bastard!

Fatima cried for three days before summoning the courage to write home about the children and what had happened. It took a while, but her father wrote back. Since none of the neighbors in Chechnya knew anything about how she had disgraced the family, she could come home, but only on one condition—she had to come alone.

Fatima took another two months to make her decision. Then one day in 2005 she walked into an orphanage in Saint Petersburg and told them that she no longer wanted her children, that she didn't need children by a Russian husband anymore, and that she had made the biggest mistake of her life by having a relationship with a Russian man.

"We were shocked. A respectable mother of Caucasus nationality brought us two well dressed, clean, but very scared children," the doctor remembers. He tried to talk Fatima out of it, but she wouldn't have it. She signed the papers and left for Chechnya the next day.

Elza P—— is right. Children do suffer the most.

Gulya and Sasha

Two-year-old Kalimat and her twenty-three-year-old Chechen mother, Gulya Morozova, are living in Russia outside the law.

Gulya has been disowned by her family, branded a "traitor." She is still afraid her relatives (nine uncles—her father left when she was a child, and her mother lives in Ukraine) will come to kill her for marrying a Russian soldier. She lives in a wood-heated, two-story house without indoor plumbing in the Rostovskaya Oblast with Kalimat and her daughter's loving father, thirty-three-year-old Aleksandr (Sasha) Morozov, a Russian contract soldier (a nonconscript, paid individual serving under contract—like our enlisted soldier), a sapper who fought in Chechnya in both wars.

Their incredible love story began in the Rai, a tiny café in the *stanitsa* of Shelkovskaya, Shelkovsky District, Chechnya. Gulya worked there while Sasha and his comrades patrolled the streets. One night he dropped in for a bite to eat. It was love at first sight.

"Something happened to me. I thought, if only I can get to know this girl, we will spend the rest of our lives together," Sasha remembers. "His friends were sitting at a table outside. He came into the kitchen. I was brushing my hair. . . . I liked him too. He was handsome. He came in every day after that, then invited me for tea, to a different café," Gulya recalls.

Sasha rented a house for Gulya, but the news spread quickly. She was shunned at the market and threatened with certain death, her windows were broken out, and bricks were thrown at her by neighbors. Sasha threw live grenades back.

In March 2001 Sasha made the decision to send Gulya to live with his relatives in Rostov, because he had been reassigned to Nozhai-Yurt and couldn't protect her anymore. But Gulya needed a passport to leave Chechnya, and it would be difficult to get one. Her birth certificate (which she always carried with her) had either been lost or stolen when she had lost consciousness after being struck by a stray bullet in 2000 in a taxi on the Dagestani-Chechen border after visiting her grandmother in the neighboring republic. Sasha obtained a substitute document, but the passport office refused to issue her a passport, either because she was considered a "collaborator" or because of bureaucratic red tape. So Sasha faked one.

Gulya was terrified of her new surroundings in Rostov: "I didn't go anywhere in the evening. I was afraid." Sasha's relatives disapproved of the relationship, and "everybody in the village looked at me—*'Chechenka'* [they would say]." Sasha came home every three or four months, stayed for a few days, and left again. Then in the summer of 2003 Gulya became pregnant.

With a baby on the way, it was vital that Gulya obtain a genuine passport so the child's birth could be officially recorded on it. Sasha and Gulya went together to the passport office, but they were immediately handcuffed, fingerprinted, photographed, and Gulya was accused of being a *shakhida* (suicide bomber).

Since Sasha was a sapper and knew all about bombs, the FSB (the Federal Security Service) was convinced that he had brought Gulya to Russia to commit an act of terrorism. It was 2003, after all: a Chechen female had blown up a bus in Mozdok (North Ossetia) that summer, two more women had killed themselves and eighteen others at a rock concert in Moscow, and another had been caught on Moscow's main street with a bomb.

Sasha's outstanding military record saved them. Gulya received a temporary passport, but only for one month. When she went back to the passport office they told her, "Get out! Girl, come back here again and we'll throw you in jail." She never went back.[6]

Leila and Stas

Two burly Chechen men stand impatiently waiting at the apartment building's entrance. Stas spots them just in the nick of time. With his heart pounding, he drops his bag of groceries, grabs his wife Leila, and they run away as fast as they can. Minutes later, they're on the first train out of the Russian city.

Leila's facing a death sentence for disgracing her family by running away and marrying a Russian contract soldier who had killed locals in Chechnya. The men at the apartment building were her relatives.

Leila and Stas (not their real names) met in Grozny's central market during the second war. Leila, who had lost her father in 1995 and a fourteen-year-old brother in the second war, and her mother were selling at the market as Stas and his unit patrolled the grounds. The scrawny, undernourished girl, who was already nineteen but looked no more than fifteen, approached Stas and his unit to sell them some beer.

"I had always dreamed of such a girl . . . such a wife. And then I looked at the smiling Leila," Stas recalls. His heart simply melted. Stas had grown up in the Kazakh city of Pavlodar, and his first love had been a young Chechen girl whose parents had forbidden marriage to a foreigner.

Leila was nearly emaciated. Stas gave her bread and fed her cans of Russian Army stewed beef, and their romance bloomed. She eventually asked him to take her away from there.

Stas's parents were kind to Leila. "I was even jealous. They gave her all the attention and constantly looked after her. Mama said to me, 'Be especially kind to her, she has lived through so much,'" Stas says. He would tuck her in at night but never cover her head. She learned to fall asleep peacefully.

Stas and Leila eventually left the village and moved to the city, where they rented a small apartment and Stas found work as a security guard. They had only been there a month when they fled with only the clothes on their back. They're safe—for now. Leila is expecting.

Zarina and Sergei

In 2005 teenager Zarina was a fugitive from home, and she too feared for her life. She probably still does.

She and her twenty-four-year-old husband Sergei, a Urals Russian policeman, met in July 2004 when Zarina's father, Said, a Chechen policeman, invited him home to dinner. Sergei was serving a six-month assignment to Chechnya at the time.

It was love at first sight. "Her eyes were like the southern nights," Sergei reminisces. He tried to obey all the rules. He never gave Zarina presents without her mother's permission; all their conversations were in front of her parents or her older sister; and he formally asked for Zarina's hand in marriage. But the answer from her parents was always the same, an emphatic "No!" So at the end of November 2004 Zarina got her own passport, and on 4 December they eloped, Zarina telling her parents that she was going to visit her grandmother.

She loved Sergei, the new jeans that she got to wear for the first time in her life, and the big, beautiful Urals city she found herself in. But her parents knew exactly where to look for her.

Said came first, insisting that she return home immediately. When she refused, he went to the authorities and accused Sergei of kidnapping his underage daughter. When that didn't work, her mother and aunt came and employed more subtle tactics. They persuaded her to come home to clear up some "family questions" created by her actions, which had caused a huge scandal in their *teip*. Zarina was told she could return to Sergei when things got resolved. But her parents didn't let her return; instead they hid her with relatives and put her under house arrest.

Sergei decided to take matters into his own hands. He went to Chechnya, used his contacts there, found out where she was being kept, and had her abducted.

The last I heard about them, they were trying to replace Zarina's passport, which she had left behind in Chechnya. She knew she had burned her bridges and couldn't return home anytime soon. She was afraid her relatives would still try to kidnap or kill her, but she was happy and determined to make a wonderful life with Sergei.

"I love him very much and want to bear his children. Who will they be, Russian or Chechen—what difference does it make? I know that they will be brave and good people—just like my Sergezha," she told the Russian writer German Petelin.

Their story first appeared on the Internet magazine *Russkiy Kurer* (www.ruscourier.ru/archive/1646) in 2006. Write-in commentary on it has been fierce ever since, much of it in support of them. Other commentary calls for their deaths and the killing of their children.

DIVORCE IS A SIN

Divorce is rare in Chechnya. Societal pressures minimize it. A family and children are respected by society if there is a father present, even if he is unemployed or the father in a polygamous marriage. The wife is expected to stick with him through thick and thin, richer or poorer, in peace and war, and even to endure his abuse if he is that kind of man.

There are serious consequences and stigmas for the divorced woman, starting with the loss of her children. The mother isn't free to simply take the children and go her own way. By tradition, they must remain with the father—who is more likely to be able to provide for them.

This is expected in Chechen society, but Russian woman too must surrender their children to their former Chechen husbands. That's what happened to celebrity pop singer Kristina Orbakaite, the daughter of Russia's singing icon Alla Pugacheva, whose former common-law husband Ruslan Baisarov kidnapped their eleven-year-old son Deni and took him to Chechnya. In September 2009 a Chechen judge, in Kristina's absence, ruled that the boy must remain with his father.

If a father dies the children remain with his family, unless the family gives permission for them to live with their mother, which is rare. Even if the children go with her, boys become part of the father's clan and are protected by it.

By divorcing, the woman also forfeits the respect she had enjoyed in society. She becomes a second-class citizen and usually returns to her family. She is obliged to hold her tongue and refrain from criticizing her ex-husband or former in-laws. Even if she had been married to a man of "weak character," she may not run him down in public. Yet young divorced women are often the object of men's gossip. Divorced women risk being punished or even killed by their own families, as divorce can be seen as shameful and disgraceful for the families.

Divorce is easier for the man, the act being concluded simply by declaring in the presence of two witnesses that she is no longer his wife. He doesn't need to go to court or state publicly why he is divorcing her. But he is obliged to pay her an agreed-upon "fine" that amounts to about a thousand dollars today. Earlier it might have been several cows.

TWO

Welcome to Hell!

I envy the dead, but I don't want to die
Zareta, a survivor

NOT TOO LONG AGO there was a little hand-painted sign nailed to a stake on the outskirts of Grozny that read, "Welcome to Hell!" I'm told a woman put it there. I don't know if that's true, but the Chechen woman has been constantly on the front lines of hell on earth since the first Russian salvos landed on Grozny in 1994. She's been bombed, shelled, strafed, mined, shot at, robbed, left homeless, imprisoned, tortured, kidnapped, raped, victimized, and had her husband, sons, and daughters taken from her. She has lost much, sometimes her mind—often her own life.

BOMBS, BOMBS, AND MORE BOMBS

Massive Russian shelling, bombing, and aerial mining of whole cities, villages, roads, forests, mountains, and just about everything else in sight in Chechnya in two wars have killed and wounded the greatest number of women. There are no statistics, official or otherwise, to tell us how many have died—although Elza P—— did tell me that near half the girls she went to school with are dead. She added that more women died in the first war than in the second. All we really know is that roughly seventy-five to eighty thousand Chechen civilians perished and over two hundred thousand were wounded in the heaviest military bombardment since World War II.

27

Painful Choices

If you believe Chechen separatists, Russia intended to annihilate the whole Chechen population with its bombardment. I reject that notion, but by today's Western standard of precision bombing, Russia clearly used disproportionate and nonselective force in both wars.

At the same time, Russia hasn't been fighting a traditional conventional army but a guerrilla one, in a campaign in which the distinctions between military targets and civilian facilities, combatant and noncombatant, are blurred and most target choices have been painful ones to make.

Chechen fighters in both wars deployed among the civilian population and under the cover of hospitals and schools, in violation of international law. And more than once they took advantage of federally declared civilian evacuation zones to escape themselves, bringing certain death down on fleeing women, children, and the elderly. Moreover, they deliberately took actions that invited Russian retaliation on whole villages and their populations. What would you do if you were a half-starved and scared eighteen-year-old draftee in a strange land at night under heavy mortar fire coming from a "sleeping" village? Probably shoot back like Russian private Arkady Babchenko did.

"We opened fire on the village, aiming at the source of the mortar shells. Our bullets disappearing in the yards of houses," Babchenko writes in his riveting memoirs of his experience as a young Russian soldier in Chechnya.[1]

Chechen forces would deploy self-propelled antiaircraft guns in the middle of villages to shoot at Russian planes, leaving the villages and their civilian populations to be punished. Fighters would disperse throughout a village, fire at Russian helicopters with automatic weapons, and then flee, giving the impression that the entire village was at war with Russia.

Practically every inhabited village had some local fighters and self defense forces, but Aslan Maskhadov, the commander in chief of Chechen forces, reinforced the Russian perception of widespread resistance when he told Russian journalist Anna Politkovskaya that every village had at least fifty combatants and thirty or so reservists, making "33,000 persons I can count on, in addition to my commanders and their staffs."

Russian warnings of imminent bombardment and appeals for noncombatants to rid their villages of fighters or leave their homes, like this one published in the pro-Moscow Chechen newspaper *Vorozhdeniye* in 1995, were commonly made:

> The war must be stopped. In villages and in districts honest citizens who respect the law must take power into their own hands. You should not wander the streets with weapons in your hand, shooting at Russian soldiers and planes. The modern, technical capabilities of the army are such that we can suppress the fire of one AK-47, groups of armed individuals, or even whole groups of fighters. . . . Therefore you should understand that armed individuals in your midst represent a mortal danger to you. Try to force them to change their minds. If they don't put down their arms, then get them out of your villages.

Another appeal to Shali residents in 1995 after an attack on an antiair-craft battery located on the grounds of the city's hospital warns: "How could it happen that in your proud settlement, without your permission, bandit formations appeared that prepare for nothing more than your annihilation? One shot from Shali and return fire will be opened upon the whole village. Remember how much unhappiness one single antiaircraft gun parked in the hospital courtyard brought? Tens of innocent people died, and the bandits that fired at the plane escaped. . . . You must immediately kick the bandits out of Shali. In the worst case, great misfortune awaits all residents of Shali. . . . Hurry up and make your choice."

Specific warnings of imminent bombardment were given with time, albeit sometimes too little, allocated for noncombatant evacuation. In early 1995, Russian helicopters dropped leaflets on the village of Novogrozny, telling villagers they had twenty-four hours to turn over fighters to Russian forces or see their village destroyed. On 15 March 1996 Samashki women and children were told they had two hours to leave before shelling began. In other cases, four days were given. On 6 December 1999 leaflets warned people to leave Chechnya's capital by 11 December: "People of Grozny. Russian troops have fully blockaded the city. To prevent casualties among civilians, we advise you to leave Grozny by 11 December. Use all the opportunities you have. Don't succumb to the provocations of bandits and terrorists."

But many people were either unaware of the leaflets or believed their odds at survival would be better if they stayed put and hid in their basements. People were frightened of what awaited them outside. "Snipers sat in the hills, and we were afraid of getting in the line of their fire," Natasha Kozyreva remembers.

Kheda Zahigova, thirty-four, regrets she didn't leave after the first bomb exploded, when two-thirds of her neighbors left. "Later, you couldn't think about it. Getting through a firing range of 'safety corridors' was much more difficult than staying put."

Malika Temirsultanova was eight months pregnant when she nearly lost her life in the "safety" corridor leading from the village of Novogrozny to Alleroi in early 1995. She had just left the village when an aerial bomb hit two trucks filled with women and children just meters in front of her. Instead of going on, she turned back and hid in the basement of a school-teacher's house.

Some women were just plain stubborn. Seventy-five-year-old Mariya Grigoryevna Shkuratova refused to leave her tiny apartment and go to the relative safety of a basement with her neighbors. "I covered my head with my hands, curled up and hid in the corner of the bathroom, praying, so that all this [bombing] would end soon," she says.

Sometimes no warning was given. A. Yakhyayev, head of administration in Duba-Yurt, says that the shelling of his village began on 31 December 1999 without any warning whatsoever. All 6,644 people stayed in the village until 7 January, when the first group left. The village was completely abandoned in early February. The army also failed to warn the residents of Katyr-Yurt before it was shelled in February 2000.

Poor Russian military targeting, errors, negligence, and sometimes even drunkenness are to blame for many civilian casualties. At the beginning of January 1995, Shali was intermittently bombed and the hospital yard housing the antiaircraft gun was struck on 3 January. That same day, Russian planes targeted a radio communications tower and missed, hitting the local market and killing several women.

"I was wounded in Shali on 3 January on Terskaya Street, not far from the market," a wounded Russian man told Human Rights Watch in February 1995:

We were in the courtyard where there were women and children. A small child ran out of the house just as the plane appeared. I saw shrapnel flying everywhere. It was a cluster bomb that landed about five feet from me, and eight bombs landed in the yard. They [the Russians] dropped eighteen bombs in and around Shali that day. The center of Shali was hit with rockets. First they hit the station. Then a group of people went there to help, and a second attack occurred. There were eight people in the yard and another twelve or fifteen in the street. Almost everyone received some kind of shrapnel wound. I covered the child with my body, as her mother had been hit with multiple shrapnel fragments.

Descent into Hell

Heavy artillery and aerial bombardment destroying much of the city of Grozny came at the beginning of the first war, in December 1994 and January 1995. Russia's human rights commissioner, Sergei Kovalyev, estimates that at least 25,000 people (about 6 percent of the population) died in Grozny from 25 December to 25 January in the new year.

Shelling killed five women and a teenage girl in the vicinity of Samashki in January and February 1995. Federal forces bombarded the outskirts of the village on 18 January, in response to Chechen shelling of their positions and to mounting casualties from guerrillas filtering in and out of the area. Then, at the end of January, came three days of shelling from tanks and helicopters and the dropping of mines.

Forty-three-year-old Tamara Mugdanova Nosipova and sixty-seven-year-old Sanipat Lyurmagomedova, along with two men, were killed on Chapayeva Street in Samashki on 31 January. Saripa Yurmagometova and her daughter Sarizha died, too. And on 2 February a land mine killed a woman and a fourteen-year-old girl.

Shelling continued sporadically until 5 February, when a cease-fire agreement was reached after village elders guaranteed that all fighters would immediately leave Samashki. They kept their promise. But the outskirts of the village was shelled again on 4 March, as a warning, after fighters attacked a federal post just outside the village. *Chechenpress* reports of a missile-launcher attack on 6 April and the killing of five hundred villagers are simply untrue.

Two more women died in the afternoon on 7 April, fifteen minutes before the deadline for villagers to evacuate Samashki expired and the federal assault began. Kulsum Musikhanova had just packed what she could carry and was on her way out of Samashki when the first shell hit. A forty-

one-year-old woman was also killed, in the yard of her home at 114 Kooperativnaya Street.

The next day five people, three of them women, were killed or fatally
wounded. An exploding shell took out a nearby water tower, claiming the
lives of Patimat Labazanova and her daughter, twenty-nine-year-old Malika
Aliyeva, on Kooperativnaya Street. Kulai Babayeva was fatally wounded in
the northern outskirts of the village, while twenty-seven-year-old Tamusa
Alisultanova received a fatal head wound from an exploding artillery shell in
the eastern outskirts of the village on 9 or 10 April. In all, shelling between
7 and 10 April killed eighteen people, six of them women. On 6 May 1995,
Malkan Suleimanova, a correspondent for the *Ichkeria* newspaper, was killed
in Shatoi during its bombardment.

In her book *The Angel of Grozny,* Asne Seierstad tells the story of a young
pregnant woman she met in a Grozny clinic who had shrapnel in her breast
because she, her husband, and their six-year-old son had been caught in the
middle of the Shatoi bombardment while making their way down a moun-
tainside. Only the mother had survived.[2]

Doctors in the same clinic were also treating nine-year-old Elisa, "a pale,
thin girl who had serious shrapnel wounds to her leg and talked in a barely
audible voice." Her native village of Chishky had come under bombardment
the night before. All of Elisa's family had perished.

On 3 June 1995, two six-ton bombs fell on Shamil Basayev's uncle's
house in Vedeno, killing Basayev's wife and child, his thirty-one-year-old
sister Zinaida, and at least nine other members of his family, mostly Zinaida's children.

Five more of Elza P——'s close friends died in 1995 and 1996. Three
members of the Malsogov family—Zara Malsogova, sixty-eight; her son
Musa, twenty-nine; and his twenty-four-year-old pregnant wife—were shot
to death by a Russian soldier in the village of Alda outside Grozny in 1995.

Imana, another friend, was killed that same year. She and her three children had fled Grozny for the relative safety of the Shatoisky District, where
they went to live with relatives. Imana was collecting water when a Russian aircraft strafing a forest gunned her down. Zula Sadayeva, a Samashki
friend and the mother of four, was getting off a bus, her arms full of groceries, when an aircraft fired on her in the Groznensky District village of Katayama in 1996.

A Doctors Without Borders 7–15 March 1996 "Grozny Situation Report" provides a snapshot of the daily perils the women of that city faced getting around town that spring:

- On 7 March, at 10 AM, a thirty-eight-year-old woman driving through the center of Grozny on her way home is struck by bullets in the left hip and right leg.
- At half past eleven in the morning, a fifteen-year-old girl who heard shooting in the street and tried to take shelter in a back room of her house is severely wounded by a grenade thrown into her house.
- Two days later, a forty-six-year-old female who ventures outside at 6 PM, following a power outage, is immediately shot in the lung and abdomen.
- On 12 March, a thirty-five-year-old woman in a car with four other people near Minutka Square is wounded in the arms and leg by a sniper after the driver stops to avoid running over two corpses in the street.
- On 15 March, a fifty-five-year-old woman receives a hip wound as she drives from Katayama to the center of Grozny. Both passengers in the car are also wounded.
- At 7 PM, that same day, soldiers manning a roadside checkpoint seriously wound a thirty-year-old woman in the arm driving a car. A second woman in the car is also hurt.

Between 6 and 14 March 1996 another seven women are admitted to Grozny Hospital No. 4 with various wounds. Two twenty-four-year-old women and one forty-year-old have bullet wounds to their legs. A forty-eight-year-old has shrapnel wounds to the small of her back. Two other women, fifty-four and fifty-nine, are admitted for kidney punctures caused by explosives; a seventy-four-year-old has severe facial burns.

Tymisha remembers that the soldiers "fired their guns in time with the music playing in their headphones just to inspire fear in us, so that we would remain in a permanent state of shock."

The slaughter goes on.

On 5 April 1996 Russian snipers shot "KS," a thirty-six-year-old woman from Tsa-Vedeno who had fled the village with thirty other people. Two girls were also killed, and a nineteen-year-old lost her leg after sniper fire hit her car.

During the heated battle for Grozny in August 1996 Zina Batalova, an obstetrician and gynecologist, crawled out of her basement and ran down a corpse-littered street, dodging bullets, to attend to a neighbor's wife, who was giving birth. Miraculously, Batalova survived, but Babchenko, working burial detail that August, remembers a fifteen-year-old Grozny girl who didn't. "I couldn't tear my eyes away from that round, dry hole in her head," he writes. "Her face is serene as if she is asleep, no torn-off jaws or rolled-up dead eyes. There's a hole the size of a fist in the side of her head where a stone hit her, driving her brain out of her skull like a piston."[3]

Across town, fleeing Russian *kontraktniki* (contract soldiers) took Satsita Gairbekova, head of the intensive care unit at Grozny's Hospital No. 9, and her colleagues hostage after their post was overrun by Chechen fighters. The soldiers figured they would do what Russia's number-one terrorist Shamil Basayev had done at a hospital he seized in Buddenovsk, Russia, in June 1995: wave white sheets out the windows and threaten to kill everybody inside unless given safe passage. Satsita negotiated a deal with the Chechen commander in charge of the neighborhood. She and the hospital staff donned white coats and became human shields to escort the Russian soldiers to safety. But "when we turned to go back, some of the soldiers started firing on us. One nurse was killed, and a surgeon was hit in the leg," she remembers.[4] More nurses died when Russian helicopter gunships pummeled Grozny City Hospital No. 4.

The First War Was Paradise

"You're going to think I'm crazy, but the first war was paradise compared to this [the second] one. During the first war, I was able to stay in Chechnya, at home. That's no longer possible." Maya, a refugee from Shatoi, told this to a Doctors Without Borders official in Duisi, Georgia, in November 1999.

Chechnya, particularly Grozny, was hit hard again with massive Russian artillery and aerial bombardment at the beginning of the second war in 1999, resulting in heavy civilian casualties and hundreds of thousands of internally displaced persons.

On 27 September four war planes bombed Staraya Sunzha, a suburb of Grozny, destroying two houses and damaging four others. Thaus Temirsultanova, her son and granddaughter, a pregnant women, and twenty-one-year-old Liza Khadzhinova, with her three-year-old girl and infant boy, were all killed in the basement of their garage. Fifty people were wounded.

A refugee convoy crossing the Terek River near Chervlennaya, thirty kilometers north of Grozny, came under Russian tank fire on 5 October 1999, killing twenty-eight people and wounding another nine women and children.

Two days later, people were digging up potatoes and picking corn for the winter when two Russian fighter-bombers high in the sky attacked the village of Yelistanzhi, leaving forty-eight dead and a hundred wounded— mostly women and children, including eighteen-year-old Imani Muzayeva, who was in her sixth month of pregnancy.

Chechen fighters bombarded villages too, sometimes in retaliation for having been kicked out of them. According to Russia's Defense Ministry, on 10 October 1999 fighters under the command of Field Commander M. Mezhidov fired mortar rounds into the settlement of Verkhniy Naur, killing and wounding forty residents. The same thing happened in the village of Oernaya, and on 12 October Chechen fighters shot thirty-two people in various villages because their residents had demanded that they leave to save them from destruction.

Russian bombardment of other parts of Chechnya followed.

In his book *Bolshaya Strategicheskaya Igra,* Chechen politician Ruslan Khasbulatov cites a fax he received from a group of "Chechen Mothers" indicating that nearly half of the thirty-one people who had died in a missile strike on the village of Yelistanzhi, Vedensky District, on 7 October 1999 were women and girls. The dead included:

1. Malkan Mukhmadova, twenty-five years old
2. Taisa Artsuyeva, ten years old
3. Shamsa Artsuyeva, fifteen years old
4. Khizhan Gekhayeva, seventy-one years old
5. Aishat Gekhayeva, sixty years old
6. Aset Saitova, thirty-eight years old
7. Madina Gabayeva, forty-three years old
8. Satsita Peterova, fourteen years old
9. Yepsa Gekhayeva, seventy-nine years old
10. Zina Durdisva, forty-three years old and the mother of eleven children

Two unnamed refugee girls, seven and eight years old, also perished in the attack, which destroyed 260 homes and wounded more than two hundred people.[5] At five o'clock in the afternoon on 21 October 1999 a Russian missile carrying cluster munitions and aimed at the notorious weapons bazaar known as "the exchange" in Grozny's outdoor central market pummeled that target, killing 140 people and wounding another two hundred, mostly women and children.

Some Russian media reporting said the missiles missed their intended target by several hundred feet, but that's incorrect. Elza P——, whose brother and sister-in-law left the market just minutes before the strike, tells me that there were no weapons physically at the market but that numerous arms dealers were standing around the currency-exchange booths at the entrance to the market, men who would gladly take your order for any kind of weapon and arrange delivery to anyone with the hard cash to pay for it.

"But who would go there to buy weapons?" I naively asked. "Fighters!" she answered.

Other witnesses, including Luiza Asukhanova, who sold fruit and vegetables at the market, says that in fact there *were* arms there, that they were being sold at several stalls at one corner of the market. Russia says there was a whole "warehouse of weapons" at the market.

"I was unbelievably lucky to have escaped the carnage," a mother of three girls, nine, seventeen, and eighteen years of age, told a Doctors Without Borders representative in Georgia on 24 October 1999:

> There were lots of people at the market, and not only those who were shopping. The Grozny market was also a place where you could meet your friends, exchange the latest bits of news, etc. At 4:30 PM, the merchants were getting ready to take down their stands when the bomb was dropped. In a fraction of a second, the market became a blood bath. Pieces of flesh were strewn over the ground; there was screaming, and wounded and dead people everywhere. The wounded were taken to the hospital. I myself helped gather up a few mangled bodies. My neighbor suffered a severed leg and lost her little girl.

Although she lost an arm, Luiza Asukhanova's fourteen-year-old daughter Sulikhan says she's lucky to be alive. Luiza and her mother had just left the market when they heard explosions. Sulikhan ran as fast as she could away from the noise. Her mother found her with a broken arm. It was bad—bone was protruding through the skin. Three hospitals and five hours later, her arm was amputated.

Uvais Yelbuzdukayev and his young daughter, as well as his cousin, were selling jewelry at the market. They were wounded, too, but survived. Shrapnel claimed twenty-three-year-old Fatima Khasuyeva's right leg: "I was lying among the corpses. Those who lived crawled away, and only the rebels picked us up and took us to the hospital."[6] Leila Migiyeva, forty-six, lost her left hand as the bus she was in passed the market. Asya Yesmurzayeva, the mother of three young children, was selling bread when she was struck by a sliver of flying metal. Tousari, Asya's mother, raced her to City Hospital No. 9 but it was full, and there was no electricity there, anyway. They were sent to the hospital in Achkoi-Martan, but there was no power there either. They went to two more hospitals before Asya got help.

A 9 December appeal to President Boris Yeltsin by the Coordinating Council of International Human Rights Organizations to stop the war said that three hundred women and children had been killed in the market strike.

But the carnage wasn't limited to the market. Missiles that missed the market plummeted into the courtyard of Grozny's maternity hospital, killing thirteen mothers and fifteen babies. Forty-one people at a nearby mosque also died. On 17 October three men and women transporting a corpse from Sleptsovsk to Katyr-Yurt were killed. At the end of October, a military target in the courtyard of a boarding school for the deaf and mute adjacent to the City Children's Hospital No. 2 in Grozny took a direct hit from planes. On 27 October shells hit the Mutayev family home in Samashki, killing Zara Mutayeva; Emina, twelve years old; L. Debryeva, also twelve; and Zara Magomedovna Barzoyeva, forty-seven. Esila Abudalipovna Debrisheva, thirty-five, was seriously wounded. Six days later, twelve-year-old Alina Derbishyeva was also killed in a missile attack. The next day, in Stariye Atagi, two planes attacked the funeral procession of sixty-five-year-old Tamara Chankayeva and her twelve-year-old granddaughter, both of whom had been killed during the bombardment of Grozny. One person was killed and five were wounded, including women.

That same month, another of Elza's friends, Turyayeva, and her daughter were shot by a Russian sniper as they ran from a dormitory in the village of Beryezka in the Staropromyslovsky District of Grozny during an aerial attack.

On the morning of 1 November head nurse Dagman Tepsurkayeva was wounded in the leg and pelvis when she, along with Khadichat Basayeva, a medical secretary, the head doctor, and a second man were fired upon by a Russian military unit when their car arrived at the main gate of the Zakan-Yurt psychiatric hospital. The vehicle's windshield displayed a white piece of paper with a Red Cross sign on it to signify a medical vehicle. They were there to look after their patients.

Outlying areas near Grozny were softened up in November. Russian forces began shelling and bombing Alkhan-Kala on 6 November in a twenty-six-day offensive that killed forty people. It's a miracle more did not perish. Underground shelters saved many. "We had already had some experience in the [first] war. We had good [underground] shelters and many people slept there. Many people slept in semi-cellar premises too," Lida Alikhanova told a Human Rights Watch representative in Pliyevo, Ingushetia, on 13 December 1999.

On 7 November Itum Kala and Bitchigui were hit by missiles for the first time, killing one woman. Nine days later, thirty-nine-year-old Aminat was wounded in the left arm and hand by machine-gun fire from a fighter plane strafing a nine-vehicle refugee convoy outside Alkhan-Yurt.

A second bombardment of Alkhan-Kala on 8 December was particularly intense. Lecha Umarkhayev's mother, Zara Umarkhayeva, sixty, along with his father and brother, were killed when an exploding shell landed on the roof of a shed in their back yard on Lenin Street, where they were busy chopping wood that afternoon. "My young sister heard the explosion and cried out. I heard her screaming and also ran toward them. . . . All three were lying on the ground. . . . First, I saw my brother. He was face down. My mother was also near. . . . She had lost two fingers and had a wound on her back. . . . We took mother to the hospital, but she died as the doctors were checking her," Lecha told a human rights worker at the Adket-20 border crossing into Ingushetia a few days later.

On 3 December a refugee column of seven cars and a bus traveling from Grozny to Goity was attacked, killing fifty women, children, and elderly persons. Taisa Aidamirova, a survivor, said that Russian soldiers came to the aid of the wounded.

On 4 January 2000 Russian planes fired on a convoy of fleeing refugees in the village of Kotar-Yurt, killing twelve-year-old Tamara Daduyeva's mother as she covered her daughter with her body. Tamara received bullet wounds to her legs and later became the ward of Khadizhat Gatayeva, who operated a home for war-orphaned children in Grozny.

On 6 January 2000 Chechen fighters entered Shali, a federally declared civilian "safety zone," and demanded that the Russian MVD (Interior Affairs Ministry) unit headquartered there leave immediately. The Russian commander called in fire support; as a result, a tactical missile warhead exploded above the central square, killing more than 150 civilians, mostly elderly people awaiting their pensions.

The same thing happened in Katyr-Yurt. On 3–4 February fighters entered the village, which had been declared a safety zone. Artillery fire and aerial bombing of the village began the next morning without any advance warning and continued through 8 February. Between a hundred and three hundred people died. Eighty percent of the village was destroyed.

A survivor, Patimat Batalova, recalls that artillery shells raining down on a road hit her convoy of Katyr-Yurt refugees, killing more than half the people—many of them women. Eighty-year-old Taisa Abakarova lost all of her family that day in the refugee exodus. She was later found in a Nazran hospital trauma ward with a badly burned upper body and two broken legs. Another mother in the exodus was forced to leave her dead baby alongside the road.

Neither white flags nor Red Cross emblems saved vehicles from Russian war planes, because fleeing fighters attached white flags and Red Cross symbols to their own cars, hoping to escape.

On 5 February 2000 Russian soldiers in the Oktyabrsky District of Grozny shot four members of the Estimorova family—Toita, Khass-Magomet, Hassan, and Khozh-Akhmed—and tried to burn their bodies.

Fifteen days later, two ambulances marked with Red Cross emblems and carrying forty civilians to safety from the village of Barzoi drove into a zone under artillery attack near Duba-Yurt, in the Shatoisky District. Three women and two men were killed, including seventy-five-year-old Dogman Giriyeva. Sixteen other people, men, women, and children, were wounded. That same month, twelve-year-old Jabrail Murtazaliyev was walking with his grandmother along the road to Duba-Yurt when a missile exploded in front of them, killing his grandmother.

Khava Khadzhimuradova, twenty-seven, the mother of three with a fourth on the way, was lucky. A Russian sniper's bullet struck her in the leg, but now she's in the hospital in Mozdok, North Ossetia, awaiting an operation. Malka, also twenty-seven, is there too, with a sniper's bullet in her leg, but she refuses to receive anesthetic during her operation because she doesn't want to risk losing the child she is carrying.

On 20 March a group of sixty civilians, mostly women and children who had been given a "safe corridor" for a day to pick wild garlic in a forest near the village of Samashki, came under artillery attack, which killed three women and wounded five.

By mid-January the Russian air force was flying sixty to a hundred sorties a day, while army aviation was conducting more than seventy helicopter flights daily, pounding fighter positions in Grozny, gorges in the Argunsky and Vedensky districts, the populated centers of Sharoi and Itum-Kala, and areas close to the Georgian border. By the end of the month, the sorties had doubled.

In early April 2006 workers doing a spring cleanup of Kirova Park near the banks of the Sunzha River in the Leninsky District of Grozny uncovered a mass grave containing fifty-seven civilian bodies. The Russian Emergency Situations Ministry dates these graves from the year 2000. Fifty-one bodies have been identified, including women. Chechnya's procurator, Vladimir Kuznetsov, concludes that these were people who died from artillery shelling and aviation bombs.

Some of them may have been the civilians retreating with Shamil Basayev and a group of two to three thousand fighters from Grozny toward Alkhan-Kala on 31 January and 1 February 2000. They walked straight into a minefield and Russian gunfire as they prepared to cross the Sunzha River bridge. "What hit us during our withdrawal were not land mines but butterfly mines that are deployed by aircraft. These mines do not need to be buried in the ground, as they resemble the color of earth," Basayev explained after his foot had been torn off by one of them. "We walked into a minefield . . . then they started shooting at us from their armored personnel carriers and with their machine guns and grenade launchers," another fighter recalls.

More than two hundred women—nurses, cooks and cleaners, snipers, and others who had earlier refused to leave Grozny—were among those killed in the exodus.

Kheida Yusupova, twenty-eight, the wife of a fighter, survived. "You didn't know where to step. We walked through blood and pieces of flesh," she told a *Chicago Tribune* reporter on 13 February 2000. Yusupova had been one of three women holed up in the basement of the presidential palace in Grozny, where she cooked and cleaned for fighters. She and her two children—Markha, ten, and Magomed, nine—left in the first group of forty civilians and 150 fighters.

Artillery and aviation bombardment of Grozny was extremely intense between 2 and 12 February 2000. It's unknown how many women died in the bombardment and subsequent Russian storm of the city, but Yasupova said that while searching for her fighter husband she came across one woman in possession of a list of sixty women and children.

In late October 2000 Zura Uzuyeva, the mother of two boys, was killed when a Russian helicopter fired a missile into the yard of her house in the Oktyabrsky District of Grozny. "My wife had just called us to dinner, and we had been sitting at the table, all four of us. My sons and I then went inside, and she stayed there in the courtyard to wash. I had hardly opened the door when the missile struck," her husband recalls.[7]

That same year, an aircraft missile claimed the lives of thirty women from the village of Mekhkety in the Vedensky District. They had been on a bus returning home from Shali after buying groceries when they were told by Russian soldiers at a checkpoint that they should turn around and go back to Shali, because it was too dangerous to go ahead. They decided to walk the remaining distance instead but soon flagged down a bus carrying village elders returning home from a meeting with Russian military commanders. The bus was hit by an aircraft missile a short while later.

"In as much as the fire came from a high altitude, the pilots couldn't see who they were shooting at in the bus flying the white flag," Zula Tolshyeva, a survivor, explains.

Students and teachers perished too. On the morning of 20 December 2000 an hour-and-a-half-long mortar attack mistakenly hit the Chechen State Teachers Institute (ChGPI) in Grozny and claimed the lives of twenty-eight people. Teachers Malika Zmayevna Akhmedova, Olga V. Klimova, and Larisa Pavlovna Tonkonogova all died that day. Three students—sixteen-year-old Madina Matayeva, seventeen-year-old Larisa Nanayeva, and twenty-year-old Aset Mustapayevna Uspanova—also perished.

The girls went into the cellar at the beginning of the attack but came out after the initial volley. They were hit when the shelling suddenly resumed. Twenty-two-year-old Malika Kagirova, nineteen-year-old Zarema Khastayeva, and eighteen-year-old Madina Atabayeva were wounded. "I only remember the sound of the explosion in my head. I fell down and began to shout because we were taught that you should open your mouth and yell to avoid shell shock," Atabayeva recalls. Shrapnel penetrated her legs.

The Chechen procurator's office determined that the attack had originated from a nearby Russian checkpoint on Sadovaya Street. Its commanding officer explained that the checkpoint had come under fire and he had been compelled to return it. The procurator described the deaths in his official report as an "unfortunate accident caused by overshot." A stone memorial to those who perished now stands in front of the institute.

That same day fifty-three-year-old Tumisha Maulatova sustained a head wound when a mortar round flew through her Grozny apartment widow while she and her daughter were making pastries to sell at the market. Zarema, her daughter, twenty-four, died.

Mistaken Coordinates

Bombardments are fewer now that the "active phase" of the war is over, but they do still occasionally occur with catastrophic consequences, particularly in the southern mountains of Chechnya.

For example, on 16 October 2001 mortar and small-arms fire wounded a woman and her five-year-old daughter in the village of Duba-Yurt after army sappers found land mines buried in the road leading into the village. The daughter died in the hospital. Later in the month shelling of the village of Goity in the Urus-Martanovsky District killed two girls, wounded four women, and destroyed sixteen houses. Four months later the village of Tsotsin-Yurt was shelled after two Russian soldiers in an armored vehicle were killed by a land mine near the village. Luba Davletkayeva died. Zareta Davletkayeva and her two-year-old child were wounded.

On 16 April 2002 two sisters, E. and K. Kassayeva, died and a teenager was badly wounded in bombardment of the settlement of Gargachi, Shatoisky District, resulting from mistaken coordinates for an enemy observation post. The Russian military is notorious for making such mistakes. Both presidents Alkhanov and Ramzan Kadyrov have demanded prosecution of those responsible for military negligence.

On 20 August 2003 thirty-six-year-old Zulai Akberdayeva, the mother of five, was badly wounded when the village of Serzhen-Yurt came under bombardment that damaged nineteen homes and destroyed one. The following month two more girls, ten and thirteen years of age, perished in a mistaken bombardment of their home in the district center of Shali. On 2 October 2003 seventy-five-year-old Aset Suleimanova was killed by the shelling of apartment houses on Tsentralnaya and Sadovaya streets in the village of Makhety.

Seven months later, on 9 April 2004, at two o'clock in the afternoon, a twenty-minute air strike on the remote mountain village of Rigakhoy, Cheberloyevsky District, claimed the lives of twenty-nine-year-old Maret Kutuzovna Damayeva (maiden name Maret Tsintsayeva) and her five children, including two beautiful little twin girls, Zara and Zura. The village of Serzhen-Yurt was struck again on 26 June 2004 by an attack that killed Rashana Kagermanova; her two daughters Kheda, eighteen, and Zhamilya, seventeen; and her husband, Lema. Their home took a direct hit from an artillery shell.

On 3 December 2004 Zareta Suleimanova, eighteen, lost her left eye and a small part of her skull when a missile from a Russian helicopter hit her house in the small mountain village of Tazen-Kala, Vedensky District. She was watching television with her two brothers while her parents were away at a funeral. One brother died instantly; the other dragged her out of the house before it collapsed. Doctors at the Burdenko Research Institute in Moscow have been able to reconstruct a portion of her left forehead, temple, and left eye socket. She has since received an artificial eye.

At least one mistaken bombardment occurred in 2005. In the early morning hours (2 or 3 AM) of 10 November the sleeping residents of Zelenaya Street in Stariye Atagi were thrown out of their beds by twelve exploding mortar shells, which seriously wounded sixty-eight-year-old Khamila Yusupova; her daughter Aimani, twenty-eight; her eight-year-old granddaughter Elina; and fifty-two-year-old Yakha Yusupov. "Everybody started running out of their houses, but not everyone made it. A young girl with the last name of Sugaipova from another family was also hurt. The shelling damaged nine homes, breaking glass, and puncturing walls with shrapnel," Khasan Yusupov, a wounded member of the family, recalls.

The military procurator promptly investigated. The next day the military commandant of Chechnya, Grigoriy Fomenko, told the newspaper *Vremya novostei* that the shelling had been unintentional. "What happened was a mistake. We meant to shell a fighter base in another place," he said. Fomenko's assistant and commandant of the Groznensky District, Anatoliy Guskov, also called the incident "a pure mistake." He conceded that the mortar fire had come from federal positions in the Shalinsky District. But Fomenko's apology did little to appease Vakhid Gadayev, the government administrator of Stariye Atagi, who said that "this is not the first time this has happened and there is no excuse for it." A group of military prosecutors, the procurator from the Shalinsky District, and other officials inspected the shelled village and opened a criminal case for "violations in arms handling regulations resulting in bodily injury."

The same thing happened on 24 February 2006, when three artillery shells landed on Lenina and Partizanskaya streets at night in the settlement of Chechen-Aul, Groznensky District, damaging two homes. No one was hurt.

Four months later, in June, at six in the morning, an hour-long bombardment near the village of Serzhen-Yurt rattled window glass and knocked doors open while frightened women and children hid in basements.

In the early afternoon on 1 December 2006 two Russian missiles struck the Gaitemirov family home on a farm in the Shatoisky District, wounding Roza Akhilgova, fifty-four; her daughter (twenty-two-year-old Zalpa Akhilgova); and two men in the family. The military procurator agreed to pay the family 97,000 rubles compensation as indemnification. Another 100,000 rubles was to be paid to the two males for their suffering.

A mistaken artillery shelling of the settlement of Gekhi in the Urus-Martanovsky District on 28 January 2008 left twenty-six homes damaged and gas and electrical facilities in the settlement in shambles. An overnight gun battle near Bamut had resulted in the bombardment of forests in the Achkoi-Martanovsky and neighboring Urus-Martanovsky districts, but somehow the gunners ended up a whole twenty-five kilometers off target, hitting Gekhi in the middle of the night.

"We woke up during the night from a powerful explosion," Zara, a resident of Gekhi, tells. "Glass was flying everywhere, and the children were screaming and crying. Then the instinct of self-survival kicked in, despite the laziness brought on by years of a peaceful life. We went into the basement and sat there for forty minutes. It seemed to me that the war had started all over again; I prayed to the Almighty that it wasn't true."

Human rights ombudsman Nurdi Nukhazhiyev appealed to the Russian military in late August 2008 to stop all bombardment of inhabited areas after the bombing earlier in the month of the high mountain settlement of Zumsoi, in the Itum-Kalinsky District. No one had been hurt, but the bombardment had forced many residents who had just returned home at the urging of Chechnya's president to flee once again.

On the night of 12 May 2009 five shells exploded in the village of Benoi, Vedensky District, following a firefight between fighters and police in a nearby forest. Luckily, no one was killed. The shelling came from a military unit on the outskirts of the village of Dishny-Vedeno and was the result of negligence in targeting.

THE HORROR OF *Zachistka*

The process of reestablishing control over whole cities and villages following the route of Chechen fighters from occupied zones claimed many more lives. This process, called *zachistka* (cleansing or mopping-up operations, and later "address checks"), carried out by Russian soldiers and police and later by pro-Moscow Chechen security forces working jointly with Russian military or law-enforcement entities, had the mission of identifying, capturing or killing Wolves still hiding among the population. It was during these operations that the greatest numbers of villagers were killed and homes destroyed, causing intense physical, emotional, and psychological pain for the Chechen woman determined to protect her family, property, and precious belongings and to preserve what could be salvaged of her shattered life.

Wartime *zachistka* operations required "up close and personal" contact with a population in an environment where the distinction between combatant and noncombatant was at a minimum blurred—and in the minds of most Russian soldiers and policemen, nonexistent. "By day, Chechens are peaceful civilians, but by night they come out and kill us," my Russian diplomatic friend matter-of-factly told me in 2007.

That was certainly true in Gudermes in 2001. "During the day, the people in Gudermes smile at us and bring us goodies, but at night they are out there shooting at us," nineteen-year-old Private Sergei Kuznetsov remembers. Gunfire could be heard coming from just about every village after dark in those days, and at night Russian soldiers shot at anything that moved.

No Chechen could be trusted. Children from fatherless families became living bombs or other instruments of death. Boys aged twelve to fourteen fired grenade launchers at tanks, dropped live grenades down open tank hatches, and put mines under tanks.

Warrant Officer Eduard Shakhazov, with the Russian 74th Motorized Rifle Brigade, still has nightmares about seeing a small boy running toward his unit and hearing the crack of a Chechen sniper rifle firing a bullet to set off the explosives on the lad's back. A little girl begging for food on the side of the road detonated the grenade under her dress when Russian soldiers stopped to give her something to eat. For a hundred dollars, Albert, the thirteen-year-old son of Yakha Ugurchiyeva, an arms dealer at Grozny's central market during the first war, walked across the street and shot policemen sitting in their car. Fourteen-year-old Zaur Abuyev and his street-kid friends carried weapons and worked as guides for Chechen fighters in Grozny. Timur blindfolded a captured Russian soldier so his Chechen fighter friend could stab him to death.

And Kazbek, a sixteen-year-old, and his gang shot a woman in the forehead in broad daylight at Grozny's central market just because she was Russian. The animals broke into a house and stabbed another Russian woman and her daughter, knifed a mullah, and shot a traffic policeman too, just for the fun of it.

Any distinction between combatant and noncombatant was further complicated by the fact that much of the civilian population aided and abetted Chechen fighters with information, shelter, food, medicine, clothing, and even weapons and ammunition.

These circumstances, plus "battlefield emotion" (to use a U.S. Army term popular in Iraq), the fear generated by Chechen female snipers and suicide bombers, and the Kremlin's priority given to avoiding the heavy casualties experienced in the first war, escalated the violence. Chechen women who survived the bombs and bullets—many of them left alone because their men had fled to safety, joined the Jihad, or died fighting—became particularly vulnerable.

There were other reasons for the violence too: ethnic prejudice and just plain hatred of Chechens by many Russian soldiers, poor military pay and training, hunger (Russian soldiers had had little to eat in the first war, too, and took food from the Chechens), alcohol, boredom, the impression of being able to break the law with impunity, and an uncaring military leadership or the inability of some officers to control their men. Finally, memories of losing the first war and the desire for revenge played a role, too.

So did a battlefield code of honor. Chechen fighters commonly killed, decapitated, and mutilated their Russian prisoners. Videotapes from the first war once sold in Grozny's market show Arab and Chechen fighters holding up the severed heads of Russian soldiers and shouting "Allah Akhbar!" Aukai Collins, an American *mujahid* who fought on the Chechen side in the first war, writes about one of these grotesque executions in his book *My Jihad:* "He [the Chechen fighter] pulled the [Russian] soldier's head back by his filthy hair and ran the knife back and forth over his neck in a ghastly

sawing motion. Bright red blood squirted out as the . . . throat was severed.
. . . A noise came from his throat as his last breath escaped through his gaping
neck. Then the Chechen simply let the soldier's head flop onto the ground.
It was tilted so far back now that it was almost completely severed."[8]

Sometimes heads of Russian soldiers would be put on stakes outside villages with booby traps to kill anyone trying to remove them. Russian soldiers found their comrades nailed to crosses, honey smeared across their bodies to attract flies, their torsos riddled with bullet holes, or their testicles cut off. In his book *Ya byl na etoi voine (Grozny 1995)* (I Was in That War) Vyacheslav Mironov tells about such things, including the nailing of a Russian soldier to a rooftop cross and the mutilation of his body: a dead soldier's body was up there, just like Jesus, his own penis cut off and stuffed in his mouth.

"Why should we consider a Chechen an honorable enemy, worthy of the protections of international law, when the animal does these kinds of things to us? They're not human!" one angry Russian officer, insulted by my stupid questioning, snapped back.

This is not to say that serious crimes haven't been committed by angry Russian soldiers and policemen. They have. Some castrated Chechens in revenge: "The commander ordered them [the men] to do a sweep through the village. All the men who could be found were herded into the square. They were thrown down in piles and then our soldiers started to hack them up. One guy pinned a Chechen to the ground with his foot, while another pulled off his pants and with two or three hefty slashes severed his scrotum. . . . In a half a day the whole village was castrated. Then the battalion moved on."[9]

Others sliced off the ears of dead Chechens and made necklaces of them. Sergeant Magonov, a soldier tried for the murder of a Chechen family in Alkhan-Kala in December 2000, cut off the ear of the teenage girl his partner had just shot. A psychologist working with Magonov said his patient had seen Oliver Stone's film *Platoon,* in which the hero, a U.S. soldier, cuts off the ear of a Vietnamese girl.

In 1995 an MVD pamphlet warning personnel against human rights violations, robbery, and other abuses during cleansing operations conceded:

Recently there have appeared cases of looting, extortion, and outrages against the civilian population by Russian forces. It is true, our forces have taken losses, but we should not allow ourselves to harden our hearts.

No one has been given the right to mete out mob law or even law and order, especially not ordinary soldiers. Looting and outrages toward the civilian population bring shame on the internal forces of the Ministry of the Interior, discredit them in the eyes of the public, and nullify the actions of the majority of forces who carry out their duties with honor.

The pamphlet demands from "all commanders at all levels and from all military personnel . . . complete obedience of all laws in [carrying out] your military duties and the enactment of strict measures against all appearance of disorderly conduct and looting of the civilian population, including bringing the guilty to justice." Above all, the code of military conduct is to be observed. "One can only fight against those carrying weapons; one can only fire upon military targets; one must spare civilians; one can only use as much force as required to carry out military activities."

Unfortunately, not all Russian commanders and their subordinates obeyed these or subsequent orders. Thousands of women lost their lives, limbs, and their cherished family treasures, personal effects, and household belongings—much of it loaded onto Russian military trucks and hauled away.

Looting became epidemic.

In his book on the first war Akhmed Kelimatov, a Chechen commander fighting on Russia's side, writes that in March 1996 "they [Russian officers and generals] filled their vehicles with furniture, rugs, televisions, video-magnetophones, and sent the stolen property by the main road outside the republic. The more valuable things [gold, money, diamonds, relics, and even icons] they keep on themselves."[10]

Shamil Basayev was able to pass through the Russian border checkpoint on his way to Budennovsk in 1995 with 185 fighters hidden in the back of two trucks by telling border police that he was carrying "war booty" back to Russia and bribing them not to inspect the trucks.

"We did it [looted] because they [the Russian military] didn't give us anything. No beds, nothing—not even uniforms—only an automatic and four clips. The rest we had to get ourselves. We took rugs, televisions and other electronic equipment. Furniture here, dishes there," Aleksandr Moro-zov admits. He furnished Gulya's house with things taken from a little *aul* (village) of about fifteen houses he helped cleanse in the Shalinsky District in the spring of 2000.

"Aviation had bombed it and they called us to cleanse it. They said it was a Wahhabi village. . . . Some houses were destroyed, some whole. Belongings were scattered everywhere; a stove with a fire still in it was sitting in the yard. Hot food on the table, but no people; no living, no dead, no wounded," he recalls of the eerie scene. So Morozov and his comrades just took what they needed.

Victimized Chechens repeatedly complain about the behavior of Russian soldiers and police. So do local government administrators. Authorities haven't completely ignored their pleas, but they haven't aggressively investigated or sought adequate punishment for those who violated the law, either. Russia's military procurator opened about 1,500 criminal cases against Russian soldiers in 1996, but only 300 ended up in military courts. Another 350 were dismissed, and 600 were suspended for various reasons.

Intending to limit the scale of arbitrariness and violence during these cleansing operations, on 24 May 2001 the commander of the Coalition Task Force in the North Caucasus, General Lieutenant V. Moltenskoy, issued Order No. 145, requiring that unit and subdivision commanders of federal forces cooperate with local administrators, military commandants, local police chiefs, and military judges of districts while conducting *zachistka* operations. Officials would be invited and be present at the command center during these operations.

Two months later Russia's procurator general issued Order No. 146, again acknowledging human rights violations and repeating Order No. 145, with additional instructions requiring the written registration of detained persons and notations as to who had detained them, when, and where they were being held. Relatives would be informed about the grounds for the detention, and complaints regarding violence against citizens, seizure, or extortion of money would be promptly investigated.

A third step was taken in 2002 when representatives of the procurator's office began attending selected operations. On 27 March 2002 Moltenskoy issued Order No. 80, which required that armored vehicles display license plates, that the senior officer of each group of soldiers introduce himself and show identification when entering a house, and that the official in charge provide the local head of administration with a list of names of all persons detained, reasons for their detention, and where the detained were being taken.

The problem is that these orders are seldom fully executed. Where perpetrators of crimes committed by Russian soldiers have been brought to justice, we can look to court records for the factual details. Where they have not, we have only the personal accounts of victims or their relatives and friends, as told to foreign journalists, human rights organizations, and international organizations, to rely on. Despite the genuine horror that people have suffered, it is possible that some of the stories have been embellished or even fabricated by an angry and resentful population, or perhaps they are even militant propaganda.

"I don't believe the gossip they tell foreign correspondents. You are a victim of Maskhadov's propaganda. This is nonsense, complete nonsense," General-Major Shabalkin, who commanded Russian soldiers in Chechnya, is fond of saying about such things. On the other hand, many Western observers and antiwar and pro-separatist activists around the world argue that Russian crimes against noncombatants in Chechnya are the result of intentional Kremlin policy. I do not believe the latter, but am I not convinced that all the stories are "complete nonsense," either.

Most Russian soldiers and policemen have served honorably in Chechnya. I have no intention of portraying all of them as lunatics running wild, looting, raping, and killing innocent Chechen civilians. But some did.

The Samashki Massacre—1995

Regrettably, the MVD's 1995 pamphlet was too late to preclude the tragic events in the village of Samashki in April 1995. Dubbed the "Samashki massacre," it was the most notorious Russian crime against Chechen civilians during the first war.

The 6–7 April Russian assault on Samashki by 250 MVD, OMON (special police), and SOBR (rapid reaction) troops met only disorganized resistance from Chechen fighters. Little property damage was done and few civilians were killed, despite claims by the *Chechenpress* that OMON troops murdered forty-one elderly men and women on 6 April. That is simply untrue. But so was the MVD's claim that three hundred Chechen fighters resisted and that fighting was intense and house to house. Only sixteen Russian servicemen were killed and forty wounded.

The greatest loss of life and property damage came the next day during mopping-up operations, when soldiers went house to house looking for straggling fighters, throwing grenades into courtyards and cellars, and detaining men of all ages, even shooting thirty of them "execution style," according to Sergei Kovalyev, who also headed the Observer Mission of Human Rights and Public Organizations in the Conflict Zone in Chechnya.

More than a hundred civilians died in Samashki's mopping-up operations. The Observer Mission's list of names includes ninety men and thirteen women. With one exception, that of eighteen-year-old Khava Gunashyeva, the 14 females on a different list of 117 dead that I saw were women thirty to sixty-seven years of age. But Japanese photojournalist Hayashi Masaaki photographed a nineteen-year-old pregnant girl who was not on my list with a stake driven through her stomach. Elsa P——, whose family was killed in Samashki, tells me that the majority of younger women had fled the village two days earlier because they were afraid they would be raped.

Khava Gunashyeva was killed along with her father by gunfire from a tank or an armored personnel carrier at her home on Druzhba Street. Soldiers then moved their bodies to the basement and burned them. Two women—Zaluba Yamirzayeva, forty years of age, who lived at No. 93 Vigonnaya Street, and Raisa Masayeva, twenty-four, No. 56 Sheripova Street—died when grenades were thrown into their homes and exploded. Nurbiya Akuyeva, forty-two, at No. 113 Kooperativnaya Street, was shot in the head. Her body was burned, too. Bata Gaitukayeva, fifty-six, and her family died when soldiers set fire to their house at 85 Sheripova Street. Another woman, Dzeki Musayeva, seventy-five, who lived at 48 Stepnaya Street, died from a stroke caused by all the mayhem.

It's unknown how the remaining women died:

1. Petimat Aliyeva, sixty-eight years old, No. 102 Kooperativnaya Street
2. Malika Aliyeva, thirty years old, No. 102 Kooperativnaya Street
3. Senipat Lyurmagomedova, sixty-seven, Chapayeva Street
4. Serizha Lyurmagomedova, forty-nine, No. 27 Chapayeva Street
5. Kulsam Musikhanova, thirty-eight, No. 2 Druzhba Street
6. Kesirt Rasuyeva, sixty-five, Sheripova Street
7. Abi Akhmadova, sixty, No. 93 Sheripova Street
8. Bata Rasuyeva, unknown, No. 93 Sheripova Street

Handicapped fifty-six-year-old Yanist Beksultanova, thirty-year-old Louisa Zubairayeva, fifty-three-year-old Raziat Amayeva, fifty-four-year-old Dagman Shuipova, fifty-one-year-old Kalisa Dazibayeva, and fifty-eight-year-old Aminat Zakiyeva all received grenade fragment wounds but lived. Thirty-four year-old Dagman Atsayeva received a gunshot wound to her chest.

Houses were looted and torched. Samashki resident Keypa Mamayeva looked out her window at 52 Zavodskaya Street on the morning of 8 April and saw Russian servicemen looting the house next door, taking away a cow, a television, and other items. The Observer Mission says that at least forty-five homes were completely destroyed by arson. Two schools were also torched.[11]

Villagers say the Russian servicemen responsible were not the young conscripts who had entered the village on 7 April but the older and poorly disciplined *kontraktniki* soldiers, many of whom were high on the painkiller Promedol (which servicemen routinely carry in their first-aid kits during combat), as evident from the disposable needles found littering the streets.

There are no allegations of rape in Samashki. There were apparently few cases of rape in the first war, although Chechen-born Umalat Umalatov tells in his book about *kontraktniki* who broke into the house of an elderly woman, stole all she had, and in front of the father raped the daughter. Nobody paid much attention to the robbery, but the father gathered up twenty-five relatives, armed them, and wiped out a whole unit of Russian soldiers to get blood revenge.

Khadizhat Gatayeva remembers three girls, one thirteen and the other two almost thirteen, whom she sheltered in 1996 after they had been raped. "Girls," she told them, "Russians are not guilty. Nationality has nothing to do with it. It's simply a horrible person who does this. They probably don't have sisters."

"After two of three such incidents, the Russian Army issued strict orders not to touch Chechen women. From that time on, they didn't search Chechen women at check points, nor did they detain, and did not bother them at filtration camps," Umalat Umalatov writes in his book *Chechnya Glazami Chehentsa*.[12]

Elza P—— did not personally know of anyone raped in the first war. But she did tell me about a special garage for public transportation in the Staropromyslovsky District of Grozny where people believed rapes took place. Her relatives lived close to the facility, which was controlled by Russian troops. At night you could hear the girls' screams. Chechen fighters destroyed the facility in 1996.

Alkhan-Yurt—1996 and 1999

In April 1996, when Russian forces surrounded Alkhan-Kala, villagers were certain they faced the same fate as Samashki, but Dr. Baiev and a delegation went to the Russian general in charge and made a deal to save the village.

When Baiev got home he found three hundred Wolves waiting for him. They had appeared out of nowhere, promising to prevent a repeat of Samashki. They wanted to hide in strategic locations around the village and shoot Russian soldiers when they entered the town. In the end they hid in a warehouse on the outskirts of the village—"just in case." The Russian general conducted his passport check and left peacefully, without incident.

The Council of Europe identified three mass killings of Chechen civilians in the second war. One was in Alkhan-Yurt in December 1999, the second in the Staropromyslovsky District of Grozny in January 2000, and the third in Noviye Aldi, a village in Grozny, in February 2000.

In early December 1999 troops under the command of Russian general Vladimir Shamanov reportedly took the lives of forty-one civilians in the village of Alkhan-Yurt, the killings accompanied by looting. There were also undocumented accusations of rape. On 1 December Maret Pashayeva, sixty-five years of age, Deti Temirsultanova, seventy, and her daughter Sordat, thirty-five, were all killed by a single grenade thrown into the basement of their neighbor's house on Suvorov Street where they were hiding. On 4 December Zara, a neighbor, found the bodies of Nabitsk Kornukayeva, a hundred years old, and her son near the entrance to their home; both had gunshot wounds to their chests. The house was burned.

Human Rights Watch received secondhand information about three rapes in Alkhan-Yurt. In a letter to the Kremlin dated 28 December 1999 the organization reported that thirty-two-year-old Zeinab had accused a Russian soldier of raping two of her close friends, a married twenty-five-year-old woman and a single twenty-year-old female.

Another woman, Zaiman, fifty-five, told human rights workers that she knew of five or six women who had been raped in a basement in Alkhan-Yurt. She alleged that conscript soldiers were often drunk and demanded vodka as well as young women, and she described how she hid herself and the neighbor's daughters in a dugout to protect them: "There were five girls in the hideout with us, three of my daughters—26, 20, and 12—and two of my neighbors' daughters, 18 and 19. We dug a pit at the end of the yard, put in a pipe to breathe though, and threw dirt over the top after the girls climbed inside. They sat in the pit [several days]."

Forty-year-old Sultan alleged that contract soldiers raped a forty-year-old female in an isolated part of town near the cemetery after kicking her husband out of the house. Elza Kasayeva was reportedly raped and murdered in her home at the 4th Liniya in Alkhan-Yurt on 21 January 2000. Four days later the bodies of Lida Taimashkhanova, her sixteen-year-old son Anzor Khashiyev, and a second male were found by neighbors in the Khashiyev's family home. Lida had not been raped, but her left arm was broken; she had a knife wound to her right thigh and several bullet wounds in her chest.

The Rape and Murder of Kheda (Elza) Kungayeva

In January 2000 Human Rights Watch presented more undocumented allegations of rape and murder in other parts of Chechnya. The United Kingdom–based Medical Foundation for the Care of Victims of Torture also reported that sixteen of the nineteen Chechen women it treated between December 1999 and January 2004 had reluctantly disclosed during counseling that they had been raped by Russian soldiers; three conceived as a result. The seventeenth woman claimed she had been forced to make sexual poses, and another was ejaculated upon.

One cannot prove or disprove these claims, but the case against a Russian tank regiment commander, Colonel Yuriy D. Budanov, for the rape and murder of eighteen-year-old Kheda V. (Elza) Kungayeva in the Urus-Martanovsky District is well documented. It stands out, but not because he was charged and convicted of rape. He wasn't.

According to Russian military investigators, at one o'clock in the morning on 27 March 2000 the commander of Division 13206, Colonel Budanov, arrived in the village of Tangi-Chu, Urus-Martanovsky District, in armored personnel carrier no. 391, together with three of his subordinates. On Budanov's orders, his men forcibly removed Kungayeva from No. 7 Zarechny Lane and drove her back to the division's encampment. At around 3 AM, Budanov strangled her in trailer 131, his quarters. On Budanov's instructions, Private Alexandr Yegorov, Sergeant Li-EnShou, and Sergeant Grigoriyev removed Kungayeva's body and buried her in an adjoining forest. Police exhumed the body at ten o'clock the next morning.

General-Major Alexandr Verbitsky, the deputy commander of the Combined Group of Forces in Chechnya, told villagers that Budanov had raped and then strangled Kungayeva. Verbitsky promised swift justice. But numerous trials, an insanity acquittal, and retrials over the next sixteen months brought Budanov only ten years in prison in July 2003, and on charges other than rape (kidnapping, murder, and exceeding his authority), despite the fact that the military's forensic investigator's official report stated that Kungayeva had been raped vaginally and anally about an hour before her death.

Colonel Budanov's subordinates testified that Private Yegorov mutilated the victim's body before burying it. Yegorov was amnestied under a government program targeting both Chechen fighters and federal forces fighting in the North Caucasus and was honorably discharged from the army. Despite massive protests in Chechnya, the criminal Budanov was freed on 15 January 2009, after serving only eight and a half years of his sentence.

Staropromyslovsky—1999

There were also cases of killing and looting in the December 1999–January 2000 Staropromyslovsky District cleansing operation.

On 28 December 1999 Issa found his fifty-six-year-old mother, Dugurkhan Archakova, and sister, thirty-three-year-old Aishat Archakova, in their burning family home in the settlement of Ivanova: "My mother was found right at the entrance to the house. The wall near the door was all damaged from bullets. My sister was lying next to her." On 19 January thirty-eight-year-old Elena Vitalyevna Goncharuk was shot in both legs and the ribs when Russian soldiers fired blindly into the basement of a garage where six women were huddled in a corner.

Two days later Kheda Makhauri, her friend Larisa, and a third woman emerged from the basement where they lived when they saw soldiers loading a vehicle with belongings taken from a neighbor's house. The soldiers ran up to the women and demanded that they empty their pockets:

> All the while, one of the soldiers was looking at my gold things; earrings, a chain, and a ring. Now I understand that we should have given them all the gold at once, though that would have hardly saved us from a bullet. Having called us "information collectors" for the militants, they ordered us to proceed with them to the commandant's office. On the way there, they stopped us and wanted to take us into a half-destroyed house. We started pleading: "Don't kill us, we have kids, we won't tell anybody what you were doing here." Submachine gunfire followed immediately.

At that moment, I was standing behind Larisa. That probably saved my life. I got a through [bullet] wound, hit my head against a stair case, and lost consciousness. I came to my senses because of a strong pain in my ear. An earring had been torn off.[13]

That same day six women and two men of the Zubayev family were found shot and burned in their family home. The house had been looted. The charred body of the mother, Zeinap Zubayeva, sixty-four; her daughter Malika Zubayeva, forty-seven, Alina, Malika's eight-year-old daughter, and Malika's sister Mariet were buried in the rubble. So were the bodies of Luiza Zubayeva, thirty-three; the wife of Ruslan Zubayev, thirty-five (also in the house); and Larisa Zubayeva, twelve (the daughter of Luiza and Ruslan); and a second male, Said-Magomet Zubayev, forty-seven. Malikah and Luiza were clutching their daughters to their breasts.

Noviye Aldy—2000

On 5 February 2000 forty-six people were shot and killed by Russian Interior Ministry personnel in the village of Noviye Aldy, Zavodsky District, Grozny. Earlier Russian bombardment and a severe winter had already claimed the lives of seventy-five residents.

The Council of Europe's Document No. 8948, dated 28 January 2001, describes the 5 February scene this way:

> On the morning of 5 February 2000, persons carrying firearms and dressed in camouflage clothing, without insignia or identification marks and aged from 20 to 35 years, appeared in the settlement, went from house to house, examined outbuildings and residential premises, and inspected documents.
>
> While these armed men were in the settlement, witnesses on the streets heard the sounds of shots. When, after a few hours, the settlement's residents began to come out of their houses, they found the bodies of their relatives and fellow-villagers, with gunshot wounds, in the streets and courtyards.

Chechen fighters had earlier passed through Noviye Aldy in their retreat to the mountains, but on 4 February, after negotiations with Russian Army colonel Lukashov, commander of the 15th Motorized Rifle Regiment, the shelling stopped and people came out of their basements. That same day

Russian military units checked passports and, according to some witnesses, warned people to get out of the village because "people with orders to kill you will soon come."

They came the next day. Malika Labazanova, a survivor of Noviye Aldy, recalls how she rushed over to see her husband's relatives on Mazayeva Street and found three dead bodies: "When I entered the yard, I saw Akhmed, he is about 70 years old, and he said to me 'There are three corpses on the street.' I ran to the gate, opened it, and the first corpse I saw was that of Azyev Aindi, an old man of 80. A few meters from him, near the gate was Koka [Bisultanova], a young woman. A bit further was Aimani [Gadayeva], who sold kerosene."

Another survivor says she heard an explosion from a shoulder-fired grenade launcher and ran out onto the street to see what had happened. She found numerous bodies, all of them her neighbors, with Russian soldiers standing around. "I turned to run back [home]. They yelled at me to 'Stop,' and then fired," she recalls. The next thing she remembers is a Russian soldier sitting beside her saying, "I didn't want them to kill you. You look like my mama." "He called his friends over and they sat with us. These soldiers saved us. Those [soldiers] who shot the people were from one command, but those who helped us, were from another."

At night the woman and her friends carried the bodies—twenty-eight in all—into a house and washed them for burial. She doesn't like to think about it now but remembers that "mainly they were shot in the head—the eyes and mouth." One woman, Gadayeva, had a bullet wound to the back of her head.

A Russian woman, Elena Kuznetsova, was killed, too. She died in her bed from a grenade explosion. Makka Dzhamaldayeva had known her well, as they had spent five months together in the basement of her house hiding from the bombs. Kuznetsova couldn't be moved for burial, because her bed had been booby-trapped.

Aset Chadayeva, then thirty-three years old, a war survivor, pediatric nurse, and now an anti-Russian Chechen political activist living in New York, painfully recalls the death of her close friend that day:

On 5 February at around noontime, I heard the first shooting in the street. We went with our father to see soldiers burning houses. Just in case they tried to rape me, I had a grenade with me. I heard the horrific screams. Ten-year-old Leila, Kaipa's daughter, a refugee from the village of Dzhalka, was hysterical, falling and rolling around on the ground, hollering and screaming in Chechen and in Russian "They killed my mama." Her brother grabbed her hand and dragged her toward our house. I gave her a tranquilizer.

By the time I finished helping her, the soldiers had already left our street. I ran to the fence, there lay Kaipa in a pool of blood, with a portion of her brain exposed. I wanted to pick her up, but she was falling apart, pieces of her skull fell off, probably the result of machine gun fire.[14]

Chadayeva testified before the Helsinki Commission that she had also witnessed killing in 1995: "I was standing in line together with some fifty people from Aldi to get water from a spring. Russian tanks were moving past us. One tank intentionally crushed a car. Inside the car were my neighbors—Yakum Shamilyov and his daughter. They were killed instantly. The Russian soldiers in the tank were drunk. They said: 'If you move from here, we'll open fire.'"

Aset wore a grenade. She told journalist Gabrielle Giroday in 2004,

We had this hand grenade at our window, sitting there for a whole winter. When I heard the Russians were coming, I taped it to my body under my left breast, because I knew if they started taking away women it would be the end of me, and I didn't want to end by being raped and dying in this way. For four days, I slept, I worked. The grenade was part of my body, a part of my body—and if they touched me, I swear to God, I'd have pulled the ring.[15]

Aset later told journalist Andrew Meier that she had bought it from a Russian soldier for four packs of Prima cigarettes: "I told Timur [her brother] I was worried about being raped." "Don't worry," her brother told her, "tape a grenade to your body, and if anyone comes at you, pull the plug."[16]

Other women carried grenades. One of them, Aizan Gazuyeva, would blow up herself and the general who had killed her husband in November 2001.

The Russian Ministry of Defense denied that army soldiers or MVD units under its control were responsible for the crimes in Noviye Aldy. Russian officials told the Council of Europe that "the investigation could find no confirmation of participation by the armed forces in the afore-mentioned events." A later reply from the military prosecutor's office of the Northern Caucasus Military District sent to Human Rights Center "Memorial" pointed the finger at Saint Petersburg and Ryazanskaya Oblast police: "It has been established that the operations of so-called 'cleansing' of the settlement of Aldy on 5 and 10 February 2000 were carried out by members of the GUVD [Main Internal Affairs Directorate] OMON of the city of Saint Petersburg and of the Ryazanskaya Oblast, which are not subject to supervision by the Military Procurators Office. In addition, the materials of investigation have been sent to the Procurator of the city of Grozny for adoption of a legal decision."

Relatives of the deceased subsequently received a "letter of certification" from T. A. Murdalov, the investigator for especially important cases with the office of the procurator general in the North Caucasus, that read: "On 5 February 2000, during a passport regime check operation in the first half of the day in the town of Noviye Aldy of the Zavodsky District of the city of Grozny of the Chechen Republic, servicemen of the RF MO and MVD units committed a massacre of peaceful residents. . . . Concerning that fact, the Main Directorate of the Office of the Prosecutor General of the Russian Federation in the Northern Caucasus is carrying out an investigation."

Chechnya's procurator tried unsuccessfully to bring at least one Saint Petersburg policeman to justice. Russia's general procurator subsequently got involved, but there is still no outcome. There are annual demonstrations in Moscow and Saint Petersburg by Russia's "anti-war movement" to bring those responsible to justice.

Duba-Yurt—2000

Duba-Yurt was also bombed, looted, and finally burned in February 2000 out of revenge for comrades killed while trying to rout Wolves out of the southern outskirts of the village.

Raisa Amtayeva, the mother of two teenagers introduced in Anna Politkovskaya's book *A Small Corner of Hell,* watched from nearby Chiri-Yurt, where she and other villagers had fled, as her house in Duba-Yurt burned. "That was the end of everything. I don't have a single photo left of our past," she told Politkovskaya.[17]

Villagers sorted through the fiery ruins for days to find any scraps left of their lives. Village administrator A. Yakhyayev, along with the Emergency Situations Ministry representative and the deputy commander of Military Unit 69771, signed the following official "certificate of inspection" confirming what had happened in Duba-Yurt:

We, the undersigned, Head of Duba-Yurt settlement Yakhyayev, A. F., MChS Representative Col. Voichenko, Yu. P., Deputy Commander, Military Unit 69771, Lt. Col. Larichyev, S. V., have prepared this certified act of inspection and joint observation of the village of Duba-Yurt testifying that columns of military vehicles (with enlisted men on board) passing through the village systematically plundered and set fire to civilians' houses.

THE TRIAL OF TWO SERGEANTS

Despite the failure to prosecute those responsible for Noviye Aldy and Duba-Yurt, a well documented cleansing-operation murder case did go to trial at the end of 2000.

Two Russian paratroopers assigned to the 417th Detached Intelligence Battalion, contract Sergeant Dmitry Magonov, twenty-three, and conscript Sergeant Alexei Sukhanov, killed an Alkhan-Kala family during a *zachistka* there in December 2000. Fifty-two-year-old Akhmet Ismailov, his wife Zinaida, and their two daughters—Fatima, twenty, and Kheda, sixteen—were all slain by Magonov and Sukhanov.

The two sergeants had been sent with their unit to Alkhan-Kala in the early morning of 15 December 2000 to capture or kill fighters led by Arbi Barayev, a notorious trafficker in people and slaves. They found only wounded fighters, but when Magonov and Sukhanov fanned out across town they were approached on the road by the Ismailov family, who asked permission to pass in order to visit relatives on the other side of town. Sukhanov let them, but then the father whispered something to his daughter Kheda, and both she and her little sister turned around and walked back home. Magonov testified in court that he thought the girls might be fighters and followed. Sukhanov in turn followed the parents, thinking they might try to warn fighters that a cleansing operation was under way.

Sukhanov claims that he entered a bombed-out building, lost his footing on a pile of bricks, let out a yell when he fell, and then heard approaching footsteps. Thinking it was the enemy he leapt out of the window, swung his machine gun around, and fired at the silhouettes he saw, killing Akhmet and Zinaida. Magonov heard the shots and ran back to find Sukhanov standing there trembling. Together they hid the bodies and then went back to the Ismailov house, where the girls were standing by the door wondering what the shooting had been all about.

"I told them that a special operation had just been carried out and that they did not have to worry about their parents. The girls went into the house to get some water [for Sukharov]. We followed them. Sukhanov went first, I behind him. I hadn't even crossed the threshold when I heard the same tone-less [because of a silencer] shots," Magonov recalled in court.

Magonov cut off the victim's ear: "When I entered the house, I saw the bloody bodies of the girls. I became angry. I remember that I took the kitchen knife from the table, went over to one girl, took her ear in one hand and slashed it with the other hand. I then wrapped the ear in cellophane and threw it away. I don't know why I did this."

Sukhanov received eighteen years at hard labor. Magonov is serving a fifteen-year sentence. Another serviceman got eleven years at hard labor for the December 2000 shooting of a woman, A. Tunayeva, and a man, M. M. Magamedov.

Four more criminal cases over the next two years resulted in a least two prosecutions and court convictions. On 10 March 2001 a Russian warrant officer was court-martialed and received four years in prison and a five-year suspended sentence for raping a woman in his barracks. Five months later, on 29 August 2001, a conscript serviceman burglarized a house in Shali, stole 1,500 rubles, and raped A. R. Dambayeva. He too was court-martialed, though only for robbery, and received five years in prison, with five years probation. In November 2001 two Russian soldiers were arrested for the 7 October killing of twenty-four-year-old Zalina Mezhidova, the mother of four, and her relative, fifteen-year-old Akhmad Gekhayev. The soldiers' helicopter had fired on Mezhidova and Gekhayev returning from their garden plot on the outskirts of Komsomolskoye. The shooters landed and removed the bodies in front of witnesses, who later staged a massive protest and secured the pledge of the Chechen government to find and punish the men.

A United Nations report cited an unconfirmed case of attempted rape in Tsotsi-Yurt on 27 July 2002. The victim's husband had helped a neighbor repair a car, which, unbeknownst to him, belonged to a fighter. At eleven o'clock the next day twenty Russian soldiers came to the house. They report-edly pinned the woman, Iman, up against the wall and threatened to kill her eleven-month-old daughter unless her husband immediately returned home. Iman's sister-in-law went out, found him, and returned home with him. The soldiers took the husband away, but some of them returned the following day. They demanded that Iman confess to being a fighter, injected her with some kind of green fluid, and then raped her, threatening to kill her and her daughter if she told anyone.

President Putin prohibited further large-scale cleansing operations in November 2002. The number of *zachistkas* subsequently declined, decreasing sharply after the summer of 2003. The smaller-scale operations that replaced them are now commonly called "passport regime checks," or "address checks," but women are still targeted. In February 2006 alone thirty-seven people were detained in address checks, including two women, on charges ranging from aiding and abetting fighters to storing arms and selling narcotics.

More targeted "spetz-operations" (special operations) hunting fighters and terrorists are now replacing "address checks." Nevertheless, women remain in peril.

CAUGHT IN THE CROSSFIRE

On 3 February 2007 the charred corpse of a Chechen woman was found in the rubble of a fifth floor apartment at No. 3 Oskanova Street in Malgobek, Ingushetia. She had died accidentally a few hours earlier in a messy police spetz-operation targeting a single fighter.

Two days later the mother of a young fighter was gunned down in her own home in Shelkovskaya, Chechnya, because her son, Salambek Bushuyev, had chosen to engage police in a vicious firefight instead of surrendering. And on 11 March 2007 Raisa Zakiyeva died when her companion, forty-year-old Apti Yukhinov, detonated a hand grenade after police surrounded their house on Krasina Street in Ordzhonikidzyevskaya, Ingushetia.

Any woman can be easily caught in the middle of a federal counter-terror spetz-operation. It can happen anytime and anywhere—when she is at home, in her car, walking down the street, shopping, on a bus, or even picking wild garlic in the forest. No place is safe or sacred. More often than not it happens simply because she is with her husband, sons, or other male members of the family who have been targeted. She rarely survives.

In January 2000 thirty-five-five-year-old Z. I. Dzhavatkhanova, an expectant mother from Nokhchi-Keloi, suddenly found herself in terrible trouble when the car she was riding in drove into a counterterror operation against a group of Arbi Barayev's fighters. She paid for it with her life.

On the afternoon on 11 January, Dzhavatkhanova and her nephew were on their way home from a tiring visit to the pediatrician in Shatoi, sharing the ride with three other people, when Russian Army captain Eduard Ulman, who had been ordered to set up a roadblock to catch fleeing terrorists, attempted to stop their car. But he failed to signal the driver in time. The captain could have shot out the tires or put a bullet in the engine, but since he had been given orders to shoot fleeing fighters—and saw a car full of people—he fired on the car, killing the driver (a schoolmaster) and wounding two other people in the arms and legs. Dzhavatkhanova and her nephew were unhurt.

For the next two hours, a very nervous Ulman pored over passports and residence registrations and thoroughly searched everybody's belongings, but he failed to find any weapons or explosives, or anything else that would in the slightest indicate that the people in his custody were fighters. He radioed his superior, Major Aleksei Perelevsky, for instructions. He was told to shoot everybody.

Ulman: "You want me to destroy [kill] them?"

Perelevsky: "Yes, destroy!"

At five o'clock in the evening Ulman told Dzhavatkhanova and the others they were free to go, but he and two subordinates, Vladimir Voyevodin and Aleksandr Kalagansky, shot everybody in the back as they turned around to walk to their car.

The North Caucasus Okrug Military Court twice acquitted Ulman and his men of murder, but in the spring of 2007 the Russian Supreme Court overturned the acquittals and ordered a new trial. This time they were found guilty, but Ulman, Voyevodin, and Kalagansky fled rather than face sentencing. They are still at large. Only Major Perelevsky showed up for sentencing. He received a mere nine years at hard labor.

In the evening on 27 December 2000 Luiza Betishyeva, the mother of two small children, was going about her usual shopping at the central market in Grozny when Russian soldiers just meters from her tried to detain a young man for questioning. But he made a run for it—straight toward Luiza and the crowded market. Bullets spat from the soldiers' automatics, tearing into them both.

On 14 October 2002 Urus-Martan resident Zaira Shakhtamirova was certain she had found quiet refuge on a homeward-bound bus at the Malgobek (Ingushetia) bus station, when suddenly a man with a grenade jumped aboard. Chechen policemen were right behind him. They fired their weapons and he detonated his grenade, killing Zaira and three other passengers.

At four in the afternoon on New Year's Eve, 2004, military servicemen and armored personnel carriers surrounded No. 16 Avtobusnaya Street in the village of Podgorny, where Wolves were hiding. The neighborhood erupted in gunfire, and residents found themselves caught in the crossfire. A woman with three small children miraculously dodged bullets from both sides as she scrambled to safety. She survived but Madina, the wife of the fighter inside the house, died along with her husband.

Ask any Chechen woman and she'll tell you never to wear camouflage clothing into the woods. It will get you killed. That's what happened to a thirty-eight-year-old elementary teacher picking wild garlic in the forest on 24 March 2007. That day MVD lieutenant colonel Aleksei Korgun and his men scouting a forest near the village of Urdyukhoi, Chechnya, detected movement up ahead. Trees obscured their vision, and the weather wasn't the best, but they were certain they saw figures in camouflage clothing bending over or kneeling, picking up something, probably weapons from a buried cache. The behavior was suspicious. And besides, only Wolves wear camouflage in the woods, Korgun reasoned.

He and his men opened fire. Thirty-eight-year-old Khaldat Mutakova was the first to fall. Zaira Kasumova, Mutakova's daughter-in-law, twenty-six, was also shot and seriously wounded. A third woman, Khaldat's sister, forty-year-old Zalpa Mutakova, screamed in horror but she was unhurt. Korgun was arrested, tried, and convicted of negligence and sentenced to three years behind bars.

You wouldn't expect your cheap car to get carjacked in Chechnya, either, but that's what happened to Madina Yangulbayeva and Khava Israilova late on the night of 21 March 2008. They were just about to arrive home in the settlement of Alkhazurovo, Urus-Martanovsky District, when four gunmen appeared out of the night and blocked the road in front of them. The Wolves, fleeing a massive police dragnet after murdering four policemen in a bloody midnight raid on the settlement, shot and wounded the two women and then stole their car.

That same summer, in mid-June, a woman out for an evening stroll was gunned down when three fighters opened fire with grenade launchers and automatic rifles on a federal convoy passing through the center of the city of Bamut. Shooting lasted only seconds, but when the dust cleared an armored vehicle was burning and the woman was lying in a pool of her own blood on the sidewalk in front of No. 15 Sheripova Street.

Women themselves become the targets of spetz-operations because they are suspected suicide bombers *(shakhidas)* or relatives of fighters and terrorists. These cases are discussed in detail in later chapters.

More often women are killed, wounded, or detained because they intentionally interfere with the detention of a suspect—defending a husband, son, brother, neighbor, or somebody else they don't even know.

Women were often successful in rescuing Chechen men during the first war. In August 1996 journalist Jim Satterwhite saw firsthand their effectiveness in springing a detainee: "Suddenly a group of women in a passing bus saw what was going on [the detention of a young man by Russian soldiers] and sprang into action. They yelled at the driver to stop the bus, ran out and pulled the young man from the military truck. They proceeded to argue with the soldiers and even ran after them waving their fists." The soldiers figured it was better to turn the young man loose rather than deal with the hysterical women.

Dr. Baiev himself was rescued by women during a confrontation with Russian soldiers over treating fighters belonging to warlord Arbi Barayev. An old woman noticing the commotion ran up and down the street shouting in Chechen, "They are holding our doctor. Doctor is a prisoner." She soon collected a crowd of thirty women, elderly men, and even a few children. "Move back, or we'll shoot," a soldier shouts, "Go back to your houses."

"But," Baiev later wrote, "the women were insistent and angry, their comments came thick and fast."

A woman holding two kids shouted, "He's treated your injured! . . . You have no right to touch the doctor! He treats women and children. Shoot our doctor and you will have to shoot us all."[18]

An old friend of Kelimatov's tells the story of a girl named Irina who, during the cleaning of the Staropromyslovsky District, came to his defense and saved his life: "They [the Russian soldiers] dragged me and the Chechen boys from the basement we had been hiding in to protect ourselves from the bombs and stood us up against the wall. That day, like the others, they killed Chechen youth for no reason to get even for their boys. Irina begged the soldiers not to shoot me. She convinced them that I was not a mujahid, but a peaceful person who had saved her life. That is how I stayed alive."[19] The girl had been arrested and the man begged Kelimatov for her release. Irina was freed.

Some Russian soldiers began shooting women who physically interfered after the Chechen female suicide bomber appeared on the scene in 2000.

On 14 January 2001, during the *zachistka* of Stariye Atagi, Zulai Demilkh-anova and other village women demanded to know why thirty-seven-year-old Kh. Elzhurkayev was being detained. Unsatisfied with the answer, they surrounded the soldiers and attempted to wrestle Elzhurkayev free. The soldiers initially beat the women off, but they came back for a second round. In the end, lethal force was used to disperse the sea of angry women. Zulai was killed, and several others were wounded.

More frequently, though, women are taken into custody along with the men they are defending. Most are interrogated and ultimately released, but some disappear without a trace.

At 6 AM on 20 April 2001 soldiers burst into the Alkhan-Yurt house of A. Dzhaubatryrova, searched the premises, and placed her son in handcuffs. She demanded an explanation, but when the neighbor was summoned for help she was also taken into custody. Dzhaubatryrova disappeared. The district administrator told her relatives that the FSB had taken her to the military base at Khankala for questioning, but the military procurator was never able to locate her.

On 14 January 2003 Anzhela Shakhmurzayeva was detained for interfering in the detention of three young men near Grozny's central square. Soldiers had ordered the trio out of an apartment building and onto the street. One man's wife rushed to his defense but was physically restrained and began screaming. Anzhela, hearing the woman's screams, ran to her rescue but was taken into custody, too.

The fates of the two women are unknown, but that doesn't mean they were killed. Human rights organizations are vocal when it comes to a woman being taken into custody but seldom make a public announcement of her release. There simply isn't enough reliable follow-up information to know what has happened to many of the women.

THREE

The Pain Continues

Each woman who has gone through these two wars can tell you. Each one has her
own kind of pain. One kind of wound might heal, but another one opens up.
Lida Yusopova, Chechen human rights activist

EVEN AFTER THE DAILY BOMBING and the massive *zachistkas,* there's
no refuge from the violence. The Chechen woman is still gunned down;
blown up by Jihadists' bombs or land mines; kidnapped or disappeared;
thrown into filthy jails and tortured; snatched right off the street for interrogation about her intentions of becoming a suicide bomber or about her "terrorist" relatives; her house burned down because she is suspected of aiding
and abetting the enemy; or killed because she behaves "immorally" or dares
to speak out against human rights abuses.

WITHOUT A TRACE

Women frequently disappear in Chechnya. Russia says that forty thousand
Chechens, Russians, and foreigners have been abducted in the republic since
the end of the Soviet Union. According to official statistics, seven thousand
Chechens have been kidnapped since 1994, but the real numbers are higher
because people nowadays are afraid to report a missing relative out of fear
for their remaining family's safety. People who file missing-persons reports
sometimes themselves turn up missing. Chechen authorities say that nearly
4,300 missing people (1,500 for the period 1994–95 and 2,800 for 2000–
2007) are still unaccounted for.

A huge number of kidnappings took place between 1996 and 1999, when Chechnya's people-for-sale trade was booming and wealthy Chechens, like foreigners, would bring a respectable profit. Chechnya has a rich culture of kidnapping for ransom. It was a traditional Chechen cottage industry in the nineteenth century, but it had become so profitable by the mid-1990s that no fewer than sixty-two gangs, with private armies and primitive prisons, engaged in a $200 million captives-for-sale trade that victimized Chechens, Russians, Jews, and foreigners alike. The business had a sophisticated division of labor, and religious contracts were concluded between those who did the physical kidnapping and the criminal entities that provided transportation, security, and ransom negotiations. Lists of names, occupations, and other vital information about people who were not ransomed but sold as slaves could be found anytime at Grozny's downtown slave market, where human beings were auctioned off like cattle.[1]

Victims were usually chosen from the wealthy and strong, but not always. Children like three-year-old Lena Meshcheryakova were even snatched from their beds.

Just before dawn on 8 October 1998 four armed men burst into Lena's house in Grozny, stole her mother's gold earrings, and took little Lena from her warm bed. Kidnappers demanded $15,000 ransom, but nine months later they reduced it to $1,000 because her Russian mother couldn't raise the money. A cruel Chechen woman had helped kidnap Lena; "Larisa cut me with a knife for losing a slipper," the child later told her mother. At the time of her release her ear was lacerated, she was emaciated, and she suffered from severe psychological trauma. She was a pitiful sight.

Kidnappers singled out Jewish children because they brought more money. The tips of Alla Geifman's fingers were chopped off and a videotape made of the act to hasten ransom payment. Alla, the thirteen-year-old daughter of banker Grigory Geifman, didn't even live in Chechnya. She was abducted in May 1999 near her home in Saratov, Russia, and taken to Chechnya.

That same summer criminals kidnapped Laura Lichtman, eighteen and an Israeli citizen, while she was visiting her granny in Nalchik, the capital of a nearby republic. A twelve-year-old Russian girl was also taken and held in a tiny, filthy underground dirt dugout until the FSB rescued her in 2000. Half-starved, her blond hair and face caked in filth, she was certain her captors had come back to kill her when rescuers lifted the steel grate from her hell. In late January 2010 Leninsky District police arrested a twenty-nine-year-old man who had participated as part of a criminal gang in the kidnapping of a fifteen-year-old Grozny girl in 1999. Police declined to release her name.

Two Chechen men went on trial in August 2007 for the 19 September 1997 abduction of Russian-born Elena Grigoryets. They intended to slit her throat and kill her family unless she paid them $200,000. Her family managed to scrape together $10,000, and Elena was released on 22 October 1997.

Multiple kidnappings of Russian and foreign women occurred between 1996 and 2002, including that of British citizen Camila Carr, who was raped, and Russian NTV television reporter Elena Masyuk; of two Russian mothers, Valintina Yokhina and Antonina Borshchova, who had come to Chechnya looking for their missing military sons in 1998; and of humanitarian aide director Nina Davidovicha, who worked for Druzba, a Russian NGO doing UNICEF work in Chechnya, in July 2002.

But there were two abductions in the spring of 1996 that didn't fit the usual for ransom pattern. Nadezhda Chaikova worked for the Russian *Obshchaya Gazeta* newspaper and traveled frequently to Chechnya. She filmed the awful things that went on in Samashki in 1995, and had close contacts with Chechen fighters. But on or about 20 March 1996 Nadezhda disappeared. Ten days later, villagers found her body stuffed neatly into a sewage pipe on the outskirts of the town of Gekhi. She was still blindfolded. She had been severely beaten and forced to kneel while a single bullet from a Makarova pistol was put into the back of her head. Nobody knows why Nadezhda was murdered. Perhaps Wolves believed the rumors about her being a Russian spy. Or maybe she was executed to silence her outspoken criticism of the Russian military.

Nina Yefimova, a reporter for the *Vozrozhdeniye* newspaper who lived in Grozny with her seventy-six-year-old mother, similarly disappeared. Both were abducted from their apartment on the night of 8 May 1996. Yefimova's body was discovered the next day in the Leninsky District of the city, her mother's body that night in an abandoned canning factory. Nina's blistering reporting on crime in Chechnya likely got her killed.

Chechen women are kidnapped, if not for marriage, by federal and Chechen police and security forces, or by criminals and Wolves for ransom to help fund their criminal groups or illegal armed formations, for use as suicide bombers, or because they have been fraternizing with Russian soldiers or collaborating with the Russian enemy or its pro-Moscow Chechen government. Women disappear because they are suspected suicide bombers or relatives of fighters and terrorists. This was especially true after the October 2002 attack on Moscow's Dubrovka's theater by nineteen Chechen women and their male counterparts, after the 2003 Chechen female suicide bomber attacks in Moscow, and after the seizure of the school in Beslan, North Ossetia, in 2004. These cases are discussed in detail in chapter 7.

The kidnapping and killing of women in retaliation for the death of Russian soldiers occurs, too. On 9 January 2002 the mutilated corpses of Ruslana Shaipova and Mayora Musayeva from Stariye and Noviye Atagi were discovered on the outskirts of a village. The frozen body of a third girl, a sixteen-year-old from Noviye Atagi, was found eight days later. Villagers will tell you that the girls were kidnapped and killed in retaliation for the landmine death of a Russian soldier on the road between Chiri-Yurt and Noviye Atagi the day before.

Unexplained disappearances, like that of a pregnant woman who drove into Grozny on 11 January 2000 to buy clothing for her baby and disappeared at a Russian police checkpoint, frequently occur. Her body, with one bullet hole to her head and two to her chest, was found four months later in the basement of a private house in Grozny. Nobody knows how she got there or why she was killed.

Similarly a Grozny nurse who disappeared in 2000 was found in a common grave in the capital in February 2001. Forensics determined that she had died from a blow to her head by a blunt object. On 16 October 2005 a thirty-one-year-old woman from Stariye Atagi disappeared without a trace. Three months later, twenty-four-year-old Markha Magomedovna Soltukhanova from the village of Tolstoy-Yurt was gone too. Nobody knows why. The following May Ina Daduyeva, a twenty-seven-year-old Octyarbsky District resident and mother of three, vanished. She had left for Grozny's city center to apply for pension certification for her nine-year-old daughter, who was suffering from asthma, and was last seen at a bus stop.

At 9 AM on 17 August 2005 masked men in camouflage uniforms took twenty-six-year-old Elina Ersenoyeva—a part-time *Chechen Society* newspaper journalist, UNICEF worker, and Shamil Basayev's widow—and her aunt from their car, put sacks over their heads, and whisked them away to a secret location. Several hours later Elina's aunt was blindfolded, put back into the car, and dropped off on a Grozny street corner. Elina called her aunt to tell her not to "raise a panic" over what had happened. Elina herself telephoned home that evening. Her captor took the phone and confirmed to her mother, Margarita, that she would be released later in the day, but she hasn't been heard from since. Two months later her mother also disappeared without a trace.

Perhaps federal or Chechen security forces seized both of them, or Basayev's associates, after his death in July, staged their disappearance in order to get them out of Chechnya to a safe place in another country.

Another woman was kidnapped, then two more, by the end of 2006. On 29 August a local resident walked into the Oktyabrsky District police station in Grozny to report that at two o'clock in the morning ten unknown men in camouflage uniforms broke into his house, threatened him at gunpoint, and kidnapped his niece—a medical student.

At the end of November armed men in Grozny and in the Naursky District abducted two girls over a weekend. A group of armed men in camouflage uniforms who identified themselves as policemen took a seventeen-year-old girl in the Zavodsky District of Grozny. The second abduction took place in the village of Chernokozovo, where armed men forcibly removed a twenty-year-old girl from her parents' home. The fates of both girls remain unknown.

Who's Doing the Kidnapping?

Unless the masked men arrive in Russian armored personnel carriers with Russian license plates and speaking unaccented Russian, it's impossible to determine who's doing the kidnapping and for what reason.

Identification cannot be determined on the basis of appearance, either, because Wolves, Chechen law enforcement personnel, and Russian police all dress alike—mostly in camouflage uniforms—wear masks, have identical weapons, and drive the same kinds of cars. Sometimes *mujahideen* purposely wear Chechen police uniforms and even flash Chechen police identification to make it look like pro-Moscow Chechen law enforcement forces are responsible for abductions. Frequently they are.

Forty percent of Chechens surveyed in a 2006 Don Women's Union study believe that federal forces are primarily responsible for abductions, 11 percent say fighters are the guilty ones, and 60 percent feel that Russian special services are doing the kidnapping.[2]

In February 2005 Russia's deputy interior minister and head of operational headquarters for the North Caucasus, General-Colonel Arkadiy Yedelyev, conceded that federal and Chechen security forces had been responsible for "unlawful detentions" and the disappearances of numerous civilians in the republic for various reasons, including criminal ones.

That May Margarita Ersenoyeva was abducted on her way home from Grozny's central market, where she had been selling all day. She was taken to a house and beaten by Ilyas, a young Chechen man. Afterward a Russian officer walked into the room, reprimanded Ilyas for hitting Ersenoyeva so hard, and promised to punish him. The officer checked her documents, made a phone call, came back, told her it had all been a big mistake, and then blindfolded her and delivered her back to the spot where she had been abducted.

But the torment wasn't over. A week later Ilyas kidnapped her again, told her that he had lost his job and a monthly salary of five hundred dollars because of her, beat her, and demanded $1,500 cash. Margarita paid up but Ilyas's men caught her again on the street a few weeks later and stole $250 and her gold earrings. They later came to the market and mugged her there, too. It's unclear if Ilyas was acting alone or with the Russian officer, but the scheme victimized dozens of market traders.

In 2006 Russia's procurator general prosecuted numerous abduction cases involving Russian policemen. The case against Senior Lieutenant Sergei Lapin, a former Nizhnevarovsky ROVD policeman, stands out.

In July 2007 Lapin was tried a second time for the beating and disappearance of twenty-two-year-old Zelimkhan Murdalov, whom he had detained and placed in an Oktyabrsky District jail cell in January 2001. Khamid Khadayev, himself a prisoner in that jail, told the Chechen court that on the evening of 2 January 2001 the "Kadet" (Lapin's nickname), together with the deputy ROVD chief, threw Murdalov into the cell. The young man had been badly beaten, with broken bones protruding through the skin on one hand. Khadayev remembers that a doctor came to the cell, bandaged Murdalov as best he could, then told police that he needed immediate hospitalization or he would die. "Make out a death certificate instead," the doctor was told. Murdalov's condition worsened during the night. He was removed, still alive, from the cell the next morning but hasn't been seen since.

Murdalov's mother and sister weren't beyond Lapin's reach either. In the fall of 2003 Rukiyat and Zalina Murdalova received political asylum in Norway, but his father Astemir stayed in Chechnya. In August 2004 he visited Norway and was interviewed on Norwegian television about the Lapin case. A few days later an unknown person delivered a note in Russian to Rukiyat and Zalina's mailbox at the refugee center in Norway, warning the family that they would soon have to answer to Lapin for their father's big mouth.

Colonel Budanov's supporters made similar death threats against Kheda Kungayeva's family, which had also immigrated to Norway in 2003. Throughout the many court trials in the years between Kheda's rape and murder and the final conviction of Budanov, Visa Kungayev (Kheda's father), Roza Bashayeva (her mother), and their remaining four children received numerous death threats from Budanov supporters and Russian national extremists supporting him. "We'll do to you what Budanov did to your daughter!" angry Budanovites shouted outside the courtroom during his trial. "The mother of a sniper!" a soldier at a Russian checkpoint yelled at Roza Bashayeva during a recent trip to Chechnya.

Calling the kettle black, Chechen president Ramzan Kadyrov has often accused Russia's ORB-2 (Operational Investigations Bureau 2), a 150-man-strong special unit made up mostly of Chechens but subordinated to the Russian MVD for the Southern Federal Okrug, of unlawfully detaining (kidnapping) people and subjecting them to cruel and unusual treatment, including torture. He has even called for the ORB to cease operations in Chechnya. So have Chechen law enforcement officials.

At a meeting of Chechen law enforcement agencies in Grozny on 4 May 2007 Chechen police officials demanded the ORB's "liquidation" in Chechnya. Noting numerous complaints of mistreatment from former detainees and echoing the Council of Europe's denunciation of the unit for its use of torture, Chechen deputy procurator Vladimir Chernyayev accused the ORB of using "cruel and unlawful methods" in interrogating detainees suspected of being separatists or terrorists. ORB officials denied any wrongdoing and said that Kadyrov was just trying to bring them under his personal control. Maybe they were right. The fact that Kadyrov personally introduced a new ORB-2 chief, Isa Surguyev, to ORB personnel on 23 July 2007 makes one suspect that he got his way.

In a meeting on 26 July, President Kadyrov told Surguyev that the unit must once and for all shed its infamous "torture cell" reputation and do everything necessary "to ensure the detainee will receive the maximum protection afforded to him by law." Surguyev assured Kadyrov that the ORB-2 "will fulfill its functional responsibilities" and that "the ORB-2 is an operational unit, not a prison," and he promised to do everything possible so that "our unit will set an example" for the rest of the MVD to follow.

In early 2009 the Human Rights Center "Memorial" reported that it had not received any reports of torture by ORB-2 and "in general the number of cases of torture of law enforcement structures in the Chechen Republic has declined sharply." That had drastically changed by the summer of 2009.

Ramzan Kadyrov's own security forces, the Security Service of the President of the Chechen Republic (commonly called the "*Kadyrovtsy*"), created by his father, Akhmad Kadyrov, and commanded by Ramzan himself, also engages in kidnappings and unlawful interrogation methods.

In February 2003 the bodies of three women kidnapped from the settlement of Goity were found torn apart by explosives. *Kadyrovtsy* are suspected. That same month explosives were also used to dispose of Seda Tsagarayeva, the sister of the late Chechen field commander Magomed Tsagarayev. She had been taken by Chechen armed men from her house in Urus-Martan and her body was later found in a forest outside the city. In a high-profile case, on 29 February and 1 March 2004 *Kadyrovtsy* kidnapped at least forty relatives, including numerous women, of Ichkeria's former defense minister, Magomed Khambiyev (now a deputy in Chechnya's parliament), to compel him to voluntarily surrender. They were held at the temporary detainment facility (IVS) in the Nozhai-Yurtovsky ROVD police station and in illegal prisons on bases operated by Kadyrov and Sulim Yamadayev.

Kadyrovtsy were also responsible for the kidnappings of twelve of Ichkerian president Aslan Maskhadov's relatives during the 1–3 September terror attack on Secondary School No. 1 in Beslan, North Ossetia. They were released after the school was stormed. Seven of Maskhadov's relatives, including his elderly sister and his niece, were seized again in December 2004. Sixty-seven-year-old Bucha Abdulkadirova was alone in her house when nine vehicles filled with *Kadyrovtsy* arrived at No. 62 Turbine Street in the Staropromyslovsky District of Grozny to take her away.

Bucha's kidnapping was not without incident. A scuffle broke out with GRU (military intelligence) personnel of the Zapad Battalion at a checkpoint when the latter accused the *Kadyrovtsy* of "stealing people" from their jurisdiction. It was only after the battalion commander personally called Ramzan Kadyrov to confirm that he had ordered Bucha to be picked up that the *Kadyrovtsy* were allowed to leave with her.

On 28 December *Kadyrovtsy* came back after Bucha's married daughter, forty-year-old Khadichat Satuyeva, and dragged her barefoot out of the house. All were held for six months in a secret prison in President Kadyrov's hometown of Tsentroi but were mysteriously released on 31 May 2005. Russia's deputy procurator claims they were freed in a spetz-operation.

Similarly, on 5 May 2005, Chechen security forces seized Chechen separatist leader Doka (Doku, Dokka) Umarov's relatives, including his wife, six-month-old son, and seventy-year-old father. Umarov's wife and son were later released, but the fate of his father is unknown. That August Umarov's sister, Natasha Khumadova, was also abducted by armed men who broke into her house. Her fate is also unknown.

President Ramzan Kadyrov apparently instructed his security services to halt abductions at the beginning of 2007, although they did not stop entirely. In mid-March 2007 he had four Chechen criminal investigators arrested for accepting a $20,000 bribe in exchange for the release of a woman's husband they had kidnapped.

That year a high-profile murder case associated with the kidnapping of a Chechen woman involved a Chechen policeman who abducted a twenty-year-old female for the sole purpose of staging the killing of a suicide bomber so he could get a promotion.

On 22 May 2007 Chechnya's procurator forwarded the case of Ruslan Asuyev and ten of his subordinates, including six policemen, to the Chechen Supreme Court for trial. All were accused of the 6 May 2005 premeditated murder of a woman identified only as "Madina." Asuyev's account of the woman's death in his official report says that she was in possession of a suicide belt and had been shot and killed before she could detonate her explosives during an attack on a police patrol. There's an alternate version, told by Human Rights Center "Memorial," which says that Asuyev made her detonate her belt. But the prosecution established that Madina died as a result of gunshot wounds inflicted at point-blank range. Investigators could not find any link between Madina and any illegal armed formation.

Questioning of Asuyev's subordinates revealed that they had been pressured by their commander to produce results in the catching or killing of terrorists. Islam Agayev, a second policeman charged in the case, told investigators that his boss had personally ordered him to kidnap a female passerby and dress her up like a suicide bomber so they would get credit for killing a *shakhida*. Madina was ordered to put on a suicide belt and cross the street. When she refused she was shot. Asuyev then telephoned the FSB to tell them that his unit had just killed a suicide bomber in a spetz-operation. Arriving sappers conveniently found an unexploded explosives belt in the woman's hand.

Asuyev, a deputy commander of an MVD security regiment responsible for protecting oil facilities, organized his rogue group of policemen, former amnestied fighters, and civilians at the end of 2004. They carried out numerous kidnappings for ransom in Chechnya, Ingushetia, and Dagestan. Asuyev's attorney dismissed the charges as part of a power struggle between the ORB-2 and the MVD Chechnya. It was, after all, the ORB-2 that had tracked Asuyev down at his hideout in the Astrakhanskaya Oblast.

There were more kidnappings after Madina's murder. On 27 December 2006 masked men took Khalimat Baytukayeva from her home in the Vedensky District. She was never heard from again. On 24 December 2008 Deniyeva, a twenty-seven-year-old woman, walked into Grozny's Leninsky District police station to report that her forty-four-year-old mother had been kidnapped by four masked gunmen who broke into her apartment on Kabardinskaya Street and forced her mother at gunpoint into a waiting car. She, too, has not been found.

In March 2009 masked men kidnapped a young girl from the settlement of Dargo, Vedensky District, in just one of twenty kidnappings in that district since the beginning of that year. Locals suspect neighboring Nozhai-Yurtovsky police.

Corrupt Chechen police collaborate with Wolves in kidnappings too. Of the fifty-two Chechen policemen fired for corruption in 2006, five were formally charged with militant collaboration. The following year Chechnya's procurator investigated eighty-eight cases involving collaboration with illegal armed formations.

Sometimes the fighter and the policemen are one and the same person, as in the case of the twenty-five-year-old Sunzhensky District ROVD policeman, a four-year veteran of the police force, arrested in early June 2007 on kidnapping and "banditism" charges.

Wolves Kidnap Too

Wolves use fictitious kidnappings to secretly recruit fighters and suicide bombers. Militants are "again using fake abductions to fill the ranks of illegal armed formations," Deputy Interior Minister Arkadiy Yedelyev told a law enforcement conference in Chechnya in July 2005. Young men and woman are reported missing when in fact they have voluntarily left home to join an illegal armed formation or become a suicide bomber.

Girls are also kidnapped against their will for suicide missions. The first publicized case of this appeared in early 2002. Zarema's policeman boyfriend kidnapped her—she thought for marriage—to blow up a Grozny police station. The bomb failed to detonate properly, she lived to tell her story, and her boyfriend was arrested. Zarema's tragedy is told in chapter 5.

On 23 June 2003 twenty-two-year-old Luiza Osmayeva, after being wounded by OMON policemen in a shootout with her two "curators" (handlers), confessed on her deathbed that she had been kidnapped five months earlier, raped, and trained to become a suicide bomber to absolve herself of her shame.

In mid-June 2005 Wolves abducted an underage girl from the Naursky District, but police quickly nabbed the two kidnappers and freed the girl. "During the course of the investigation, the detainees admitted that they took the girl on orders from [militant leader Doka] Umarov with the goal of preparing her to become a suicide bomber."

A rash of kidnappings like this followed in the fall and winter of 2005 and early into 2006; all of the victims were snatched off the street after leaving home or as they were returning home from school.

At the end of September 2005 a mother reported that unknown men had forced her middle-school-age daughter into a car at 5 PM as she was walking down Pervomaiskaya Street in the Leninsky District of Grozny.

Then on 10 December 2005 sixteen-year-old Madina Auduyeva disappeared on her way to Middle School No. 50. Twenty-one days later two girls, Markha Saburayeva and Aishat Atakayeva, one seventeen and the other fifteen years old, both residents of the Isti-Su settlement, Gudermessky District, left their house together and haven't been heard from since.

Two more teenage girls went missing in early March 2006—one eighteen years of age from the Gudermessky District and the other, Khava Mudayeva, twelve, from Grozny's Leninsky District. Two adult women were reported missing that month, too. On 21 December 2006 twenty-two-year-old Zaira Amirova from the village of Staroshedrinskaya, Shelkovsky District, disappeared without explanation.

There's no proof that any of the victims, other than the Naursky girl, were kidnapped for suicide missions, although FSB director and National Anti-Terror Committee chairman Nikolay Patrushev did tell the Federation

Council on 22 June 2007 that terrorists had planned to use suicide bombers in some of the thirty terror attacks that the FSB had thwarted in recent months.

Unlike Khava Mudayeva, the fifth-grader at Groznenskaya School No. 60 who disappeared on 1 March 2006, the fates of the other four girls are unknown. Khava was murdered by her cousin because she threatened to tell on him for smoking. Her body was found with eight stab wounds in an abandoned kindergarten school on Kosiora Street in the Leninsky District of Grozny.

Wolves kidnap for other reasons too. A Chechen woman told the British Medical Foundation for the Care of Victims of Torture in 2004 that she had been taken captive and forced to nurse their wounded. She was thankful when Russian soldiers rescued her, but then they raped and beat her because she had helped wounded Chechen fighters.

Natasha and the Endangered Women of 2009

I had real hope for Chechnya in 2007. Kidnappings were way down and it seemed that Kadyrov and the Russian government were finally making real progress in addressing the problem. Only nine abductions had been officially registered between January and September 2007, whereas Human Rights Center "Memorial" reported twenty-five kidnappings, compared to 187, for 2006 in the territory it covers. "Memorial" even said, as we have seen, that the number of cases of torture had declined "sharply."

My hope began to fade with the forty-two officially reported abductions in 2008. But Senator Torshin was full of optimism when I met with him the following spring. Grozny was being quickly rebuilt and there were (he said) fewer than a hundred fighters left in Chechnya. I was told I could finally go for a visit now that the ten-year designation of Chechnya as a "zone of counter-terror operations" (KTO) had been lifted (on 16 April). I had been trying since 2006.

But within a month suicide bombers had returned to Grozny. Twelve would blow themselves up by year's end. Kidnappings (at least twice as many as in 2008) and murders like those of Natasha, Rizvan, and others soared. There would be over 50 bombings (compared to 35 in 2008), and 80 shootouts; 175 Wolves would be killed and 135 captured (compared to 67 and 104 in the previous year); 73 policemen would be shot dead and 151 wounded (compared to 26 and 96 in 2008); and nearly 300 civilians would be killed and 200 wounded in terror and counterterror-related violence by the New Year.

After a brazen May suicide bombing in Grozny an embarrassed and angry Kadyrov swore there would be no more dialogue with fighters, no more offers of amnesty to induce fighters to return to a peaceful life—only certain death—and that families would be held directly responsible for the actions of their fighter relatives. "Don't accept the notion that family members don't know the whereabouts of fighters. Even if they refuse, they must not be left alone," Kadyrov instructed his security forces. These dangerous developments put the Chechen woman at the greatest risk for violence since the 2003–2004 campaign against female suicide bombers (discussed later).

The new cycle of violence quickly claimed its first victims. Natasha Estimirova was kidnapped and murdered because of her high-profile human rights work—even President Medvedev said so. After Anna Politkovskaya's death, Natasha became "Little Stalin's" most outspoken critic on everything from serious human rights violations, Kadyrov's forced dress code for women, and accusations of debauchery and immoral behavior of today's Chechen woman, to the rock stars he invited and treated to lavish gifts. Natasha was deep into multiple investigations of state kidnappings and police death-squad murders in the months before she died. The 7 July execution of Rizvan Albekov in his underwear in the Akhkinchu-Borzoi village square because he was suspected of aiding Islamic extremists weighed heavily on her mind. Natasha's public exposé on this absolutely enraged Kadyrov.

The 5 July murder of newlywed twenty-year-old Madina Yunusova, who police allege was an Al-Qaeda emissary and a suicide bomber who had fired a machine gun at them when they came to arrest her and her husband for plotting to assassinate President Kadyrov, was another of Estimirova's embarrassing (for the Kadyrov government) cases.

Days earlier Madina had been wounded and her forty-year-old husband killed in a police spetz-operation. They had been married all of one week. She survived, even spoke to her mother by phone from her hospital bed, but early in the morning of 5 July men in camouflage uniforms barged into the room, disconnected her life support, and dragged her out of the hospital. Madina's shroud-wrapped body was dropped off that afternoon at a neighbor's house (her own family home had been torched the day before by Kadyrov's arsonists) with written instructions to bury her "without noise" (that is, without making a big public scandal out of it).

To top it off, Natasha had also been busy collecting information on kidnapping cases to be presented before the European Court of Human Rights.

Little Stalin considered Estimirova a traitor. "Memorial—this is an organization invented to destroy Russia. . . . People who work for them are not patriots of Russia. How can a person born in Russia, living in Russia, say such bad things about their nation?" Kadyrov said in a 23 September 2009 interview with the newspaper *Zavtra*.

After Natasha's body was found, Human Rights Center "Memorial"'s chief Oleg Orlov promptly pointed an accusing finger at President Kadyrov: "I know, I am sure, who is guilty of Natalya Estimirova's murder. We all know this person. He is called Ramzan Kadyrov. He is the President of the Chechen Republic."

Kadyrov vehemently denies any involvement in her death: "Why would Kadyrov kill a woman nobody needs," someone "who has no honor, dignity, or shame?" he told a Radio Liberty interviewer. But in Kadyrov's Chechnya, that is reason enough to kill.

Natasha's open defiance of authority and outspoken advocacy of women's rights must have played a part, too. In February 2009 Grozny's mayor, Muslim Khuchiyev, the author of the "scarf law," summoned Estimirova to his office. But he was forced to meet her outside because she refused to wear a head scarf and so wasn't allowed into the building. "I will not put on a scarf," Natasha texted Human Rights Center "Memorial."

Khuchiyev was angry because she was pushing for the prosecution of a close relative of his in the rape of two little girls. Natasha had sought out the mother, persuaded her to prosecute, and even hired a lawyer for the woman. Thanks to Estimirova, the rapist was convicted and got fourteen years.

Khuchiyev made it perfectly clear during his meeting that the "state" was very displeased with her. So did an angry Kadyrov when he and Khuchiyev met with her at the Palace of Youth on 31 March. Kadyrov dressed her down about her public statements against women being forced to wear a head scarf in public places, telling her that only "loose women refuse to wear a head scarf" and that she "must understand there's no place for you here." He also informed her that she was being removed as chairperson of the Grozny Public Council for Assistance in Ensuring the Rights and Freedoms of Citizens. He had appointed her to that position at the beginning of 2008.

"Kadyrov directly threatened her in a private conversation and she took it seriously. . . . He threatened and insulted her and considered her his personal enemy," Orlov says.

Estimirova had been repeatedly warned by her friends—and enemies. Just days before her murder Adam Delimkhanov, a Russian State Duma deputy and Kadyrov's right-hand man, who often commands spetz-operations, openly threatened, on Grozny television, all human rights workers:

> There are certain people who call themselves 'human rights defenders,' who actually help these militant scum, these criminal-militants, who work for them and do their dirty work, and promote their politics.
>
> But I know the mood among the security services, the society. I know what the simple folk are saying. They're saying that the claims made by these people [human rights workers], and a certain Aushev and others, in other words, what they're saying and doing, their evil deeds are no better than those of the militants hiding out in the forest.
>
> These people [human rights activists like Natasha] are confusing the people with their rhetoric, are deceiving them. But they won't fool the people. They won't succeed in this. Truth and justice will always prevail. . . . Our soldiers here, commanders, our guys are always asking me, 'what do these people [activists] want?' and I tell them that they're not worth a ruble to me.
>
> God willing, we will hold responsible all those who support evil. Each one of them, be they Chechen or Ingush or whomever, should know, that they will pay for their words.

Natasha paid.

Her neighbors saw and heard everything, but fear and the threat of police reprisals gripped them. They could not save her. Human Rights Center "Memorial" tracked down two women who observed from the window of their apartment building the four men grabbing and punching Estimirova. "We don't remember the license plates. But a woman was walking behind Natasha—a local. She might be able to tell you more," the women told "Memorial."

Investigators pieced together a sketch of the women and canvassed every apartment in the building, but people would not open their doors. Police found her but only after the building was emptied and the sketch compared to the appearance of everyone, standing at attention outside the building. It was fruitless; she remembered nothing. Kadyrov's supporters, on the other hand, argue that Estimirova's murder was a "well-planned provocative action" carried out by Jihadists to embarrass him and Chechen authorities and to "destabilize the whole of the North Caucasus."

Two more high-profile murders quickly followed.

Barely four weeks later, in the early afternoon of 10 August, five men identifying themselves as policemen entered the Grozny office of the "Save the Generation" NGO and handcuffed and took away Zarema Sadulayeva, the NGO's director, and her husband Alik Dzhabrailov. Their bullet-riddled bodies were found at 4:30 the next morning, neatly stuffed into the trunk of a car left at the entrance to a busy rehabilitation center in the village of Chernorechye, in the Zavodsky District of Grozny. Like Natasha, both had been shot in their heads and chests.

"I can't imagine why anyone would want to murder the woman who provides much needed aid and psychological support to invalid children, orphans, and war victims," Kadyrov told journalists, but he suggested that her husband's former membership in an illegal armed formation may have had something to do with it.

Alik had spent four years behind bars for being a fighter and had only recently been released. Procurator investigators believe that relatives of people he might have murdered (policemen) killed him for blood revenge. Since his wife witnessed the kidnapping and killing she was killed too they reason. But why did these same men come back to her office later in the day to seize her computer, cell phone, and her husband's car if they were only out for revenge?

Nevertheless investigators concluded on 1 December that Sadulayev had been killed only because "armed men posing as policemen were after Alik" and because "she volunteered to go with him [when he was kidnapped]."

State kidnappings in Chechnya are usually done quietly, in the middle of the night, but these seem to be deliberately public, in front of large numbers of eyewitnesses, as if designed to intimidate and instill fear in the population. "See, this will happen to you too if you support fighters," Rizvan Abukhadzhiyev's executioners told stunned residents as they watched Rizvan's illegal execution.

The 8 June 2009 kidnapping of a young girl in front of a huge crowd of shocked and terrified traders, shoppers, and children at Grozny's new Berkat shopping center was very public—and theatrical. "I and a friend were just getting ready to sit down in our seats in *marshutny* taxi no. 12 when all this took place," one eyewitness told the website www.Kavkaz.memo.ru *(Kavka-zsky Uzel)*. "All of a sudden, from all sides, soldiers and people out of uniform ran up and grabbed the young girl. Some of them tried to strike her with their hands and feet; all wildly crying out and yelling that it was necessary to kill her."

"What happened two days ago at Berkat defied explanation and normal behavior. The crowd in military uniforms and without [in civilian clothes], armed, threw the girl into a car. 'She should be cut. Give me your knife,' one of them said and ran away and came back with a knife. We thought that they were going to cut her right there," another eyewitness, Ibragim, told the media. A third kidnapper grabbed a grenade.

The men shoved the kicking and screaming girl into a car and disappeared. Nobody interfered because "people understand that in this case they might also be counted in the ranks of the 'accomplices of terrorists.' Our police don't know how to work normally. . . . They behaved shamefully," Ibragim added.

THE FILTERED

Detained women in wartime Chechnya were usually taken to one of the "filtration points" (FPs) set up to interrogate suspected combatants and to isolate and identify members of illegal armed formations and their "accomplices" (people who help fighters). The FPs became yet another source of misery, suffering, humiliation, degradation, torture, and even death for Chechen women.

These facilities came into existence by Presidential Decree No. 2166 (dated 9 December 1994) and MVD Order No. 247 (dated 12 December 1994) to establish separate confinement for Chechens at the MVD's SIZO-1 and SIZO-2 detention facilities.

Numerous FPs were set up throughout Chechnya and elsewhere, including the notorious "PAP-1," the MDOHQ (Main Directorate of Operational Headquarters), and the seventy-person "Stolypin [railroad] wagons" in Mozdok, North Ossetia. The principal FPs in the second war were located at Chernokozovo in the Naursky District of Chechnya and in Grozny. Khankala and other military bases were also used.

Thousands of suspected fighters, snipers, suicide bombers, members of illegal armed formations and their "accomplices," and innocents passed through Chernokozovo after it was established in 1999 in the punishment isolation ward of an former maximum-security penal colony. At least one cell at Chernokozovo was specifically designated for women.

Zura Bitiyeva, an antiwar activist, spent twenty-four days there after she and her teenage son were taken into custody at their home in Kalinovskaya, the Naursky District, on 25 January 2000. She later described her cell as small, capable of holding only from three to ten people, and unheated. She claimed she was fed and given water once a day but given hardly any medical attention. She filed an application with the European Court of Human Rights concerning her "torture" immediately after her release.

Bitiyeva was murdered in 2003. She had resumed her antiwar activities in 2001 and at the end of March was executed, along with her husband Ramzan, their son, and her brother in their home in the settlement of Kalinovskaya, Naursky District, by fifteen men wearing camouflage uniforms and masks. Her daughter, now living in Germany, survived the massacre by hiding in an outbuilding. Crouched in horror in a corner, she heard the shots and later found her mother and the rest of the family with their hands and legs bound, dead of bullet wounds to their heads.

An Ingushetian man who spent fifteen days at Chernokozovo remembers a second cell for women. He couldn't see it, but he could hear the screams. "Their pain was very great." He says that he suffered less from his own beatings than from the cries of these women.

Kelimatov never saw the women, either, but during a visit to the filter in the former PTU (technical school) No. 6 he could hear the "harrowing female screams and moans" coming from one of the cells where women were being interrogated.[3]

An elderly woman describes her own experience at Chernokozovo:

There were other women together with me in the cell. Aminat B (Bakhayeva), a young girl, was kept there for two months. They detained her while she was on a bus transporting wounded people. She was just a fellow traveler. Svetlana [Kozlova] was detained when leaving Grozny. Polina Nikolayevna [Filipova] was detained in Shatoi on suspicion that she was a sniper. She was born in Latvia and was thirty years old.

Together with us, there was a seventeen-year-old Chechen girl, Eliza [Timirsultanova] from Urus-Martan on 27 January 2000. She was in shock when brought in and slept for three days. Most likely, she had been poisoned with a drugged drink at Khankala. She was accompanied by Lola [Daurbekova], who said that Eliza had been raped by several men. On the fourth day, she [Eliza] started having epileptic fits, but medical doctors paid no attention.

There was also a pregnant woman called Aminat in the cell. She was arrested on her way to Grozny at a police post after a letter written in Russian urging her neighbor to look after her apartment was found. She had a medical certificate warning that she was in danger of miscarrying. Her labor started three days later, and she was taken to a hospital. Eliza was released together with her.[4]

A second girl from Urus Martan, fourteen years old, detained on a bus at a checkpoint, died in Chernokozovo. She was among sixty females being held in cell no. 25. Another was twelve-year-old Luiza Magomedova, also from Urus-Martan, who was also accused of being a Chechen sniper. She died, too, but not in prison. Relatives found her body days after her release.

Umalat Umalatov writes about a thirteen-year-old girl and her ten-year-old brother incarcerated on "document" charges (not having passports) in January 2000. The girl was raped.[5]

The British Medical Foundation for the Care of Victims of Torture tells of a Chechen woman they treated who witnessed her cellmate commit suicide following rape.

In another case, a five-thousand-ruble bribe bought the mother and two daughters of an incarcerated woman a five minute visit, but when the eldest daughter, fourteen, came to visit she was put into the cell too. She was released days later, "half alive," after being allegedly raped.

After the initial barrage of terror attacks in June 2000 Shamil Basayev threatened to carry out more attacks if women and children were not immediately released from Chernokozovo and other facilities like it. They weren't released, but the attacks would have come anyway.

Nurses Malika Edisultanova, Zarema Khasimova, and Aminat Alayeva, along with Dr. Omar Khambiyev (the Ichkerian minister of health and the brother of Ichkeria's defense minister, Magomed Khambiyev) and twenty-four other members of Khambiyev's medical team were taken into custody and put in the Mozdok filtration center on 2 February 2000. All were later released.

A lucrative "cottage industry" sprang up around these FPs. Every power broker or influence peddler imaginable figured out a way to make money from all the suffering. Women who showed up at the FP to seek information about missing loved ones were often made to pay bribes to prison guards just to scan detainee lists or to pay middlemen who claimed to have special connections with FP guards and officials. Sometimes families, even whole villages, were made to pay for the release of detainees.

There were also secret prisons and temporary FPs in which women were held, some of them nothing more than pits in the ground, less than two meters deep, covered with logs; the same kind of pits had been used earlier by Arbi Barayev and the other people traders to hold Russians for ransom and slavery. Pits like these could be found on the outskirts of the village of Khatuni in the Vedensky District. Rosita, a middle-aged woman from the village of Tovzeni with children and grandchildren, accused of sheltering militants, spent twelve miserable winter days in one of them. She sat on the earthen floor. "Her legs were drawn up under herself." But the soldier guarding the pit felt sorry for her and threw in a piece of carpet for her to sit on. "I put it under myself. That soldier is a human being too."[6]

Seven women, one of them pregnant, all of them relatives of suspected fighters, were filtered through a temporary facility near the the village of Assinovskaya and the "Kavkaz 1" border-crossing checkpoint into Ingushetia.

An illegal secret prison was located in the basement of the former Internat (school) for the Deaf on Minutka Square in Grozny. It was discovered when the Operative Group of Oktyabrsky District of Grozny MVD abandoned the building on 26 May 2006. Between 1999 and 2003 the building was occupied by the Temporary Department of MVD Oktyrbrsky District and Sibirskiye *OMONovtsy* (OMON policemen). At least one woman, Luiza Bapayeva (or Barayeva), who remains on Chechnya's official list of missing persons, was held there in April 2000. Former prisoner and survivor Alavdi Sadikov remembers seeing Luiza and hearing her screams. Her fate is unknown, and the building has since been demolished.

Another secret prison was, and probably still is, in Tsentroi, Little Stalin's hometown. Both Khambiyev's and Maskhadov's relatives were held there. Tsentroi was also mentioned by Dick Marty, the Assembly of Europe's (PACE) rapporteur investigating secret prisons, in a press conference on the subject in the summer of 2007.

Despite official denials, secret prisons like these still exist in Chechnya and elsewhere in the North Caucasus.

THEY SHOOT INFIDELS AND TRAITORS

The brutal killings of Russian families living in Chechnya; journalists; pro-Moscow Chechen government administrators; Chechen women who hid wounded and deserting Russian soldiers, spied for Russia, or refused to carry out their missions as suicide bombers; wives, children and relatives of pro-Moscow Chechen policemen; and others such as faith healers and those who refuse to help Chechen fighters have been regular features of both wars and the years leading up to them—and still are.

The bottled-up hatred for Russians boiled over with the revolutionary fervor of the Dudayev regime in the 1990s and left more than 21,000 men and women of Russian families dead and others fleeing for their lives.

On 24 October 1992 S. T. Sinyayeva, her husband, and family members were loading up their belongings to move back to the Stavropolskaya Oblast when a group of armed Chechen men showed up at her home and demanded money. They refused to give it to them, so the criminals shot her husband and brothers dead. The following May V. N. Rezanova failed to show up for work at the Grozny chemical plant; her colleagues dropped by her house after work to find out if she was sick. They found no sign of her or her husband, only a Chechen family living in the house who politely told them that the nice couple had moved to Astrakhan. But they couldn't be found there either.

On 8 June armed Chechen men broke into the house of seventy-six-year-old Z. A. Pikalyeva and her daughter, L. I. Pikalyeva, murdered both of them, and then burglarized the house. Seventeen days later, armed Chechen men shot and killed P. Gocharova, a sixty-year-old widow, and confiscated her apartment on Verkhoyanskaya Street in Chernorechye.

The killings resumed that fall. On 9–10 September 1993 thirty-eight-year-old I. M. Raspopova and her elderly sister were slain in their house and their bodies were dismembered. A similar murder took place on 23 October when A. A. Ivanova, a Russian store assistant, and her daughter were slaughtered in their home. Their throats were slit and their bodies hacked up.

This campaign of brutality—and the theft of cars, personal belongings, and more 100,000 apartments and homes—designed to drive the Russian population out of Chechnya accomplished its goal. Many of those who refused to leave paid with their lives. On 25 July 1995 upon returning home from their summer cottage, V. I. Tarintsyeva, a mother of three, was gunned down in front of her husband and four-year-old daughter. That same summer at Grozny's central market an angry young man grabbed a young Russian woman by the hair, shoved a pistol down her throat, and pulled the trigger. She and two Russian soldiers had tried to abscond with stolen video-tapes from the market: they had stopped to buy some tapes, found the price too high, just took the tapes, and were about to leave without paying. The seller asked them to pay, and the girl snapped at him, "'You can do with-out it, you black mug.' Then, an instant later, a young man of an intellectual appearance came up, grabbed the girl by the hair, and shot down her throat. She fell, and he shot down the officer who was next to her, ran into the mar-ket pavilion, and was lost in the crowd."[7]

In the fall of 1997 twenty-five-year-old Ramzes Gaichayev and twenty-two-year-old Rustam Khalidov, together with brothers Rizvan and Kharat Magomadov and a fifth criminal, broke into the house of a Russian fam-ily in the *stanitsa* of Chervlennaya, raped the mother, Elena Zemlyakova, in front of her husband and ten-year-old son, then chopped her up with an ax. Next they killed the husband and the boy. They killed an old Chechen woman and committed another eight murders, one rape, and four robberies before they were caught.

Chechen criminals at the beginning of the second war tried again to take the apartments of the few Russians still in Grozny. A gang held retired engi-neer Larisa Petrovna hostage, demanding that she sign over her apartment to them. She refused, but they let her go. In May 2003 two teenage mili-tant recruits, Umar-Ali Akhayev and Vladimir Ilyin, murdered three Russian women, eighty-eight, seventy-four, and thirty-eight years of age, all residents of the Naursky District and invalids—just to gain "practical experience" in letting blood. Russian women were chosen because there would be no pos-sibility of blood revenge.

I don't recall many cases of Wolves murdering whole Russian families in Chechnya in recent years. They certainly did in Ingushetia in 2007, but not in Chechnya until 17 August 2009, when a family of five, three women and two men, were found in their Pervomaiskoye apartment with multiple execution-style gunshot wounds. But two children, one and a half and three years of age, were spared.

Many Chechen women hid wounded Russian soldiers in the first war, but those who did were often targeted by militants.

"Taking advantage of a peaceful lull, the Marines [naval infantry] . . . headed for the outskirts of the village where, according to intelligence reports, a local woman was hiding gravely wounded soldiers. When their car pulled up at the house, the headlights lit up a soldier who was hanging on the gate. Nearby, there was another soldier lying in a pool of blood. The woman was found on the floor behind the stove naked and mutilated. A slip of paper on her forehead read: 'Russian pig,'" Yu. V. Nikolayev writes in his book *The Chechen Tragedy*.[8] "Everybody in the city [Grozny] knows how the Dudayev rebels avenged themselves on a woman who hid wounded Russian soldiers in her house for several days. The woman was shot shortly after she had handed over the wounded to a hospital. Evidently, that was meant to be a lesson to others," Nikolayev writes elsewhere.[9]

Wolves shoot and burn women alive who spy for Russia. They cut off their heads, too.

A woman and her husband were shot to death in Chernorechye in August 1996 for providing information about their neighbors and Chechen fighters operating in the area. Wolves burned to death Desha Abdulkerimova for spying. At around midnight on 10 August 2005 fighters shot two women and burned several houses in the village of Dyshne-Vedeno, Vedensky District. Eight fighters entered Abdulkerimova's house at No. 5 Pochtovaya Street, tied her up to her bed, poured gasoline all over her, and lit a match. They also executed fifty-year-old Aizan Abdulsalamovna Satayeva because she didn't have any money to give them. Fighters went to her house at No. 51 Rechnaya Street in Dyshne-Vedeno and demanded 100,000 rubles, but when she said she didn't have it the commander gave the order to shoot her. She cried and begged for mercy. One of the men shot her in the head after the commander repeated the order.

Militant Ilyas Dashayev beheaded a woman who confessed to him to being a spy for Russia. According to the investigative materials sent to Chechnya's Supreme Court for his trial in early July 2007, Dashayev, a member of a military *djamaat*, in October 2001 kidnapped three civilians from Grozny, accusing them of cooperating with and providing information to the police. When one finally did confess, Dashayev took a handsaw and cut off her head.

The killing of pro-Moscow Chechen civil servants and collaborators is common. Between 2000 and 2006 the Chechen procurator's office opened seventy-one criminal cases for actual or attempted assassinations of Chechen government officials. On 18 October 1999 Wolves shot forty people in the *stanitsa* of Znamenskoye for cooperating with Russian military forces. There were similar attacks in Ishcherskaya. On 4 August 2000 a bomb was put in the family home of Isita Gayribekova, head of the Nozhay-Yurtovsky District administration, wounding her and her brother but killing her sister. Two months earlier Gayribekova had participated with five other Chechen women in the Russian-hosted Council of Europe's "Seminar on Democracy, Rule of Law and Human Rights" held in Vladikavkaz, North Ossetia. Top Russian Ministry of Justice, procurator, MVD, foreign affairs, and human rights officials had also participated in the event.

That winter Wolves began circulating leaflets promising to kill any local government administrator who cooperated with Russian officials. Just before noon on 9 November 2000 a gunman walked into the Alkhan-Kala administrative building and shot two women, seriously wounding both of them. He killed the district administrator, Yusha Tsuyev. The same fate befell Tsuyev's successor, a woman, Malika Umazhayeva. Exactly two years later to the month, on 29 November 2002, she was executed by four masked men who forced their way into her house, took her to a shed out back, and shot her in the head. On a Sunday afternoon eleven days later neighbors found the bodies of Zura Koliyeva, the deputy administrator of Alkhan-Kala, and her husband in their home at No. 7 Beregovaya Street in Alkhan-Kala. Both had been shot execution style.

"They kill Chechens who work with the authorities. At night it is awful. Sometimes we don't even sleep here [at home], we go to friends," Natasha Khibulina, forty, who works in a government pension office, told a *Washington Post* reporter in 2001. The bloody campaign against collaborators widened that year when the wife and daughter of a Chechen policeman were murdered by a militant commander who publicly claimed credit for the executions, saying that he had killed the two out of revenge for the policeman's collaboration with pro-Moscow forces.

On Sunday night, 18 July 2004, more Wolves broke into the home of twenty-nine-year-old Tamara Khadzhiyeva, leader of the Shalinsky District branch of the Edinaya Rossiya political party, and shot her in cold blood. She had already survived a kidnapping in the first war and had received numerous death threats since becoming the party's district head in 2002. Her assassination was clearly linked to her work in campaigning for the pro-Moscow Chechnya constitutional referendum that was coming up for a vote.

On 10 October 2005 police found the bodies of a nineteen-year-old Chechen female and her policeman boyfriend, both of whom had been kidnapped eleven days earlier. Witnesses say that three men in camouflage uniforms and in broad daylight had forced the girl, who worked as a secretary to the administrative head of the district, and her boyfriend into their car. On 4 December 2008 Wolves killed Khaji Saidullayev, the government administrator of Agishty, his wife Taus, and their son Salman, and set fire to the family home. On 23 November 2009 an assassin walked right up to forty-five-year-old police lieutenant colonel Roza Almazova, the chief accountant for the state narcotics control office, standing in the yard of her house, and put a bullet into her head.

Women who change their minds about becoming suicide bombers are also the targets of militant wrath. This was the fate of Larisa Dzhabayeva and Asama Dzhamburayeva, whose bodies were found in a forest near the village of Komsomolskoye, Gudermessky District, on 24 June 2003. Both had been shot in the backs of their heads after being raped. The FSB says they had been trained at a camp for suicide bombers and had been members of the illegal armed formation commanded by Umar Dzhabayev. Investigators believe the women were killed either because they refused to carry out their missions or were suspected of spying for Russia and having participated in Dzhabayev's death. A forty-year-old-man detained by police confessed to participating in the deaths of the two women.

On 6 November 2006, Wahhabi militants broke into the home of Elena Goryachenko, a forty-year-old Chechen woman and well known doctor and faith healer in Ingushetia, and shot and killed her in front of her son because they believed faith healing is a sin. The scenario repeated itself on 14 August 2008 when thirty-seven-year-old Chechen card reader and fortune teller Elza (Aizan) Yesmurzayeva was shot and killed in a drive-by shooting. Gunmen in a car opened fire on her with automatic rifles as she walked along Gazdiyeva Street in Nazran at 6:30 in the morning. She had received multiple threatening notes from militants warning her to cease and desist from her practice.

WHEN JIHADISTS STRIKE

Chechen terror targeting Russians outside Chechnya has claimed thousands of lives. But innocent women—foreign, Russian, and Chechen, even little girls—are victims of Chechen terror inside Chechnya. Police don't keep a gender body count, so it's impossible to say how many victims there have been.

The worst attack on foreign females in Chechnya came in the early morning hours of 17 December 1996 when five foreign International Red Cross nurses were shot to death in their sleep at the newly opened Red Cross field hospital in Noviye Atagi, south of Grozny. Before dawn eight men in masks and camouflage uniforms, armed with silenced weapons, crept into the hospital and executed Fernanda Calado, a Spanish nurse; Ingeborg Foss and Gunnhild Myklebust, both Norwegian Red Cross nurses; Nancy Malloy, a medical administrator with the Canadian Red Cross; and Sheryl Thayer, a New Zealand Red Cross nurse. The terrorists were never found.[10]

On 12 September 2000 a truck bomb in the Oktyabrsky market in Grozny killed a Chechen woman and her daughter.

Significant numbers of Chechen female government workers are killed, wounded, and maimed in terror attacks that often involve Chechen female suicide bombers targeting pro-Moscow Chechen government administrative buildings.

A bomb hidden in the Russian administrative building in Grozny in December 1995 killed eleven people and wounded another sixty, many of them women. There were significant female casualties in the 27 December 2002 truck bombing of the main Chechen government administrative complex in Grozny. Lidiya Kozlova, an administration employee, and Tatyana Shevelyeva, a consultant to Chechnya's head of government, were among the sixteen dead in the initial body count. Out of a preliminary list of thirty-five wounded, eleven were women. They included deputy premiers Zina Batyzheva and Lida Doshukayeva, Galina Batmanova, Shukran Dzhabrailova, Malika Ismailova, Lidiya Ludanova, Tamara Murtayeva, Fatima Murtayeva, Muminat Khabzayeva, Galina Pozdnyakova (a Ministry of Justice official), and Elena Svetovatchenko. The role of a fifteen-year-old girl in this terror attack is discussed in chapter 6.

The bloody scene repeated itself in May 2003 when Chechen Zarina Alikhanova and two male suicide bombers crashed their explosives-laden truck into Nadterechny's district government administrative building in the village of Znamenskoye, killing sixty people, including many female administrators who had survived the Grozny attack and moved their offices to Nadterechny. More Chechen women died in May, when female suicide bombers tried to kill Chechen president Akhmad Kadyrov outside a mosque in Iliskhan-Yurt during an afternoon religious festival attended by 1,500 people. The following month six more people were killed when a man and a

Chechen woman attempted to drive their KamAZ truck filled with two metric tons of explosives into the main MVD police building in Grozny. Thirty-six others, mainly women just walking down the sidewalk, were wounded.

On 27 July 2003 Sara Magomedova and Berlant Zakriyeva, both residents of the Kurchaloyevsky District, and a passerby were killed by female suicide bomber Imana Khachukayeva in the village of Tsotsin-Yurt. The following spring Shamil Basayev assassinated Akhmad Kadyrov during World War II Victory Day celebrations at Dinamo Stadium by detonating a bomb built right into the newly renovated structure. The 9 May morning blast snuffed out the lives of six other people, including a still-unidentified eight-year-old girl, and wounded fifty-four others. Tamara Dadashyeva, Chechnya's beloved female singer, who was on stage with Kadyrov and had just finished singing "My Chechnya," narrowly escaped death in the attack. Her left arm was wounded, her right leg was fractured, and her face was badly lacerated by flying cement chips.

Even going out for a Sunday afternoon bicycle ride can be dangerous. On 19 July 2006 a girl riding her bicycle past a suspicious car being inspected by police in the village of Znamenskoye became the fourteenth casualty when the booby-trap artillery shell inside the vehicle exploded.

I strongly suspect terror is to blame in what appeared to be toxic poisoning of ninety people, mostly school girls, in the Shelkovsky District in 2005.[11] On 25 September twenty-four children were admitted to the district's hospital for what doctors initially diagnosed as a "nerve paralysis" gas attack at a school in the village of Staroshchedrinskaya. Within a week eighty-six more people had become sick, including nine women and even a policeman. Vakha Yesilayev, the head doctor at the district hospital, ruled out food poisoning, concluding instead that "maybe terror is responsible since the children show signs of toxic poisoning." District administrator Khusein Nutayev was certain it was nerve gas. It looked like somebody had been experimenting with a chemical agent.

Fourteen-year-old Dinara was the first to collapse at the school after becoming overwhelmed by a chlorine bleach–like smell and experiencing shortness of breath while standing in a cafeteria line. The same thing happened to twelve-year-old Zareta Askhova right behind Dinara. Symptoms included shortness of breath, frequent headaches, vomiting, diarrhea, physical weakness, periodic asthmalike seizures, fainting, sometimes nosebleeds, pain in the joints and stomach, epilepsy-like convulsions, stomach gas, difficulty in swallowing, numbness in the arms and legs, extreme sensitivity to smells, acute cramps, hallucinations, and hysteria. Infections of the stomach tract, liver, and gall bladder were also reported in thirty-five children.

Subsequent testing found traces of ethylene glycol (antifreeze) in the blood of some patients, but doctors could not explain how it had gotten there. Then, without waiting for the results of all laboratory tests to come back, psychiatrists at Moscow's prestigious Serbesky Psychiatric Institute decided that it was not toxic gas after all that was causing the sickness but psychological stress caused by ten years of continuous war in Chechnya. Zurab Kikalidze, Serbesky's deputy director, called it a "psychological infection" and explained that it had spread because "when one person feels bad, then a second gets sick, and so forth." A government commission established to investigate the sickness invented the term "Pseudo Asthmatic Syndrome" to explain the symptoms. But Chechnya's deputy minister of health, Zaur Musuluyev, does not buy the diagnosis. Chechnya's human rights ombudsman Nurdi Nukhazhiyev also says that it is "not a final diagnosis" and commented to *Dosh* magazine in 2006 that "everybody laughs at the official analysis because if it were true then all the population in the mountain regions of Chechnya should be in hospitals." Shelkovsky was a peaceful district compared to fighting that had taken place in the mountains. Nukhazhiyev says, "There was almost no fighting there [in the Shelkovsky District]."

The first deputy chief of the Emergency Situations Ministry for Chechnya, himself a member of the special commission, Colonel Akhmed Dzheikhanov, told the media that "the diagnosis of Pseudo-asthmatic Syndrome is a preliminary diagnosis and there is still no unified agreement among doctors [as to what the cause of the sickness is]." District head Nutayev also doubts the official theory: "I have not seen a single diagnosis put in writing and signed by a concrete doctor. They talk about the sickness being caused by psycho-emotional stress, pseudo-asthmatic syndrome, and other things, but not one doctor has taken official responsibility for any kind of diagnosis."

The sickness persisted. In February 2007 doctors in Nalchik, Kabardino-Balkaria, treating a group of children unanimously concluded that the children were in fact suffering from toxic poisoning. Elena Shelchenko, the head doctor at the "Nart" Sanitorium in Nalchik told the website www.Kavkaz. memo.ru in February 2007: "Children visit us from Chechnya every year and nobody has ever demonstrated psychological trauma [of this kind], despite the fact that many have lived through the war. And when these [Shelkovsky District] children came to us from a relatively peaceful district of Chechnya, it became clear to us that we are not talking about 'mass psychosis' but mass poisoning."

Dr. Leonid Roshal, Russia's most influential pediatrician, also stated publicly in February 2007 that he did not believe psychological trauma was the cause of the sickness. "Many people are convinced that fighters are testing some kind of new poisonous substance," Isa Amayev, a forty-year-old resident of the Sunzhensky District, told journalists. But those fighting Russia accuse the Kremlin of experimenting with new kinds of bacteriological and chemical weapons and "trying to sterilize Chechen girls."

Suspicions that it was a terror attack were reinforced when a similar "mysterious disease" exhibiting many of the same symptoms showed up at a Nazran, Ingushetia, PTU institute in February 2007. This time a stronger smell was detected. As in Shelkovsky, the sickness persists, but the Serbsky Institute is again saying that it is the result of "hysteria"—however, nobody is able to explain the cause. One Nazran doctor diagnosed it as "hysteria" caused by some kind of nerve gas.

I am still waiting for a final diagnosis. In the meantime, more women are being killed in terror attacks.

On 19 March 2008 two women, Yangulbayeva and Israilova (their first names are unknown), were seriously wounded during a carjacking by Wolves trying to escape a police dragnet in the village of Alkhazurovo, Urus-Martanovky District, after terrorizing the settlement all night. A month later, on 20 April, two little girls, six and seven years of age, were killed in a militant attack on the car in which they were traveling on the Tsa-Vedeno highway. No one else was hurt. The attack was likely targeting Chechnya's human rights ombudsman Nurdi Nukhadzhiyev, who was not in the car. Four and a half weeks later, on 9 August 2008, an unidentified woman making a purchase at a kiosk in the city of Bamut was wounded when militants attacked a Russian military convoy going down the main street.

On 31 July 2009, two Chechen women out for a stroll were wounded by a homemade bomb that somebody had put next to a dentist's office in Urus-Martan. Twenty-one days later, on 21 August, at 1:10 in the afternoon, a female passerby was wounded by a male suicide bomber on a bicycle targeting four policemen in the Leninsky District of Grozny.

MINES, CRIME, AND ACCIDENTS

Minefields, crime, and freak accidents kill and maim Chechen girls and women too.

There are more than 500,000 mines left in Chechnya. In April 2006 Robert Drouen, director of the International Committee of the Red Cross (ICRC), presented Chechen officials with figures indicating that 3,045 people had been killed and wounded by mines and unexploded ordnance since 1994. Of those, 696 were fatalities, with 572 women killed and wounded. That figure may be low. Other information suggests that more than seven hundred civilians died from mines in the first war, while 2,500 were wounded.

In 2000 mines killed an estimated 719 people. Olara Otunnu, the UN special representative for children and armed conflict, estimated in June 2002 that between seven and ten thousand people had been maimed by land mines in both wars.

On 1 June 2001 a pregnant medical student was on her way home from exams when she stepped on a land mine, losing both of her legs and her baby. A UNICEF study published in July 2002 indicated that nearly two hundred women were killed by mines that year.

The figure continues to climb. A month before the 2006 ICRC report two women and a twelve-year-old girl were picking wild garlic in a forest outside Dzhugurty in the Kurchaloyevsky District when one of them stepped on a homemade mine. A woman and the child died. Another woman gathering wild garlic on the outskirts of Balan-Su, Nozhai-Yurtovsky District, stepped on a mine and was seriously wounded. Every year one or two women who go into the forest to gather food for their families are killed by land mines or other explosive devices.

Mines are not only in forests. In March 2006 a woman cleaning up her yard in the settlement of Noviy Benoy, Gudemessky District, set off a mine. She survived. On 15 October 2007 thirty-six-year-old Taisa Aduyeva died when she stepped on a mine during a visit to the grave of her relatives in a remote area of the Itum-Kalinsky District. Yusup Khalidov, a seventh-grader, remembers the day his mother and father were killed by a land mine on the side of the road. It was 1 June 2001, when he was in the third grade. His parents set out in the family car toward Urus Martan to sell cucumbers. They were stopped at a military checkpoint and told they couldn't go any farther. They backed up onto the shoulder of the road and hit a land mine.

Violent crimes as well as accidental shooting by drunken Russian soldiers result in more senseless loss of life and wounding. On 1 October 1999 Anna Alenova's throat was cut by a man she was trying to pull off her husband, whom he was repeatedly stabbing because of a dispute over a car. Aslan Larsanov, her killer, was finally caught and sentenced to thirteen years at hard labor in June 2008. On 25 December 1999 a Russian soldier shot and wounded A. V. Yeltsova. He was charged with the careless handling of firearms and sentenced to one year of suspension from military service and a 10 percent reduction in pay. A month later two soldiers were sentenced to nine and twelve years, respectively, at hard labor for killing B. Kh. Shankhullayeva and badly beating her sister during an attempted robbery of their house in Khankala.

On 10 December 2000 a serviceman shot and killed A. Tunayeva and M. M. Magomedov, for which he has been imprisoned. On 15 April 2001 Sergeant Vladimir Andreyev was sentenced to eighteen years at hard labor for killing two women in the village of Dargo "for hooligan motives." A couple of months later, on 12 June 2001, a Russian policeman from Saratov got into an argument with A. Gaeryekova and shot her. Gaeryekova's death is classified as "death by negligence."

On 13 December 2001 forty-six-year-old Luiza Betergiriyeva, a Russian-Chechen Friendship Society employee, was killed at a roadblock outside the town of Argun. She had wanted to interview people in the hospital there but was told that the town was blocked off. For unknown reasons, soldiers opened fire on her car after it had turned around and started to drive away, killing her and wounding her driver.

Drunkenness, the thirst for vodka and beer, accounts for more deaths.

In February 1995 Russian soldiers shot Abaz and his wife Koka Saigatova in the *stanitsa* of Goryachevodska for refusing to sell them vodka. On 22 December 2000 Russian soldiers went to the house of sixty-five-year-old Masani Shakhguiriyeva, a peddler of alcohol in the village of Redukhoi, and called out to her to bring them vodka. When she appeared and said she was completely out, a soldier fired a burst of bullets at her feet, wounding her. A military court charged him with the illegal use of a firearm and suspended him from military service for six months.

The next spring three drunken Russian servicemen went AWOL to look for vodka. Since nobody would give them any, they broke into N. D. Talalayeva's house. She screamed and ran out into the street. A sergeant shot her.

Her neighbor, Khatimat Nazayeva, dragged the wounded woman back into her house. The sergeant followed them inside and killed them both. Later in the year Aishat Suleimanova, a sixty-two-year-old grandmother who lived on Khankalskaya Street in Grozny, and her family were awakened by a 2 AM knock on the door by OMON riot policemen demanding beer. "We need beer," they said.

"We don't sell beer," she replied.

"Give us beer," they retorted.

"We don't allow beer in the house," she insisted.

"OK, Grandma." Then they left. They came back an hour later and shot her.[12]

Also in 2001, a fourteen-year-old Chechen boy murdered two women. The motive is unclear. Questioned by police after his arrest in the Zavodsky District of Grozny for stealing on 9 September 2008, the now twenty-two-year-old confessed that he had murdered two women seven years earlier.

In June 2002 an unknown gunman shot and killed twenty-three-year-old Kh. Makhmayeva at the Grozny market. Another unknown shooter killed twenty-three-year-old A. Batashyeva and thirty-year-old T. Khadzhiyeva in the settlement of Naurskaya. And on 28 February 2007 two unknown persons fired grenade launchers at the house of a woman in Grozny, wounding her. The motive in each of the attacks was unclear.

On 15 December 2003, during a drunken rampage, Chechen national Rizvan Paiduyev raped and robbed a seventy-year-old woman in her house in Chervlennya, Shelkovsky District. Caught in August 2008, he was sentenced to four years behind bars. On 29 June 2007 Milana Balayeva, the wife of Baudi Yamadayev, and her forty-one-year-old mother-in-law were shot multiple times at point-blank range with a Makarova pistol in their apartment on the recently rebuilt Mozdokskaya Street in Grozny. Only Belayeva, a well-known singer, survived the attack, but she sustained serious wounds to her face and abdomen. She died eighteen days later without ever regaining consciousness.

Police say the motive for the killings was likely a dispute over the apartment, but I have been told by people who know friends of hers that it had more to do with her refusing the affections of Ramzan Kadyrov. Rumors also circulated that Sulim Yamadayev, Baudi's brother, had ordered her killed because Milana's public behavior was too "vulgar," an embarrassment to the Yamadayev family.

Just before midnight on 5 August 2006 two armed men in camouflage uniforms and masks broke into the Grozny home of twenty-eight-year-old Lilia Asukhanova and shot Ramzan, her policeman husband, three times in the chest. Then they demanded gold and money; the terrified woman didn't have any. "Then give us the car keys, or we'll kill her [Lilia's daughter had walked into the room]," they said, putting a gun to the little girl's head.

She wasn't hurt. The assassins took the keys and left the house, joined two more men in the yard, and got into their car to leave. They didn't get far—Lilia, who had never fired a gun before, grabbed her husband's Kalashnikov and sprayed the car with bullets, thirty in all, killing one man and seriously wounding the other three.

"I don't know how this happened," Lilia says. "It was as if a voice inside me was saying: 'kill them.'"

A fighter wanted for the murder of a woman was captured in Grozny on 9 August 2007.

On 4 April 2008 an armed man in a mask and camouflage uniform in a car traveling down Proletarskaya Street in Grozny shot and killed a woman walking on the sidewalk in what was clearly an execution killing. The man threw his weapon out the window of his car and sped away. On 4 December 2008 a group of unknown gunmen broke into the Sadulayev house in the village of Agishty, shot and killed fifty-eight-year-old Taus Sadulayeva, her seventy-two-year-old husband Khozhi, and their thirty-two-year-old son Salman, then set the house on fire. Eighteen days later eight gunmen in masks broke into the home of Judge Aktamirova, a federal district court judge, in the Zavodsky District of Grozny, held her and her husband at gunpoint, and robbed them of over a million rubles ($18,000) and valuable jewelry. On 15 March 2009 a man in the settlement of Prigorodnoye, Groznensky District, murdered his sister Zairayeva. It's unclear whether or not she was murdered for "immoral behavior."

Freak accidents, assaults, suicides, and "various circumstances" cause deaths too.

On 6 October 2000 in Khankala, Russian "serviceman Z" lost control of his armored vehicle and collided with a passenger car, killing two female passengers, A. Sh. Tatashyeva and Tatayeva. A military court convicted and sentenced him to five years in prison with four years probation and suspension of driving privileges. In February 2006 the Chechen Center for Public Information reported that eleven people had died in January, one of them a woman, due to "various circumstances." On 8 July 2006 ten-year-old Malika Yandarova was playing in her backyard when she was struck and killed by a stray bullet. A similar shooting occurred on 7 June 2008 when an eight-year-old girl playing in the yard of her apartment building in the Oktyabrsky District of Grozny died from a bullet wound to the head; a man visiting a traffic policeman friend in a neighboring apartment building had accidentally discharged the policeman's pistol, the bullet crashing through the window and into the yard below.

On 9 January 2007 seventy-six-year-old Saman Abzuyeva was attacked and badly beaten by several young men who lived in the neighborhood as she was walking to the market in Argun. An attempt to persuade her to drop the investigation into the abduction and murder of her son by Chechen police was probably the motive for the attack. In June 2007 a woman in her fifth month of pregnancy took her own life in the Staropromyslovsky District after learning of the death of her husband, killed by a land mine. In mid-September 2007 Polish border guards found the bodies of three Chechen girls, ages six, ten, and thirteen, in the high Bieszczady Mountains after spotting their emaciated mother carrying her two-year-old daughter near the town of Uztrzuki Doine, at the foot of the mountains near the Ukrainian border. The woman and her four children had tried to cross illegally into Poland but got lost in the mountains. Her other children had died from starvation and hypothermia in the wet mountain snow.

An earthquake in Chechnya in October 2008 claimed the lives of seven people, including fifty-three-year-old Amina Alabayeva when the ceiling of a bread store fell on her. A month later a six-year-old girl was raped and murdered by a teenage boy, age fifteen. Investigators found the body of the little girl with stab wounds and evidence of rape in the home of her forty-three-year-old unemployed mother in Shali. On 31 January 2008 a forty-year-old mother and two boys, ten and seventeen, were wounded when someone threw a grenade into the yard of their home in the settlement of Goity. On 21 January 2009 a tragic accident in Grozny involving a head-on collision between a BMW and VAZ car resulted in the deaths of six people, including a mother and her two-year-old child.

Gas leak explosions caused by old, worn-out pipes in apartment buildings and private houses commonly kill women. On 1 December 2009 a twenty-five-year-old woman died from burns sustained in a gas-leak explosion at her house in Gudermes. Her two-month-old baby was badly burned but lived.

Earlier in the year, in February, seven members of the Babiyev family were seriously burned when another leaky gas pipe exploded. The mother and six of her children, including two girls, ten and thirteen years of age, were badly burned. Their mother died in the hospital.

In November 2008 a thirty-six-year-old woman and her two-year-old daughter in the Shelkovsky District received first- and second-degree burns trying to light a gas stove, and in May 2008 a woman and a man were hurt in a gas explosion in the village of Mesker-Yurt, Shalinsky District.

FOUR

Baking Bread

*I baked bread, handed out arms and ammunition, and sometimes
my husband would allow me to shoot.*
Larisa, a fighter

THE CHECHEN WOMAN is the principal victim of war violence, but she
has also perpetrated violence, even unimaginable violence. Sometimes she
has no choice but to fight. Women who find themselves in the mountains—
for whatever reasons, perhaps only because they wish to remain with their
fighter husbands—carry water, cook, clean, wash, nurse, keep up the morale
of the men, and sometimes shoot, too.

There have been hundreds of these women, fewer than Russian soldiers
imagine but not figments of "battlefield mythology," either, as some Western observers assert. Female fighters served in most of the Chechen units led
by major field commanders like Shamil Basayev, Salman Raduyev, and Ruslan Gelayev. At the same time, Said S—— tells me that he knew commanders
who would not allow women near their men—"They were not welcome."

Little is known about most of the women. People don't like to talk about
them. The majority are dead. Some have been captured, tried, and imprisoned. Three or four have voluntarily surrendered. Several received hero med-
als, others returned home to resume peaceful lives or assume noncombatant
roles. Some are still in the mountains. All, along with their predecessors,
the legendary *boyevichki* (fighters) of the nineteenth-century Caucasus wars,
inspire others to fight.

SINGING SONGS AND BEATING PANS

I disagree with those who argue that there has never been a tradition among Chechen women of taking up arms. That notion ignores the heroines of the nineteenth-century Caucasus wars who fought at Dadi-Yurt, Akhulgo, and other Chechen villages attacked by Russian tsarist forces, not to mention the legendary Taimaskha Molova, who for ten years eluded tsarist armies until she was finally captured in 1842.

In 1819 Dadi-Yurt was an *aul* of about two hundred houses situated on the right bank of the Terek River. In September tsarist forces surrounded it in preparation for an assault. Chechen history books and legendary songs tell of valiant women like Dadi Aibika, the daughter of the *aul*'s founder, and Amaran Zaza, who sang songs and beat copper pans in front of the mosque to inspire Dadi-Yurt's male defenders, only to die themselves impaled on bayonets with fighting *kinzhals* (knives) wet with Russian blood clasped in their hands.

Legend has it that Dadi-Yurt's girls cut off their cherished long braids, slicing them up into bullet-sized bits to stuff into empty gun barrels when ammunition ran out. General Yermalov recalls in his memoirs how these women fought furiously when his soldiers entered their homes. Female prisoners were taken, but as his force was crossing the bridge over the Terek River on 15 September forty-six of them pounced on Russian soldiers and threw themselves and their conquerors into the abyss below.

This ultimate sacrifice is still remembered and honored in Chechen song, poetry, history, and now an official holiday. In 2009 President Kadyrov designated the third Sunday of September as an official annual holiday—Chechen Women's Day—in honor of Dadi-Yurt's forty-six women and today's Chechen woman.

Women and children fought with the same vengeance during the 1839 siege of Akhulgo, a mountain *aul* linked by a long, wooden plank bridge spanning a deep gorge. Days of beating back Russian attacks in that hot June summer exhausted Akhulgo's food and water supply, decimating the population. In a final attempt to take the *aul* the Russian general, Count Glasse, launched a three-pronged attack. One group of soldiers attempted to scale the steep cliffs of the ravine, but Chechen sharpshooters picked them off. Soldiers in a second group traversed the ravine floor below but soon found boulders raining down on their heads. A third group made its way along a precipice only to face hundreds of screaming, charging women and children who had been hiding in the caves. Wielding *kinzhals*, the women slashed away at the intruders on horseback while children hacked at their legs and feet. Even after the *aul* was overrun the seemingly helpless prisoners—nearly a thousand of them, wounded women, children, and old men—snatched bayonets from their guards and fought to the death.

The fearless Nadezhda Durova, better known as "Taimaskha Molova from Gekhi," became a legend of the Caucasus wars in her own time. Fighting from the Black Sea to Derbent, for ten long years General-Lieutenant Falafeyev and his soldiers tried to defeat her. They finally succeeded in 1842. On 15 April 1842 Molova commanded a Chechen unit subordinated to Akhverdy-Magoma, a deputy of the famous Imam Shamil, in a battle with Russian soldiers near Bolshoi Yandyrki, Ingushetia. She was captured and later sent to Vladikavkaz. But Tsar Nikolas, having heard long before of Molova's exploits, ordered that she be brought to Petersburg. It's unknown how long she remained there, but Molova so captivated the tsar and tsarina that they presented her with gifts of a gold necklace with pearls, a hundred rubles, and her freedom. She returned to the Caucasus, but she never fought again.

THE SHOOTERS

"I will kill you slowly because I love to. First, I will shoot you in the leg—the knee is best—then I will shoot you in the hand, then in the balls. You had better be scared. I'm a master sport champion [biathlon sharpshooter] you know," the soft, accented radio voice of "Masha" echoed somewhere deep in the mountain forests of Chechnya in 1995, instilling cold fear in the hearts of already scared young Russian officers.

Soldiers feared and hated these "White Stocking" snipers, whose classic trademark was said to be a bullet to the crotch and whose principal virtue was patience, willingness to wait for hours, sometimes days, for a Russian officer to come along. The girls didn't get their name from wearing sexy *belye kolgotki* (white pantyhose) but from the white sports pants worn by highly skilled Soviet biathlon sharpshooters from the Baltics.

This combination of fear and hate fed myths, fantasies, anecdotes, stories, and even inspired movies about the skill, cold bloodedness, beauty, and yet ugliness of these White Stocking snipers. For example, Anna, the star of the

Russian film *Kavkazskaya ruletka* (Caucasus roulette), is stunningly beauti-ful. She is a hardened White Stocking sniper, Russian by nationality, who escapes from her vengeful Chechen husband who vows to kill her after she kidnaps their young son and runs away to Moscow.

But the two snipers portrayed in Alexandr Nevzorov's 1997 film *Chistil-ishche* (purgatory) are anything but beautiful. The film about trapped Rus-sian soldiers in Grozny on 4 January 1995 opens with a tall, ugly woman in her early thirties with long hair braided into a ponytail and another blond woman (about the same age) with short hair. They are standing in a second-story window picking off Russian soldiers one by one as the wounded crawl out of a burning hospital bus.

A sniper with a long bulbous nose and face caved in under one eye laughs and congratulates her partner as they kill. One scene shows them shooting a soldier in the crotch. "Did you hit him in the balls?" the ugly one asks.

"Of course!" her companion replies.

Then they count out the wad of hundred-dollar bills their Chechen commander has given them for their work. "Are you from the Baltics?" a Chechen *mujahid* asks in another scene. "Yes!" she nods.

Shamil Basayev put together a whole "battalion" of these women drawn from the Ukraine, Belorussia, Siberia, Moscow, and one or two from the Baltic States. There were also Chechens in this battalion commanded by Basayev's cousin Medina Basayeva. Another battalion was called "the Djokhar Dudayev Regiment." These women and their male counterparts wrought havoc on Russian soldiers entering Grozny in 1994 and again in 2000. "Heavy air and artillery bombardment doesn't seem to slow the hail of bullets from the Chechen snipers' rifles," journalist Yuriy Bagrov wrote in a dispatch from Grozny on 20 January 2000.

The biggest myth about White Stocking snipers is that they were all biathlon sharpshooters from the former Soviet Baltic republics. Former Chechen president Yandarbiyev told the newspaper *Nezavisimoye voyennoye obozreniye* in January 1999 that he had known of only two Baltic "volun-teers," a Latvian and a Lithuanian. Yandarbiyev called them volunteers, but girls who could shoot straight came to Chechnya for the money. "In six months I could earn enough to last a lifetime," a Chechen female sniper proudly told her interrogator.

I only know a few of their names, but I do know what happened to most White Stocking snipers whom Russian soldiers captured alive. They were executed on the spot by slow death, which explains why few criminal cases were brought against them in the first war.

One sniper caught in the Argun Gorge in the first war was "abused for ages, raped, and then a grenade was put into her vagina. She was blown to pieces," Russian Army private Andrei told the Committee of Soldiers' Mothers of Russia in a postwar interview.[1] Another was a pretty twenty-five-year-old woman with white skin and fair hair down to her waist. "We didn't rape her," her executioner told the Soldiers' Mothers, but "we did tie her arms and legs between two BTRs [armored vehicles] and pull her apart"; all the while she was screaming, "I hate Russian pigs!" A third was "tied to a tank and dragged along the road until all the flesh had been ripped off her." Yet another was caught and tied to a tree. "Two kilograms of C4 trotil [TNT] explosives were placed under her. A slow burning wick, four to five meters long, was then lit so she could see it burning. She had no fear whatsoever," the Russian soldier remembers.

Private Andrei's unit caught two more snipers in Grozny. "One woman began to shout that she hates Russians. She was shot on the spot. The other pleaded 'Let me go!' The soldiers took her up to the fifth floor of a house, tortured her, then tied a grenade to her and ran downstairs. She had asked 'Let me go,' so we did—she was sent in all directions; she didn't even reach the ground." "A fifth was offered up to us by our officers," Andrei remembers. "They told us we could all rape her before she died. None of us wanted to rape her, and none of us did. We shot her instead. A few weeks later we found out she was Ukrainian. She turned out to be the cousin of one of the men in my group."

"Stretching" was the favored method of execution. "I remember a Chechen female sniper. She didn't have any chance. We just tore her apart with two armored personnel carriers, having tied her ankles with steel cables. There was a lot of blood, but the boys needed it. After that, a lot of the boys calmed down. Justice was done, and that was the most important thing for them."

In Grozny, Private Nikolai even killed a Russian woman eight months pregnant because he thought she was a sniper: "We [the Soldiers' Mothers] asked: Did she cry? Did she ask you not to kill her? 'Yes', he said, 'she was crying, she fell down on her knees, shouting, asking me not to kill her. But how can I leave her alive if in an hour she would pick up an automatic [Kalashnikov rifle] and begin shooting?' However, he wasn't sure himself whether she was a sniper or not."

A Russian female doctor serving in Chechnya describes in the film *White Raven* how a female sniper in Grozny who had shot Russian soldiers in the back of the knees was captured, raped, and killed.

These acceptable methods of dealing with female snipers helps explain why Russian Army colonel Budanov believes he did nothing wrong in raping and strangling eighteen-year-old Elza Kungayeva, whom he accused of being a sniper, picking off his men one at a time. Budanov said in his 22 June 2001 court testimony that his regiment had advanced halfway across Chechnya without losing a single man but that at Duba-Yurt a lone female sniper—Kungayeva—had begun killing his officers. General Vladimir Shamanov, now governor of the Ulayanovskaya Oblast, agrees: "She wasn't just a girl, but a sniper, an enemy, who took the life of more than one of my officers." But the military prosecution told the court that there was absolutely no evidence that she had ever been a sniper or that any member of her family had undertaken any kind of anti-Russian activity.

Passions soar over this subject. As recently as 2006 a Russian woman was killed by a Russian Chechnya war veteran because she told him she had been a White Stocking sniper. During a drunken employee party at a furniture factory in Ulyanovsk, Russia, thirty-seven-year-old Elena Skoryatina claimed that she had been a sniper for the Chechens. Denis Saurin, her killer, told investigators that he had been chatting with friends at the party about the atrocities committed by Chechen terrorists when Skoryatina interrupted and started arguing with him, claiming that Chechens were fighting for their freedom.

"She said that Maskhadov and Basayev were good people and in the end, said she had been a sniper with Chechen fighters and taken out our boys. The light dimmed in my eyes and I thought, I have to take revenge. I thought [to myself] 'Skoryatina is not leaving this party alive,'" Saurin remembers. He beat her, then put her right (shooting) eye out and cut off the index (trigger) finger on her right hand, as well as the middle finger on her left hand (used by snipers to make an obscene gesture after a good shot).

"She cried and begged for mercy, but I couldn't stop—the faces of our boys killed by Chechen snipers stood before my eyes," Saurin told investigators. He stripped the woman, shoved the fingers he had cut off into her vagina, and then slit the woman's throat. Saurin and his brother disposed of the body in a bag of sawdust.

Skoryatina could not have been a Chechen sniper: she was near-sighted and had never left her native town of Ulyanovsk for more than a week at a time. Investigators concluded that her story was either a sick joke or "drunken bravado."[2]

The names of some White Stocking snipers are known. In May 1995 Russian intelligence learned that Svetlana Korzhikova and a group of female snipers were active near the settlement of Assinovskaya. Akhmed Kelimatov was given the task of neutralizing them. On 17 May he located Korzhikova's position, drew her fire by raising his cap on a stick above his head, then called in Russian artillery fire on her. When the smoke cleared Kelimatov found the wounded girl with tears streaming down her cheeks. A sniper's rifle with twenty-four notches on the stock was by her side. He writes:

Seeing my anguished look and the cap in my hand, she uttered: "first time and, it seems, my last."

When I asked her how she got herself into this mess, she abruptly answered: "When the USSR collapsed, life became very difficult. Many people looked for work. It was difficult for me to leave my family, but I had to find work and there was no employment. Then the 'buyers' showed up [and said] I could earn money. [But] I feel sorry for the children."

Kelimatov "gave her to the boys [the other three men in his unit] for entertainment" after he finished questioning her.[3]

Budennovsk's Nurse and the School Girl

In 1995 Shamil Basayev took two of his women along on his first suicide mission into Russia. On 14 June Basayev, thirty-year-old Raisa Dundayeva, and Tamara Topchayeva, sixteen, along with 140 other fighters concealed in the back of two large KamAZ trucks, crossed the border from Chechnya into the Stavropolsky District of Russia, heading for Moscow. But they got only as far as the city of Budennovsk because, according to Basayev, he ran out of money to pay bribes to the police: "I only had $100 left [after paying off the border guards] in my pocket when we got to Budennovsk, so we had to change our plans. . . . We wanted to go to Moscow, to go there for a little while and watch Russians bombing Moscow. But our operation failed because of the greediness of local [Budennovsk] police officers. We just didn't have enough money to pay them off. That's why they started picking on us and escorted us back to GUVD [police headquarters] . . . in Budennovsk."

Basayev seized Budennovsk instead, beginning with the police station. After a nasty gunfight with police and a few Russian soldiers in the town, he rounded up 1,600 hostages and marched them to the city's hospital. "We decided to take as many hostages as possible. . . . We don't care when we die. What is important is how [we die]," Basayev told the media. Thus began a sixteen-day ordeal that left 148 hostages dead and 415 people wounded, compelled Russia to agree to a cease-fire with Chechnya, and made Chechen national heroes out of Basayev's women.

Raisa Dundayeva was a pretty Ukrainian woman in her thirties, a long-time resident of Grozny, and, according to Russian intelligence, Basayev's secret lover. The other was the teenage Tamara Topchayeva, a sniper. But it was Dundayeva who raised the green Islamic flag of victory over Budennovsk's city hall. Otherwise, she kept a low profile. A *Sevodnya* newspaper reporter who was at Budennovsk vividly remembers that "she kept her face masked" and that "Raisa refused to talk to reporters, except to give her name and say only that she was a nurse." Journalist Sergei Topol was there, too, and remembers "a woman [Dundayeva] with a cowboy handkerchief covering her face leaning up against the door jamb [in the hospital], beside her a grenade launcher."

On the second day of the siege Basayev demanded a press conference at which he repeated his demands that Russia cease combat operations in Chechnya, withdraw its troops, and enter into negotiations with President Dudayev. Five days later, after two failed stormings of the building, Russia conceded and gave Basayev, his women, and the rest of his battalion escorted passage back to Chechnya. He took 139 volunteer hostages with him. One of them was a *Moskovskaya pravda* reporter who talked briefly with Dundayeva, confirming that she had been born in the Ukraine but had lived all of her life in Grozny. Raisa claimed she had lost three children at the beginning of the war.

Dundayeva arrived home to a hero's welcome. Basayev personally pinned Ichkeria's highest medal, the coveted *Koman Sii* (Honor of the Nation), on her. He also gave her an apartment in the Oktyabrsky District of Grozny. Despite ultimately falling out with Basayev over money, she lived there in peace until June 2000, when Russian forces took Budennovsk's "nurse" into custody while she was asleep in her bed.

The *Moskovskaya pravda* reporter photographed the teenager Topchayeva cradling a Kalashnikov rifle on the bus home from Budennovsk. During Dundayeva's court trial, one of the hostages testified that a woman in Basayev's group told her that she had been born in Kazakhstan. This was Topchayeva. She too received a medal for Budennovsk but says that "after Budennovsk they [Basayev and his group] abandoned me. They didn't give me an apartment and left me without work." She must have received some money because she bought a small café, which prospered for a while. But then the radical Wahhabis came along and burned it down because she served alcohol. She married, too, but her husband soon took a second wife and eventually abandoned her.

Russian forces captured Topchayeva in 1996, but she was never tried for terrorism because she was exchanged for four Russian soldiers being held by the Chechen side. She voluntarily surrendered to Russian forces in the Nadterechny District in November 1999. By that time she was broke, destitute, and living in an old, abandoned museum.

Dundayeva and three of her Budennovsk compatriots were tried and sentenced by a Stavropoly court in October 2001. She told the court that she had played a very "modest role" and had done "nothing special" at Budennovsk—simply cooked, washed, and nursed the wounded. She admitted that she carried a Kalashnikov rifle but said, "I didn't even fire my weapon."

Dundayeva's primary defense rested on her claim that she never wore the medal that Basayev gave her because "there was nothing to be proud of." She pleaded with the court, "Please understand, I am not a terrorist. I was like a speck of dust in the field. When I was a girl they made me marry a man fifteen years older who used narcotics and died from them. Now his relatives won't have anything to do with me, and I don't even know where my son is." As to how she had become involved with Basayev and his men, "It was purely accidental," she said. "I didn't have any close relatives around. There was nobody to guide me down the right path in life."

The prosecution's witnesses said that after Budennovsk, Dundayeva complained to nearly everybody that her service there deserved a lot more than just the medal and apartment Basayev gave her. Basayev promised her money, as he did to everyone in those trucks, but she never got her share. "Money spoiled Basayev," Dundayeva testified, "causing many of those who had been with him to start to mistrust him and even turn their back on him because of his pathological stinginess with money."

The court put Dundayeva away for eleven years. The prosecutor proved that she had burned the Russian flag at Budennovsk and that she was guilty on ten counts of banditry, kidnapping, hostage taking, terrorism, belonging to an armed band, and illegal possession of firearms.

Raduyev's She-Wolves

Said S——, whose office was just down the hall from Raduyev's, remembers that the "loudmouth" (Raduyev) always had women hanging around his office; two or three could be found there most anytime. In January 1996 Raduyev took eight of them with him to Kizlyar, Dagestan, a city of about forty thousand people located northeast of Grozny. There he too seized a hospital, taking twice as many hostages as at Budennovsk.

Only a few of the women lived to return home. "Lolita" (Elena P——, Russian authorities never released her last name), a White Stocking sniper and the infamous recorded voice of "Masha," was one of them.

Ten months earlier pretty twenty-two-year-old Elena had arrived in Argun, Chechnya, from the Ukraine with the hope of earning quick money for her wedding. She was no biathlon sharpshooter but she was a good shot, so she was assigned to a fighting unit headed by Abdul Khadzhiyev-Aslambek, one of Basayev's field commanders. It was Aslambek who nicknamed her "Lolita" for her youth, beautiful hair, pretty grey-green eyes, and pure white skin. She also had a gold tooth and an "intelligent looking face." She was simply stunning.

Lolita was an obedient girl. She cleaned, cooked, cared for the wounded, and learned to shoot better. In a few months she completely forgot why she had come to Chechnya. She fell in love and married a Chechen field commander, but a Russian bullet ended the marriage in the summer of 1995.

After her husband's death Lolita threw herself into her new profession as a sniper. It's said that she took revenge for her loss by shooting Russian soldiers in the crotch. She made few friends outside the close circle of Chechen fighters who became her only family. She kept photographs of them. One photo reads: "To the nurse, Shamil Basayev."

In January 1996 Lolita became a terrorist when she accompanied Raduyev and two or three hundred "Lone Wolves" to attack the Russian air base in Kizlyar. Lolita's participation in the attack on the base and then on the Kizlyar hospital only became known in early 2000, after Raduyev's capture, when a letter was discovered among his belongings asking the head of the Oktyabrsky District to give her a two-room apartment for service in Kizlyar.

"Wolves have come to you!" Raduyev called out at the air base. But Russian forces hit back hard, and Raduyev's Wolves were forced to withdraw into the city, where they seized a four-story hospital and maternity ward and other strategic buildings. Wolves rounded up hostages and herded them into the hospital until the count numbered a satisfactory two thousand or so people. Horrible things went on in that hospital. Anna Romashchenko later testified at Raduyev's trial that her son Pavel, a policeman who was on duty at the hospital, was murdered, savagely mutilated, and incinerated in the hospital's furnace. Raduyev booby-trapped the building with bombs and demanded that Russian troops withdraw from Chechnya or he would kill everybody. I was glued to the television in Moscow. A defiant Raduyev told us that "we can turn this city into hell and ashes." Lolita and other snipers controlled a bridge across the Terek River, as well as two high-rise apartment buildings near the hospital.

As at Budennovsk, a negotiated settlement was reached. Raduyev agreed to free most of the hostages in exchange for the agreement of several high-ranking Dagestani officials to become volunteer hostages on his escape buses back to Chechnya. Eleven buses and two large trucks transported Raduyev, Lolita, the other seven women and fighters, and their hostages. But near the Chechen border the Russian military demanded that Raduyev free his human cargo. When he refused, a Russian helicopter answered with gunfire, forcing Wolves to take cover in the nearby village of Pervomaiskoye.

A four-day Russian bombardment ensued, and 153 of Raduyev's fighters were killed. He tried once to break out of the encirclement but failed. In the early morning hours of 18 January seventy fighters and sixty hostages tried a second time and succeeded with the help of reinforcements sent by Maskhadov and Basayev. Raduyev and what was left of his men, hostages, Lolita, and the other women made their way through minefields and Russian gunfire to Raduyev's secret hideout in Novogroznensky.

Lolita started a new life after Pervomaiskoye. Musa Charayev courted her; he was a tractor operator before the first war and sold wine for a living, but by the spring of 1996 he had become a well known field commander. They married and went to live in the mountains. Lolita participated in all of her husband's attacks on Russian forces. One day she called her parents in Konstantinovka; her mother fainted at the sound of her voice. That summer Lolita's father and brother died from eating bad mushrooms. She acquired a false passport and went home for the funeral.

Soon after the war finished in August 1996 Lolita bore Musa a son. Maskhadov gave her husband a piece of the oil industry in Chechnya while she built a profitable customs-control business. "I inspected trucks, prepared documents, that kind of thing; nothing special," she recalls. But Russian intelligence claims she also hunted Russian spies in 1997 and 1998. Tragedy befell Lolita once again in March 1999, when Musa was murdered. He was found shot in the back near an oil pipeline.

Lolita was one of two snipers whom Igor Tkachyev tried to prosecute. Tkachyev led the special group of investigators for Russia's general procurator that brought charges against 430 combatants at the beginning of the second war. She was arrested at the Ishcherskaya train station on the border between Chechnya and North Ossetia in January 2000. Lolita was in possession of a stolen passport in the name of a Donetskaya Oblast woman. Her interrogation videotape shows that the previous five years had taken their toll on her physically. She was no longer the beauty she had once been; she looked far older than her twenty-seven years, and her voice had become deep, like a man's. Interrogators describe her behavior as "vulgar."

Tkachyev was unable to prosecute Lolita because she fell under Russia's amnesty program. But, he says, everybody was so afraid of her that nobody would testify against her anyway. Lolita was sent to prison for two years for belonging to an illegal armed formation and possessing a stolen passport. Her subsequent fate is unknown.

Birlant is another woman who accompanied Raduyev to Kizlyar and survived. Right after the bitter battle for Grozny in August 1996, which Chechen forces won, the website www.amina.com described the twenty-something woman in this way:

> Dressed in dirty black jeans, a T-shirt and a floppy camouflage hat, a single woman fighter stood out among the Chechens resting in the shade of the trees outside their new headquarters in Grozny last month. Clearly in a position of authority, she was shouting orders to the men and listening to petitions from civilians.
>
> Dark circles ringed Birlant's eyes, but otherwise she gave no hint of the horrors of the previous two weeks' fighting in Grozny. Taciturn about her own exploits, she had nevertheless confirmed her place as the most redoubtable woman fighter in Chechnya. Her toughness is daunting.

Birlant's fate is also unknown. I could find no one who could or would tell me what happened to her after 1996.

A third woman, a video photographer by the name of Khazman (Raisa) Umarova, also made it out of Pervomaiskoye alive. Umarova's videos from Pervomaiskoye were shown on Chechen television. She was the only person reporting from inside the embattled village. Some sources say she managed to sneak through Russian encirclement into the village to find Raduyev, but according to the *Amina* website she was in Kizlyar and filmed the action there, too.

The 2004 Russian video *Chechensky Kapkan,* aired on Ren TV, shows two women on Raduyev's buses headed toward Pervomaiskoye. The video is likely Umarova's work. One woman (perhaps Birlant) is tall with a full face and large, round reflecting sunglasses; she is wearing a black scarf and a camouflage uniform. She is sitting on the right side of the bus next to the window and looking directly into the camera. Next to her on the aisle seat is a boy holding two rocket launchers. Lolita, wearing a black and yellow floral headscarf and a black leather coat, is sitting on an aisle seat on the left side of the bus. A Kalashnikov is in her lap, her hands folded over it.

Umarova was raised in a village in northeast Chechnya, studied philology, and joined the Youth Committee of the Chechen Republic of Ichkeria in 1991. Her film "career" began in April 1995 when a British journalist, himself denied access to Samashki, gave her his video camera and insisted that she go there to film Russian operations. She smuggled it in under her dress. After Samashki Umarova traveled to other battle sites, filming everything for Dzokar Dudayev's *Presidentsky kanal* television broadcasts.

In an *Amina* interview prior to the second war Umarova said she and her friends had always supported the idea of independence, but today she says she looks back on those days of innocence with incredulity: "If I thought I would go through all this, running everywhere and seeing all that I have seen, I would never have believed it. . . . People are amazed because I used to be frightened of everything, even of people raising their voices."

"Always poised, a smile lighting up her face, she rarely talks of the horrors she has seen, but when she does, the intensity of her emotion turns her eyes to black holes of despair. It is that passion that drives her to record what is happening in Chechnya for history. Like the fighters, she says she is a *smertnik,* ready and willing to die in the fight for independence," the website writes.

Umarova now lives in Western Europe. In 2006 the Ukrainian embassy in Paris denied her a visa to attend a conference to establish an "anti-imperialistic front." At the end of that year, she was listed as one of four board members of the Belgium-based DAGAN International Charity Foundation, which says that its mission is to "contribute to the reimbursement of losses caused by the Russian colonial war against the Chechen nation, after the latter has declared the restitution of its historical statehood." Mairbek Vachagayev, Aslan Maskhadov's former press secretary, told me that she, along with Akhmad Sardali, runs the *Svobodny Kavkaz* (Free Caucasus) website.

Asya and Anya

In his pictorial book *Open Wound*, Stanley Greene tells the story of a twenty-two-year-old fighter/nurse he met in Itum Kale in July 1996 after he was taken captive by *mujahideen*. His captor, Chechen field commander Daoud, accused Green and two of his colleagues of spying on them, for which he said they should be executed. But Asya, a woman fighter in the unit, came to their defense and "ultimately saved our lives," Greene says.

Asya's story is that of yet another Chechen woman kidnapped for marriage at the age of fourteen, when Chechnya was still part of the Soviet Union. One night a complete stranger broke into her house when her parents were away, threw a bag over her head, and dragged her to a waiting car. When she refused to marry him, he "spoiled her." In the end, she became his wife because her parents agreed to accept a payment of $2,300.

Asya eventually fell in love with her kidnapper-rapist-husband and had a little girl, but his physical abuse forced her to take the child and run away to her sister's in Grozny. When Asya refused to return to her husband her mother-in-law came and took the child away and her husband divorced her. But Asya was determined to make a new life. She went to nursing school and met her second husband at the hospital where she worked after graduation.

Asya was at that hospital on 11 December 1994, when Russia launched its military operations into Chechnya. In late December Russian forces bombarded Grozny; street-to-street fighting began shortly after that. Chechen forces were commanded by former Soviet Army colonel and Chechen chief of staff Aslan Maskhadov from the basement of the Presidential Palace in Grozny. On 17 and 18 January Russian Su-25 aircraft bombed the Presidential Palace, killing many fighters. Maskhadov abandoned the palace on the 18th.

Two weeks before Maskhadov's departure Asya, who was then six months pregnant, and her mother went to nurse the wounded and dying in the palace. "She nursed the wounded in corridors amongst dead bodies, bombing debris and human waste," Greene writes, finally fleeing with Maskhadov and the others into the mountains on 18 January. A month later

Asya returned to Grozny to nurse fighters still in the bombed-out city. She gave birth to a baby boy and her former mother-in-law, now unable to take care of her first child, returned Asya's little girl to her. Asya stayed in Grozny, but her new husband took the children and left to escape the war.

Asya told Greene that she had personally executed a captured Russian soldier because he was talking in his sleep about what his patrol had done to Chechens they had captured. "She took a gun and shot him dead, unable to hear his confessions," Greene writes. Two other Russian soldiers were pushed off a cliff, and a fourth had his throat cut in a public circle of Chechen fighters. "He begged, he cried, he swore at us and called us bad names," she recounts, "but it was not terrifying to kill him because the Russians had done far worse things than we did. I felt only hatred."[4]

Greene describes Asya as "tall, slim and agile with wide, clear, brown eyes, wearing the soldier's striped t-shirt and combat trousers instead of the traditional long dress and scarf. Like most women in Chechnya, she sported a green velvet beret, the uniform of the Chechen fighter."

"We will never stop, we will fight them to the last," Asya swore. A superb picture of Asya in a blue-and-white-striped shirt, dark pants, and a camouflage jacket, holding a Kalashnikov rifle, is found in Greene's book and on his website.

There is also a photograph of a second fighter, Anya, in Greene's book—a very pretty girl with classical Chechen features sitting on a prayer rug with her Kalashnikov in front of her. The caption reads: "Anya in prayer. She is a Chechen fighter who was injured in the war. She believes that war is like a drug—she cannot imagine life without her Kalashnikov."[5]

The Pride of Her Grandmother

In early December 1997 the FSB and the Moscow region Anti-Organized Crime Directorate arrested two young women who had arrived in the capital by train from Grozny carrying twenty-six pistols, silencers, and ammunition. In 1999 eighteen-year-old Anya Klinkyevicha was nearly caught doing the same thing.

Anya was born and grew up in Moscow's upscale Patriarchy Ponds neighborhood. She obeyed all the rules at home and did well in school. This slightly built, pretty teenager was simply an angel, the pride of her grandmother. Anya's mother, Margarita, was wealthy. She was the financial director of Russia's "Loto," and Anya's father, Aleksandr, was the Loto's general manager.

Anya fell in love with a nineteen-year-old Russian policeman and at the age of sixteen gave birth to a little girl. Despite the difficulties of being a young mother she finished school, but then things started to go wrong. Her husband was arrested for stealing and was sentenced to seven years in jail. They divorced.

At eighteen Anya enrolled in the expensive Moscow Chemistry Institute, only to drop out and enter a pedagogical institute a few months later. She didn't stay long there, either. One day she walked into the dean's office in tears, saying that her parents had been killed in an automobile accident and that she needed her tuition money back so she could take care of her little girl. "We returned everything," the dean recalls.

But Anya didn't go home. Instead, she sent a letter telling her mother that she was going far away for a while to earn money: "I'm going to Chechnya to earn good money. I'm tired of asking you for a hand-out all the time. I'm an independent woman now. I'm leaving and will return in a few years." What Anya didn't say was that she had fallen in love with a handsome black-haired Chechen boy from Grozny named Eduard and was going home with him.

Anya and Eduard were married and lived with his Wahhabi family. She converted to Wahhabism. Eduard schooled her well in Chechen tradition, and then introduced her to Sultan Saayev and Wakhid Turpulkhanov, two former Chechen Shariah security personnel. "Listen to them and everything will be fine," Eduard told his obedient wife. "Remember, I love you."

They in turn assigned Anya to Yakhita Ibragimova, another veteran female fighter from the first war, for Anya's further education. Yakhita took Anya under her wing and enrolled her in the Caucasus Islamic Institute (run by the infamous Arab fighter Samir bin Salekh al-Suweilem—alias al-Khattab—a veteran of the Soviet war in Afghanistan who had come to Chechnya in 1995 to again fight the Russians). The year was 1999. For three months Anya intensely studied Wahhabi ideology at the institute and general fighting tactics at Khattab's training camp in Sergen Yurt, and then chose sniping as her military specialty.

"Don't worry about me and don't come looking for me. Everything is ok. I am in a great training camp. I like it very much, especially the shooting and hand-to-hand combat," Anya wrote to her mother.

Anya had an interesting "diploma project." While other graduates made raids into Dagestan, her assignment was to smuggle guns into Moscow, just like the girls in 1997 had done. One morning she boarded the

Moscow-bound train with a sports bag filled with ten pistols and a disassembled automatic rifle. Yakhita accompanied her. Anya passed her final exam with distinction, receiving a thousand dollars and a Zhigule car as graduation presents. She was told that a war with Russia would soon come and that she would be paid $250–$500 for every Russian officer she killed. In the meantime, she would smuggle arms into Moscow. A friend's apartment served as an armory.

She was the perfect gun runner because she was small in build, young, and cute. No one would ever suspect her. But one day all that worked against her when she caught the eyes of two young, flirty policemen at Moscow's Vladikhino subway station. They asked for her passport and address registration and emptied her handbag. A pistol clip fell out. "I just found it," she told them in her innocent voice. They took the clip and sent her on her way.

A few months later the same policemen spotted her again, but this time her name was Antona Valyeva. "I said to her jokingly, I could shoot you on the spot, right here and now, if I wanted to," the flirty policeman said. "Shoot me and I'll shoot you back." she replied, also with a flirty grin.

Later, during interrogation, she admitted that once she had even smuggled explosives into Moscow, but the police "couldn't put her in prison for words," so they let her go again. Anya promptly returned to Grozny, but only for a little while.

In January 2000 Ruslana Ibragimova (Anya's new name) was positively identified as a White Stocking sniper. She wore the unmistakable trademark of a single earring and had a bad bruise on her shoulder. Dressed in jeans and a coat but without her rifle, she was detained along with her brother-in-law following a sniper attack on a Russian Army column in Grozny. "My husband is Chechen and I've come to see him," she pleaded with Russian officers in her quiet voice. But twenty-two sniper bullets for a Dragun rifle and sniper paraphernalia in her bag gave her away. "I found the bag," she tried to explain. But no one listened. Anya was tried and sentenced to prison, but because the prosecutor couldn't prove that she was a member of any particular illegal armed formation she only received a three-year sentence. Under Russian amnesty law she was released within a month. With her pretrial prison time, Anya spent a total of nine months in jail.

When she got out Anya went to stay for a while with her grandmother in the Tulskaya Oblast but again ran away to Grozny. She wrote in her departing letter to her dear grandmother: "I have an obligation there. Forgive me, but I can't do anything else. I will earn money so we can live comfortably. I will return and everything will be ok. Don't try to find me. I'll get in touch with you. P.S.—I ask your forgiveness one more time, but I really do love you and grandpa and I want to be with you."

She never returned home.

Larisas I & II

In her book *Chienne de Guerre: A Woman Reporter behind the Lines of the War in Chechnya,* Anne Nivat, a French journalist who snuck into Chechnya to report on the second war, recalls her encounters with two female fighters she met near Grozny in February 2000. Both have the first names of Larisa. I will call them "Larisa I" and "Larisa II."

Larisa I is a twenty-six-year-old woman who proudly calls herself a sniper. She helped Nivat maintain her cover as a Chechen woman and delicately navigate her way toward Grozny. Nivat describes her as looking older than her twenty-six years, tall, strong, with "hands like a bricklayer." Nivat explains that Larisa I had left Grozny before the fighting became intense because "she jokingly said[,] . . . 'The boys [fighters] insisted'" that she go home to Noviye Atagi and raise her two-year-old daughter, whose father had died two months earlier in Grozny.[6]

They harped on it constantly. "Larisa, for the sake of your daughter get out of here, leave us," Larisa I told Nivat. "I asked: And what will I do in the village. I will be thinking about you all the time. But they insisted: Larisa, you must stay alive so that you can raise your children, so that our people will not disappear."

She was sent home but "the boys" told her that she could work for counterintelligence in Noviye Atagi. "That's OK, but a little boring. In the city I did everything; I was a sniper, and when it came my turn, I cooked kasha [a kind of oatmeal], was a nurse, and mainly spent all my time alongside the boys," she explained to Nivat, who goes on to say that Larisa I would make a good spy: "She conducted herself well, like a true spy, knew where Russian posts were and how to get through them."

Nivat only got about ten kilometers from Grozny, as far as Alkhan-Kala, where in February 2000 she met twenty-year-old Larisa II, a beautiful girl who "had a turned up nose, bright lipstick and shining eyes," and who "even under a uniform and white camouflage clothing had a feminine figure." Larisa II was with wounded fighters fleeing Grozny for the mountains to the south. Nivat says she spotted her clutching a Kalashnikov to her chest at the end of the corridor at the hospital in Alkhan-Kala where Dr. Baiev worked.

Larisa II was very talkative; she had plenty to say about her life and *gazovat* (Jihad), that she had "dreamed about participating in *gazovat* ever since she was a little girl," and that the war against Russia is "fair and necessary, and will stop only when Allah wants it to."

"Earlier we cut off their heads, and now we will once and for all destroy them. . . . As long as the war continues, I will remain in the unit. And even if my brothers or those from my *teip* order me to return home, I will not obey them," Larisa II emphatically told Nivat.

Neither Larisa II's father nor her three brothers, who lived in Grozny, gave her permission to fight. She obtained that right only by marrying a fighter. She had a romantic suitor in October 1999 at the beginning of the war, but then in November she was kidnapped by fighters and was married off to a man eighteen years her senior. He was wounded during the exodus from Grozny. "No, I'm not in love with him, but everyone respects him, and thanks to him I have received the right to fight," Larisa II confesses. Nivat calls her a "young fanatic." Regarding children, Larisa II told Nivat: "We will have little *mujahideen* who will have one goal, and that is to get even for us."

Like Larisa I, the second Larisa helped fighters in Grozny: "I want to help them in any way I can. In the city I baked bread, gave out arms and ammunition, and sometimes my husband would allow me to shoot. . . . Now what I am most afraid of is not the Russian bombs, but my former fiancé coming after me," she admits.

"Cleaners" in the Exodus from Grozny

Larisas I and II weren't the only women in the February 2000 exodus from Grozny; there were more than two hundred of them—cooks, nurses, fighters, and snipers. According to prosecutor Tkachyev, several suspected female snipers turned up.

One of them was the unassuming, full-figured woman with a rifle slung over her shoulder pictured in Sergey Melnikoff's "The Chronicles of Hell" photo exhibition on Chechnya. But when Tkachyev saw them none were armed, and there wasn't enough bodily evidence (a bruised shoulder, a blackened eye) left to prove in court that they were snipers. "True, we did send one to a filter, but the bruise around her eye was almost cleared up. Another suspected sniper turned out to be pregnant, and a third had a badly torn leg. All the rest claimed to be cleaners. It was pointless fooling around with them anymore, so they were simply let go," Tkachyev recalls.

Thirty-year-old Latvian-born Polina Filipova was not the sniper Tkachyev sent to the filter at Chernokozovo, but she ended up there anyway in 2000 after being arrested in Shatoi as a sniper. Her name was mentioned by Zura Bitayeva and an elderly woman who had both been in Chernokozovo with Filipova. Her fate is also unknown.

Birlant Ananbekovna Abukarova and Lipa Adianovna Biluyeva

Ousam Baysayev, a Chechen Radio Liberty reporter, told me during the screening of the film *Burning Sun* in Washington, D.C., in May 2007, that two female fighters were among the seventy or so remnants of Ruslan Gelayev's group who surrendered to federal forces at Komsomolskoye in March 2000. He couldn't remember their names.

I found them in Johann Feindt and Tamara Trampe's documentary film *White Ravens: Nightmare in Chechnya*. Russian video clips shot at Komsomolskoye show twenty-five-year-old Birlant Ananbekovna Abukarova and twenty-three-year-old Lipa Adianovna Biluyeva kneeling in a field with the other prisoners.

Both are skinny and the hair on their heads is knotted. Neither is dressed in camouflage fatigues like other fighters; both wear clean, fresh clothing that they had clearly changed into before surrendering so they wouldn't look like fighters. One is wearing bright-colored, blue-and-white-speckled outerwear, while the other is dressed in black with a white shirt.

The commentator identifies one as Chechen and the other as Russian, but both have Chechen names and I was told by Chechens in the audience that they were Chechen. One had a hopeless, blank stare, as if knowing she was going to die; the other still had life and hope in her face. One died at Komsomolskoye, the other at the Russian military base at Khankala.

Women of the "Martyrs' Brigade"

At 10 PM on the night of 21 June 2004 hundreds of Chechen, Ingush, and other North Caucasus fighters in stocking masks, camouflage, and police uniforms, calling themselves the "Martyrs Brigade," seized police checkpoints on the Kavkaz federal highway, and then swept into Nazran to attack strategic targets. These included the republic's MVD police headquarters, the 137th Russian Border Guards barracks, and the old KGB headquarters now being used as an FSB dormitory. Within an hour dozen of corpses littered the streets, most of them policemen and government officials.

Al Jazeera television reported that the raiders got away with at least two truckloads of weapons and ammunition: 300 pistols, 322 automatic riles, 22 grenade launchers, 5 machine guns, 190 hand grenades, and 63 ammunition clips. Some of the stolen weapons were used in the terror attack on Secondary School No. 1 in Beslan, North Ossetia, less than three months later.

Chechen women participated in the attack. Eyewitnesses say they heard the women shouting, while another told investigators that he personally saw several women help raid the Kommunalnaya Street MVD weapons and ammunition depot just before midnight. Exactly how many women participated in the Nazran attack and who they were remains a mystery. None were among the thirty-five or so casualties, nor were they counted among the five fighters captured. But two were among the twenty-two suspects police rounded up in the first days after the attack. Authorities would not release their names.

Aina Yunusova and Raisa Zakiyeva

In 2005 nineteen-year-old Aina Yunusova (alias "Fatima") and Timir Aslambekov (alias "Orel") were both members of Bislan Madayev's illegal armed formation, but neither expected a hundred counterterror policemen to show up at their safe house in the village of Mayakovskoye on 12 October. Police surrounded the house and demanded that the couple immediately surrender. What authorities didn't know was that Aina and Timir had made a pact never to be taken alive: they would die together, in each other's arms, first. They embraced for the last time, and then Timir pulled the pin on his grenade.

On 11 March 2007 Raisa Zakiyeva, identified by police as a *boyev-ichka,* and her companion, forty-year-old Apti Yukhinov, also chose martyrdom over surrender when faced with capture in Ordzhonikidzyevskaya, Ingushetia.

The story has repeated itself hundreds of times.

Malikat Dadashyeva and Zama Mansuyeva

On Saturday night, 15 December 2007, twenty-one-year-old Malikat Dadashyeva, along with two fighters—Aslanbek Alisultanov, twenty-two, and Rezvan Mikahilov, twenty-five—died in their apartment on Dudayev *Boulvar* in Grozny in an hour-long gun battle with police. All were wanted for attacks on police. The media reported Dadashyeva as the owner of the apartment, but she was probably Rezvan Mikahilov's wife.

An identical scenario played out on Slavanskaya Street in the Leninsky District of Grozny a month later when nineteen-year-old Zama Mansuyeva, Uvais Techiyev, and two other male fighters were killed in a bloody predawn police spetz-operation. Chechnya's interior minister, Ruslan Alkhanov, explained that Mansuyeva had been a member of Techiyev's illegal armed formation, which had conducted attacks against federal forces and policemen in the settlement of Stariye Atagi (Groznensky District), Noviye Atage (Shalinsky District), in Grozny, and elsewhere. He called Mansuyeva a *boyevichka,* but a posting on the MVD's official website (www.MVDinform.ru) on 15 January 2008 listed her as a noncombatant "accomplice."

Malkan Chagayeva

On 28 July 2008 Malkan Chagayeva and Adam Abdulayev died in a noontime gun battle with police in a forest near the settlement of Gordaly, Chechnya. A police spokesman identified her as a fighter, but only Abdulayev's Kalashnikov rifle was found at the scene. Malkan was likely Abdulayev's wife. The remaining fighters escaped after killing two policemen and wounding three more.

The Anonymous

There are hundreds of female fighters whose names remain unknown.

A female survivor of the 26 November 1994 bombing of Grozny remembers seeing an armed Chechen woman in a group of fighters who hauled in a truck-mounted ZSU-23/4 antiaircraft gun to shoot at Russian aircraft. She described the fighter as dressed in pants and camouflage and as having "a very gallant look about her." Another was a wanted thirty-year-old Azerbaijani woman in Shamil Basayev's unit who tried to flee Chechnya as a refugee with a kidnapped baby in her arms at the beginning of the second war. A twenty-nine-year-old Chechen woman, like Topchayeva, voluntarily surrendered. Two Chlyabinsk journalists, Olga Bagautdinova and Aleksandr Utrobin, both held hostage for ransom in Chechnya in early 1997, describe a female fighter in an article about their ordeal published in the 25 August 1997 issue of *Vecherny Chelyabinsk*. The caption of a photo of this middle-aged woman identifies her only as a "female *boyevichka* with her granddaughter." She was wounded in the August 1996 fighting in Grozny. The name of the middle-aged sniper in Melnikov's exhibit is unknown.

Twenty-five-year-old Zarina Pukhayeva, a hostage in the September 2004 terror attack on the school in Beslan, North Ossetia, says that a "woman of Slavic appearance, a female sniper, participated in the siege of the school." She saw her on the second day but not after that. "She had a rifle, she was a sniper! She had light hair in a ponytail. I didn't see anything else of her, not even in the photographs of the dead fighters," she told the court that tried Nurpasha Kulayev, the only Beslan terrorist captured alive. Kulayev denied that there had been a female sniper among the terrorists but remembers having been asked about one during the investigation.

On 28 January 2007 police in Ordzhonikidzevskaya, Sunzhensky District, arrested an unidentified thirty-nine-year-old woman on terrorism charges. A police spokesman said that "she had participated in attacks on military units on the territory of the North Caucasus" but didn't say which ones or when. Both Interfax and Gazeta.ru reported that she had earlier been an "accomplice" to the commander of the Chechen women's sniper battalion known as "Djokhar Dudayev's Regiment" in the first war.

An unidentified woman whom Chechen police detained with two male colleagues on 1 September 2007 turned out to be a former "assistant" of Chechen field commander Rustam Basayev. Chechnya's interior minister says she had worked for Basayev for some time and that he had planned to employ her as a suicide bomber; those plans failed to materialize because he was killed in a spetz-operation.

In early January 2008 two unidentified women, along with several male fighters, escaped from an elaborate police dragnet in the Tabasaransky District of Dagestan. They had been spotted with nine or ten fighters in the village of Kheli-Pendzhik on 8 January and later near the Rubas River, but then they miraculously disappeared into the mountains through heavy snow and in freezing temperatures.

On 23 October 2008 police picked up an unidentified former female fighter who in 1997–98 had belonged to the Chechen unit commanded by Ruslan Gelayev. She had long ago come down out of the mountains and was gainfully employed as a cook in a café in the Staropromyslovsky District of Grozny.

THE "ACCOMPLICES"

Women in noncombatant roles also play a critical part in the Jihad. Without relatives, without their families to supply them, Wolves couldn't survive.

Called *posobniki* (accomplices) by Russian law enforcers, these women may be former fighters like Larissa I who are lucky enough to return home alive. For the most part, though, they are ordinary women of all ages who—because of family commitments, ideological or religious beliefs, the need for money, or just plain hatred of Russians and Ramzan Kadyrov—collect and pass on intelligence about the location and movement of federal and local police forces, serve as money couriers, participate in counterfeiting operations, sell narcotics, store arms and explosives, and provide food, medical supplies, clothing, equipment, cell phone cards, and safe houses to fighters. Their involvement is both short and long term.

They number in the thousands and are found in every age group and just about every household, since most women in some fashion or another have supported family members fighting Russia in the two wars. They serve in the present Jihad too.

Mountain Justice

"There's not one family which doesn't have relatives [fighters] in the forest," Ramzan Kadyrov told a televised meeting of his government ministers on 9 August 2008. "They pass on information to their family members in the woods. . . . They warn them. . . . They bring them food, help them, and the rebels kill our policemen and burn our houses." Of course, not all families support their Jihadist relatives, but Little Stalin thinks they do and says that they must be punished: "Those families who have relatives in the forest are also participants in crime; they too are terrorists, extremists, Wahhabis, and devils. Some of them publicly denounce their relatives [rebels] in order to be left alone [by the police], but secretly support them."

Four years earlier then–Deputy Prime Minister Ramzan Kadyrov, in a Russian NTV television interview, had promised to punish these families lawfully: "We will punish their relatives according to law. They help bandits, but they say that they are helping their relatives, their brothers and sisters. No, they help bandits. We will punish them according to law. And if there is no such law, we will ask for it, we will turn to the Russian State Duma and they will pass such a law so that it becomes possible to punish. Otherwise, the war in the Chechen Republic will never end."

Kadyrov never did get his law, but he punishes families anyway by having his *Kadyrovtsy* burn down their houses—"mountain justice" (revenge) he calls it. Organized arson is the preferred method.

On 2 May 2004 *Kadyrovtsy* torched the home of forty-five-year-old Taus Buzurkayeva in the village of Alleroi, Kurchaloyevsky District. Two days later she was detained and accused of supporting her fighter son. She didn't disappear, but now Taus has no place to live. At least the arsonists who burned down the home of Vakhid Murdashev and that of his mother on 1 December 2004 were thoughtful enough to bring a team of firemen along to ensure that neighboring houses did not catch fire. The Murdashev family was targeted because Ramzan Kadyrov had come across a videotape of Vakhid, President Maskhadov's former chief of government personnel, nodding his head in agreement when Maskhadov allegedly ordered the assassination of Ramzan's father, Akhmad Kadyrov—"mountain justice" again at work.

Late at night on 23 December 2004 *Kadyrovtsy* broke into the home of seventy-year-old Mandat Turlayeva on Nagornaya Street in the village of Novogrozny and escorted Mandat and her husband, their daughter, and four small grandchildren out of the house, allowing them to take only their passports, and then set fire to it. One of Mandat's sons is a fighter. The home of Mandat's second daughter, Leila Turlayeva, had been burned down a week earlier, and her son had been kidnapped.

More or less identical methods are usually used in each arson. First, police come and search the family home, maybe several times. At the same time, the family is summoned to the police station to be given a little talk about all the terrible things that can happen to them if the fighter in the family doesn't come down out of the forest. The family is held personally responsible for bringing the fighter home.

Some parents are so terrified that they actually go into the forest to hunt for their children. Bad things happen to them there. In September 2008 Azam A—— (not her real given name) set out afoot for the deserted village of Tazyn-Kale in the Vedensky District, thinking that her son might come out of the woods to meet her. She had only walked a short distance when a minivan filled with masked men pulled up, grabbed Azam, and took her to a nearby house where they beat her about the legs and accused her of being an "accomplice." Ultimately she "confessed" to the police and was given a one-year suspended prison sentence in December 2008.[7]

If the fighter in the family doesn't return home, masked men in camou-flage uniforms arrive in the middle of the night, herd the family to safety or kidnap some of its members, pile the house furniture into a heap, douse it with gasoline, and set a match, torch, or Molotov cocktail to it. Homeless, the family is made to denounce and disown their fighter relative at a public meeting or at the local mosque. Sometimes they are asked to leave the vil-lage. Of course, not everybody's house can be burned, but Human Rights Center "Memorial" says that the homes of twenty-six families whose chil-dren ran off to the forest were burned in 2008.

Once, when asked about the practice, Kadyrov's spokesman replied: "We have no information regarding what you are talking about, so we cannot help you." But Grozny's mayor, Muslim Khuchiyev, was vocal enough when he warned families in a televised meeting on 16 August 2008 that "the evil which is done by your relatives in the forest will return to you and your homes. Each of you will feel it on your skin."

Wolves retaliate, targeting relatives of the *Kadyrovtsy* and policemen who help them. One angry female arson victim promised, "That's not the end of it. They think they're masters because they have guns and power. But just wait until the weather gets warmer. They too have relatives." On 12 April 2004 Wolves entered the village of Ishkoi-Yurt, Gudermessky District, with a prepared list of villagers who work for the police and security services. They killed seven *Kadyrovtsy* and policemen and burned four houses. They would have burned all the homes on their list, but the relatives of policemen talked them out of it by promising that the men would quit their jobs.

Three hundred fighters marched into the village of Alleroi, Kurchaloyevsky District, on 23 September 2004. One group, led by Akhmed Avdarkhanov, entered the house of the local *Kadyrovtsy* commander, Suleiman Abuyev, and told his mother that they were going to set fire to her house. They said they were also going to torch the house of her second son, a former police-man who had already been killed in a shootout with fighters. Avdarkhanov burned the first house but let the second stand so the family would at least have someplace to live. Fighters burned nine houses that night.

On 10 August 2005 *mujahideen* burned police sergeant Khalis Turayev's home at No. 91 Ushayeva Street in Dyshne-Vedeno. His wife and five young children were dragged out into the street and told that if her husband continued to work as a policeman the whole family would be killed. That same night Wolves torched a second house in Dyshne-Vedeno, at No. 25 Skolnaya Street, belonging to policeman Alikhan Altemirov. They took his mother, Khavra Gazaliyevna Altemirova, and his two brothers outside, tied them up, and demanded their car keys. Khavra didn't have them, so they riddled the family car with bullets. She was also told that her family would be killed if Alikhan didn't quit his job.

In mid-June 2008 fighters torched the house of a policeman in the village of Musolt-Ali, Shatoisky District, killed a responding policeman, and wounded several more. A month later, on the night of 13 July 2008, sixty Wolves entered the village of Benoi-Vedeno, Nozhai-Yurtovsky District, and burned the houses of Zamid Umarov; Khamid Umarov, his son; and his grandson Almaksud. Both had worked in Kadyrov's security structure. That December Jihadists came in the middle of the night and executed Khaji Saidullayev, the government administrator of Agishty, and his family, burning their home.

House burnings intensified after suicide bombers attacked the heart of Grozny in May 2009. At five o'clock in the morning on 18 June 2009 masked men in camouflage uniforms entered the village of Engel-Yurt in the Gudermessky District and burned two houses on Kh. Muradilova Street belonging to the Baisuyev family, because a son, Sheik Baisuyev, had been positively identified in a firefight with police. The men burst into the homes, kicked the families out onto the street, stole their valuables, seized passports, and then burned the houses. The state arsonists waited to leave until everything was engulfed in flame.

Other arsonists burst into the home, also in Engel-Yurt, of Baisuyev's sisters, Maki, forty-four years of age, and Medno, forty-two, who lived apart from their husbands, and burned it. Ten days later, on 28 June 2009, masked policemen visited Magomed Dadilov to take him away. They were followed the next day by twenty men who drove all the residents and children who lived in the same courtyard as Dadilov into a neighboring house a safe distance away, and then set fire to Dadilov's house. This time the arsonists left before it burned to the ground, so neighbors were able to put out the fire and save the walls and the roof. Dadilov admitted to having given a ride to Abubakar Musliyev, a fighter, in the summer of 2008. Musliyev's family home was also burned.

Madina Yunusova's Argun family home was burned, too. Her parents were brought to the Argun ROVD for questioning on 3 July. The next day men in camouflage uniforms burst into their home, locked them in an outbuilding, and then set fire to the house. It burned to the ground. At the end of July Rustam Mukhadiyev's mother's house in the city of Argun was burned down after he killed several high-ranking Chechen policemen in a suicide bombing at Grozny's theater–concert center. And after two bicycle bombers killed four Grozny policemen on 21 August Little Stalin, over local television, again promised "mountain justice." "They killed four policemen. Now, it's necessary to find their relatives and punish them."

Holding relatives *directly* responsible for terror attacks became government policy a month earlier. Grozny's Mayor Khuchiyev told fighters' relatives in a public television announcement: "Yesterday, the President told us and we are telling you that from the 16th [of July]. . . . [Y]ou will be responsible for the stability in your districts, whether it is the Staropromyslovsky District or the Leninsky District. If something happens there, any incident at all, anything bad, that these devils [fighters] have been getting up to, then it will be the father, the brother, or the sister of a member of an illegal armed formation living in this district who will pay for it."[8]

But punishment now goes beyond house burnings. In February 2009 Natasha Estimirova reported that pensions and child-support payments are no longer being made to some fighters' families. This is true in the Sunzhensky District, but people in the Achkoi-Martanovsky District and the districts of Grozny are also filing complaints with the procurator's office about nonpayment of benefits rightfully due to them. And lately Little Stalin has just been killing their children on sight. "I swear to Allah. If they do not bring their children [the fighters] home, I will not let them live on this earth. They have to either take their bastard children home and put them in a pen or kill them. I swear to Allah! We won't even detain them, but will just kill them on the spot. Then we won't even let anyone say their names."[9]

Couriers and Counterfeiters

I have been tracking the arrests of "accomplices" since 2006. A few hundred, particularly in the Vedensky District, Shamil Basayev's home district, have been caught and prosecuted.

Two women have voluntarily surrendered. On 24 August 2007 forty-seven-year-old Magomeda Deniyeva, a resident of Dargo, walked into the Vedensky District police station and confessed, becoming, in the words of one Chechen police spokesman, "the first female militant in the ten years of war with Russia to voluntarily come forward to turn herself in." A year later a twenty-four-year-old woman who said she had helped fighters in the Shel-kovsky District in 2002–2004 also stepped forward.

Deniyeva's background is typical of most female "accomplices." She was never a fighter, but for three years (from 2003 to 2005) she supplied Wolves in her native Vedensky District with food and clothing. Fighters gave her money to buy what they needed and arranged delivery. Deniyeva hoped to receive amnesty by voluntarily coming forward. Those who are caught get stiff jail sentences.

Some women specialize in couriering or counterfeiting currency. Malika (alias "Yesira") Vitaliyeva, Basayev's cook in the first war and a veteran of the Chechen Wahhabi movement who helped organize and participated in the October 2002 terror attack on the Dubrovka theater, became particularly skilled at couriering money from Baku, Azerbaijan, to Chechnya to pay fighters.

Aina Sidgaliyeva, the accountant for the Urus-Martan military *djamaat* commanded by Khingizhkan Gishayev, wasn't so clever. On Friday, 27 November 2009, Chechen police nabbed Aina as she was about to go into a bank in Astrakhan, Russia, to collect a huge amount of money for fighters' winter salaries. Russian intelligence had learned that Gishayev regularly received monthly private donations by wire transfer from Poland and that in mid-November Aina had gone to Astrakhan and picked up $50,000 that had been deposited in her personal bank account there. This time, Chechen police and the local FSB were waiting.

Aina and her bodyguard, Bekmagomed Saigatov, commander of Wolves in Urus-Martan, arrived by car in Astrakhan and rendezvoused with Musa Khaikharoyev, their local contact. The next morning all of them went to the bank. Police intended to make the arrests after Aina had collected the money, but her experienced bodyguards outside the bank became suspicious and bolted like scared rabbits. Police grabbed Khaikharoyev first, Saigatov was shot after he tossed a grenade, and Aina tried to blow herself up with a homemade grenade she kept in her purse. It didn't work; she sustained serious wounds to the face and stomach but survived. Aina is married to Anvar

Labazanov, a fighter born in Kazakhstan who had served in Chechnya as a contract serviceman, was captured by Wolves, and then joined them. She became acquainted with him during one of her excursions to meet with Gishayev.

The counterfeiting of Russian rubles and U.S. dollars has always been a big producer of cash for Wolves. It's used to buy weapons, to exchange for real money, and, in the last few years, even used to pay the salaries of Chechen fighters. The printing of counterfeit U.S. dollars began in Argun and Grozny in 1996. Within two years Chechen-counterfeited U.S. dollars flooded banks in Siberia, the Far East, and the Volga regions, forcing the Russian government in 1996 to take a million counterfeit U.S. hundred-dollar bills out of circulation in the Primorsk region.

When the Russian Army moved back into Chechnya in 1999 it closed down counterfeiting operations, but it never found the plates used to make U.S. dollars and production was soon back in full swing. This became evident when Grozny police caught twenty-five-year-old Zarema Khasuyeva and her thirty-eight-year-old male companion, Bakayev, smuggling over $300,000 in counterfeit into Chechnya on 22 September 2003. The money was meant to disrupt the upcoming Chechen presidential election. Police found the counterfeit dollars, which Bakayev said he acquired from "various criminal groups," in a secret compartment in his car.

By 2004 Chechen women were widely circulating counterfeit hundred-dollar bills in stores and at markets. In early October police in the Russian city of Sevastopol arrested two women in possession of large amounts of "high quality" counterfeit U.S. hundred-dollar bills. The following fall police at the Chechnya/Dagestan border confiscated nearly $700,000 from two groups running counterfeit dollars into Chechnya. A man and a woman working as a courier team were nabbed with $500,000 in their possession. Several hundred thousand-ruble notes were also taken from the woman. The money was meant for fighter payrolls.

On Saturday, 24 March 2006, a thirty-five-year-old unemployed woman walked into the Antoshka store on Kirova Street in Karabulak, Ingushetia, and attempted to buy food with counterfeit thousand-ruble notes. Organized-crime police took her into custody and found an additional 219,000 rubles in counterfeit thousand-ruble notes at her home. Two months later police busted up another major counterfeiting ring being used to finance North Caucasus terrorists. Twenty-five people were arrested, including several women. Subsequent searches netted forty million in counterfeit thousand-ruble notes and more than $310,000 in counterfeit U.S. currency.

It's becoming more and more risky to operate as couriers and counterfeiters. On 21 October 2007 Argun police arrested a twenty-four-year-old woman who had been working as a currency courier for only one month.

Intelligence Collectors and Generalists

Wolves have a well-developed human intelligence (HUMINT) capability in Grozny and elsewhere. During the wars women served as intelligence collectors because they could move around more easily than men.

Women who earlier worked in Grozny's central market and other local street markets picked up information from loose-lipped Russian soldiers and MVD servicemen on assignment to Chechnya. For example, on 30 November 2007, police in the Staropromyslovsky District of Grozny arrested a female market trader who had provided information about the locations and movement of federal forces during Shamil Basayev's 1999 invasion of Dagestan.

Most female "accomplices" work as generalists. One of those was Natalya (Kheda) Khalkayeva. On 20 September 2004 a federal sweep of Urus-Martan targeting *mujahideen* operating under the command of the Emir of Grozny, Yunadi Turchayev, snared a small, pretty, oval-faced thirty-one-year-old woman. Born in the Limansky District of the Urals-Kurgan Region in southwestern Siberia, Khalkayeva lived in Grozny but often traveled to Urus-Martan to visit her parents.

All three of her brothers had been members of Arbi Barayev's kidnapping ring but fled abroad shortly after the second war began. Khasan, the oldest, kidnapped the son of a wealthy Krasnodar businessman for a million-dollar ransom in 1998. He lived for a while in the United Arab Emirates (UAE) but returned to Chechnya in 2001 to fight and was killed. A middle brother, Khusein, lives in Austria, and the youngest, Khamzat, is in Malaysia, where I am told he raises funds for the Chechen Jihad.

An FSB search of Khalkayeva's Grozny apartment turned up a Turkish-made satellite telephone that had been purchased and registered in the UAE, a suicide belt containing one kilogram of Semtex plastic explosives and shrapnel, and a forged passport. According to the FSB, Khalkayeva shared the use of the telephone with Turchayev. She used it to keep in touch with fundraisers and financial supporters in Australia, the UAE, Germany, Czechoslovakia, Poland, Turkey, and Austria. Ilya Shabalkin, head of the regional command center for counterterror operations in the North Caucasus, adds that she was also engaged in the training of suicide bombers. Khalkayeva was charged with belonging to an "illegal armed unit" and with the "illegal acquisition, transfer, sales, storage, or carrying of weapons, ammunition, or explosives." But if FSB investigators are correct, her role was far richer; a role that included collecting and couriering money for the recruitment and training of suicide bombers.

A Warm Bed and Hot Meals

Women sympathetic to the Jihad or who need a little extra cash hide fighters in their homes, particularly during the bitter cold winter months when it's just about impossible to survive in the mountains and there's little tree cover for concealment.

At four in the evening on 2 October 2005 at least a hundred Chechen FSB, Anti-Terror Center (ATTs) personnel from Grozny's Staropromys-lovsky District, and police surrounded Zarema Burayeva's Grozny house at No. 37 Ivanova Street, finding and shooting her fighter brother-in-law hiding there. Twenty-four-year-old Zarema had hidden the wounded Supyan Arsanukayev in the attic of the house the day before. Police found him with a grenade in his hand on the roof of the house trying to escape. After confiscating the family's money (nine thousand rubles), a television, computer, and other valuables, the government personnel arrested Zarema; her two brothers, Ali, eighteen years of age, and Baudin, twenty-one; and her mother Satsita, who were also in the house. Satsita was released the next day, but Zarema, Ali, and Baudin disappeared without a trace.

During an address check on 20 October 2005 police discovered a woman providing sanctuary to fighters in her home at No. 26 Kirova Street in the village of Pervomaiskoye. Four months later Argun police arrested a woman sheltering a fighter. In February 2006 two unidentified women were taken into custody during address checks on charges ranging from aiding and abetting fighters, storing arms illegally, and selling narcotics to support terrorism.

On 22 March 2006 police in Khasavyurt, Dagestan, picked up a thirty-four-year-old Chechen woman at the city's central market and charged her with being an "accomplice." "Kerta" was wanted for providing fighters commanded by Field Commander Abdulkamirov with safe houses and food. Police say, "The detained woman also served in a communications role." An MVD spokesman later explained that she had been a runner for Abdulkarimov's fighters. On 5 May 2006 police detained a thirty-nine-year-old woman from the settlement of Yelistanzhi, Vedensky District, as a suspected "accomplice." According to Russia's MVD official website, "For the past five years, this woman kept arms, ammunition, and acquired food products, medicine, and clothing for terrorists." Interrogators learned from the woman the whereabouts of a significant arms and explosives cache outside Yelistanzhi. There police found 5 homemade bombs, 32 grenade-launcher projectiles, 4 grenades, and 260 rounds of 5.45 mm caliber ammunition. The cache belonged to her brother, who was a fighter.

Eight days later, on 15 May, the FSB made an astonishing discovery: they found Dokka Umarov's personal bunker and an explosives cache in a dugout under the house of a thirty-one-year-old female in Assinovskaya. Unfortunately Umarov was not there. The woman's brother had been a fighter; he had been killed the previous January. In early June, the MVD's website reports police in Sagopshi, Dagestan, had taken a forty-seven-year-old Chechen woman into custody for aiding and abetting fighters commanded by A. Taziyev. Two years earlier she had provided him with the home addresses of policemen marked for assassination.

There were fewer arrests of female "accomplices" reported in early to mid-2007, but on 21 October 2007 police detained a fifty-year-old woman who worked as a librarian in the village of Yeshilkhatoi. She had served since September 2007 as an "accomplice" to the Selim-Khamas group of Wolves operating in the district. The arrest of a second Yeshilkhatoi woman for providing food to fighters under the command of Bimurzayev came on 19 November. That same day a fifty-six-year-old woman in the settlement of Gukhoi, Itum-Kalinsky District, was also taken into custody for providing food and medicine to fighters.

At least ten women were arrested as "accomplices" in 2008. On 7 February police detained a twenty-nine-year-old woman on Zheleznodoroznaya Street in the city of Argun for storing arms and ammunition and providing food and a safe house to fighters under the command of Managyev and Yeskiyev. Four days later police arrested two more women in the village of Goryachevodsk who were said to be working with four fighters in "preparing a terror act."

In early May the case against four Vedensky residents—a woman identified as Khitiyeva and three men—who served as "accomplices" was sent to the Shalinsky District court for trial. Khitiyeva had been recruited in November 2006 by Beksolt Istamulov, a Chechen immigrant to Austria who was responsible for organizing foreign "financial channels" and providing material and technical support to Chechen fighters. She dispensed clothing and shoes, $12,000 in cash, a notebook computer, watches, and CD players to fighters.

At the end of July police picked up a "young woman" accused of providing *boyeviki* operating in the district with food and intelligence information on the movement of federal forces and local police. Almost a week later, on 6 August, a twenty-four-year-old woman from Kizlyar, Dagestan, voluntarily turned herself in to Shelkovsky District police, telling them that she had aided and abetted fighters operating in the Shelkovsky District. Investigators said that "the young woman from 2002–2004 was an 'accomplice' to members of a band formation commanded by Danilbek Alkhazurov, who was killed in 2005." On 22 October police caught a fifty-six-year-old Tazen-Kala woman walking in the woods with a plastic shopping bag filled with men's clothing, a hunting knife, and food. She was taking the items to her fighter son.

On 19 December three women, aged twenty-one, twenty-three, and twenty-five, were arrested in Argun for providing Visit Batayev, a fighter, with food and a safe place to sleep for nearly two months. He had been killed by police in the apartment of one of the women at No. 29 Stepnaya Street in Argun two days earlier. Two more arrests came on 26 May 2009, both residents of the Shalinsky District who had provided food, information, a bed, and transportation to fighters commanded by a certain Saikhanov. Another Vedensky District woman, twenty-nine years of age, was taken into custody on 1 October 2009 for having provided food to fighters from April to June. On 11 January 2010 Grozny police arrested a twenty-four-year-old woman who at the age of fifteen had aided and abetted fighters in 2001.

FIVE

The Sisterhood

Sisters, the time has come. When the enemy has killed almost all our men, our brothers and husbands, we are the only ones left to take revenge for them.
Khava Barayeva, 9 June 2000

AT A LITTLE PAST 9 PM on Wednesday, 23 October 2002, at least nineteen women and twenty-two men charge through the front doors of the sprawling House of Culture (the Dubrovka theater) at the corner of Dubrovskaya and Melnikova streets in an obscure industrial suburb of Moscow. They're not starring actors in the second act of the family hit musical *Nord Ost* that is entertaining a sellout crowd of 711 spectators inside but Chechen terrorists, members of Shamil Basayev's "Riyadus-Salikhin [Fields of Righteousness] Reconnaissance and Sabotage Battalion of Shakhids."

"You are hostages—We've come from Chechnya. This is no joke! We are at war!" Movsar Barayev, the leader of the group, shouts as he leaps onto the stage. Spectators think it's a joke, just part of the musical, until Barayev fires a volley of bullets into the ceiling. Meanwhile, the Dubrovka women disperse according to their well-rehearsed scripts, each taking a predesignated position in the spectator hall. Explosive belts are strapped conspicuously to their waists, each belt containing more than a kilogram of explosives. The women mix with the hostages to ensure maximum visibility, control, and casualties.

The next forty-eight hours are eventful and tragic. A suspected female FSB agent who walks into the building is executed, and two women terrorists recklessly fire their pistols at a hysterical young man who bolts from his seat, throws a glass Coca-Cola bottle at a terrorist, and runs down the aisle toward the exit screaming, "Mama! I can't take it anymore!" The shooters miss him but hit another man in the left eye, and also a woman.

For three days television screens worldwide would flash pictures of these mysterious women dressed in their long black robes, their faces veiled, and their fingers on detonator buttons. Russian sensationalist journalists hastily labeled them "Black Widows," desperate Chechen women whose husbands had all been killed by Russians soldiers and had come to Moscow to seek blood revenge.

Barayev skillfully promoted the widow image among the hostages. The Russian writer Eduard Topol describes one of these exchanges in his book *O lubvi i terror ili dvoe v dubrovke:*

> You see that short woman on the balcony? That's my aunt, Zura, the widow of uncle Arbi, whom you killed. Sveta, who is in the auditorium, we call her Sekilat, was an actress and is the sister of my friend Movsar, whom you killed two years ago. . . . He was married to Maryam [Khadzhiyeva], she is here too. . . . The widows of Zelimkhan and [Rezvan] Akhmadov are also here. Zaira . . . buried her brother. One leg and the head, that is all, nothing else was left of him. We in Chechnya don't have any families left.

Blood revenge for a husband or another male member of the family killed or brutalized by Russian soldiers, uncontrollable grief and despair, destitution, and a feeling of nothing left to live for became the popular explanation for why these and dozens of other Chechen women began killing themselves in suicide missions.

But how well do the Dubrovka women fit the "desperate housewife," "grieving widow" mold? And what about the nineteen Chechen female terrorists who immediately preceded them—and those who followed? Were they all desperate housewives and grieving widows too? Who exactly were these women?

THE ORIGINAL THIRTEEN

The first war spawned at least thirteen female terrorists. I have already discussed Raisa Dundayeva, Tamara Topchayeva, and the other eight women who participated in the horrific attacks on Russian hospitals in Budennovsk and Kizlyar.

To advance his personal vendetta against the Kremlin, Salman Raduyev toyed with the idea of dispatching females to attack Russia when he sent Aset Dadashyeva, Fatima Taimashkhanova, and a third woman to blow up train stations in Armavir and Pyatigorsk, Russia, in April 1997. Russian spies were everywhere in Chechnya that year, and Raduyev's publicly announced plans in April to blow up "whole Russian cities" were either exaggerated or compromised. Instead he ordered female members of his newly formed "Djokhar's Way" terror unit to plant bombs in two railway stations in southern Russia.

The 23 April 1997 bombing of the Armavir train station waiting room killed three people and wounded nine. The bomber was never caught. Nearly ten years later, on 27 January 2007, the FSB came to the Mekhstoy temporary refugee camp in Ordzhonikidzevskaya, Ingushetia, and arrested Malika Chabiyeva for her alleged role in the bombing. "They're taking me with them," Malika, trembling, told her sister Aza, who also lived at the camp, as she was led away. "Why?" Aza asked. "I don't know, it must be some kind of mistake," Malika said hastily as she looked back at the masked men.

The FSB also rounded up Malika's other sister, Asya, as well as Asya's employer, a woman who owned a café. They wanted to know who Malika's friends were, what she had been doing in 1996–97, and whether she knew a woman by the name of Elbika. Asya instantly recognized the photograph of the woman the FSB showed her as someone who rented a house in Ordzhonikidzevskaya and visited Malika often to ask her to walk her (Elbika's) little girl to kindergarten.

Malika's visit with the authorities was not a short one. "I had hoped they were only taking me to the local police station, so when we drove out of Ordzhonikidzevskaya onto the highway, I became very scared," she later told Human Rights Watch. "There, we entered the secured grounds of a large new building. I didn't know it was the FSB—I only understood this later on. They interrogated me, asked about my family and about a woman by the name of Elbika who lived in the same tent camp with us at the very beginning of the war and who, according to them, was a rebel fighter."

The day after Malika's arrest a military spokesman informed the media that she had been detained for questioning concerning the Armavir attack.

Malika was also accused of being an "accomplice" to the commander of the Chechen women's sniper battalion, the Djokhar Dudayev Regiment, in the first Chechen war, and she was suspected of participating in attacks on federal forces in the second. But Malika's relatives insisted that she was innocent, that she could not possibly be a terrorist because she had never been to Armavir or even to the Krasnordarky Krai, where Armavir is located, and that in the period between the two wars she had simply sold produce at Grozny's central market. Malika was released on 28 March 2007, her arrest a case of mistaken identity. She had looked like someone in a video that Elbika herself had sent to police after two other innocent women had been falsely accused of the Armavir attack.

Five days after Armavir Aset Dadashyeva and Fatima Taimaskhanova detonated a bomb in the Pyatigorsk railroad station, killing three people and badly wounding thirty. Greed motivated them. Dadashyeva testified at Raduyev's 2001 trial that she had been personally instructed to carry out the attack by Vakha Dzhafarov, the commander of Raduyev's army, and promised a three-room apartment and money for it.

When it came her turn to testify, Taimaskhanova acknowledged that she personally knew Raduyev and had even been photographed with him. She had often visited his office and sometimes had seen explosive devices on his desk. She also knew that he had planned a series of "actions to frighten Russia" and to mark the first anniversary of Djokar Dudayev's death in a 1996 Russian missile strike. Taimaskhanova confirmed that Vakha Dzhafarov had insisted that she and Dadashyeva carry out the 28 April 1997 attack, for which Raduyev promised to reward them handsomely. Pyatigorsk was picked as a target only because one of them had once lived there. Both are now sitting out long prison sentences in the Volgorodsky maximum-security prison. Dadysheva left three children behind, Taimashkhanova one.

Would Taimashkhanova have participated in the Dubrovka siege if she had been given the opportunity? Probably. "If I had lost all my family. Then I would have nothing to live for and maybe I would have gone there [to Dubrovka] too. I don't know. I would go where the fighters are, where I could act against those who had killed my family," she told a Russian reporter from her prison cell. Dadysheva is not so sure: "It [Dubrovka] was very disturbing. At the same time, I did this thing [bombed Pyatigorsk]. But I acted stupidly, and there were those innocent people who suffered."

THE PRICE OF PARADISE: KHAVA BARAYEVA
AND LUIZA MAGOMADOVA

The Chechen female suicide bomber made her debut in the summer of 2000, ten months after Shamil Basayev invaded Dagestan, declared Jihad on Russia, and started the second war in Chechnya—and a little more than two years before Dubrovka.

Russia accused Basayev of training women for suicide bombings as early as March 2000. His close associate, Arbi Barayev, the notorious kidnapper, people trader, murderer, and Wahhabi Islamic fanatic, delivered three months later. On 9 June Barayev filled a large KamAZ truck full of explosives and sent seventeen-year-old Khava Barayeva and her best friend, Luiza (Kheda) Magomadova, sixteen, on the first female suicide mission in Chechnya, targeting the Alkhan-Yurt OMON commandant's headquarters.[1]

"I know what I'm doing," Khava Barayeva told her parents in a prerecorded videotape before going on her mission. "Paradise has its price and I hope this will be the price for Paradise." Her purpose was to inspire others to Jihad. "Prepare yourself to meet your all-mighty Lord and purify yourself. We hope that those who claim to be men will follow in your footsteps and go to Jihad without hesitation. You will be an example for all those men," Barayev told Khava as the videotape rolls. Turning to the camera herself, Khava implored, "I sincerely request that all of you go to Jihad for the sake of Allah and expel the Kifir [Russians] from our country as Jihad is as obligatory for every Muslim [in Chechnya] as prayer. A large number of women are involved in Jihad now, and I hope that all men will go for Jihad and not take the woman's role by staying at home."

She further encouraged women to join Jihad: "Sisters, the time has come. When the enemy has killed almost all our men, our brothers and husbands, we are the only ones left to take revenge for them. The time has come for us to take up arms and defend our home, our land from those who bring death to our home. And if we have to become *shakhids* for Allah we will not stop. *Allah Akbar!*"

Luiza took her turn in front of the camera, too, "I request something from my sisters in Islam—do not stay at home, go for Jihad for the sake of Allah. Jihad is now as obligatory upon you as prayer, and it is time for women to be fighting alongside their men. We must not play and waste our time, but work hard to please Allah. Going to the battlefield with our *mujahideen* brothers will be support for them and victory will come sooner, *Inshallah!*"

Khava's video is in three parts. Part I shows her sitting on a couch at Barayev's home in Alkhan-Kala, reading aloud from the Koran and discussing the merits of living and dying. Barayev shot Part II himself as Khava and Luisa were preparing to step into their explosives-laden truck. The final segment was taken by someone standing alongside the road about a hundred meters from their target. It shows the truck barreling down to the police base, with policemen at the checkpoint yelling and shooting. Then the explosion—the massive explosion—and chunks of metal and human body parts go flying into the air.

Russia claims Khava and Luisa killed only two policemen, but Barayev said at least twenty-five Russian policemen died. The casualty count wasn't important—Khava's purpose was served. The small and unattractive girl became an instant inspiration for men and women both, someone who would be forever immortalized on film, in extremist poetry, and in a song that would become the battle hymn for all those who would follow her.

"Barayeva" was not Khava's real last name. It was Zhansurkayeva; her mother had died when she was very young, leaving her to be raised by her father until the soft-spoken Barayev came along and spun his web of manly charms on Khava, as he had on all his wives. All women were attracted to him. "He is handsome like the devil," the women would say. Because of Chechen tradition Khava hadn't been close to her father, but he nevertheless tried unsuccessfully to extricate her from Barayev's clutches. But Khava fell in love with this handsome man who had converted her to Wahhabism, made her his lover, manipulated her every thought, plied her with narcotics, and finally sacrificed her. Silva Saidulayeva, Barayev's fourth wife (she married him four months before he died), remembers Khava well. "Every time she walked past our quarters, I looked at her and thought to myself: What a meek, timid, and well brought up girl she is."

Any notion that Khava's act was an isolated "incident" of terrorism was dispelled on 2 and 3 July, when more suicide bombers—both men and women—threw Russian forces into a state of panic with nearly simultaneous suicide truck bombings on Russian police and military installations in five Chechen cities. Kidnapper-turned-terrorist Ramzan Akhmadov, who commanded this operation, publicly proclaimed that "these were planned actions to carry out terrorist acts." Ichkeria's propagandist Movladi Udugov claims that six hundred Russian soldiers were killed in these attacks, but Russia's official body count is under one hundred.

Until November 2001 you could buy videotapes of the attacks. The videos, called *Chechnya from the Ashes* and *Russian Hell in the Year 2000,* could be purchased in CD-Rom from Azzam Publications for twenty dollars. They show live footage of the operations, ambushes, and remote-controlled landmine and roadside bombings of Russian military vehicles in 2000. That summer and winter suicide bombers—Basayev boasted that there were more than five hundred of them—were paid to become martyrs in the name of Allah, or were coerced or shamed into doing so, or did so willingly. Old women, teenage girls, even children were recruited.

THE "SWEET SIXTEEN" BOMBERS

Mareta Dudayeva

In December 2000 sixteen-year-old Mareta Dudayeva attempted to drive an army Ural truck into the Leninsky District police station in Grozny, but guards opened fire on the truck, wounding its kamikaze driver and stopping the vehicle in the nick of time. "Everything will blow up now!" Mareta screamed as she bolted from the cab and tossed a grenade behind her. But the half-ton of explosives in the back didn't detonate. Some information says that Mareta later died from her grenade wounds, but I've been told that she survived and is sitting out a ten-year prison sentence somewhere in Russia.

Why did she do it? She was unmarried and none of Mareta's immediately family had died during the war, so it's unlikely she acted out of personal revenge. Her police report says that she was drugged. But Mareta claimed during interrogation that she had been forced to do the dirty deed by fighters of deceased field commander Magomed Tsagarayev who threatened to kill her relatives. Later on she changed her story, saying that Tsagarayev's widow had hired her to do it for revenge. A third version says that she had been filmed being raped—making her unsuitable for marriage in Chechen society—and was blackmailed into doing the job to absolve herself of "her sin."

Aizan Gazuyeva

Aizan (Aiza, Luiza) Gazuyeva was the same age, sixteen, when she blew herself up to kill the cruel Russian general responsible for her husband's death in one of the most horrible places on earth, Urus-Martan, a former Wahhabi stronghold.[2]

Between 1997 and 1999 Urus-Martan was the center of Islamic Wahhabi extremism in Chechnya, a place where neither President Aslan Maskhadov nor his feeble law enforcement organs dared go. Many Dagestani Wahhabi families moved there after the first Chechen war. In 1997 a few hundred of them took over a local school, built a mosque, and began recruiting young people for religious and military training in Khattab's terrorist training camps. By 1998 Urus-Martan had become a closed city and, for a while, was home to Maskhadov's opposition leaders Shamil Basayev, Salman Raduyev, Khunkar Israpilov, and Arbi Barayev.

It was still a nest of extremist activity in 2001, one of seventeen cities and villages actively supporting Chechen and imported Arab terrorists. Russian forces frequently cleansed the town. Aizan's father and brother were taken away once but later released. She had already lost an uncle and two cousins in the war.

Aizan's family was poor. Her parents wanted a better life for their young daughter, so they arranged her marriage to a man six years her senior who could adequately support and protect her. Aizan had only been married a little over six months when her husband was picked up in a cleansing operation. Going from one official to the next, and finally to the man in charge of the Urus-Martanovsky District himself, General Geidar Gadzhiyev, Aizan tried desperately to find out what had happened to her beloved husband. General Gadzhiyev was known for his harshness with Wahhabis. He had even been promoted for it. Sometimes Aizan would be let in to see him, sometimes not, but she always got the same answer—"Nothing is known about your husband's fate"—despite the fact that Gadzhiyev had flashed her husband's passport on public television after the cleansing operation. Aizan's family says that one day she went to the general's office and he told her: "I killed him myself with my own bare hands." She never went back.

Yulia Yuzik in her book *Nevesty Allakha* tells a different story—one told "in secret" to her by a Chechen policeman. According to this version Aizan's husband was beaten severely during interrogation, but the FSB ultimately determined that he was not the person they were after and that he had no relationship with radical Wahhabis. Nevertheless, he was not freed. Then one day General Gadzhiyev ordered Aizan to be brought to his office, where her husband was waiting. Seeing him, she began to weep and plead with Gadzhiyev to let him go. But instead Gadzhiyev disemboweled him, grabbed Aizan by the hair, and shoved her face into his ripped-open intestines.[3]

Aizan tried desperately to overcome her grief, which was compounded by the recent loss of her brother, an invalid who had lost his leg in the first Chechen war and had been shot by Russian soldiers earlier that spring. She went into a deep depression, withdrew, and stopped talking to neighbors and friends. She wasn't able to discuss her grief with her mother, who was away in a refugee camp in Ingushetia, and "I couldn't talk about it with Aizan because, according to our customs, daughters and fathers do not talk [about such things]," her father says.

For General Gadzhiyev, 29 November 2001 began like any other day. He set out early for an official meeting at town hall. Afterward, he found himself surrounded by a crowd of angry people demanding answers about missing relatives. He made a few statements then started across town square. Aizan approached him, but bodyguards blocked her path. "Do you remember me?" she yelled to him. "Get out of my way, I'm not going to talk to you," he retorted. That's when she detonated the grenades under her dress, and Gadzhiyev and his guards fell. He died in the hospital two days later.

In an analysis of Chechen female suicide bombers I did for the Washington, D.C.–based Center for Defense Information in December 2004, I concluded that Aizan's suicide was a purely spontaneous act; but if Yuzik is correct, Aizan too was manipulated by a "curator" sent by those organizing terror. According to Yuzik, an unidentified man had appeared at Aizan's house early on, urging her to take revenge for her husband's death. He gave Aizan religious books, took her to "secret meetings," then put a plan in her head and supplied her with the grenades to kill Gadzhiyev, for which he received $200,000.

Zarema Inarkayeva

With the grenade she carried around, Aset Chadayeva could very well have been another Aizan Gazuyeva if Russian soldiers had tried to touch her. There were probably hundreds of other women who would have liked to strap grenades to themselves, but sixteen-year-old Zarema Inarkayeva wasn't one of them. She was tricked into bombing a Grozny police station in early February 2002 by her Chechen policeman boyfriend. Some information says that Zarema was kidnapped and, like Mareta Dudayeva, was told that her family would be killed if she didn't do the bombing. But according to Yuzik, who befriended Zarema, her Chechen policeman boyfriend recruited and dispatched her.

At 3 PM on 5 February a car with two men and a girl stopped a distance away from the targeted police station. It waited for a second car, driven by Shamil Garibekov, Zarema's boyfriend. When he arrived he reassured the terrified girl: "You're brave, I know you can do it." Shamil handed Zarema a bag containing the bomb with explicit instructions to carry it on her shoulder and not to remove it under any circumstance. She was to walk into the ROVD building, go upstairs, and enter the office of police official Zaurbek Amranov. Shamil would do the rest. Zarema reluctantly entered the building but, unable to find the official's office, sat the bag down on the floor and scurried away. Shamil triggered the bomb, but it failed to fully detonate. Zarema lived; doctors had to remove shrapnel from her hip, but that's all.

Zarema's boyfriend had courted her for months, and then in December 2001 kidnapped her; for the next two months he kept her under guard with three other girls in an apartment. Three men and Shamil guarded the girls around the clock. Zarema assumed that Shamil had kidnapped her for marriage, but she told him she wasn't interested because "my mother should know first," and besides, "I didn't have anything to wear for the wedding." Shamil drugged her food to calm her down, collected her belongings from her mother, and then informed Zarema they were married. "That evening I slept with him as a wife," Zarema recalls. "I understood that I couldn't escape. They guarded me. One man was always there. Then I started to cook and wash for all the men who lived in the apartment." Soon Shamil began to share his "wife" with the other men. Zarema was kept segregated but overheard the men trying to convince the other girls to do "something terrible." They refused. The girls disappeared days before she was sent on her mission; their bodies were later found in a dump.

After the bombing Zarema lived in the police station under protective custody for four months because her parents refused to let her come home. After all, she was unmarried, had lived with a man, and so was now "spoiled" and a significant embarrassment to the family. Everybody would have been better off if she had been killed.

Zarema's fate is a mystery. Yuzik kept in touch with her by telephone and mail for a while. After the police station Zarema went to live with her aunt in the Astrakhanskaya Oblast, but she didn't stay long in the quiet village. She left for Khasavyurt, where she worked as a waitress in a café and became a prostitute.

THE DUBROVKA "SISTERS"

Passports and other documents found on some of the Dubrovka women, as well as what is now known about their personal histories, reveal something about how they were recruited and why. I concluded in a 2004 interview with the online magazine *Russia Profile* that the Dubrovka siege was very much a family affair. I haven't changed my mind. But it was also about betrayal, deception, greed, and the exploitation of teenage girls; about friendships, allegiances, the lonely, the sick, and the poor. It's a complex and tragic story. It's also a complicated tale about the intricate working of the Chechen extremist underground.

It's still unclear how many women participated in the siege. The Russian media has reported twenty-four names. Only nineteen are on the government's official list, published in early 2003, but the list is not completely accurate, either. Some not on the list have since been confirmed as being at Dubrovka, and one name is repeated with a slightly different spelling. The investigative report by Viktor Kalchuk, the Moscow procurator's office chief investigator for Dubrovka, lists twenty women, two of whom were not on the official list because they remain unidentified. Only sixteen identifications are positively confirmed by police and morgue photographs. Most were not strangers to the FSB. More than half had been detained and interrogated during cleansing operations in Chechnya earlier in the year.

The Widows

At least three Chechen women were widows.

There's no morgue photo of twenty-two-year-old Maryam Buvaisarovna Khadzhiyeva from the Oktyarbrsky District of Grozny, but Barayev personally pointed out "widow Maryam" to the hostages. Her husband, Movsar Aliyev, had been killed by Russian soldiers in 2000 when they wiped out his entire unit of forty-five men commanded by the Arab mercenary Abu-al-Bakar. After his death Maryam and their young child went to live with her husband's Wahhabi family. Maryam became very close to Movsar's sister, Sekilat (Zara) Aliyeva, who was also at Dubrovka. Maryam being the younger, she looked up to her sister-in-law and likely followed Sekilat to Moscow.

Barayev also identified Sekilat, who was not a widow but was in the theater to avenge her brother's death. She was also identified by a genuine passport and bus ticket found on her body, and in morgue photograph no. 2024. She was shown on television as the dead terrorist with her head on her left arm, leaning forward over the back of an auditorium seat.

Born in Kazakhstan on 2 January 1977, Aliyeva studied in a Russian school in the Dzhambulskaya Oblast, later moving with her parents back to Chechnya. Sekilat's passport lists her address as No. 132, Sadovskaya Street, Oktyabrsky District, Grozny. She bought her bus ticket in Khasavyurt, Dagestan, on 16 October 2002, to come to Moscow the next day. Aliyeva was neither a widow nor destitute but gainfully employed in the history department at the Chechen State University. In the mid-1990s she studied in the acting faculty at the university. The staff there remembers her well. "She never missed a class, she was modest, and correct—and talented," Heidi, the rector's assistant, recalls.[4] Heidi also remembers that in 1997–98 Sekilat started to wear the traditional Islamic veil demanded by the Wahhabis. Although the family considered itself Wahhabi, her friends did not see her as a radical.

After graduating in 1998 Sekilat enrolled in a Grozny business-management training program, but her studies were interrupted by the second war and Movsar's death. After his death she required medical treatment for depression. Wahhabi friends of the family in Baku were happy to pay for it. Before leaving for Moscow Sekilat left a note behind for her mother promising to save a special place in heaven for her. "I thought she was safe in Baku," Sekilat's mother later told reporters. She had been happy that her daughter had found psychological help. Maryam, on the other hand, had simply run away and disappeared, deserting a small son, which worried Sekilat's mother more.

One of Arbi Barayev's six widows, the only one without children, Maryam (Zura) Marshugova, was also in the theater. "She's the short woman on the balcony—my aunt, Zura, the widow of my uncle Arbi [Barayev] whom you killed," Barayev told hostages. The FSB says that "Zura Arbi Barayeva" (Marsugova) commanded the women at Dubrovka, but Kalchuk is certain it was another terrorist, Malika Vitaliyeva, Basayev's trusted "cook" from the first war and a principal organizer of the Dubrovka siege, who was in charge.

Zura babysat an eighty-eight-pound bomb in the middle of the Dubrovka spectator gallery. "Barayev's aunt sat with the bomb, while we [hostages] formed a circle around her, guarding the evil machine," Tatyana Popova, a surviving hostage, writes in her book *Nord Ost*.[5] Zura demonstrated nerves of steel and iron discipline: "She was always calm, never shouted, which was all the more frightening. . . . She worked like a machine, without showing any external emotion, without sleep, and practically without eating."[6]

To hostage Irina Filipova, Zura Marshugova "seemed to take pleasure that she was in this situation, that people were listening to her and wanting to talk to her, that she was in control." Once, Marsugova jumped up, pointed her pistol at a man, and demanded that he show her his passport. He gave it to her. She looked at it and gave it back. Then she walked over to a grey-haired man and asked, "Mister, are you Georgian?"

"Yes, I am Georgian."

"Your passport please!" Like before, she looked at it and simply handed it back. The man's wife, sitting next to him, then jumped up and said, "I'm also Georgian, and my grandfather and mother are Georgian."

"Do you have a passport?"

"No!"

"Then sit back down!"

And that was it. "The *terroristka* suddenly abandoned the idea of establishing our identities," Popova says.

Marshugova is not on the official list of dead terrorists, nor is she on Kalchuk's list, nor am I aware of any morgue photos of her. Yuzik says the woman, twenty-five to thirty years old, escaped alive along with Vitaliyeva and the widow of Zelimkhan Akhmadov and fled abroad. Her younger sister told OMON policemen who searched the family home that she had gone to Azerbaijan to visit relatives.

Because she was a Barayev widow Marshugova had earlier been detained and questioned by the FSB. Her husband had died the previous summer in a federal assault on the house in which he and eighteen of his men had been holed up. Wounded, he tried to escape but fell in the yard. Two of his men hid his body in a pile of bricks. When Zura and her mother showed up in Alkhan-Kala to bury him, angry townspeople armed with pitchforks, spades, sticks, and stones met the convoy and refused to let it pass. Pelting the truck carrying his body, the mob yelled, "Take him to the dump!" Traditional Chechen law forbids burying murderers in cemeteries.

The second widowed wife of prominent Chechen field commander Zelimkhan Akhmadov was present in the theater too. A month or so earlier Zelimkhan's bullet-riddled body was found in a car between the villages of Goity and Chechen-Aul, his death the result of a blood feud. He had not been shot by Russian soldiers.

The unusual beauty of this black-eyed, veiled woman, with her hand constantly on the detonator button of her suicide belt, infatuated NTV television reporters. "Why did you come here to die? Don't you feel sorry for innocent people?" one of them asked. "Women, old men and children are killed every day in Chechnya—and it means nothing [to you]," she answered in a stern voice. "Why did you choose this place to carry out a terror act?" they further enquired. "By the will of Allah we chose it!" she retorted.

Akhmadova was childless. A fighter remembers her saying that she had no purpose in life after Zelimkhan's death. By Wahhabi tradition a widow should mourn four months and nine days, after which she should think about finding a new husband. But friends say Akhmadova had no desire to remarry. Still, her presence at Dubrovka had nothing to do with extracting revenge for her husband's death.

Newlyweds and Wives

Far from grieving widows, at least seven of the Dubrovka women were married; five of them were newlyweds, thanks to *djamaat*-arranged marriages to fighters just before the siege. Three newlyweds were pregnant and four had longtime associations with one another.

Thirty-eight-year-old Raiman Khasanovna Kurbanova, whose valid passport was found on her body, had married two months before Dubrovka. Yuzik interviewed Raiman's cousin, a Chechen policeman, who said that she had been married before but that her first husband had divorced her because Raiman failed to bear children for him. Months before Dubrovka the local *djamaat* arranged her marriage to a Dagestani fighter; as his property and obedient wife, she followed him to Moscow.

Raiman had returned home to the village of Novoterskoye from the Rostovskaya Obast at the age of twenty-seven to take care of her sick mother. Raiman's policeman cousin says that she was an antiwar activist, that she went along to all the meetings of the antiwar movement, and had difficulty talking about anything else. She was a devout Wahhabi who had attended Islam University and, like Sekilat Aliyeva, wore the traditional Islamic garb in the interwar years. "She wanted to stop the war, to do something for her people. Maybe she wanted to become a hero for her people like Joan of Ark," Raiman's cousin says.

Kurbanova was a close friend of at least three other Dubrovka women, the sisters Aiman and Koku Khadzhiyeva and Zareta Bairakova, with whom she made trips to Moscow in April and June 2002. Aiman Vagetovna Khadzhiyeva, twenty-eight, and her younger sister, Koku Vegetovna Khadzhiyeva, twenty-six, had also recently married *djamaat* fighters. Both were psychologically disturbed and pregnant.[7] Aiman's valid passport and bus ticket to Moscow, purchased in Khasavyurt on 16 October 2002 for travel the following day, were found at Dubrovka. A badly scribbled note on the ticket reads, "meeting 24 [probably 21] 10.02 Luzhniki." She was on the bus with Sekilat Aliyeva. We don't know if Koku traveled the same day. Police found Koku's passport and a Moscow Metro card that had last been used at 9:39 PM on 22 October. There was no bus ticket in her possession.

Aiman was born on 26 July 1974 in the village of Tepliye Kluchi, Kasharsky District, Rostovskaya Oblast, but had returned home in 1995 to live with her mother, Kheda, in the village of Staraya Sunzha, close to Grozny. Her sister Koku returned home that year too. Their mother told Yuzik that her daughters came to her, a month apart, at the end of the summer of 2002 with the news that they were getting married, collected their belongings, and abruptly departed. Aiman returned a short while later to say that she was going to Turkey to buy some goods to resell in Grozny, but she never returned home again. Kheda, who never saw Koku again either, admits that she broke off relations with both girls because they rushed off to get married right after their father died, "leaving me alone."

Despite their late ages both Aiman and Koku, like Kurbanova, conveniently found Wahhabi fighters to marry that summer too. Koku married a *mujahid* from the Dagestansky *djamaat,* while Aiman married one from the Groznensky *djamaat.* These and other marriages that summer suggest a pattern in the recruitment of at least some Dubrovka terrorists.

Aiman and Koku were identified and targeted because both were unwell, were "outcasts" in their own society, and had no chance of having better lives with husbands and children. Neither had been married before, and by the ages of twenty-eight and twenty-six it was unlikely they would ever get married. Moreover, both were ill. Koku had tuberculosis, while Aiman suffered "frequent panic attacks" and "severe headaches" and was being treated for a mental illness. They too, as obedient wives, followed their husbands to Dubrovka.

Twenty-nine-year-old Aset Vakhidovna Gishlurkayeva had been a widow but, like the other three women, also entered into a *djamaat*-arranged marriage before Dubrovka.[8] The FSB says that she was the common-law wife of Timur Kantashyev, the "head of a criminal group." Though religious, a Wahhabi, and also involved in the "antiwar movement," Aset came from a well-to-do family in Achkoi-Martan and earned an economics degree with high marks from the Chechen State University. She was far from a destitute housewife.

In 1997–98 she worked as the secretary to Achkoi-Martan's police chief. Kalchuk says that she was also a member of an illegal armed formation headed by one of the Ganiyev brothers. Therefore, she likely knew at least two more of the Dubrovka women, Khadchat and Fatima Ganiyeva. She was already known to the FSB, as she, along with Malizha Matayeva, had been detained in Achkoi-Martan during a spring 2002 cleansing operation there.

Gishlurkayeva left home at the beginning of October, telling relatives she was going to Rostov for treatment of a breast tumor. She went to Saint Petersburg instead, departing from Nazran, Ingushetia. She lived there for the rest of the month with two men, another woman, and a child. The men drove her to Moscow a few days before Dubrovka. Her mother and the small son she had left behind fled to Azerbaijan after Dubrovka.

Twenty-six-year-old Zareta Dolkhayevna Bairakova may have also wed just before Dubrovka.[9] Human rights journalist Tamara Uzumkhadzhiyeva, who interviewed her parents, says that she left home on 29 September after a knock at her apartment door and a brief visit by an older woman (likely Yesira Vitaliyeva) and two armed men. Zareta's mother was in prayer and didn't hear the conversation between her daughter and the woman. Zareta called out to her mother to say that she would be back in fifteen minutes and left with the woman. Zareta's mother remembers the visitor had on dry boots, which meant that she had come by car, as it was raining outside.

Zareta never returned. Two armed men in camouflage uniforms came instead to tell her father that she was getting married to one of their relatives and would be living in the village of Dargo in the Vedensky District. He just assumed it was a marriage by kidnapping. The new husband should have brought presents for the family, but given the fact that the Vedensky District is a long way away and since it is dangerous to travel there, the family didn't think any more about it.

Neighbors say Zareta was bright and attentive. She was tops in school, but instead of going on to university she helped her invalid parents financially by selling at the market in Grozny. She left behind her parents, a sister, and three brothers. Two of them, Baudi, twenty-three, and Murad, twenty, are suspected illegal armed formation members. The family last heard from the two boys when they were working in a logging camp in the Irkutskaya Oblast. In 2002 the youngest brother was fifteen years of age.

Zareta, too, had earlier been detained and questioned. On 17 October she bought a bus ticket in Khasavyurt, departing for Moscow two days later. That ticket, her valid passport, and a note reading "meeting 27 [also probably 21] October 2002, Luzhniki," were found on her body. I have been told that several of the girls who only arrived in Moscow a couple of days ahead of Dubrovka had been instructed to rendezvous at the well known Luzhniki Stadium on 21 October. In photographs of the dead Dubrovka terrorists published in the media Zareta is lying back in her seat with explosives in her lap. Hers is morgue photo no. 2031.

Blond-haired, eighteen-year-old Marina (Madina) Nebiyullayevna Bisultanova was married too. She is on the official list and was positively identified by her parents in morgue photos. Yuzik says she was not a destitute housewife but a trapped girl who was used and abused by her husband and kidnapped by his fanatical Wahhabi friends from Baku. But according to Kalchuk, "she fell under the influence of Vitaliyeva and was recruited by her." Still other information says that Ruslan Elmurzayev—a mysterious character, a former Urus-Martanovsky ROVD policeman, a Basayev emissary, the man in overall charge of the Dubrovka operation, and himself a Dubrovka terrorist—personally recruited Bisultanova. Presenting himself as Khunov Fauda, a businessman from the Karachayevo-Cherkessiya Republic, he reportedly made a business deal with her to buy discounted goods in Baku for resale at Grozny's market.

Bisultanova was born in Grozny on 21 December 1983 but moved to Baku, Azerbaijan, with her family at a young age. At eighteen she married, but her father, who returned to Chechnya with his wife and two other daughters to live in 2001, went back to Baku two and a half months before Dubrovka and snatched his unhappy daughter away from her abusive husband. Marina's husband refused to let her live in peace, making numerous trips to Chechnya to cajole her into returning to Baku. Two of his friends, Vitalyeva and Elmurzayev, came for her a final time after dinner on 30 September. Her father was away from the house, but Marina told her mother that friends had come to ask her to go to Baku with them to buy some merchandise. She turned them down. "I grabbed her handbag, just in case, so she wouldn't go," her mother says.[10]

But Marina was told that she didn't have any choice. Ruslan was wait-ing in his black Volvo. He was dressed in an MVD uniform and was in pos-session of a special police *propusk* (pass) signed by police general Anatoliy Yezhkov permitting him to travel freely in Chechnya. Marina's father later searched for her among the Wahhabi community in Khasavyurt, but to no avail. He also tried unsuccessfully to find Vitaliyeva, who was known to the family and who, he says, also "recruited the girls." Five days later he received a package containing Marina's clothing with a note that read: "Dear Mama and Papa. I have gone to Baku for merchandise, I will return in 10 days. *Mamochka, Papochka,* I love you dearly. You know that I will always be there for you. Marina."[11]

Little is known about Liana Musayevna Khusenova except that she was born on 31 October 1979 in the *stanitsa* of Naurskaya, had been married to a Wahhabi fighter who died in the war, and had recently moved to Gro-zny. According to Zaira, Yupayeva's mother, who knew her, Liana was not a widow, but other information says her husband died fighting. She, too, had been earlier detained and questioned by the Naursky FSB office. Khusen-ova is on the official list, with a note that a valid passport was found on her body, but she is not on Kalchuk's list. He names a Luiza Alavdinova Khuse-nova with a birth date of 2 August 1968 and says that she was the sister of Baudin Bakuyev. Kalchuk's Khusenova is likely the married name of Aishat (Luiza) Bakuyeva.

Amnat Isuyeva is not on the official list, either, nor is she on Kalchuk's list—but then, he did say that two female terrorists remain unidentified. She was frequently discussed in the media as a Dubrovka participant. According to that information, Amnat had long ago married and moved to Petropov-loskoye, but during the first war her husband died from medical complica-tions. Her husband's friend, a Wahhabi leader, took care of their three girls for awhile but eventually took them away from her, forbidding her from even seeing them. In the fall of 2002 she moved in with relatives. She again asked to see her children but was refused, so she made arrangements with a schoolteacher to give her eldest daughter a letter saying that she was get-ting married soon and that the daughter would soon have a little brother. Amnat said she would return in a few days to get her daughter and they would live happily ever after. According to friends, her new husband was there in the theater with her. She had been seen with Aishat Bakuyeva ear-lier in the year.

Schoolgirls and Family Betrayals

Sixteen-year-old Aimani Kurbanova, the pretty girl from Grozny with the doll-like face, was the second youngest female terrorist at Durboka. It's unknown if she was related to Raiman Kurbanova. Aimani had never been married. Despite her youth and beauty, she was strict and stern with the hostages; her pistol always at the ready. "She was raised on Allah. . . . [G]ive her the order to detonate her bomb and she will do it immediately—that would be her ultimate happiness," Barayev warned hostages in the theater. Nothing else is known about her or how she was recruited. She is on neither the official list nor Kalchuk's list.

The youngest Dubrovka terrorist, Khadchat (Milana) Sulumbekovna Ganiyeva (morgue photo no. 2038), was a devout Wahhabi. Born on 1 April 1986 she was unmarried, little more than a child. A valid passport and a round-trip ticket from Makhachkala, Dagestan, to Moscow on 18 October with a return date of 27 October were found on her body. Like the others Khadchat was shot in the head by Spetznaz (special purpose) forces during the rescue attempt. In police photographs she is lying on the auditorium floor with her eyes open. Relatives describe Khadchat as a quiet, shy, and obedient girl from a large Muslim family who lived in the Wahhabi stronghold of Assinovskaya in the Achkoi-Martanovsky District of Chechnya.

"Before the war we lived well," Raisa, an older sister, remembers. "But the war ruined everything." Years of fighting made it difficult for their father to feed the family, so the children worked the land to make ends meet. Clothing was handed down. Khadchat was the middle child. Her father was the dominant figure in this devout Wahhabi household, which prayed five times a day. The children both respected and feared him.

After Dubrovka federal forces destroyed the family home. The family now lives in Baku, where Khadchat studied Arabic at the insistence of her father, who is fluent in the language. Prayers in Arabic scribbled on the walls of the destroyed family home can still be seen.

There are three versions of Khadchat's path to Dubrovka. Yuzik says that she was identified by her close friend and fellow Dubrovka terrorist Zura Bitsyeva, twenty-two, as a possible recruit, prompting a *djamaat* representative to approach her father with a moneymaking proposition. If he would allow Khadchat to participate in a mission "to scare President Putin" into negotiating with Ichkerian president Maskhadov, the family would receive $20,000 and guaranteed relocation to Baku when the mission was completed. No blood would be spilled, but if something did go wrong, Khadchat's father would still have nine children left and money to feed, clothe, and shelter them.

According to a second version I heard in Moscow in 2003, it was Khadchat's older brother Rustam Ganiyev, one of Basayev's field commanders, who sold Khadchat and Fatima for a thousand dollars each for the mission.

Inspector Kalchuk has a third version, that Khadchat joined the fighting unit headed by her brothers Rustam and Ibragim and "in 2001, was detained on suspicion of carrying out an attack on the Assinovskaya [train] station." She was detained again in May 2002 during a cleansing of Assinovskaya but was let go.

Khadchat bought a bus ticket to the capital from Khasavyurt three days before the Dubrovka siege.

The name of her older sister, Fatima, twenty-seven years of age (born 1 November 1975), also appears on the 2003 official list—and on Kalchuk's list. Although the official list states that Fatima's valid passport was found, Yuzik says she was mistakenly included on the list of dead terrorists because Khadchat had a temporary address registration in Fatima's name in her possession. There are no morgue or other photos of Fatima.

Raisa, the third sister, reportedly asked for federal protection and was moved out of Chechnya to avoid being forced into becoming a suicide bomber.

The credibility of this brotherly betrayal is in doubt because of what Zarema Muzhikhoyeva, the 9 July 2003 "Tveskaya bomber," had to say about Raisa sixteen months after the Dubrovka siege. In an interview from her prison cell with *Izvestiya* reporter Vadim Rechkalov in early February 2004, Zarema, who also lived in Assinovskaya, asserted that it was this same Raisa who had put her on the path to becoming a suicide bomber.

Raisa was well connected. "Everybody knew she had links with fighters. She was special, and she didn't try to hide it," Zarema told Rechkalov. Zarema naturally went to Raisa when she decided to become a suicide bomber. She was very helpful. Raisa gave the aspiring *shakhida* the handbook *The Moment of Death* and other Wahhabi literature, coached her, and then turned her over to Rustam, who introduced Zarema to Basayev.

But Ilya Shabalkin, the Russian commander in charge of counterterrorism operations in Chechnya, told reporters that Raisa was constantly plied with mind-altering drugs and was not conscious of what she was doing and therefore should not be held responsible for her actions. "She was sent to distant relatives in another region of Russia and for all practical purposes, at the present time, has no contact with the Republic of Chechnya," Shalbalkan told reporters when asked about her.

Twenty-five-year-old Zaira Bashirovna Yupayeva (morgue photo no. 2017), born on 17 May 1978 in the Naursky District, was also sold by a family member. She was not a widow—although she had lost a brother, Akhmed, in fighting in 2000. It's uncertain if she was married. Yuzik says she did marry not long before Dubrovka, but even if that's true, it didn't play a role in her recruitment. Fatherly betrayal did.

Zaira lived with her little sister, mother Lyuba, and Bashir, her father, who later confessed to the FSB that he had given his consent for Zaira to participate in "some kind of a spetz-operation in Moscow" in exchange for $30,000 compensation if anything happened to her. He too was betrayed. After Dubrovka he received nothing for his daughter, who was found with a bullet in her head. Like Ganiyeva, Zaira, who was described by her mother as naive and trusting, had been identified as a possible recruit by her childhood friend and fellow Dubrovka terrorist Madina Dugayeva.

Zaira disappeared from home on 30 September. She went to a relative's wedding in Kalinovskaya, and then accompanied the couple back to the Naursky District. They put her on a bus home the same day, but Elmurzayev, in his black Volvo, intercepted the bus before it could reach Sapogi. He removed Zaira and put her into his car, where her friend, Madina Dugayeva, was waiting. Madina would comfort Zaira and explain that her father had given his permission for her to go to Moscow with them. Zaira probably had no knowledge of the operation's details, nor is it likely that she went to Moscow knowing that she would never return home.

The following day two men, one of them a mullah from Komsomolskoye, showed up at Zaira's house with two hundred dollars and a note in her handwriting addressed to her mother saying that she had left for Grozny to get married to a man from the Belgata *teip*. But her mother knew better and demanded to know where her daughter was and who had sent the note. She later determined that Vitaliyeva had passed the note on to a man identified as Akhmed Khamzayev in Berkat-Yurt, who had in turn given it to the mullah to deliver. Lyuba confronted Khamzayev, threatening to call the FSB, but was quickly silenced with the threat of bodily harm.

The Ringleaders

Three women played key roles in organizing and recruiting the Dubrovka sisters. Full-figured, forty-one-year-old Malika (alias "Yesira," "Misi") Rashidkhanova Vitaliyeva (born 19 March 1960) is not on the official list, but her description by Moscow's deputy procurator as a "bandit who made a career out of developing the women's part of the war" and her inclusion in the Kalchuk list confirms her presence in the theater, although there is no public record of her body having been found.

Yesira was neither a widow nor a desperate housewife but a disciplined and loyal Basayev follower going back to the first war. Kalchuk describes her as a "cook for Basayev's unit," while "her task [for Dubrovka] was to recruit girls as suicide bombers and during the attack act as head of the female terrorists." Yuzik and others believe she escaped from Dubrovka.

Vitalyeva was a busy woman in the early fall of 2002. Planning for Dubrovka began that summer, with a 6 June military conference cementing an alliance between Maskhadov and Basayev. They spent twenty days together hammering out the details of a new unified military structure and discussing and developing a unified plan of combat operations that included a change in military strategy and a terror strike at the heart of Russia. Basayev proposed a terror attack on the "lair of the enemy in the heart of Moscow." There was agreement that the attack should be more spectacular than the apartment building bombing in 1999 and should involve large numbers of civilian casualties.

Basayev conceived a plan to establish a special suicide unit—the "Riyadus-Salikhin Reconnaissance and Sabotage Battalion of Shakhids"—to do the job. To facilitate entry into Moscow the unit would be much smaller than the one he had organized in 1995. This time members would go to Moscow not as a group but individually. Also, nearly half the unit would be young women, which would facilitate infiltration since women were seldom stopped by the Russian police for document checks. Seasoned fighters would make up the other half of the battalion.

Vitaliyeva recruited many of the girls for the Moscow mission. She was also responsible for ensuring that they got to Moscow and for taking care of them once they arrived. They needed places to stay, so at the beginning of October 2002 modest "Khava Erbiyeva" (Vitaliyeva's alias) went to the Kalita-Grad real estate agency to rent apartments for "relatives" coming from Dagestan for medical treatment. She found three large apartments,

No. 22 Vorontsovskaya Street, No. 15 Festivalnaya Street, and No. 4, Corpus 1, Yelevatornaya Street.

But Vitalyeva's role was even more significant. Much of the preparation for the attack had to be done in Moscow, including the acquisition of schematic drawings of the target, the collection of critical security information, visits to target sites, and even dress rehearsals.

Russia's parliament was the original target picked by Shamil Basayev, but three alternative targets had to be chosen when the field commander he had assigned to lead the siege was killed in Chechnya. Vitaliyeva calculated that a concert hall or a theater—any location where security would be minimal but there would be lots of people—would be ideal. She selected three potential targets: the Moskovsky Dvorets Molodyozhi (MDM) Theater, where *42nd Street* was playing, the Estrada Theater, and Dubrovka. She also scouted out the targets and videotaped each, but Elmurzayev made the final selection.

Twenty-four-year-old Madina Movsarovna Dugayeva, the devout Wahhabi resident of the Naursky District and the confident, beautiful woman in traditional Islamic black garb and veil with the pistol in her hand seen in Russian television footage, recruited her childhood friend Zaira Yupayeva.

Dugayeva, who played the "senior sister" role at Dubrovka, preventing panic among the younger girls, was born in the village of Samashki, Achkoi-Martanovsky District, on 13 January 1978. Her brothers were all fighters, living in either Azerbaijan or Turkey. Only her sick mother and underage sister remained at home.

Madina's valid passport was found in her handbag at Dubrovka. Along with it were four tattered photographs, identification (issued on 27 April 2001) as an assistant in the Department of Acting Arts at the Chechen State University, and two postcards with the messages, "To my dear sister Madina from your one and only unforgettable sister Iman, 27.04.2001," and "Congratulations on your birthday. I wish you happiness. With love, Amina and Mama, 13 January 2002."

Dugayeva is on both the official list and Kalchuk's list but not in any morgue photographs that I saw. According to Yuzik she was promised an escape along with Vitaliyeva and the others. Yuzik was told about this by a fighter from the settlement of Stariye Aldy, who was personally acquainted with the widows of Arbi Barayev and Zemlimkhan Akhmadov. Maybe that's why Dugayeva never once removed her mask in the theater.

Twenty-two-year-old Zura Rezvanovna Bitsiyeva (morgue photo no. 2019) also recruited girls. Using her real passport, this attractive, professionally trained business executive assistant, "who could easily fit into a miniskirt or tight jeans," came to Moscow on a bus from Makhachkala on 16 October with several other girls. Zura, a devout Wahhabi who never wore jeans but, according to Kalchuk, "Wahhabi clothing," was born in Samashki on 22 April 1980. She moved to Assinovskaya with her mother and older sister after the 1998 death of her father in a drunken knife fight with her brother. The family was poor and rented a house. A secretarial diploma from Grozny Professional School No. 23 was found, along with her bus ticket and valid passport, on her body.

The fact that she had a return ticket dated 27 October led some investigators to conclude that she had planned to return home in eleven days, but that is unlikely in light of this note left behind for her best friend: "By the will of Allah, I have left for you know where. I cried my eyes out and swore to Allah, I could not eat or even communicate with anybody. But suddenly I found khadis, where 'prorok' [Mohammed] forbid the mourning for more than three days, and, with difficulty, I calmed down. I will soon meet him in heaven. . . . I have one important request. Please keep the faith to the end. By the grace of Allah, we will meet in Heaven."

The administrative secretary of the state farm in Assinovskaya describes her as very religious, always wearing a veil (in the interwar years), and very quiet, almost timid in manner, keeping to herself. She was good friends with Khadchat Ganiyeva, Zaira Yupayeva, and Madina Dugayeva.

Zura was detained along with Khadchat Ganiyeva in the May 2002 cleansing operation in Assinovskaya.

The Fighter, the Pharmacist, and the Grandmother

Thirty-one-year-old Malizha Daudovna Mutayeva is described by Kalchuk as an "officer in a women's resistance battalion during Dudayev's regime." Unfortunately Kalchuk doesn't elaborate on her earlier role in the women's battalion. People who knew her called her "Captain," but that could just as easily have been a nickname instead of her official rank. Matuyeva is on the official list, but spelled "Mugayeva" (an obvious typo). Her valid passport and a bus ticket to Moscow from Makhachkala, departing 22 October, were found on her body. She is also identified in a morgue photo and is on Kalchuk's list.

Malizha Mutayeva was born on 30 October 1971 in the village of Valerik, Achkoi-Martanovsky District. In 2002 she lived at No. 1 D. Vednovo Street in Assinovskaya with her mother Sovdat, invalid father Daud Ferzauli, and her sisters Luiza, eighteen, and Madina, fourteen. She also had an older half sister, Naapskhan, the daughter of her father's first wife.

Malizha's mother says she never married but did have a suitor she was in love with who died in 1994. After he was gone she wasn't interested in marrying and stayed at home and did house work and cooked. "She baked wonderful pies. She seldom went anywhere," her mother says. Other information says she was married to a fighter and had a child. Sovdat told Yuzik that Malizha left home at the end of September because she had found a job in Nazran. She seemed "calm, even happy" at that time.

Thirty-four year-old Aishat (Luiza) Alavdinovna Bakuyeva from the village of Ilinovka, east of Grozny, was in the theater too. This is likely the Luiza Alavdinovna Khusenova, born on 2 August 1968, whom Kalchuk includes in his list (Khusenova being Bakuyeva's married name). Bakuyeva was far from a desperate housewife. She was a successful pharmacist and businesswoman but had lost four brothers in fighting, including the well-known Baudi Bakuyev, who had been a member of Arbi Barayev's gang and had played a role in the kidnapping and murder of Russian general Sphigun in 1999. Baudi died in a GRU spetz-operation in 2000. Shortly afterward two other brothers, Aslan and Idris, were killed too. The last brother, fifteen-year-old Daud, was arrested as a suspect in a bombing in northern Grozny. He was murdered and his body thrown away without a proper Muslim burial.

Neighbors say that Bakuyeva became a little more distant and withdrawn with the death of each brother. She would no longer cry at funerals—just stare—and she stopped attending prayer services. Then one day in the spring of 2002 Aishat sold her kiosk in Grozny, packed a suitcase, and told her friends that she was moving to Moscow to start a new life. That was the last anybody saw of her.

Police major Igor Alyamkin of the Nizhegorodsky Moscow branch of the OVD completed the paperwork for her Moscow address registration on 20 August 2002. His failure to check her family's background, and corruption charges, later landed him in jail.

It's unknown if Aishat was divorced or if her husband was still living at the time of the Dubrovka siege. Only her mother, Datu, and a sister,

Aisha, are left from this large family. Bakuyeva is not on the official list or on Kalchuk's list, but she is in morgue photo no. 2006.

Forty-three-year-old Yakha Khamidovna Meferkhanova, who lived in Moscow, was the oldest of the Dubrovka sisters. An official Moscow address registration (for Otkrytoye Shosse) was found on her body. She is on the official list but not on Kalchuk's list. Her marital status is unknown.

Svetlana Gubaryeva, a hostage who lost her thirteen-year-old daughter Sasha and her American fiancé, Sandy Booker, at Dubrovka, vividly remembers her: "Standing beside me was a Chechenka about forty-five years of age. She had come by contract, and told us about her life. She had a twelve-year-old son that they took from school and he disappeared." Gubaryeva saw a kind side to Meferkhanova: "She had a mobile telephone and she gave it to us to call. We guessed that they [the terrorist leaders] would have yelled at her if they had known."

Unknowns

There are four Dubrovka sisters about whom little is known. Eighteen-year-old, Seda Seitkhamzatovna Elmurzayeva (born on 3 April 1984), Ruslan Elmurzayev's wife, sister, or relative, is both on the official list and Kalchuk's list. Her valid passport was found at Dubrovka.

A valid passport with Moscow registration and a notation that she had been issued a foreign travel passport, as well as a small prayer book in Arabic, was found on the body of twenty-five-year-old Fatimat Mukhamedovna Shakova (born on 6 May 1977). She is on the official list but not on Kalchuk's list.

Similarly, twenty-four-year-old Zaira Basirovna Bityeva (born 17 May 1978) was found with a valid passport with the words "Israpilova Dagmara from Rubezhnoe" written on the cover. She is on the official list but not on the Kalchuk list.

Finally, eighteen-year-old Aminat Khamzatgovna Tushayeva (born on 28 October 1984) is not on the official list but is identified on Kalchuk's list.

WE'RE READY TO DIE

Barayev and his *shakhidas* repeatedly threatened hostages with certain death. "They work in shifts," he told Mark Franchetti of the *Sunday Times*. "Those on duty have their finger on the detonator at all times. One push of the button and they will explode." Another time Barayev blurted out, "Two widows are ready to blow themselves up; the situation might turn into a blood bath at any moment." When a *shakhida* placed a grenade between hostage Nastya Kruglikova's cousin and her aunt, Nastya asked, "What's going to happen. Are you going to blow us up?"

"No, it will be OK—well, maybe you will be blown up, but at least you won't know anything about it," the *terroristka* replied.

Hostage Aleksandr remembers that a girl on the balcony grabbed a grenade in one hand and two battery wires in the other and then told everybody to pray. "She then started to chant." He thought it was the end.[12] Hostage Vitaliy recalls, "When they slept, they had a pistol or a grenade in one hand, and a detonator in the other. One sneezed and hostages around her dropped to the floor."

"We'll toss grenades at you if there's a storm [assault]," a female terrorist told Pavel, another hostage. Oksana was terrified of the "Black Widow" standing next to her. "She was very aggressive, waving her pistol in front of my face all the time, showing her power." Zinaida says what disturbed her most was that "she [a *shakhida*] was constantly playing with her grenade."

All the Dubrovka women were vocal about their desire to die. "It would be a present for me if I died for Allah now," one told a hostage. "My whole family was killed. I have buried all my children. I live in the forest. I have nowhere to go and nothing to live for," another alleged. A *shakhida* confirmed that she didn't want to die, but "I am ready to do it for Allah." A third said that "it doesn't matter if I die, here or there [in Chechnya]. My husband and children have all been killed, so I have nothing to live for." One girl kept repeating over and over, "'We're going to heaven, We're going to heaven.' I got the impression she had lost her mind," Zinaida recalls. Alla, another hostage says: "The *shakhida* woman sitting next to me said her brother was killed last year, and she lost her husband six months ago. 'I have nothing to lose; I have nothing left. So, I'll go all the way with this, even though I don't think it's the right thing to do.'"[13]

Popova says that the Dubrovka women were all well disciplined and in control of themselves, despite the fact that conditions in the theater were unbearable. It was very hot and the Chechen women were wearing heavy clothing with black scarves and sometimes even masks over their heads. The heavy explosive belts around their waists made it difficult for them to breathe. "I had the impression that they never slept. I was struck by their powers of endurance. . . . Despite the tremendous psychological stress they were under and certain death hanging over their heads, they joked among themselves, even laughed."[14]

Some hostages saw a softer side. "Many of the [Chechen] women cried and I wondered, who will shed more tears, us or them? I saw them weeping, but they tried to hide their tears. They were afraid to die just like everyone else," one hostage says. Nastya Kruglikova also remembers the younger girls crying. An older woman, Asya, possibly Aset Gishlurkayeva, also told her not to be afraid: 'Please don't worry.' She hoped they would give up, that there would be a conversation with the government and it would end well." Irina Filipova remembers that "Some cried. One of them told me her parents had sold her into it [terrorism] and she didn't want to blow herself up."

"I saw a young girl which sat to the left of me. She didn't raise her voice once. . . . The women with the bomb talked to us, even allowed us to go to the toilet without waiting," Zanaida recalls.[15]

Vitaliy recalls, "I was getting cold and a Chechenka asked me 'Where's your shoes?'"

"I gave them to somebody."

"Show me!" she said.

"To one of yours. I pointed, it was Yasir," Vitaliy recalls.

Anya adds, "She yelled [to Yasir], 'We didn't come here for that! Give them back now.' And he gave them back [to Vitaliy], these [are] American army boots, super boots, that sell for around $200."[16]

"One even gave us water," Oksana remembers.

The sleeping gas pumped in under the stage by the police at the beginning of the storming of the building failed to knock out everybody at once. When the twelve Alfa and Vymel antiterror units entered the theater they engaged male terrorists in close-quarters combat in the corridors and on the stairs. Russian snipers took out terrorists standing near windows.

It's still unclear why Barayev, who was in an upstairs room splicing together his videotape of the theater siege, didn't detonate the bombs. The "Black Widows" would not have acted without his order. A male hostage featured in the documentary film *Terror in Moscow* remembers "one of the Chechen women kept reassuring us, saying, 'Don't worry. Without the order, I won't set off the bomb.'"

Apparently, they never got the order from Barayev. Electronic jamming may have prevented him from communicating it. Then, too, the terrorists may simply have decided to draw as many Russian Spetznaz into the theater as possible, fight to the very end, and then detonate the bombs. However, one hostage concluded they didn't want to kill anybody. "It was clear that they were not *shakhidi*—they wanted to live."

Shamil Basayev says there was another reason they didn't detonate their bombs—they couldn't! The detonators were "nonfunctional," "sabotaged." Akhmed Zakayev claims that Barayev's group had been infiltrated by an FSB agent. Anna Politkovskaya said that it was a GRU agent.

CASE CLOSED!

Some terrorists must have escaped. Russia's deputy interior minister said initially that an unknown number had fled but that one was picked up standing among a group of journalists outside. Other police sources said initially that about ten got away. Retired Army general-major Aleksandr Lyakhovsky says that the male terrorists were supposed to escape by means of an underground tunnel, leaving the young women behind to set off the bombs and create a diversion for their escape. Attorneys for Dubrovka victims point out that the 2006 chief investigator's report says that there were fifty-two terrorists involved in the attack but that only forty died in the storming of the theater. But the procurator general maintains that none escaped, that there were never more than forty-one terrorists, and that all were killed.

On 15 March 2006 the newspaper *Kommersant* printed a sensational story citing a document signed by the Moscow procurator's office saying that the investigation into the attack had confirmed that a Dubrovka female terrorist identified as Z. A. Daurova had managed to escape. Two days later the procurator's office issued a statement of clarification, explaining that Daurova had not escaped from the theater because she had never been there. Instead, she had been part of a backup group that was to conduct a series of diversionary terror attacks in the city to coincide with the theater's siege.

Besides Daurova another female suicide bomber belonged to this group, but her name is unknown. Four male members of the group were caught and convicted in 2004, including Alikhan Mezhiyev, who told of Daurova's role.

According to information published by the website www.NEWSru.com on 15 March 2006, Ruslan Elmurzayev telephoned Mezhiyev and asked that he spend the evening with two of his "relatives" who had just arrived in Moscow from Chechnya. Mezhiyev proceeded to pick up the two girls not far from the Dubrovka theater and started out for Elmurzayev's apartment. But about twenty minutes into the trip Mezhiyev became stuck in traffic near Okhotny Ryad. The news about the theater siege came over the radio while he was sitting there.

Hearing this, Daurova and her companion told Mezhiyev to drop them off at the closest subway station, which happened to be the Lenin State Library stop. Mizhiyev says that the women showed him their suicide belts and said they were going to blow up the station, but he wouldn't let them. Instead he took them to the apartment of another member of the group, Aslan Murdalov, where they changed clothes and ditched their belts.

In *The Wolves of Islam* I tell a slightly different version of events based on Mezhiyev's March 2004 trial testimony. Mezhiyev testified that Elmurzayev had called him on the mobile phone and asked to be picked up at the Kristall Casino on Proletarskaya Ulitsa because he had been in an automobile accident. But there had been no accident. When Mezhiyev arrived Elmurzayev instructed him to deliver the women with him to Pushkinskaya Square, in the center of Moscow; there they were to blow themselves up to coincide with the siege of the theater. But on the way Mezhiyev heard the news that the theater had already been taken; he aborted the mission and put the women on a homeward-bound train.

Kalchuk tells a third version. In it, the two bombers were supposed to carry out terror attacks in "populous and significant community areas" of Moscow for the purpose of causing further panic in Moscow, and Mezhiyev was to mount the operations. But after Dubrovka was seized, security around the city became so tight that Mezhiyev and the girls decided it was too risky to go ahead with the mission and called Elmurzayev in the theater to get his permission to call it off. A short while later, Elmurzayev telephoned back to tell him to buy train tickets for the girls instead.

In this version, Mezhiyev handed the women's belts over to H. H. Sobraliyev, another member of the team, who hid them in his Volkswagen Golf car, which he then loaned to his former wife. She and two of her male friends found the belts and tossed them into the Moscow River. Police recovered the belts on 25 and 26 October.

Authorities long kept the Dubrovka theater investigation open because they were looking for Daurova and two males also connected with the siege. They never found them. The case was finally closed in June 2007, because "the whereabouts of the three suspects is unknown."

SIX

Mountains of Bodies

*They showed me the mountain of bodies at Tushino. I saw for the first time
what it would look like. If I told you that I felt sorry for
them you wouldn't believe me.*
Zarema Muzhikoyeva, suicide bomber

DUBROVKA WAS A WATERSHED EVENT, creating a new dynamic, with
two fundamental and qualitative changes taking place on the Chechen side.
First, terror became the strategic weapon of choice. Second, Shamil Basayev
escalated the war by adopting the Palestinian model of suicide terror against
civilians.

"Black Widows" would soon return to Moscow, but time to regroup,
recruit, brainwash, and prepare a fresh cadre of capable women was needed.
So was cash—operations outside the North Caucasus would be costly. If
Dubrovka cost Basayev $50,000, which he claimed it did, payments to the
families of dead terrorists cost him several times more. But given the global
publicity Dubrovka generated, a healthy injection of foreign capital from
Osama bin Laden and others would soon be on its way. In the meantime,
shakhidas would hunt closer to home.

HUNTING MARIONETTES AND INVADERS

Alina—27 December 2002

In the early afternoon of Friday, 27 December 2002, three suicide bombers
crashed their large KamAZ truck and a UAZ jeep filled with a mix of ammo-
nium nitrate and other explosive material through the quadruple security

barriers guarding Chechnya's central government administrative complex in Grozny, the most heavily fortified structure in all of Chechnya. The first explosion left a twenty-foot-wide crater; the second was closer and tore off the entire façade of the building, as well as imploding several floors of the beautifully renovated four-story complex. Forty-eight people died instantly. The rubble trapped more. Within days the death toll had climbed to eighty-three, with over 150 people hospitalized, many of them missing limbs and crippled for life.

The bombers' vehicles bore Russian military license plates. Eyewitnesses say the drivers wore Russian military uniforms, looked "Slavic," spoke Russian, and flashed Russian military IDs as they maneuvered in and out of the maze of security checkpoints on the way to their target. But Basayev tells a slightly different story: "Yes . . . those behind the wheel were dressed in military uniforms, but a Chechen family—a man forty-three years old, his son, seventeen, and daughter, fifteen, carried out the bombing."

His details are a little off. What Basayev didn't say was that the driver of the truck, Gelani Tumriyev, was really one of his own field commanders, who had been given $18,000 to buy the truck, the jeep, and two tons of agricultural ammonium nitrate (for the explosive mix) from a farm in Ingushetia for the terror attack. Tumriyev's daughter, Alina, fifteen (she may have been as young as thirteen), rode beside him in the truck, while his friend Nural followed in the jeep.

Alina had had a pitiful childhood. Six years earlier Gelani had stolen her away from her Russian mother, Maria Volodina, who lived in the Russian city of Yaroslav. Ilyas had been born to a different Russian woman. Tumriyev kidnapped him too. Gelani Tumriyev was far from the ideal Chechen father. He neglected to provide financially for his children and only occasionally visited them. But he was good at hiding his two families from one another, at least until he took Alina and her half brother back to Achkoi-Martan to live with him. Multiple attempts by the mothers of the children to rescue them failed. It was easier for the boy; Ilyas adjusted to his new environment. But Alina never did. The child missed her mother. She begged her father to let her go home, but he stubbornly refused. Even attempts by Tumriyev's relatives failed to persuade him. Instead, he set out to convert Alina and her half brother to Wahhabism. Perhaps he succeeded. Anna Politkovskaya believed that Alina intended to avenge the death of her half brother, who had been killed fighting Russian soldiers in 2000.

Another explanation, equally as sinister, is that Tumriyev sacrificed his daughter for the good of the mission—a Chechen girl in a KamAZ truck might be suspicious, but a young Russian girl with distinctive Slavic features would not. She might even facilitate passage through Russian police checkpoints. Then too, Alina's job may have simply been to push the detonator button. But Basayev says he did that himself: "I pushed the button on the remote control explosive devices that were in the vehicles. I was watching from a distance and when the vehicles disappeared from eyesight and entered the premises of the puppet administration compound, I pushed the button." In those final moments, Alina probably didn't even realize what she was about to become.

"Juliet"—12 May 2003

Basayev put the finishing touches to his master terror plan, code named Operation Whirlwind, in the spring. In Chechnya he would kill as many "infidel occupiers, invaders," and their collaborators ("marionettes," as he called them) as possible, eliminate the pro-Moscow Chechen leadership before the October 2003 Chechen presidential election and the December parliamentary elections, and demonstrate that he and Maskhadov were as much in charge of Chechnya as President Putin and Akhmad Kadyrov.

Basayev targeted "marionettes" who survived the Tumriyev family attack first. A real Black Widow, Zarina Alikhanova, eager to end her miserable life, was dispatched for that. Born in Kazakhstan, Zarina was the only child of a Chechen officer in the Kazakh MVD and an Ingush mother who was a successful business woman in Almati. She studied at a German school. She excelled in dance and ballet, even starring as Juliet in a Prokofiyev production of *Romeo and Juliet* at the Alma Altinsky Opera and Ballet Theater.

"Juliet" met her "Romeo," Ramzan, a former Soviet Army officer and Dudayev National Guardsman, in Grozny during a visit to her aunt there in 1993. From the beginning, their young lives were destined for tragedy. They wed and dreamed of opening an exclusive ballet school, but then the first war came along and even in battle Zarina could not bear to leave "Romeo's" side, cooking and washing for him and nursing the wounded in his unit—sometimes even shooting too. Ramzan had no money after the war, because he wasn't being paid. They lived in poverty but refused to stop dreaming. Ramzan thought about quitting the Guards and opening a small hotel in his native Itum-Kalinsky District, but once again war stole everything, and like before, Zarina was by his side—until they walked into a minefield near Komsomolskoye in January 2001.

"Romeo" died in "Juliet's" arms as she carried and dragged him from the minefield. Her spirit was broken after that. Neighbors say she often spoke about how she wished she had died in that minefield too, about how she yearned to be by "Romeo's" side. That kind of talk didn't go unnoticed by Wahhabi suicide bomber recruiters eager to help, for the sizeable recruitment stipend they would receive.

At 10 AM, on 12 May 2003, Zarina and two male comrades slammed their KamAZ loaded with agricultural nitro, cement, and aluminum powder into the metal barrier protecting Nadterechny's district government administrative building, nearly demolishing the structure and destroying most of the adjoining FSB building and eight nearby village houses. "Shards of glass were flying all around us . . . and there were screams and moans from the many wounded women," a survivor with a bandaged and bloody head told a Russian television audience that night. "Juliet's" one-ton bomb killed sixty people, including six children and government administrators who had temporarily moved their offices from Grozny to Znamenskoye. Two hundred sixty-nine victims were wounded, and 111 people were hospitalized, fifty-seven of them in critical condition.

Akhmad Kadyrov demanded answers: "Where did the explosives come from?" Federal forces had stopped the truck more than once to check the driver's documents, but "no one bothered looking in the back." The story was a familiar one. A later official government version said that the explosives had been hidden under bags of cement, and that's why they hadn't been found.

Basayev was on a roll. In only two strikes his *shakhidas* had already killed 169 "marionettes" and wounded 579 more. The body was crippled. Now, he would cut off its head.

Satan's Servants—14 May 2003

The dead were still being collected in Znamenskoye when two "Black Widows" disguised as journalists approached the heavy security cordon surrounding Akhmad Kadyrov, Chechnya's chief administrator, as he was about to sit down with VIP guests at an afternoon religious festival attended by 15,000 people outside Iliskhan-Yurt.

Akhmad Kadyrov had earlier warned his security staff that *shakhi-das* might be lurking in the crowd. "It concerns some three female suicide bombers. . . . The information that an attempt is being prepared came from the special services. A recommendation has been made to me to be more vigilant," Kadyrov told Interfax following a visit to the United States for a United Nations General Assembly meeting. U.S. intelligence may have supplied that information.

The women had all the right credentials and equipment—press passes and shoulder bags, along with microphones and a video camera. "Let us through, we want to catch Kadyrov's last words," one of them shouted as Kadyrov's personal bodyguards intercepted them. That's when the bomber pushed her detonator button. The nail-embedded explosives around her waist shredded her torso into tiny bits of flesh, leaving only her head, and killed twenty-six other people, including a second *shakhida,* Zulai Abdurza-kova, fifty-two. One hundred fifty people were wounded. Though drenched in blood, Kadyrov, shielded by his bodyguards, four of whom had been killed, walked away unscathed.

"On a day like this, only Satan's servant could make an attempt on the lives of peaceful people, women, children, and the elderly," the tough but shaken Kadyrov told his public. "One tried to approach me after they were unsuccessful in getting close to the leader of Chechnya's anti-extremism movement Ramzan Kadyrov." Later on Akhmad Kadyrov said that two women had tried to kill him, but a third woman, their "curator," age fifty, had died too.

Four women were at the epicenter of the blast. Authorities were quick to identify forty-six-year-old widow Shakhidat Baymurodova (maiden name Abalayeva) as the perpetrator, but forensics would later prove that she was a victim, not the bomber. She died from only a small shrapnel wound to the temple. Baymurodova had been present because she was searching for her missing son and had a bag full of money to give Kadyrov to help her find him. Shakhidat's sister, seventy-year-old Aimani, was searching for her son too and died with Shakhidat.

Authorities later identified the real killer as Larisa Musalayeva, thirty-one, from the village of Kirov in the Zavodsky District of Grozny. She, like Alikhanova, had been easy to recruit. Relatives say she happily volunteered to kill Kadyrov to get revenge for her brother's death at the hands of Kady-rov's security forces the previous fall. Her brother Imran, who had been accused of helping organize the 27 December Grozny bombing, had blown himself up with a grenade on a bus full of people after being wounded in a gunfight with Kadyrov's men at the bus station in Malgobek, Ingushetia.

As before, Maskhadov played Arafat's role, denying any responsibility for the deadly Znamenskoye or the Iliskhan-Yurt attacks: "The [Ichkerian] President does not lead people who blow up themselves and others," he said.

But Basayev does! Despite failing to claim his main prize—Kadyrov's head—Basayev proudly took credit for killing civilians, proclaiming, "By the grace of Allah, *mujahideen* fighters from our suicide . . . brigade carried out two successful operations against the Russian occupiers and their local lackeys."

"We are the warriors of Allah," cried Basayev, promising that "this [terror] whirlwind will soon be everywhere."

Chechnya's interior minister claimed to have intelligence showing that Basayev had trained thirty-six more female suicide bombers. He was busy building a rich cadre of suicide bombers—men and women. The coming months would be ample proof of that, but he declined to confirm or deny Alkhanov's numbers. Instead, he promised to dispatch a few of them "beyond the boundaries of Chechnya" to attack military targets. He kept his promise.

Patience Kills—5 June 2003

For two days Samara resident Lidiya (Lida) Khaldykhoroyeva patiently stalked her prey, deliberately passing up tempting, though less valuable, targets near the Prokhladny Russian air force base in Mozdok, North Ossetia. But when the regularly scheduled base bus carrying helicopter pilots flying combat missions into Chechnya stopped at a railroad crossing to pick up its last load of passengers for the day, the girl, wearing a light overcoat with her shrapnel-filled bomb hidden underneath, smiled and politely asked the bus driver to let her on. He refused. That's when she detonated her bomb, killing herself and eighteen others, and wounding twenty-four, mostly female technical personnel who worked at the base.

An autopsy of Khaldykhoroyeva's brain fragments would determine that she had been under the influence of a psychotropic drug, perhaps because she was a last-minute replacement for another female, the infamous "Tverskaya Street bomber," Zarema Muzhikhoyeva, who had become ill with severe sinusitis and could not carry out the attack herself. Muzhikhoyeva confessed from her prison cell that she was supposed to have been the Moz-dok bus bomber but was sick that day, so Khaldykhoroyeva took her place. Her story was confirmed by Basayev associate Magomed Kodzoyev after his arrest for organizing the attack.

Yet Another Woman in a KamAZ—20 June 2003

By now, you would think, a Chechen woman driving a KamAZ truck would be shot on sight. At the very least, it seems inconceivable that a man and a woman in a big truck full of explosives could still freely transit Russian territory. But they could with the assistance of greed and corruption at security check points, and the terror attack on 20 June proved it. This time their target was the multistory ORB/ SOBR MVD police building around the corner from the procurator's office in Grozny.

The scenario was identical to Grozny and Znamenskoye. A man and a still unidentified woman crashed a KamAZ truck through the outer perimeter metal fence but failed to penetrate the large barriers providing a second defense around the building, falling short of their target by three hundred feet. Police fired into the truck's cab and detonated over nine hundred kilograms of explosives. The explosion killed six people and wounded another thirty-six, mostly residents of adjacent apartment buildings.

Death Is the Only Way Out—23 June 2003

Three days later, twenty-two-year-old Luiza Osmayeva died in a Grozny hospital after a shootout with police. The woman and two Chechen men dressed in camouflage fatigues had been in a Russian Army minibus headed to their target in the center of the city when OMON police intercepted them. A shootout ensued, killing both men and wounding Osmayeva.

Luiza lived just long enough to tell that she had been kidnapped in February, raped, and trained for four months to become a suicide bomber. She was also four months pregnant. Hers is a classic case in which a woman is shamed into becoming a suicide bomber because she is doomed to be shunned by her family and the rest of Chechen society because she has been raped, is unwed, and is pregnant to boot. "For me, death is the only way out. . . . Nobody needs me now. They [the handlers at the suicide camp] told me I was unclean and should go do my duty [kill myself]," she said in video-taped testimony on her deathbed.

KINGS AND CLOWNS

My Dear Zhaga—5 July 2003

It was a warm, sunny day in Moscow. It was also the Fourth of July, 2003, and I was on my way to the airport for a meeting with my publisher the next day. The manuscript for *The Wolves of Islam: Russia and the Faces of Chechen Terror* was finished. I expected an attack in Moscow soon, but I didn't imagine that on 5 July Basayev would begin an intensified terror campaign that would leave another 215 dead (including 14 suicide terrorists) and 530 people wounded over the next eleven months.

I heard the terrible news as soon as I arrived home: two of Basayev's female suicide bombers had blown themselves up at a Moscow rock concert—the annual Krylya (Wings) beer and rock festival at Tushino airfield.

The beautiful weather that Saturday brought out 40,000 young rock fans. The punk-rock group King and Clown was in full swing when twenty-year-old Zulikhan Yelikhadzhiyeva arrived at Tushino. After a long wait in the ticket line, she passed through the ticket verification and alcohol control checkpoints and headed for the line of people waiting at the security checkpoint, the last obstacle between her and the sea of spectators already on the airfield.

"She had a classic figure, but she was dressed a little strange," Alexei, a teenage boy behind her in line, recalls. "Despite the heat, she was wearing a light coat with something a little bulky, maybe books or a cosmetic bag, underneath. I couldn't tell."

Thirty feet from the metal detectors and the bomb-sniffing dog, the girl who had attracted Alexei's attention stopped abruptly. Taking out her mobile phone and saying something to somebody at the other end, she caught the eye of a vigilant young policeman. When she adjusted the bulky weight under her coat, he led her by the elbow out of the line. "That's when there was a small firecracker-like explosion," eyewitnesses recall. Zulikhan fell.

"What's your name, where did you come from?" the dazed policeman asked the girl lying on the ground in a pool of her own blood. The two pounds of plastic explosives in the suicide belt around her waist had only partially detonated, leaving a gaping hole in her stomach. "Leave me alone, I've failed. . . . I'll not meet Allah now," the girl sullenly replied, taking her last breath.

Minutes later another explosion, a hundred times more powerful, rang out. A second *shakhida,* Zinaida (Marem) Aliyeva, twenty-six, standing in the ticket line, had detonated her bomb, instantly killing eleven others. Seven more people died later in the hospital. The crowd, spellbound by the performance of the rock group Krematorii (Crematorium), hardly noticed the "loud clap" outside. "All I saw was a cloud of smoke," one spectator recalls. Nothing was left but Aliyeva's head and parts of her upper torso. Police let the show go on to avoid mass panic and a human stampede.

Zulikhan and her friend Zinaida had come to Moscow on a flight from Ingushetia in mid-May and rented an apartment together. Their arrival had attracted the attention of the police, but since a thorough search of their apartment had failed to turn up anything suspicious—and since their passports were in order—the women had been released.

Zulikhan's passport, found at the scene, identified her as a twenty-year-old unmarried girl from the city of Kurchaloi, Chechnya. But Yuzik says she had already been married twice to "Arab mercenaries," each one killed. But that's not why she went to Moscow. Before Zulikhan disappeared from home in early 2003 she had lived in Kurchaloi with her father, a younger sister, younger brother, and a stepbrother, Danilkhan, her same age and a fighter. Another brother, Magomed, was the "emir" of fighters in the Kurchaloyevsky District. Neighbors say that Zulikhan was a quiet and disciplined girl, "well known for her beauty." She enrolled in medical college in 2002 and studied hard. They describe her as a cultured girl, a "modern girl."

But Zulikhan did the forbidden—she fell in love with her stepbrother, Danilkhan (or "Zhaga," as she intimately called him). Several months before her appearance in Moscow she ran off with him to Dagestan. Yuzik says Zulikhan's parents thought she had been kidnapped by fighters, but Muzhikhoyeva, the next suicide bomber to appear in Moscow, said Zulikhan's parents had disowned her after she ran away with Danilkhan. The need to honorably absolve herself of the guilt and shame of this incestuous relationship with her stepbrother, so they could be together in paradise and escape the wrath of her relatives on earth, motivated her to become a *shakhida.* April 2003 entries in her diary, as well as an undelivered letter to Zhaga found in her pocket at Tushino, show that she saw martyrdom as the only way to get to heaven and be with Zhaga. Contrary to what the media reported, Danilkhan did not force her to become a suicide bomber, but Magomed did provide her the mechanism for "absolution."

"My dearest Zhaga is leaving this evening," she wrote on 14 April. "I will miss him terribly, but soon he'll come for me. . . . We had such a happy time today, but something within my soul isn't right. I laugh, but inside my heart cries. . . . This night I cried myself to sleep. I need him so much." The next day she writes: "Zarema, Nuseiba, Khadishta, and I laughed and joked. But all the time my heart was aching and wanting Zhaga so much. He doesn't understand how much I love him, how I would give my life for him if I had to. I don't fear death as much as I fear falling into the hands of my relatives."

Her departing letter to Zhaga says:

I have only one request of you; that you forgive me my little Zhaga. Don't think that I don't love you and don't think of you. I don't have anyone besides you in this world and it is for that reason that I became a *shakhida* on the path of Allah.

Please, I beg you; don't punish [take blood revenge] on anybody [for what I have done]. I am doing this on my own free will—nobody made me do it. . . . I don't want to live in this filthy world and go to hell. I am so fearful of this and of dragging you with me.

We are pushing one another into hell and for that reason we must go to paradise together. Makhmad [Zhaga], give my things to somebody. You are everything that I have. And if you like, I will show you there just how much I love you and will love you. Besides Allah and you, I don't need anybody else. . . . Nothing else matters to me; not here, not there.

She begged Zhaga to give up his guerrilla fight with Russia ("Let Allah judge them, not you") and become a *shakhid* too so they can be together:

Don't go to the forest [to fight] or anywhere else, just pick up a [suicide] belt and become a *shakhid* on the path to Allah and we will be together. . . . Don't live on this earth Zhaga. Come quickly to me. I will anxiously await you and will never let anybody else have you. Leave everything and everybody behind. They will get what they deserve from Allah; he will judge them, not you. Please, I am on my knees begging you to become a *shakhid*. I will anxiously wait for you. I love you, love you, and will always love you there in the sky.

Zulikhan was pregnant, all the more reason to become a *shakhida,* because of the shame of having a child out of wedlock. Zhaga never did do what Zulikhan wanted; he was captured two months later and is still serving a jail sentence.

All that is known about Zinaida Aliyeva (Yuzik identifies her as Marem Sharipova), the second Tushino bomber, is that she had lived with her fighter husband in the mountains and had become pregnant but was made to abort her baby on orders from her husband's commander. Then her husband was killed in a firefight, so she was left with no reason to live—at least, that is the story Zulikhan told Zarema Muzhikhoyeva.

What's in Your Bag?—9 July 2003

Four days after Tushino, on 9 July, twenty-three-year-old Zarema Muzhikhoyeva, an Ingush by birth from the village of Assinovskaya, began a long and strange seven-and-one-a-hour terror ordeal up Tverskaya Ulitsa, Moscow's main street.

There are two versions of Zarema's story, both told by her—the first to police right after her capture, the second to *Izvestiya* reporter Vadim Rechkalov a month before her March 2004 trial. Zarema initially told police that her mission was to blow up the Pushkinskaya Square McDonald's or the Yelki-Palki restaurant on Tverskaya Ulitsa, whichever had more customers. But in the *Izvestiya* version, her target was the smaller Mon Kafe, located at Mayakovskaya Square.

Zarema's ill-fated mission began at the Kremlin's Red Square at 4 PM. Her curator—Lida (Black Fatima) in the first version but a man, Igor (Ruslan), in the second—gave her explosives and several hundred rubles and dropped her off near the church of Vasilya Vlazhenovo with instructions to catch a cab to her target. Carrying her heavy bomb in her big, leather shoulder bag, Zarema did as she is told.

But in the first story the taxi driver took her to the small McDonald's beside the Central Telephone and Telegraph building on Tverskaya Ultisa, not the Pushkinskaya Square McDonald's at the top of the hill. If you have ever been to Moscow, you know the difference in the crowds at the two places. (The Pushkinskaya Square McDonald's is probably the busiest McDonald's in the world.) Not knowing her way around, it took her some time to make her way up Tverskaya. She eventually found Yelki-Palki, but the vigilant presence of the restaurant's security guard at the door scared her away. She turned around and headed down the steps and through the underground passageway to get to McDonald's on the other side of the street, but she found security guards in the passageway too, so she went back up to the street from which she had come.

For the next four and a half hours Zarema wandered around, not knowing what to do. At 10 PM, exhausted and scared, she walked into the Mon Kafe, sat down, opened her bag, and tried to detonate her bomb. But the bomb didn't go off. She went outside, checked the tumbler (on/off switch), went back inside, and tried again. Then she became hysterical and screamed in a mix of Russian and Chechen that she was going to blow up the place.

How she ended up an hour later at the upscale Imbir restaurant at No. 1 Tverskaya-Yamskaya is unclear. One media report said that Zarema and a Chechen man, Zarub Daduyev, left the Mon Kafe together and went to the Imbir with the intent of finding a more crowded restaurant to blow up. At 11 PM Dadayev entered the restaurant. Zarema waited outside, but then the police arrived.

Newspapers reported that Zarema yelled "I'll blow this place up!" as police demanded that she put down her bag. They then reportedly grabbed and handcuffed her and laid her bag on the sidewalk. But video film from an adjacent bank's security camera shows that she put the bag on the asphalt in front of the Imbir restaurant herself, then walked over to the bank's guards and said something to them. They or the Mon Kafe guards then detained her, and the police showed up only to put the handcuffs on and take her away.

For the next two hours the FSB tried unsuccessfully to destroy the bomb using a robotic hydro-canon. Thinking that it must be a dud, a young FSB explosives expert decided to get a closer look. The bomb blew up in his face.

Zarema told Rechkalov that she had made up nearly everything in her first statement to police, including the existence of Lida (Black Fatima), because she thought the court-appointed attorney who had visited her in jail right after her arrest was really someone sent by Igor. Zarema claimed that she took Lida's name from the *shakhida* who blew herself up in Mozdok on 4 June 2003, the imaginary scar on Lida's lip from Igor, and other parts of Lida's physical description from a Russian woman she had seen on Tverskaya Ulitsa. She had made it all up because she wanted Igor to believe that she really did try to detonate the bomb. She realized that her attorney was not someone sent by Igor only later when she heard the details of Lida's description broadcast over her prison-cell radio.

In the *Izvestiya* version Zarema says that she never entered the Mon Kafe at all but sat at a table outside the restaurant's entrance as she had been instructed to do. She didn't order. When a waiter approached her, she stood up and walked away. Then she went back to her table. She tried to make herself look suspicious so she would get caught. Once when a man from another table approached she got up and walked to the other side of the street and stood between two cars. There she opened the pocket of her bag and fooled with the tumbler—"to kill time, so Igor's people following her wouldn't get suspicious." She again returned to her table. Zarema finally got the attention of two guards standing inside the restaurant's doorway by making faces and sticking her tongue out at them. When they approached, she stood up and backed off.

"Do you have a passport?" one of then asked.

"No!"

They took another step forward and asked, "Are you Russian?"

They got a second "No!"

"What do you have in your bag?" they asked.

"Explosives!" Zarema answers. "A suicide belt."

They shout: "What? You're lying!"

"So I opened my bag, took a step forward and showed them," she says. "They told me to get out of there, so I walked away."

Zarema had flown into Moscow from Nazran on 3 July using her own passport. In the first story Lida picked her up at Vnukovo Airport and whisked her away to a safe house in the village of Tolstopaltsyevo, a little over a hundred kilometers outside Moscow. In the *Izvestiya* story, she took a cab to the Rus café near the Paveletskaya Metro station, where Ruslan (who now calls himself Igor) was waiting for her, and from there they went in his car to Tolstopaltsyevo. However, in her court trial, the taxi driver said that he took her straight to Tolstopaltsyevo from the airport.

She stayed in the house at Tolstopaltsyevo with Igor (Ruslan) and Andrei (real name Arbi Khabrailov, age thirty-four), "our bodyguard and explosives expert." The owner of the house testified in court that he had rented the house to one Igor Saayev, whose real name was Ruslan Saayev, thirty-three, and who was later killed in Chechnya in a gunfight with police.

The day after Zarema's arrival in Moscow Igor brought Zulikhan and Marem to stay with them. Igor came home the evening of the Tushino bombing and asked if Zarema had seen the news on television. "They showed me the mountain of bodies at Tushino," she says. "I saw for the first time what it would look like. If I told you [Rechkalov] that I felt sorry for them you wouldn't believe me. Frankly speaking, I felt sorry for Zulikhan more than the others because I had seen her alive that morning. And if you really want the truth, I felt more sorry for myself."

Zarema went through the ritual videotaping the night before her mission so everybody back home could see that she was a hero. Igor gave her the customary black dress, scarf, a veil, and a piece of paper with a message, written in big letters, which she had to read in front of the video camera. As the videotape rolled, she read from the paper, held by Igor: "My day has come. Tomorrow, I will go against the unbelievers in the name of Allah, in the name of myself and you, and in the name of peace."

Igor promised to give her grandparents a copy of the tape, because she wanted them to know that she was a "good girl after all, and that I wouldn't bother them anymore."

She got her bomb instructions the next morning after prayers. They were technical and tedious. Andrei told her that she would not wear a suicide belt around her waist but carry her bomb in a shoulder bag. Then he explained how he had attached the four detonators to the bomb to ensure that the Tushino problem (failure of Zulikhan's bomb to fully detonate) would not happen again; how he had made technical modifications to ensure maximum destruction; how the wires were attached; and how to use the on/off tumbler (switch) to detonate the bomb. Finally, "Andrei told me that I should stand up, face toward the café, and rest the bag on my breast before switching the tumbler to 'on,' so the force of the explosion would reach the people inside."

When the instruction was over Zarema dressed up to look like a modern Moscow girl—in new blue jeans, T-shirt, sneakers, a baseball cap, and dark sunglasses. "I looked in the mirror and liked the way I looked. I had never dressed this way. For a moment I was happy," she recalls, before she and Igor left for Moscow.

Zarema was charged with terrorism, murder, criminal conspiracy, and unlawful possession of explosives. Her attorney said that she intentionally tried to get caught and did not attempt to detonate the explosives and therefore was not guilty of terrorism. The *Izvestiya* story conveniently built that defense. To further back up her story Zarema said that she had been sent to Mozdok a month earlier to blow up a military bus there (the one Lidya attacked) but couldn't do that either. "I understood then that I could never do such a thing." She said she made up a story about the bus not arriving on time as an excuse for not carrying out the bombing. She also claimed she couldn't do it because she was sick. Zarema also says that she would have run away from Tolstopaltsyevo, but Igor constantly reminded her that his people were watching the house. She was afraid they would kill her, a death that would not land her in heaven. So she decided to get caught and hide in prison instead.

Zarema helped the MVD and FSB find explosives in Moscow, Ingushetia, and Chechnya, and she provided information leading to the arrest of thirteen of Basayev's people. Acting on her information, police raided the single-story house and garage in Tolstopaltsyevo, where they found a half-dozen suicide belts buried in the backyard. But in court the prosecution stuck to Zarema's original story. The government's chief investigator testified that Zarema had told her that she had come to Moscow specifically to carry out a terror act and that she had planned to blow up the Pushkinskaya Square McDonald's. However, if the court testimony by bomb experts is true, she may well have changed her mind. They say that the detonators on her bomb were attached to two separate tumblers, so that if one did not work the other one would. "She could have detonated the bomb if she had really wanted to," they concluded.

The jury found her guilty on all counts. Hearing the verdict, she stood up and shouted: "When I get out of jail in twenty or twenty-five years, I'm going to come back and blow you all up! You made a terrorist out of me and I will come back and finish what I didn't do on Tverskaya." But the judge's lighter sentence of twenty years in a general woman's prison instead of the customary "strict regime" may have made her change her mind. "Do you understand the sentence?" the judge asked. "No problem, your honor," she said, smiling.

Judge Peter Studner linked Zarema's act of terrorism to the fact that she had joined a Wahhabi *djamaat* in Chechnya in December 2002 and six months later had become a member of a group organizing terror acts in Grozny. He said that she had been carrying at least seven kilograms of explosives and had twice tried to detonate the bomb on Tverskaya Ulitsa.

Zarema claims that money, not religious conviction, motivated her. She recounts in the *Izvestiya* article how her mother had abandoned her when she was ten months old and her father died when she was seven. Her husband, a businessman twenty years her senior, was killed in a business dispute while she was pregnant, so in good Chechen tradition her in-laws took her little girl when she was born and gave the child to her dead husband's brother to raise. Zarema lived with her grandmother, because her own home had been destroyed by artillery fire in the second war.

Zarema says she was desperate to get her daughter back. She had relatives in Moscow she could stay with, so she concocted a plan to steal her grandmother's jewelry, valued at eight hundred dollars, to finance a new life. She took the jewelry, hidden at her aunt's house, and sold it at an Ingush market for six hundred dollars, then went to collect her daughter on the pretext of a visit. Her mistake was leaving a note telling her plans to her grandmother, who summoned relatives to intercept her and the little girl at the airport.

Because of the huge family scandal Zarema had created her aunt told her that it would be better if she were dead. So she thought, "What a great idea!" Zarema figured out a way to die with dignity and, at the same time, repay her eight-hundred-dollar debt. She went to Raisa Ganiyeva for help. Zarema heard that a martyr's family would receive a thousand dollars. By killing herself Zarema would be able to pay off her debt and have a little left over for her daughter. It was all so logical.

THE INFERNO

Suicide Belts Made to Order—27 July 2003

After an early summer of hunting in Moscow, "Black Widows" briefly returned to the hunt, closer to home.

On 27 July 2003 twenty-six-year-old Imana Khachukayeva walked up to the base in Totsin-Yurt, Chechnya, that housed Ramzan Kadyrov's special security unit to get even for the killing of her brother by his security forces. But observant guards ordered her to halt and fired warning shots. That's when she blew herself up, in what seems to have been a spontaneous act, except for her Wahhabi-crafted suicide belt. Any grieving woman now seemed to be able to get her hands on one.

The Hospital—1 August 2003

Five days later, on 1 August, fifty Russian soldiers, doctors, and nurses perished when yet another explosives-laden KamAZ truck (the fourth in nine months) rammed full speed into the 58th Army's Military Hospital No. 458

in Mozdok, North Ossetia. The structure turned into an instant inferno. The truck bomb, driven by a man, with a female passenger controlling the detonator, was able to completely destroy the four-story block building in which all military personnel wounded in Chechnya were cared for. The structure was defenseless because the hospital's security commandant had failed to erect concrete security barriers, in violation of a direct order by the minister of defense.

A Fighter of Nogai Nationality—15 September 2003

It happened again on 15 September. A man and his wife attempted to crash their lighter GAZ-53 truck into the newly constructed three-story, concrete FSB building in Magas, Ingushetia. But their three-hundred-kilogram bomb blew up five meters short of its target. Nevertheless the explosion killed three and sent the building's roof flying, broke windows, knocked down doors, and destroyed much of the interior. It also put a huge hole in the ground and left a tangled mess of cars in the parking lot. A man and a woman, both sitting in cars parked near the building, perished instantly. A third person died at the hospital. Another twenty-eight people were hospitalized.

Emir Assasula, the self-described "Ingush Chief of Staff" of Basayev's Islamic Brigade, told kavkazcenter.com that the attack had been a joint operation with the "Stavropol staff" of the Islamic Brigade and that the operation had been carried out by a fighter of Nogai nationality and his wife.

Yessentuki—5 December 2003

A series of homemade bombs hidden at bus stops and on railroad tracks in the fall of 2003 targeted commuters, including university students traveling on a train near Kislovodsk in southern Russia, killing six people and wounding thirty on 3 December.

Two days later three *shakhidas* and a man attacked a train packed with students and other passengers as it departed from the station in Yessentuki at eight o'clock in the morning. The huge explosion ripped the carriage in half, killing forty-two people and hospitalizing two hundred others. The remains of a male bomber were found with hand grenades still taped to his legs. Two bombers jumped from the train just before the explosion. The third woman survived the blast but later died in the hospital. Police never released any of the names.

WHERE IS YOUR STATE DUMA?

Dirty Shoes—9 December 2003

On 9 December 2003 I was sitting in my office on Tverskaya Ulitsa just before noon when another of Basayev's *shakhidas* struck just down the block, around the corner from the Russian State Duma. "Where is your Duma?" she had asked a businessman coming out of the main entrance of the National Hotel at the intersection of Makhovya and Tveskaya streets. But her bomb had cut his answer short. The explosion all but demolished her body.

"I saw these bits of flesh, these fatty chunks of flesh scattered everywhere. It was just ——ing awful," a British traveler at the hotel told the *Moscow Times* newspaper. The bomber's head was all that was left, close-up photos of which were published in the *Kommersant Daily* the next day.

A second woman, originally thought to be an accomplice, died too, as did three passersby. The fifty-year-old businessman's body was found face up in front of an expensive Mercedes parked at the hotel's entrance. A uniformed parking lot attendant and a woman in a black dress fell farther from the car. A sixth person passed away on the way to the hospital. Fifteen others were wounded and hospitalized. One eyewitness saw three young girls "trying desperately to get to their knees, but who kept falling back because their legs wouldn't support them. Soot covered their faces and the head of the third girl was very bloody."

I tried but couldn't get close enough to get a good look.

A single female bomber had carried out the attack. Fifteen minutes earlier, two women, one later positively identified as the bomber, had asked a man near the Lenin State Library Metro station how to find the Russian State Duma. He didn't know. The unidentified bomber, in her mid-thirties, had explosives and bomb components identical to those found at Tushino and on Tverskaya Ulitsa hidden in a black shoulder bag like the one carried by Zarema Muzhikhoyeva.

The bomber was identified nine months later as twenty-four-year-old Khedizhi Mangeriyeva, the widow of Chechen field commander Ruslan Mangeriyev, who died in a firefight in the village of Avturi in the early summer of 2003. Dirt from her shoes indicated that she had come from the western region of the North Caucasus. No DNA testing was done, but her parents, Ramzan and Malika Magomadova, positively identified her head.

The bomber's "curator," described as an older woman, short in stature, was thought to be the same "Black Fatima" that had figured in the Tushino and Tverskaya bombings. A new police sketch of her was nearly identical to the one taken from an eyewitness at Tushino.

The bombing came only days after elections to the Russian State Duma—her likely target. For some reason she detonated her bomb early. The attack might also have been intended to mark the ninth anniversary of the start of the 1994–96 war with Russia. But kavkazcenter.com and Maskhadov's "Press Office of Ichkeria's Foreign Ministry" said that neither was the case. Both initially alleged that the bombing had been "organized and directed by Russian secret services and military intelligence for propaganda purposes," just as "the FSB was responsible for the Yessentuki train bombing" days earlier. At the end of the month, though, Basayev acknowledged that "they [both bombings] were pre-planned combat operations . . . carried out by our brigade's fighters."

The Emergency Squad Girl—5 March 2004

Basayev planned more attacks in Moscow but Zara Murazaliyeva, one of his suicide bomber recruiters, foolishly spoiled one of them. Moscow police arrested her in early March 2004 for failure to have the required Moscow address registration and for possession of a small amount (196 grams) of "Plastit-4" explosives. She says they planted it.[1] A Moscow city court found that she had been trained in a suicide-bomber training camp in Baku run by Chechens and that she had come to Moscow in September 2003 to recruit teenage girls for suicide bombing. On 19 January 2005 she was given nine years behind bars for preparing a terrorist act, involving other people in a terrorist plot, and illegally acquiring and storing explosives.

Zara's presence in Moscow had first attracted the attention of police when they picked her up in December 2003 in a routine passport check for failing to register her Moscow address. She had done nothing suspicious, but in light of the earlier Tushino bombings, police decided to keep an eye on her anyway. A Chechen policeman with the Moscow Directorate for Fighting Organized Crime Control (UBOP), Said Akhmayev, kindly arranged her release and offered to put her up in an apartment that he said belonged to a friend. It was equipped with secret audio and video surveillance.

Over the next few weeks investigators learned that Zara liked to hang out in places frequented by girls sixteen or seventeen years old and talk to them about Islam and the injustices of the war in Chechnya. Police became suspicious that she might be trying to recruit suicide bombers.

Zara, along with two teenage Russian girls she had befriended, (Darya) Dasha Voronova and Annya Kulikova, both of whom had recently converted to Islam, soon moved into a small apartment on Boris Galyshkin Street, in the Yugo-Zapadnaya region of Moscow. According to the court, Zara recruited the girls to become suicide bombers in a plot to blow up the ritzy Okhotny Ryad underground shopping complex in Moscow. They visited the multilevel underground complex together in January and February, and Zara took numerous photographs. Police recovered twelve photos of escalators taken on 3 January 2004. They also taped sixteen secret video and audio cassettes of conversations and songs by a Chechen musician calling for Jihad. The videos show Zara glorifying Jihad and suicide bombings to Dasha and Annya. Several books on Islam and Wahhabi literature were also taken from their apartment.

The girls told the court that Zara had cast a "strong psychological spell" over them. They read Wahhabi religious literature together every evening and went out to pray at a mosque on Prospekt Mira. Dasha wrote in her diary after meeting Zara: "Albina [the name Zara used] came to me and Annya, two stupid girls who were raised in riches, to help us understand the religious character of this war. I walked around in comatose when I remembered her words about how Chechens hated Russians. But I will participate in Jihad. I will fight, and begin to defend these oppressed people in the far corners of the mountains."

In court, Dasha recanted her earlier incriminating statements to police. "Nobody prepared me to become a *shakhida*," she told the judge, then, looking at Zara, said: "I was simply under her influence twenty-four hours a day. She commanded us in the minutest detail, and her stories stirred intense emotion." Dasha said she had given up Islam: "I wouldn't say that I have undergone tremendous change in the last few months, I just don't observe Islam anymore."

Annya, on the other hand, came to court dressed in a headscarf and traditional Muslim dress and said that Zara was an old friend, that they had lived together in a *djamaat*, studied Islam, and engaged in religious rituals together but had never had any discussion about a terror act. She contradicted her earlier statements to police. "Why?" the prosecutor asked; "I didn't correctly understand the investigator," she replied. The court questioned the girls' parents. Dasha's father testified that his daughter had fallen under Albina's strong influence. When the court asked him why he didn't remove his daughter from the apartment, he wasn't able to answer.

Zara's mother told the court: "I didn't want Zara to come to Moscow. I was afraid for her because she didn't have any friends here. But she got a job [as an insurance agent] and I visited here at the end of February. Days later, I saw over television that she had been arrested with explosives in her possession. I don't believe she had explosives. In her childhood they called her the 'the emergency squad [girl]'—she helped everybody. Now she needs help." Her mother said the family had no close relatives who had suffered either in the first or second wars and that therefore her daughter had no motive to become a *shakhida*.

Zara told a different story. She said she was framed, that she had been stopped for a document check in Kitay-Gorod and that police at the station planted the explosives. They fingerprinted her and promised to let her go. After she washed her hands and picked up her purse to leave, she noticed it was heavier than before. She was stopped on her way out the door and asked to open her purse. Two bricks of plastic explosives wrapped in foil were found inside.

When asked if she would like to make a statement before the judge retired to consider the verdict, Zara accused investigators of making everything up. Then she said, to applause in the courtroom, "There will never be any victory if you fight terrorism this way."

Zara had been born in the Naursky District of Chechnya. At the time of her arrest she was registered as a student in the "third course" of the day-time department of the Linguistics University of Pyatigorsk but was working as an insurance agent in Moscow. Until she left for Moscow in September 2003 she lived with her family in the *stanitsa* of Naurskaya. Her brother Ilyas is a junior police sergeant there.

As horrible as the terror attacks in the winter of 2002–2003 were, they still did not extract the kind of "maximum damage" that Basayev had promised Russia after Dubrovka. That required a super-sensational act of terrorism. The 6 February 2004 bombing of the Green Line subway train by a male suicide bomber, which killed fifty people, didn't qualify either; even the 9 May 2004 killing of President Kadyrov by a bomb cemented into a pillar next to where he was speaking at Grozny's Dinamo Statium wasn't enough. I finished writing *The Wolves of Islam* in the early fall of 2003, predicting that "the Kremlin should expect such an event before the first anniversary of the Dubrovka siege." I was wrong; it came eleven months later.

TOY SELLERS OF THE "ISLAMBOULI BRIGADE"

Nine Seconds—24 August 2004

Go to the market in Grozny and you might still bump into a *shakhida;* it's been a fertile breeding ground for them. But it's hard to imagine that anyone could commit more heinous crimes than four market sellers who visited Moscow in the summer of 2004.

On 24 August 2004 Siber Airlines Flight 1047 bound for the Russian resort city of Sochi with forty-six passengers and crew aboard departed Moscow's bustling Domodedovo airport on time at 9:40 PM. A second airliner, a Volgo-Aviaexpress Tu-134 flying to Volvograd with forty-three passengers and crew, followed forty minutes later. Shortly before eleven o'clock both planes fell out of the sky, their tail sections blown away by powerful explosions, killing ninety passengers and crew.

The planes' flight recorders and wreckage showed no signs of a hijacking or an assault on cabin crews but did indicate nearly simultaneous explosions (nine seconds apart) in the passenger cabins—one in seat 19F (near the rear of the plane on the right side) on Flight 1047, the other in seat row 25, also on the right side on the Tu-134. Traces of the explosive Hexogen were found in both planes at the crash sites in the Rostov and Tula regions.

Reminiscent of the 9/11 attack on America, an entity claiming to be the Al- Qaeda-associated "Islambuli Brigades" proclaims on the Internet:

> We in the Islambuli Brigades declare that our *mujahideen* managed to hijack two Russian planes with a team of five *mujahideen* on each plane, and the *mujahideen* were crowned with success despite problems they initially encountered.
>
> Russia's slaughter of Muslims is continuing and will not stop except for a bloody war. Our *mujahideen* were able with God's help to deal a first strike, which will be followed by other operations in a campaign aimed at helping our Muslim brothers in Chechnya and other Muslim countries enduring Russia's atheism.

But was this really the work of the same group that assassinated Egypt's President Anwar Sadat in 1981 and claimed responsibility for the attempted assassination of Pakistani finance minister Shaukat Aziz in July 2004? Maybe, but first investigators wanted to know who had been sitting in seat 19F and whether there was a link with anyone on the Volgograd plane.

As the investigators began to piece the puzzle together they learned that thirty-seven-year-old Satsita Dzhebirkhanova, from the Kurchalo-yevsky District of Chechnya, had occupied seat 19F. Sibir counter personnel remembered her well, because she had been the last passenger to be seated on the plane; boarding registration had closed. She had no carry-on luggage. Her Grozny flat mate, twenty-seven-year-old Amnat (Amanat) Nagayeva, from the rebellious Vedensky District of Chechnya, was on the Volgograd plane. Evidence quickly pointed to the probability that Chechen *shakhidas* had killed again, not an Al-Qaeda cell.

Still, this was a grave development, because with forged visas (in 2003 you could buy one at Moscow's Sheremetovo airport), "Black Widows" might just as easily have boarded one of the weekly flights from Moscow to New York, Washington, D.C., London, or Paris. I flew out of Sheremetova earlier that summer and saw a mother and young boy with a toy pistol in his pocket successfully pass through the first security checkpoint at the airport. The "gun" wasn't found until boarding began. The mother was yelled at, "fined" on the spot, the "weapon" was confiscated, and the boy was still crying as they boarded the plane.

If lax airport security was responsible in this case, it was also to blame for the attacks. A missed flight, a helpful ticket scalper, negligent airport security, a bribe-taking, and a complicated sequence of events and mishaps made the downing of the two planes possible.

According to the court case against the negligent police captain who failed to properly process the two women through security, Amnat, Satsita, and two other Chechen women—Amnat's sister Rosa, twenty-nine, and her childhood friend, twenty-seven-year-old Maryam Yusupovna Taburova—flew to Domodedovo from Makhachkala, Dagestan, together, arriving at 7:45 PM on 24 August. All four had left Chechnya two days earlier for Baku to buy school items to sell at Grozny's central market. They were last seen at the Khasavyurt bus station waving goodbye to a friend.

When they arrived at Domodedovo Rosa and Maryam rushed outside and disappeared. A car was waiting for them. Inside, Amnat, and Satsita sought out Armen Arutyunov, a ticket scalper and former employee of Sibir airlines now peddling black-market tickets. Though not part of the conspiracy, he sold the girls tickets to Sochi and Volgograd.

But there was a problem. Satsita could only get a flight out the next morning. That wouldn't do. She desperately needed to be on Flight 1047, so she could be in the air at the same time as Amnat, but check-in registration had already closed. However, Arutyunov spoke with his old friend Nikolai Korenkov at the Sibir counter, who for a thousand-ruble note put Satsita on Flight 1047. Then Amnat ran into difficulty. She was supposed to take Sibir Flight 1167 at 9:21 PM but also failed to make it before boarding closed. Arutyunov booked her on the 10:20 PM Volga-Aviaekspress Flight 1303 to Volgograd.

How the two women coordinated the detonations of their bombs within nine seconds of one another remains a mystery. The more important question, though, is, how did the girls get their bombs aboard the planes? Presumably they wore suicide belts, but air force general Vladimir Mikhailov believes the explosives were smuggled aboard by airport personnel and the suicide bombers just activated them.

Negligence had allowed Amnat and Satsita to bypass the normally stringent security check. Police captain Mikhail Artamonov's subordinates did take the women aside, collect their passports, and turn them over to him, but for unexplained reasons—perhaps because they looked like just two sweet girls in a hurry to catch their flights—Artamonov let them proceed, for which he is now serving prison time.

Chaos reigned at the airport that night. Passengers scrambled to catch their flights after being delayed by the huge traffic jam on Kashirskoye Shosse caused by an explosion at a bus stop. Someone had deliberately detonated a bomb to disrupt traffic or, as investigators speculate, Rosa or Maryam blew up the bus stop instead of boarding a bus to Domodedovo and blowing up the bus, as they had been supposed to do.

Amnat's and Satsita's passports were found at the crash sites. Satsita's body was in tiny pieces, while Amnat's severely damaged torso was found in the aircraft's tail section. Most of the other bodies were "whole." Arutyunov and airline counter personnel positively identified both Amnat and Satsita from family photographs.

In early September *Rossiiskaya Gazeta* caused a stir by reporting that Amnat could not have been aboard the aircraft, because she had been found alive, selling toys in the Rostovskaya Oblast. Local police said the passport used in her name at the airport had been a fake. But the FSB quickly refuted this.

The girls had no previous criminal record and had been unknown to authorities. Six months earlier Amnat, Satsita, Rosa, and Maryam had rented an apartment together in a dilapidated building across the street from the market in Grozny. A woman with grey eyes and long, flowing, pitch-black hair, Amnat was born in 1974 in a large brick house in the little village of Tevzan in the Vedensky District but had lived for a long time in Russia's Rostovskya Oblast. Her father died in the 1980s. The family moved back to the Vedensky District before the second war to get Amnat away from a foreigner she had secretly married.

The Nagayev family was large. Besides Amnat and Rosa there was a third sister, Amina (Asma), who lived at home, and a fourth sister, Bayan, who lived in Moscow, and six brothers. One of the boys, Uvais, a fighter, disappeared in 2001; according to the village head unidentified armed men took him from the family home in the spring. Amnat's older brother, Isa, said Amnat may have been seeking revenge for Uvais's death, but police discount this motive.

In an interview with *Komsomolskaya pravda*'s Dmitriy Steshin, her younger sister Amina described Rosa as a "quiet, kind girl, who never talked about such things (terrorism). Rosa was very sick." Rosa's mother Taos told *Russia Newsweek* reporter Oleg Rashidov in an interview in Tevzan, "She was an epileptic for the last five years. Look at the photographs; she was in bed all the time. She only became better recently, and her sisters began to take her to the market in Grozny."

In the middle of August Rosa's thirteen-year-old son had been picked up during a cleansing operation in the village of Alkhan Kala. Rosa bought his freedom for $2,500, but not before he had been tortured with cigarette burns on his back and between his fingers.

Satsita Dzhebirkhanova was divorced and had eight sisters and two brothers living. A brother, Saidkhamzat, who had worked in the Shariah court and was active in the Peoples of Dagestan and Chechnya Congress, was killed in 1998 in Dagestan. Basayev had sent him there to do something, but somebody shot him and his three bodyguards. Her other brother, Khusein, says that Russians had nothing to do with Saidkhamzat's death and that therefore revenge can be ruled out as a motive for his sister's act of terrorism.

Satsita was childless. Her father died from cancer in 1995, her mother from an acute illness in 2001. Until she moved to Grozny Satsita lived in her father's house in the village of Mairtup with the widow of her brother. She began selling at the market in 2003. According to Khusein, she had never been to Moscow or flown on an airplane before, but the FSB says that's not true, that she and Maryam Taburova often visited Moscow and that Satsita even had temporary address registration there. Khusein last saw his sister two weeks prior to the attack. She came home and asked about the family but was in a hurry to leave. She didn't stay the night as she usually did.

Maryam Taburova's mother, who also sold at the market, lived with the four girls in Grozny. She last saw her unmarried daughter at 6 AM on 22 August. "That morning she behaved normally. I didn't see any strange people hanging around my daughter. Nobody visited us. At the bazaar she didn't become acquainted with anybody suspicious. Nothing changed, nothing in behavior or clothing. There were no Wahhabi books at home. I don't think she even had any books" (she couldn't read), her mother told reporters.

Maryam had been to Baku only once. This time she had 20,000 rubles of her own money and some cash that her sister had given her to buy school items, brief cases, underwear, and the *bantiki* hair ribbons that little girls like to wear.

Rizhskaya—31 August 2004

Hardly any Russians canceled their flights because of the crashes, but panic sometimes spread whenever a Chechen woman boarded a Russian plane. Two women wearing Muslim clothing on Russian charter KrasAir Flight 2212 preparing to depart from Sharem el Sheikh, Egypt, at 11:45 for Moscow on 31 August were booted off for "acting suspiciously." They had prayed and then locked themselves in the aircraft's toilets. Passengers demanded that the pilot remove the women from the plane. He did.

Back in Moscow the scene at the Rizhskaya subway station looked like a giant meat grinder had been at work. Seven incomplete bodies lay on the ground at the station's entrance. One was disemboweled; another was missing an arm. Ripped pieces of wet human flesh and puddles of blood littered the filthy sidewalk. The leg of the suicide bomber was next to a burned-out car; her head, catapulted by the blast, was somewhere else. Some of the fifty-one dazed and wounded, among them eleven women and eight children, were sitting or trying to stand but toppling over. One boy walked a few meters, then fell. Three more would later die in intensive care.

The FSB immediately identified Amnat's sister Rosa as the bomber. Days later she was "positively" identified by "medical records which confirm that she had a scar on her skull identical to the one found on the recovered head." Other reporting said she was identified by her "fingers." Authorities would shortly recant these statements.

The bomber, whoever she was, arrived at the Rizhskaya subway station at 8:08 PM and had intended to go inside but, seeing two policemen at the entrance checking passports, hesitated. She caught the eye of police sergeant Aleksei Yegorov, who headed straight for her. That's when she turned away, walked between two cars, and detonated the bomb.

One eyewitness says he thought she threw the bomb under a car. Another, Alexei Bordin, remembers: "I walked out of the Krestovsky store [across the street] with my mother when a white car—I didn't see the make—blew up. People came running out of the Metro with fire extinguishers and tried to put out the blaze, then there was another explosion and the car again rocked." A second car caught fire, setting off secondary fuel-tank explosions and breaking glass out of the Metro entrance and the Krestovsky store.

After denying that they had had anything to do with it, the "Islambuli Brigades" claimed credit for this attack too. A 31 August Internet posting read:

> We in the Islambuli Brigades declare our responsibility for this operation, even though we denied it before because the news had not reached us by that time
>
> This heroic operation, as we warned you, is an extension of a wave of support and assistance to the Chechen Muslims. Allah willing, this will continue with coming waves until we humiliate the infidel country known as Russia and launch attacks on the evil Putin, who had carried out the slaughter of Muslims time and again ever since he took a tyrannical leadership position.

But the FSB says that "Muslim Society No. 3"—headed by Basayev subordinate and Karachai *djamaat* leader Achemez Gochiyayev, the mastermind behind the 1999 apartment-building bombings, which killed hundreds—was the real terror group behind the attacks.

How does the FSB know? One of the bomber's victims was her handler and a known subordinate of Gochiyayev's. On 26 September Moscow's deputy procurator, Vladimir Yudin, told a television audience that the bomber had had an accomplice named Nikolai Kitkeyev, a Wahhabi resident of the

Karachyevo-Cherkessiya Republic, who was killed at Rizhskaya. He was initially identified as Nikolai Samygin, but when no one came to claim his body at the morgue police became suspicious and checked him out further. Forensics determined that Samygin and Kitkeyev were the same man, leading investigators back to Gochiyayev and the conclusion that he had organized the terror attacks aboard the planes.

WE DON'T WANT TO KILL CHILDREN—
1–3 SEPTEMBER 2004

With the celebration of colorful balloons, bouquets of flowers, music, glowing children in their fresh, new school uniforms, and the crowd of proud parents and onlookers, there was an especially festive atmosphere on the sunny morning of 1 September at Secondary School No. 1 in Beslan, North Ossetia. It was, after all, the beginning of the new school year. But screaming armed men and "Black Widows" quickly spoiled the 9 AM festivities in the school yard.

The scene became surreal.

Twenty-one-year-old Kazik Torchin and others remember bearded, masked men, armed to the teeth and crying "*Allah Akhbar,*" jumping out of a "tented" GAZ-66 truck and firing into the air, shooting a fleeing girl and a father who had pulled a pistol out of his pocket to defend himself. The gunmen began to round up a thousand human beings.

A grotesque masked terrorist stood in the doorway of the school chanting, "Russians, Russians, come here," cynically beckoning children with handfuls of chocolate candies. Elsewhere, "Black Widows" in their long, flowing black robes with suicide belts strapped around their waists and pistols in their hands headed straight for the courtyard and the formation of children, who tried to run away but couldn't, because their exit was blocked.

How many "Black Widows" did Torchin and others see? He swears there were four. But shock might have played tricks with his mind. Zaur Dzafarov saw only two, but then his vision was blurred by men throwing smoke grenades while "trying to encircle us." Russia says there were only two—Rosa Nagayeva and Maryam Taburova. Narpasha Kulayev swore in court testimony that only two women joined militants at a training camp in the woods near the Ingushetian village of Psedakh the day before the siege. Surviving hostage Larisa Mamitova, a mother and doctor, also says that she saw only two but didn't see the body of the second one among the terrorists she was later asked to identify. Other court testimony says there were more and that some escaped.

Vasily K——, a member of a Southern Federal Okrug Spetznaz unit participating in the rescue mission at the school on 3 September, swears there were four female suicide bombers but that three escaped. Radio Ekho Moskvy reported that two "Black Widows" dressed in white medical uniforms blended in with the fleeing hostages during the 3 September rescue attempt. Other information says one wore a "light-colored dress" she had taken from a dead hostage. Still more information says a disguised "Black Widow" headed straight for the hospital with the wounded hostages but, seeing the police cordon, turned around, catching the eye of an observant policeman, who promptly arrested her. NEWSru.com's chronology of events had her arrest at 5:33 PM on 3 September. *Izvestiya* reported that Spetznaz servicemen who stormed the building on 3 September "succeeded in taking four rebels alive, including one woman." Identification of the "Black Widow" blown up on the first day of the siege as the wife of dead Chechen fighter Mairbek Shibekkhanov is also cited as evidence that there were more than two.

What is known for sure is that two *shakhidas* died on the first day of the siege and only two bodies were found in the school's rubble after the federal storming on 3 September.

How did they die?

The commander of the unit that attacked the school, "Colonel" Rasul Khachbarov, blew them and a male terrorist up in the late afternoon on 1 September because they rebelled against taking children hostage, Kulayev told the court. But hostage Zalina Dzandarova said that the two women blew themselves up in the school corridor, along with some male hostages, because they could not stomach killing children. The "colonel" had promised to kill children first if adult hostages started any trouble.

Senator Torshin says that the explosion that killed the female terrorists was the first one in the school and that it took place between three and 3:30 PM on 1 September, following a heated argument between a *shakhida* and a fighter about using hostages as human shields.

C. J. Chivers, in his award-winning article on Beslan, *The School,* recounts hostage Karen Mdinaradze's gruesome tale about how the two *shakhidas* died. It was evening, and Mdinaradze had just been taken to the main hall, where two veiled "Black Widows" and a male terrorist were guarding other hostages. "There was no warning. One second she was standing there, a veiled woman in black. The next she was not, having been torn apart in a roaring flash. The explosives cut her to pieces, throwing her head and legs into the geography classroom. Much of her flesh splashed along the walls. Shrapnel and heat shot out from the belt, striking the men in the corridor as well as another terrorist who guarded them, who was knocked to the floor. The other *shahidka* was also pierced with shrapnel. She fell, blood running from her nose."[2]

One "Black Widow" had earlier visited the bathroom. Fatima Tskayeva was hiding there with her baby and remembers that the terrorist was "menstruating and upset." Fatima says, "The *shahidkas* seem to have been deceived, as if they had not known they would be targeting children." That's surprising, considering that one of them had earlier threatened to shoot Azamat Tebiyev, ten, and other children for hiding cell phones instead of handing them over to her as instructed: "One of the female terrorists searched us for mobile phones. She told us that if she found a phone on anyone, that person and three more nearby would be killed."

The deaths of the two *shakhidas* and the others marked the beginning of many bloody episodes in the school over the next two days. Larisa Mamitova and her son, thirteen-year-old Tamerlan Toguzov, took medicine from the bag of a dead female terrorist to treat the wounded hostages. She did a wonderful job. But two hours later, terrorists began shooting from fifteen to twenty of the strongest male hostages and throwing their bodies out the windows to the ground, seven meters below. The next day "Abdullah" (his real name was Vladimir Khodov), the terrorist in charges of hostages in the gym, made a shocking proposal to replace a dead *shakhida* with a live hostage. He had taken a shine to hostage Larissa Kuzhiyeva—a woman he thought must surely be Chechen or Ingush and a Muslim, because she was dressed in black. She was mourning the death of her husband.

"There's an extra suicide belt," he tells her. "If you will put it on and wear the veil I will free your two children [Zaurbek, seven, and Medina, twenty]."

"Can I have some time to think about it?" she asks.

"Sure, go and sit! You have time," he replies. Back in the gym she told the other hostages about Abdulah's offer. "They said that maybe I should do it." She didn't.

Except for the symbolism it's hard to imagine why any of the "Black Widows" were at the school. Their suicide belts weren't needed, given the sophisticated string of bombs that hung between the two basketball hoops in the gym and the male explosives team that attended to them. Their tasks inside the school were trivial. They collected cell phones, cameras and video equipment, escorted hostages to the toilet, filmed events, and helped guard the hostages.

Their presence only made sense to deter a hostage rescue attempt and for the message it sent—that it was Basayev's Riyadas-Salikhin Reconnaissance and Sabotage Battalion of Shakhids that was responsible for the siege, and that the situation should be taken seriously.

Three hundred seventeen hostages died, 186 of them children.

Natalya Estimirova—Life and a
beacon of truth extinguished.
© *Dylan Martinez/Reuters/Corbis*

Welcome to Hell!
Courtesy Sergey Melnikoff

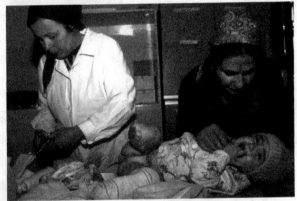

A mistaken missile strike in 2004 killed 29-year-old Maret Damayeva
and her five children, including twins Zara and Zura (on the right).
Courtesy Natalya Estimirova

Young mothers in front of their destroyed Grozny apartment building.
Author's collection

Wartime "basement people." The sign reads: "children and
people [live] here." Writing on the wall reads: "The blind,
women, invalids, people, and children [live here]."
Courtesy Sergey Melnikoff

A "hot meal" in wartime Chechnya. *Author's collection*

A wartime "summer kitchen."
Courtesy Sergey Melnikoff

The Morozov family. Gulya has been branded a traitor and is afraid relatives will try to kill her for marrying Sasha, her Russian policeman husband. Kalimat, their daughter, was born in Russia. *Author's collection*

Малика и Джамиля

Malika Temirsultanova was eight months pregnant with Dzhamiliya when a Russian aerial bomb hit trucks filled with women and children just meters in front of her. She narrowly escaped death. *Author's collection*

Inside the secret prison of the Temporary Department of MVD Oktyrbrsky District and Sibirskiye OMONovsty in the former Internat (school) for the Deaf on Minutka Square in Grozny. *Author's collection*

Chechen women staged hundred of rallies like this one (above
and opposite page) in Grozny on 1 July 2005, begging
authorities to return their kidnapped and missing children.
Author's collection

The Ultimate Sacrifice. Dadi-Yurt's women pounced on the backs of tsarist soldiers and threw themselves and their conquerors into the abyss below.
Author's collection

Chechen female snipers like this one reeked havoc on Russian soldiers in Grozny. *Courtesy Sergey Melnikoff*

The FSB identified 27-year-old Maryam Taburova as one of the Beslan school's "Black Widows." "But there were no Wahhabi books at home. I don't think she even had any books (she couldn't read)," her mother says. *Author's collection*

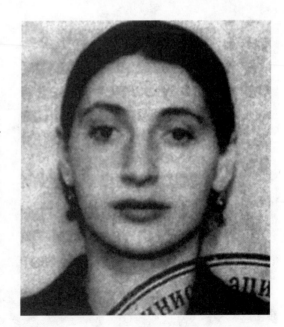

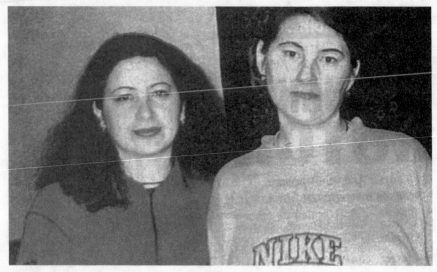

This family photo of airliner suicide bomber Amnat Nagayeva and her sister, Beslan terrorist Rosa, was taken in happier times. Rosa suffered from epilepsy.
Author's collection

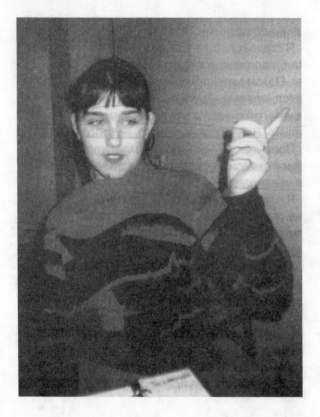

Sixteen-year-old Zarema Inarkayeva was tricked by her boyfriend into bombing a Grozny police station. She lived there in protective custody for four months after the bombing because her parents refused to let her come home.
Courtesy Yulia Yuzik

body is carried from the "Wings" rock concert and beer festival at Moscow's Tushino airfield. [F]ourteen spectators were killed by the July 2003 "Black Widow" attack there.

Courtesy Ilya Pitalyev

The court said 22-year-old Zara Murtazaliyeva was recruiting teenage girls for suicide missions when she was arrested for explosives' possession.
Author's collection

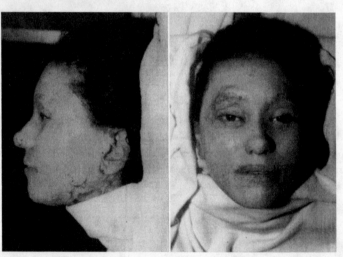

The head of the "Dirty Shoes" bomber, Khedizhi Mangeriyeva, is all that remained of this "Black Widow" who killed six people in front of Moscow's plush National Hotel in December 2003.
Author's collection

SEVEN

I'm Not Who You Think I Am

But I'm the mother of a two-year-old. I'm far from being
who you're talking about [a suicide bomber].
Milana Ozdoyeva, January 2004

WE HAVE INFORMATION

"WE HAVE INFORMATION that you want to become a *shakhida*," the mysterious man, who identified himself as Mikhail Yevseyev from the FSB, told twenty-two-year-old Milana Ozdoyeva, a fighter's widow, as she sat in her mother's office in Katyr-Yurt on that cold 5 January day in 2004. "But I'm the mother of a two-year-old! I'm far from being who you're talking about," Milana retorts. "You had better keep a close eye on your daughter!" the stranger advised Milana's mother as he turned and strolled out the door. Fourteen days later, masked men come for Milana. She disappeared and she is still missing.

Failed Measures

The humiliated FSB and MVD faced enormous pressure in 2003–2004 to stem the epidemic of suicide bombings. The crude, mostly random, measures adopted after the truck-bomb attacks of 2000 had proven woefully inadequate to deal with the new dynamic created by Dubrovka. More focused, preemptive measures, as well as better intelligence, means of psychological intimidation, and collective punishment were needed.

There had been good intelligence in the spring of 2000 that Shamil Basayev was training females for suicide missions against Russian military and police targets in Chechnya. The 3 June federal raid on Grozny's Mozdokskaya Street market was intended to preempt just such an attack.

Forty-six-year-old Nura (Nina) Said-Alviyevna Luluyeva, a nurse, kindergarten teacher, and wife of a Chechen judge, and her two cousins, Raisa and Markha Gakayeva, were selling strawberries at the market that morning when dozens of masked men in camouflage uniforms descended upon them and other women, pulled bags down over their heads, and hustled them into waiting armored personnel carriers. Concerned citizens summoned Chechen police and the district administrator, but 'they were informed that a lawful spetz-operation was under way. They could do nothing.

When Luluyeva and her cousins failed to return home after twenty-one days, Chechnya's procurator opened a criminal kidnapping case. But it was' too late. The women's bodies were later found in a mass grave of forty-seven people in Zdorovye, an abandoned holiday village on the outskirts of Grozny less than a kilometer from the Khankala military base. Forensic tests would show that Luluyeva died from multiple skull fractures inflicted by a blunt object—probably a gun butt.

If the debuts of Khava Barayeva and Luiza Magomadova as Chechnya's first female suicide bombers just four days after Luluyeva's arrest are any indication, the wrong people were killed.

The market was targeted again in late November. This time only two women were grabbed because a near riot broke out when a few greedy Russian soldiers began plundering sellers' booths. One made off with six hundred dollars' worth of Khava Magomadova's merchandise, while three others absconded with boxes of Zarema Abubakarova's precious vodka, cartons of cigarettes, and VCRs.

Random detentions of suspected female terrorists continued but with little real success in identifying and preempting *shakhidas*. To the FSB's embarrassment, most of the Dubrovka women had been detained and interrogated at least once during spring *zachistkas* preceding the theater's siege.

The search for *shakhidas* became more focused after Dubrovka. The families of terrorists and women of dead fighter husbands and brothers living in Chechnya and elsewhere in Russia begin to be targeted, and the burning of terrorists' family homes became the approved punishment and warning to mothers to keep close eyes on their daughters. But it was the Tumriyev family's killing of eighty-three civil servants in the December 2002 bombing of the Chechen government complex that intensified Russia's hunt for suicide bombers, both female and male.

The Lists

The FSB seemed better prepared in the new year, if only because it began working from prepared lists of *shakhida* suspects.

I don't know why fifty-nine-year-old Petimat Gambulatova and her three lovely daughters—Salmatu, thirty-nine; Luiza thirty-one; and Liza, twenty-nine—topped the FSB's 2003 January list. It's around midnight on 4 January and the married girls are spending the night with their mother when masked men in camouflage uniforms enter the Staropromyslovsky District family apartment (No. 11) at house No. 123 on Mayakovskovo Street and roust everyone from their beds. The intruders are clearly agitated, having gone to two wrong apartments (Nos. 10 and 55) first. The sleepy family gathers in the living room, and the masked man in charge begins reading from a list:

> Petimat Khumparovna Gamulatova!
> Luiza Shitayevna Musayeva!
> Liza Shitayevna Musayeva!
> Salmatu Shitayevna Musayeva!

"Put on warm clothing. It's cold outside," he instructs them, as well as Gambulatova's twenty-seven-year-old son. Only Magomed's wife, Milana, who is breast-feeding her two-year-old, is left behind. All disappear without a trace, and they will still be missing at the end of 2004.

Four other names—Madina Aladamova and Elza Adiyevna Gaitamirova, both thirty-one; Luiza Mutayeva, twenty; and Seda Khurikova—are also on the January list. They disappear too.

The routine is the same in each case.

On 9 January Russian-speaking men show up at the Aladamov family home on M. Mazayeva Street in the village of Stariye Atagi and ask for Madina. She had just returned from Georgia, where she worked for a humanitarian organization assisting Chechen refugees in Georgia's Pankisi Gorge. Since the gorge is home to an odd collection of Islamic holy warriors, Chechen fighters, murderers, drug runners, and arms traders and is used as a springboard for new guerrilla and terror attacks on Russia, Madina would have valuable information to share. Days later she is found in handcuffs, with a bag over her head and disoriented but alive, on a street corner in Argun. Madina declines to speak about her ordeal.

Elza Gaitamirova was the mother of four young children, two through nine years of age. On 15 January Elza and her mother return home from Urus-Martan to find two Zhiguli cars without license plates parked in front of their family home at No. 31 Budennovo Street in the village of Gekhi. Masked men placed Elza in handcuffs.

She was used to the routine. This was Elza's third visit from the FSB. She had been picked up earlier in October and held at the Urus-Martan ROVD temporary detention facility for two days. Then on 1 December, she had been summoned to the ROVD and questioned in Urus-Martan and in Grozny for a month. Elza's husband had disappeared three years earlier after being detained by police.

Eighteen-year-old Luiza Mutayeva, the sister of Dubrovka terrorist "Captain" Malizha Mutayeva, was next. On 18 January twenty masked men came for her. The visit was not unexpected. The 1:40 AM visitor to the family's temporary housing (the family home had earlier been blown up) in Assino-vskaya informs Luiza's mother, Sovdat, that "a passport check is under way." She hesitated. "Open the door! We have an order!" a threatening voice commanded. She obeyed.

Once inside, the masked men scoured everybody's passports, looking for any imperfection. "I thought they were getting ready to leave," Sovdat recalls. Then men in the bedroom instructed Luiza and her little sister Madina, fifteen, "Get dressed! Grab your scarves, it is cold outside." Madina began to sob and asked, "Where are you taking us?"

"Don't be afraid; come along with us to the car. We'll question you there and then let you go," the commander answered. But Luiza objected. "No! She's not going anywhere. I'm the only one going with you!" she said, pushing Madina back into the room. "OK!" came the reply.

Twenty-six-year-old Seda Khurikova, the sister of killed Field Commander Magomed Tsagarayev (he trained *shakhidas* in 2000), was last on the January list. Masked men took Seda from her Urus-Martan apartment on 28 January. Thirteen days later her body, minus hands and a head, severed by an explosion, was found in a forest on the outskirts of the village of Belgatoy in the Shalinsky District. Villagers had caught a glimpse of a car entering the dark forest. Then they had heard an explosion. They knew what to look for. Weeks earlier four people had been blown to bits in exactly the same spot.

Federal forces subsequently detained and interrogated dozens of women. Lida Yusupova, who ran the Human Rights Center "Memorial" office in Grozny, says that many were later released but that others remain missing and that the bodies of some like fifteen-year-old Aminat Movsarovna Dugayeva and her thirty-three-year-old relative Kurbika Said-Khasanovna Gekhayeva (Zinabdiyeva), both of whom were taken from their homes in the Shatoisky District on 17 May 2003, were later found.

The night that Dugayeva and Gekhayeva disappeared a military spokesman went on Chechen television to say that they had been detained at No. 12 Skolnaya Street in Ulus-Kert because of their involvement in the Dubrovka theater siege conspiracy—that is, they had helped recruit Dubrovka women.

Operation Fatima

Operation Fatima, designed to help ferret out potential female suicide terrorists, kicked off on 9 August 2003. Russian Interior Ministry *prikaz* (order) No. 12/309, issued a month earlier, had ordered the targeting of women dressed in traditional Muslim headdress and head scarves for special checks. Women in traditional dress, particularly those who looked pregnant (it might be a bomb instead of a baby), and those passing through police checkpoints, were to be thoroughly searched.

The profile of a potential female suicide bomber published in the Russian media said that a Chechen woman who had lost her husband and several family members in the wars, was between the ages of twenty and thirty-five, and had a European appearance and a higher education was most suspect, "especially if she wears a headscarf and a long dress, doesn't look at men, and tries to cover the bare parts of the body"—all sure signs of being a Wahhabi.

Operation Fatima disturbed human rights activists, who say it did little more than cause more arbitrary detentions, torture, and gender-specific violence, not to mention wasting the taxpayers' money. But Russian officials counter that it prevented multiple terror attacks, despite the "inconveniences" and the expense.

Chechen FSB and police informants now found themselves pressured more than ever to identify *shakhidas,* and law enforcers used "enhanced measures" to interrogate captured fighters to find out what they knew. Every young lady became suspect. The littlest thing aroused suspicion—a found photograph; recognition received during the Dudayev or Maskhadov years; being in the company of someone who's relative or friend was a suicide bomber; attending a fighter's funeral; a goodbye letter sent by a suicide bomber; a misspoken word on the telephone—anything.

In July the FSB wanted to know why thirty-four-year-old Aishat Said-layeva, a kindergarten teacher, had been photographed posing with fighters in an old photo they found in her belongings. Later in the summer, a fare-well note mailed months earlier by a Dubrovka terrorist to a friend got the recipient four days in jail, four days of interrogation, and a promise that she would be the prime suspect if another suicide bombing took place. That fall, masked men came for sixteen-year-old Luisa (Elza) Katsayeva. Neighbors, demanding that she be safely returned to her parents, demonstrated at the "Caucasus-1" federal checkpoint on the Rostov-to-Baku highway, but her fate is unknown.

Elina Gakayeva, nineteen, a student in the physics and mathematics department of the Chechen State University in Grozny, was luckier. On 26 September, Russian soldiers found her standing in front of the university's main building. Five days later she was returned home unharmed after a huge crowd of students, relatives, friends, and neighbors demonstrated in front of the Chechen administrative complex. That same month, *Novaya gazeta* reports, Russian intelligence had learned of thirteen *shakhidas* being trained in the Vedensky District, among them a fifteen-year-old "being prepared by an older man."

In October the FSB wanted to know the whereabouts of Lipkhan Basayeva. Masked men arrived and entered her house at No. 96 Kaluzhs-kaya Street in Grozny's Staropromyslovsky District but found only her tenants, who allege they were then beaten. In his written response to a Human Rights Center "Memorial" enquiry about the tenant's' allegations, Chechen MVD colonel A. S. Dakayev says that his investigation deter-mined "unidentified masked men did, in fact, visit Basayeva's residence, but nothing illegal took place." He further noted, "For your information, I should notify you that Basayeva Lipkhan is an active supporter of the Dudayev and Maskhadov regimes" and "that on 11.02.1997 she was deco-rated with the order *Koman Sii* (Honor of the Nation) Dakayev added in an attachment to his Russian superior in the Southern Federal Okrug, "The

MVD, regards the political convictions of Lipkhan Basayeva [as] legitimate grounds for our search for her."

Basayeva was an antiwar demonstrator during the first war and later worked in the Ichkerian Ministry of Foreign Affairs. "Memorial" says she received Ichkeria's Honor of Nation award for her "peace making work" in the mid-1990s, and since 2000 has worked for them and lives in Ingushetia.

Scorched Earth

Russia was losing the war on terrorism to suicide bombers. If *shakhidas* killed at least 220 civilians in 2002, they claimed the lives of nearly twice as many in 2003. Casualties were mounting and the threat was growing exponentially. Angered by the December 2003 Yessentuki train bombing, Russia's interior minister, Boris Gryzlov, told the Russian public that the Russian government had had enough. "The earth will burn beneath their [the terrorists'] feet. These animals will never feel safe anywhere," he promised. But the target proved elusive. It wasn't always widows and sisters of dead fighters—or women from Wahhabi families—who became *shakhidas*. Yet efforts to put together an alternate profile were futile, so the net was simply cast wider. Every time a fighter died and left a widow or a sister behind, her name would be added to the "lists," which were becoming lengthy and cumbersome. It became impossible to keep track of everyone.

Something else was added too. Law enforcers were now expected to turn up their own *shakhidas*. Promotion depended on it. That's what landed police commander Ruslan Aushyev in jail, and it contributed to the widespread abuse of power and arbitrary detentions that Human Rights Center "Memorial" talks so much about.

"Milana Ozdoyeva was detained [on 19 January] in connection with the criminal activities of her former husband," Achkoi-Martanovsky's District deputy procurator wrote in his official response to "Memorial's" enquiry regarding her disappearance, but he acknowledged that he had no idea of her whereabouts. Ozdoyeva had been questioned the previous April about her intentions of becoming a suicide bomber. In December FSB agents paid her parents a visit to determine her location. Then, four days after the exchange with Yevseyev in her mother's office, he showed up at Milana's doorstep to accuse her of letting somebody use her passport to travel in Russia. It wasn't true—she produced her passport to prove it.

Another seven suspected *shakhidas* were rounded up in January 2004. Two more were taken in February. Satsita Kamayeva, twenty-three, was removed from her house on Aviatsionnaya Street in Grozny on 4 February. Twenty days later Urus Martanovsky District police arrested "Madina" on terrorism charges. Then on 23 March 2004 masked men kidnaped sixty-year-old Yakha Mintsayeva from her Oktyabrsky District home. She was released three days later after traders from the market where she works picketed and demanded her release. She had earlier bought the freedom of her sons who had been detained. Twenty-three-year-old Aminat Soslambekova, the sister of a convicted murderer who had been wounded in a shootout with police, was taken from her brother's guarded hospital room in Ingushetia on 18 April 2004. Her interrogators demanded to know the names of fighters, *shakhidas*, Wahhabis, and their whereabouts, and they warned Aminat to tell everything she knows lest she become one of those who "disappeared without a trace." But 3 May brought her release.

The hunt for *shakhidas* reached a fever pitch with the August 2004 downing of the two Russian airliners and the September events at Beslan.

A nationwide "all-points bulletin" went out for Satsita Dzhebirkhanova, Maryam Taburova, and Amnat and Rosa Nagayeva after it was learned that they had flown into Moscow together on 24 August. The logic was simple: if it really was Amnat and Satsita who blew up the planes, Rosa and Maryam might be planning terror attacks in the capital too.

Maryam was of particular interest, because no one in her family had been killed in fighting in Chechnya. Shariah law says that if there are no men left in the family a woman has the right to carry out blood revenge for the killing of her male relatives. But this was not the case with Maryam. However, she did have "ties" with Wahhabi families living in her home village. The Yeshurkayev Wahhabi clan, whose head is serving a long prison sentence, is well known in Maryam's village, and the clan is active in Baku, where the FSB believes Maryam and the other girls were recruited. Baku figured prominently in the recruiting of yet another Chechen *shakhida*.

Just as everybody's eyes were glued to their television sets for Beslan developments the MVD announced the arrest of another "diehard Wahhabi" *shakhida* recruiter, a forty-five-year-old Chechen woman from Karegi Aul. This arrest, plus a shocking letter from quiet sixteen-year-old Medi (Medina) Musayeva to her mother, triggered a frantic hunt in the Rostovskaya Oblast for Medi and her suspected recruiter, thirty-four-year-old Luiza

Magomadova. The message in Medi's letter to her mother was unmistakable: "Don't worry about me. I've left for good. We'll meet in Paradise."

The head of the FSB's press office in Rostov announced on 2 September that the FSB was looking for the two women from Shali, but noted, "I want to underscore that we are not calling them terrorists who are ready to commit a terrorist attack in the near future, but certain signs oblige us to seek help in determining their whereabouts. Documents of these women or elements of their appearance could be used by other people." The oblast was blanketed with photos of Medi and Luiza, while the television repeatedly flashed bulletins about them. It worked. Both were arrested on 7 September, one in Argun, the other in Shali. The arrests were accompanied by FSB proclamations that both were confirmed suicide bombers trained by a subordinate of Basayev's who had helped organize the Beslan attack.

Medi was cooperative, telling investigators that Luiza had simply introduced herself one day while returning home from a soccer game; that she lived just down the block; that they had become close friends; and that Luiza had invited her to Wahhabi "women's meetings," where they read Wahhabi literature, discussed sacrificing one's life for Allah, and snacked. Then one day, out of the blue, Luiza had said to her, "It's time to go to the forest." Along with another girl her own age, two adult women, and a man, Medi was kept hidden in a basement somewhere in the Russian city of Rostov. But soon Basayev's emissary came to tell Medi to go home, because police photographs of her were plastered in public places everywhere.

Medi's recruiter, Luiza Magomedova, was born in the Rostovskaya Oblast and is well known there. Tatyana Ikhova, chief of the MVD's polyclinic personnel department in Rostov, remembers her from fourteen years ago, when Luiza worked at the polyclinic after finishing medical technical school. Luiza had a boyfriend then, a Russian man, but her parents forbade her to marry the foreigner. Bitter, she returned to Chechnya in 1991.

Just days after Medi's and Luiza's arrests the photos and names of a fresh new crop of *shakhidas*, seventeen in all, were publicly circulated and published on the website www.rambler.ru. But fourteen of them were medical doctors and personnel employed in Ingushetia by the Los Angeles–based NGO International Medical Corps (IMC). Were they terrorists too?

It was all a terrible mistake. The postings were supposed to have been removed from the MVD's wanted list back in February, when they first appeared, with information that the women could be planning a terror attack similar to the one on the Green Line subway train in Moscow on 6 February 2004 that killed fifty people.[1] A formal apology had even been made after the State Duma deputy for Ingushetia queried Russia's general procurator about the matter. Nevertheless, everything reappeared on the 9 September FSB's "be on the lookout" list, this time prompting the International Helsinki Federation for Human Rights office in Moscow to write a letter to the Kremlin expressing concern for the safety of the doctors and nurses.

No one is able to explain how the original photographs of the women submitted with their IMC employment applications ended up in a weapons cache belonging to Kh. Tazabayev, the head of a terrorist group, but the situation was cleared up for good this time. However, there's no mistake about thirty-seven-year-old Khalimat Sadullayeva, a housewife and mother of four little children who was living with her mother and sister-in-law. She was conspiring to conduct a terror act and was arrested in September too. "Someone [one of the masked men] pointed at her and said [in Russian] 'That's her,' and then three men took her away without explanation," Madina, her sister-in-law recalls. Khalimat's parents too insist that it was a big mistake. "To be a *shakhida* you need to have someone in your family dead. She didn't have any victims," her father says. But Khalimat's own house had been burned to the ground earlier in the summer during a firefight between fighters and police, raising suspicions about her.

Three more trained *shakhidas* were arrested on 8 and 9 September. A thirty-four-year-old and a woman ten years younger were charged with terrorism. Police found a bomb made from a 1.5-liter bottle filled with explosives, shrapnel, and an electronic detonator in the home of the third woman, thirty-six years old.

In Argun a woman selling at the local market, identified only as "Myalkhaziy," was detained as a suspected *shakhida*. Cute thirty-one-one-year-old Natalya (Kheda) Khalkayeva was also arrested in September on multiple charges, including training suicide bombers. I said earlier that she bought the satellite telephone used by the emir of Grozny, Yunadi Turchayev, to coordinate terror attacks on Russia. In January 2003 he assembled a group of suicide bombers to carry out attacks in several Russian cities. The FSB foiled that plot but missed the May 2003 attack on the regional administrative building in Znamenskoye that Turchayev organized for Basayev.

That December twenty-eight-year-old Irina Saidullayeva became a terror suspect too. at Around midnight on 2 December, after she had been tailed for almost a week, armed men in masks and military uniforms and speaking "unaccented Russian" entered the family home at No. 15 Lenina Street in the village of Sernovodsk, Sunzhesky District, gagged and bound everybody, then forced Irina into their waiting car.

She survived. By Irina's own account, she was held for four days in a trench covered with wooden boards and deprived of sleep and food. Every time she fell asleep guards would rudely awaken her. "Cry a little and beg us nicely, and maybe we'll give you some food," her captors would tell her. Irina's brother, Imran, had been shot and killed in a police raid on the family home five months earlier. Irina herself had been wounded in that raid. This time she was fortunate. On the fourth day of her captivity a plastic bag was pulled down over her head and she was placed in a car, which was driven around for hours. Then suddenly it stopped. Her captors got out but she was ordered to sit still. Irina just knew she was going to be shot right then and there. The silence seemed to last an eternity. Then somebody opened the door and snatched the bag from her head. It was Ramzan Kadyrov. "Congratulations! You're free!" he told her. She was speechless. The Sunzhensky District police chief drove her home.

Post-Beslan

I was told by a respectable American academic at the February 2005 Association for the Study of Nationalities (ASN) Conference that the religious leadership of those fighting Russia had sworn off the further use of suicide bombers after Beslan. I wasn't convinced. Beslan might make *shakhida* recruitment more tedious, I thought, but I was certain that suicide attacks would continue as long as Basayev's evil heart was beating.

Indeed, he planned two major attacks for the spring. One was a repeat of the December 2002 Chechen government complex bombing, but good Chechen police work thwarted it. The other was a copycat of Beslan, but this time the school was in the neighboring republic of Kabardino-Balkaria.

Twenty-two-year-old Achkoi-Martan resident Madina Saidrakhmanovna Mitrayeva and Shukran Khasanovna Isayeva, nineteen, both from Grozny, were just hours away from driving the KamAZ truck filled with 1,200 kilograms of explosives into the Chechen government building complex. What they didn't know was that the two men who were delivering the truck to them had fallen into police hands and revealed not only plans of the attack but the location of their hideout in nearby Sernovodsk. Shortly after

4 PM on 6 May hundreds of law enforcers moved in. They instantly killed Magomed Khaidayev, the emir of the Sunzhensky *djamaat,* and his subordinate. Surrender wasn't an option for the girls, so one of them grabbed a grenade and detonated it, killing them both.

That same day Staropromyslovsky District police engaged a *shakhida* in a standoff in front of the district police station. Demands to remove her suicide belt went unheeded. She hesitated, then charged. A volley of bullets felled her, but she detonated her bomb anyway. No one else was hurt. The FSB says the bomber had been recruited for Dubrovka but for unknown reasons hadn't participated. Police arrested a "Black Widow" recruiter (other reports say instructor) two days later.

At the same time Terrorist "chatter" hinted that Wolves were planning something big. Human intelligence indicated that it might be a copycat Beslan attack. Then it was confirmed—in early May the FSB identified School No. 18 in the city of Cherkessk, Karachyevo-Cherkessiya Republic, as the target of a six-person suicide battalion involving two Chechen teenage *shakhidas* who had earlier been reported missing by their parents.

On 14 May seventeen-year-old Diana Saparovna Katchiyeva and Aina Arslanovna Bekeyeva, nineteen, were in the company of Timur Kubanov, thirty; Murat Laipanov, twenty-eight; Kazim Kecherukov, thirty-five; and Khapani Uzdenov, forty-five—men who are neither their husbands or relatives. They had become the target of an intense two-day spetz-operation targeting their fifth-floor apartment at 29 Khetagurova Street in Cherkessk. Everybody was killed.

The FSB produced "irrefutable proof" that Katchiyeva and Bekeyeva had been trained suicide bombers getting ready to go on a killing spree at the school. After all, the girls' apartment did look like a small bomb-making factory. Explosives were everywhere. Investigators found seventy detonators, two hundred microchips for use in improvised explosive devices, assembled homemade bombs, and other bomb making equipment and materials. You could hardly make your way through it all. Katchiyeva, Bekeyeva, and their four male companions were reportedly subordinate to the terrorist Achemez Gochiyayev, a fugitive still wanted for organizing the 1999 Moscow and Volgodonsk apartment building bombings—although sources in the Turkish Chechen diaspora tell me he is dead.

The respite in suicide bombings in the summer and fall of 2005 wasn't because Wolves had sworn them off but because the FSB and the MVD were getting better at what they do and because Basayev was busy planning the October 2005 terror attack on Nalchik, Kabardino-Balkaria's capital. The attack killed ninety people, but his *shakhidas* were not involved.[2] The Kremlin's amnesty program thwarted three suicide bombings in 2006. National Anti-Terror Committee (NAK) statistics for the year show that three *shakhida* women were among the more than two hundred Wolves who voluntarily surrendered.

Basayev's death on 10 July 2006 while moving a truckload of explosives left his *shakhida* battalion brigade without its commander in chief and in disarray. It would be nearly three years before it could be successfully resurrected. Nevertheless, Russia's *shakhida* hunt went on relentlessly.

In midafternoon on 27 January 2007 masked men came to the Mekhstroi temporary refugee settlement in Ingushetia to arrest thirty-eight-year-old Malika Mikailovna Chabiyeva. After midnight on 18 May 2007 Chechen police took Zulikhan Malsagova from her home on the 8th of March Street in the Oktyabrsky District of Grozny. Police had already arrested her husband for collaborating with fighters. Her fate is unknown. On 1 September 2007 a women who had worked as an "assistant" for the deceased illegal-armed-formation leader Rustam Basayev was arrested along with two male members of his group. Chechnya's police chief Ruslan Alkhanov says the men intended to employ her as a *shakhida*. The following March, an unidentified forty-eight-year-old local woman, a member of the Nadterechny *djamaat* who had been on Russia's wanted list for terrorism since October 2001, was captured in Pervomaiskoye, Groznensky District.

WHY WOMEN KILL THEMSELVES

I was asked in a 2005 Russian Profile interview why Chechen women kill themselves in suicide attacks. I could easily have said that they are all desperate widowed housewives seeking revenge and have been done with it. But the answer is much more complex, and it has as much to do with the practicalities of why Wolves adopted suicide terrorism to fight Russia in the first place as it does with why women agree to carry it out.

The answer has four dimensions.

The economics of suicide terror is the first. Suicide terrorism is the cheapest kind of warfare, requiring minimal monetary, material, technical, and human investment—all practical considerations important to any group short on cash and the manpower necessary to fight an overwhelming enemy in conventional ways. It's also a practical means of fund-raising. Basayev understood perfectly well that sensational, suicide terror is the best way to attract the financial investment of Osama bin Laden and other Islamic extremist organizations, constituencies, and benefactors. Major attacks like Dubrovka and Beslan generate huge sums of money. A Russian diplomat told me that he is certain the real purpose of Dubrovka was to raise money. Inclusion of Dubrovka in Al-Qaeda's November 2002 list of targets struck since the 9/11 attack on America shows that either Shamil Basayev made a suitable impression on the Islamists' commander in chief or that Russia was an Al-Qaeda target all along.

Osama bin Laden has contributed millions to the North Caucasus Jihad, but it's impossible to determine exactly how much. The U.S. government will only say that it is "a substantial amount of money." Bin Laden himself admits to personal investment. He told a Pakistani journalist in 1999 that it is his "moral duty to provide [Chechen fighters] with every kind of help."

Bin Laden's public endorsement of both Dubrovka and Beslan, as well as his call in October 2004 for Muslim's worldwide to financially support the Chechen Jihad, demonstrate that Basayev's Riyadus-Sakhalkin Shakhida Battalion stood tall among global Islamic terrorist organizations. Movladi Udugov, the Ichkerian ideologist who runs the www.Kavkazcenter.com website, even touted it as the front line of Muslim fighters worldwide. "We are ready to become the vanguard of the Muslim nation and the defenders of Islam worldwide," he proclaimed on the website in 2003 after Osama bin Laden called on Muslims everywhere to "deploy on all fronts" to fight the evil "Crusader Coalition." Udugov always did like to exaggerate.

By the end of the summer of 2002 suicide terror had become the necessary Chechen force multiplier, because cash shortages, losses on the Chechen side, and the disarray of Chechen fighting forces had limited other options. There was another factor too. Wolves still had good access to arms, but they had been complaining for some time about shortages of ammunition, and their attempts to acquire more powerful weapons had proven futile.[3] "I swear to Allah, if the Russians or Americans will give us cruise missiles or intercontinental ballistic missiles, then we will not be using suicide attackers or trucks loaded with explosives," Basayev publicly proclaimed on 2 June 2003.

The killing power of suicide terror and the ability of the Chechen female suicide terrorist to target precisely and inflict high casualties constitute a second dimension. "Chechen women are a greater threat to our national security because they carry out more dangerous operations," then Vice Premier Ramzan Kadyrov told a Chechen television audience on 11 May 2005.

Women in Russia have a distinct advantage as bomb-delivery vehicles because they don't arouse as much suspicion as men and can more easily penetrate target areas. The macho male Russian policeman is still ill equipped psychologically to deal with the female terrorist, because he has difficulty imagining that any woman can be a threat. It's still rare to see a Moscow policeman stop a woman and ask for her *dokumenty* unless she is pretty and his intent is to flirt with her. When I left Russia in June 2004, the daily *proverka* (passport checks) at the subway stations and in the *perekhods* (underground pedestrian passageways) still targeted primarily dark-skinned young men.

There are other tactical as well as sociological considerations for deploying women. The life of a Chechen woman may be traditionally worth two men in traditional Chechen society, but wartime attrition of males has changed that equation. Chechen women are more expendable as combat assets, especially since they significantly outnumber men and there is a large pool to choose from. There are many widows who will probably never remarry and lots of young single girls who may not marry at all. The lower social status of widows, single women, and unmarried teenage girls in Chechen society make them attractive recruitment targets. Females who have been raped, divorced, shunned by their families, or otherwise marginalized by society are particularly easy prey.

The psychological devastation of suicide terror on the targeted population is a third dimension. In any society a suicide attack by a woman has more psychological impact than one carried out by a man. Ultra-shock is the intent—to instill mass fear, anxiety, and panic ultimately destabilizing the targeted society, is the ultimate goal.

It worked well for Basayev at Budennovsk. If he hadn't thought about it before, media coverage of the siege gave him exactly what he needed to force Russia into a cease-fire in 1995. Russian politicians and journalists flocked to Budennovsk, and there was a daily feeding frenzy of bloody events freely broadcast over Russian television. I watched in disbelief as Prime Minister Chernomirdin, live over Russian television, begged Basayev not to kill the hostages. The unfettered press quickly exposed the government's weakness, the lack of preparedness of the police forces, and brought quick concessions.

Russians have since developed considerable psychological resilience to terrorism. By and large, people tell me that terrorism is "something we have to live with—a nuisance." I used to advise my friends to take the first or last car on the Moscow subway trains; I felt terrorists would be more likely to strike the middle car, to inflict maximum casualties. But my fatalistic friends would tell me, "That's ridiculous; if it's your turn you're going to die; there's nothing you can do about it."

The fourth dimension goes to the heart of the question of why Chechen women kill themselves. Just about everybody has a strong opinion on this subject.

Those fighting Russia and their sympathizers, who blame Russia and former president Putin for everything bad that has happened in Chechnya, say that revenge, the invasion of Chechens' homes, kidnapping, and the loss of husbands and other male family members, destitution, desperation, and ruined lives drive women to suicide terror. "It's the inevitable response to the most crude, the most terrible crimes that Russian forces have committed against Chechen civilians, principle among these being rape," Imran Yezhi-yev, head of the Chechen-Russian Friendship Society, alleges. He's dead now, but Abu al-Waleed, a Saudi-born Basayev advisor, appointed commander of the Wolves' "Eastern Front" in 2002, used to say that Chechen women were killing themselves because Russians were "raping, humiliating, and threat-ening them in their homes." The University of Cincinnati's Mia Bloom says that "in Sri-Lanka, Chechnya, and Turkey a lot of women who were raped became suicide bombers because it brought shame on them in their commu-nities. The only way to regain their honor was to die." Akhmed Zakayev, the "Vice President of the Chechen Republic of Ichkeria," asked an 18 June 2004 London audience, "How can anyone be surprised that our youth—a brother whose sister was raped, a son whose father was tortured to death—ignore our sermons of moderation and join the ranks of desperate suicide avengers?"

It's odd that they put rape by Russian soldiers at the top of the list. I have not found a single case of a Chechen woman becoming a suicide ter-rorist because she or any member of her family or friends had been raped by Russian soldiers. There are no suicide notes left or good-by letters sent to friends to that effect, nor have parents claimed that daughters became *shakh-idas* because of having been raped by Russian soldiers. Nor have any of those suicide bombers captured alive said they planned to kill themselves because they had been raped by Russian soldiers.

But I did find two females raped by Chechen fighters who became suicide bombers. Luiza Osmayeva is one of them; the other was a girl kidnapped for marriage whose name I do not know.

Others commentators like Human Rights Center "Memorial's" Oleg Orlov says that kidnappings by federal forces and the horror of *zachistkas* are to blame for the suicide bombings. Anna Politkovskaya has said that the brutality of the Russian assault and the mopping-up operations "pushed Chechen women over the edge." Zainap Gashayeva, a longtime Ichkeria supporter and anti-Russia activist who heads the *Echo Voiny* human rights organization, says the women kill themselves because "a normal person can only take so much humiliation and violence before they take desperate measures."

But Dr. Baiev believes that suicide bombings are "largely motivated by a desire to take revenge for a family member killed by the Russians. People who have lost everything think they have nothing more to live for. They are desperate. Blood revenge, rather than religious extremism imported from the Middle East, governs the violence." Anne Nivat elaborates: "These women are driven by despair, they know they have lost everything. . . . They have lost a husband, a cousin, a brother, a father, a son and they have nothing more to lose, they understand that the war is far from being over and they think it is easier to die."

Two Fallacies

Blood revenge is clearly what drove Aizan Gazuyeva and Imana Khachukayeva to their acts of violence. It likely also motivated Maryam Khadzhiyeva, Sekilat Aliyeva, Maryan Marshugova, Aishat Bakuyeva, Larisa Musalayeva, Zinada Aliyeva, Khedizhi Mangeriyeva, and other women. But to say that the desire for personal revenge is what drove all the women, or even most, to suicide terrorism is incorrect.

Grenades are easy to get hold of in Chechnya. Remember how Aset Chadayeva carried one taped to her body during the cleansing of Noviye Aldy, just in case? If personal revenge was the principal motivator for all or most suicide bombers, there should have been many more spontaneous acts of rage directed at officials responsible for the deaths of their husbands and loved ones, instead of highly planned and organized acts of terror against innocent Russian civilians. Rarely is Chechen female suicide terrorism a spontaneous act of desperation.

Nabi Abdullaev is right when he says that "it is the existence of the organization [Basayev's Riyadus-Salikhin Reconnaissance and Sabotage Battalion of Shakhids], rather than existence of grievances, that determine the occurrence, scope, and pattern of suicide attacks." The resurrection of the battalion and the resumption of suicide bombings in 2008–2009 supports that.

It's unlikely that most of the *shakhida* women of 2000–2005 would have become suicide bombers had Basayev's network of local representatives not worked so diligently to identify, target, and cultivate them, capitalizing on their personal needs, weaknesses, grievances, friendships and allegiances, family obligations, traditional Chechen culture, and Muslim beliefs. The organization was skilled at brainwashing—Ramzan Kadyrov says "hypnotized and stuffed full of drugs [injected with opium]"—many women into believing that dying for Allah like this would give higher meaning to their time on earth, provide redemption for their sins, purify their spirits, reunite them with loved ones, and reserve special places for them in heaven. Khava Barayeva's logic made perfectly good sense.

If Chechen ethnographer Zalpa Bersanova is correct, there's another factor arguing against Chechen women deciding by themselves to take revenge on innocent Russian civilians. She says women do not blame ordinary Russians for their despair. Bersanova told a Washington, D.C., Radio Free Europe/Radio Liberty audience in August 2004 that her research had found no correlation between personal wartime losses and the expression of resentment toward ordinary Russians. Rather, respondents "saw the Russian people as victims of their government too."

Without the "organization" there would have been few *shakhidas*. They didn't exist during the first war, which was equally, if not more brutal, but the Riyadus-Sakhalin Battalion didn't exist then either.

The second fallacy is that all these women were widows of men killed by Russian soldiers. It's the Russian media's fault. They coined the ominous term "Black Widows" to describe the Chechen females at Dubrovka, but it quickly became the generic reference for all Chechen female suicide terrorists, regardless of marital status or family losses. It's been good propaganda play, though. As Nabi Abdullayev aptly puts it: "Black Widows have now become a high-value franchise, and it will be strategically unwise for rebels to jeopardize its integrity."

"But they're not black widows!" Atle Takayev, a Chechen police chief in Grozny, insists. "What these women are doing is not patriotism. . . . They just making up these stories about themselves." Takayev is mostly right. Of the fifty suicide terrorists I identified, less than half were widows, and of those, not all of their husbands died at the hands of Russian soldiers, either.

No Single Profile

There is no single profile for the Chechen female terrorist. Even her ages (sixteen to forty-eight) are as different as her reasons for becoming one. Many reasons motivated the women.

Khava Barayeva said she was doing it to inspire others to Jihad. The idea is that self-sacrifice is the litmus test of commitment to Allah and to the cause, making heroes and heroines out of those who kill themselves.

Most of the women came from less than desperate families. Some owned businesses; many were highly educated and even gainfully employed. One was a medical student; others were teachers and professionals, one a pharmacist. Few were destitute. None came from poor refugee camps, and none were living in abject poverty, except perhaps Zarina Alikhanova ("Juliet").

Nevertheless, money clearly motivated some and their families. Like so many other things in these wars, this has been about money. When Basayev handsomely rewarded the families of martyrs, suicide bombing became a way to provide for loved ones left behind. The Tveskaya Street bomber Zarema Muzhikhoyeva needed money to repay her grandmother for the stolen jewelry. She also needed to redeem herself before her family. And the Wahhabi families of Dubrovka terrorist Khadchat and Fatima Ganiyeva, and Zaira Yupayeva, sold the girls for large sums of cash.

Zarema Inarkayeva, Marina Bisultanova and other girls, were kidnapped by their boyfriends or estranged husbands and forced to become *shakhidas*. Luiza Osmayeva was kidnapped, raped, and impregnated. She became a *shakhida* to redeem herself from her "sins." "They [her handlers] told me I was unclean and should do my duty," she said before she died.

Others, like Dubrovka terrorists Aiman and Koku Khadzhiyeva, Raiman Kurbanova, and Aset Gishlurkayeva were terminally ill, psychologically disturbed, or social outcasts. They were targeted by local *djamaats* and married off to fighters who would participate in Dubrovka and take them along. Being obedient women, they followed. Alina Tumriyeva was probably dragged along by her father.

Zulikhan Yelikhadzhiyeva sacrificed herself because of forbidden love, and perhaps others because Basayev personally asked them to. "He is an idol for many Chechen women. . . . We perceive these sympathies with Basayev even in the women we ourselves use. They work for us, for counterintelligence, but sympathize with Basayev," a Russian counterintelligence officer confessed.

The Wahhabi religious connection is the most common thread. Several *shakhidas* came from the Wahhabi stronghold of Assinovskaya. Others were from Wahhabi families elsewhere. Almost all passed through some kind of Wahhabi orientation, indoctrination, or training, either in the family or at Wahhabi women's meetings.

Shakhidas ARE BACK!

The "Riyadus-Salikhin Reconnaissance and Sabotage Battalion of Shakhidass" has been resurrected. Out of at least thirteen known suicide bombers in the North Caucasus since September 2008, seven have been women. Four carried out terror attacks, and police have killed and captured another three.

I began to see the warning signs of a *shakhida* revival in the early summer of 2008, when updated "lists" of women who could become suicide bombers began to be circulated. The new lists are more cumbersome than ever. One (for the Gudermessky District) alone contains 166 names. Very detailed information is given, including full names (some maiden names); birth dates; a few with passport numbers and issuing authority; in many cases, full addresses; and such additional information as eye color, length and color of hair, body language observed during questioning (wringing of the hands, etc.,); the kind of car driven; and whether the woman is a widow of a dead fighter. Two entries are suspected suicide bomber recruiters (Luiza Magomadova's name is still on the list), and one is thought to have already been trained as a suicide bomber.

In mid-September a male suicide bomber drove his car filled with explosives into the Russian Defense Ministry's "Yug" Battalion base in Vedeno, killing one serviceman and wounding eleven others.

Two weeks later, just after eight in the morning on 30 September, a woman in a car packed with forty kilograms of explosives on Kartoyeva Street in downtown Nazran detonated her car bomb just as the motorcade of Ingushetia's interior minister, Musa Medov, passed by. He survived.

Medov's armored car was engulfed in a fireball but sped away. At least four civilians received shrapnel wounds and were hospitalized. Fragments of the bomber's car and her body parts were scattered fifty to sixty meters away.

A month later, Moscow police begin a frantic search for forty-one-year-old Raisa Abdulkadyrovna Tumriyeva, Gelani Tumriyev's sister. Operational intelligence indicated that she intended to blow herself up at a public event during the upcoming November holiday celebrations. Bulletins throughout the night of 30 October alerted policemen that Tumriyeva was already in Moscow. The warnings were accompanied by her picture and passport data:

Raisa Abdulkadyrovna Tumriyeva
Date of Birth: 21 July 1967
Birthplace: Achkoi-Martan, Achkoi-Martanovsky District, ChIASSP
Passport No: [blocked out]
Passport Issuing Office: OVD, Leninsky District
Date of Issue: 12 March 2003

Moscow police never did find Tumriyeva, but the *Moskovsky komsomolets* newspaper reported that she was the suicide bomber who detonated a bomb a week later in Vladikavkaz, North Ossetia, killing twelve people and wounding thirty-eight.

Authorities have yet to publicly confirm that Tumriyeva was in fact the *shakhida* who on the afternoon on 6 November 2008 detonated a five-hundred-gram bomb after she got off one bus, wondered around awhile, then started to get onto another bus. The woman's head, parts of her feet, and fragments of her suicide belt were strewn around Kuibysheva Street near the Druzhba Theater. The *shakhida* had taken a long time to determine where to detonate her bomb. Eyewitnesses say she strolled up to the Druzhba, which was full of children, then hung around the entrance to the Globus Market right across the street for a while, and even attracted the attention of apartment building residents by loitering too long in front of their building. Bus driver Ostan Ketsoyev recalls that she sat in the back of his minivan, was dressed in black, and was on edge and aggressive the whole time she was in his vehicle. She even spat at him when she got out.

The attack bore all the earmarks of the 2003 Mozdok military bus bombing. The case is still unsolved. Victims' relatives complain that they know the bomber passed through several police checkpoints to get into North Ossetia, but who she was and who ordered the attack remains a mystery.

There would be one more suicide bombing—this one by a male bomber in May—before Wolves made public the revival of the Riyadus-Salikhin Reconnaissance and Sabotage Battalion of Shakhids. That revelation came on 29 June 2009, when Doka Umarov took credit in the name of the "Sabotage Battalion of Shakhids" for the 22 June suicide car-bombing attack on President Yunus-Bek Yevkurov.

Everyone assumed it was a female who nearly killed Yevkurov. "It was the wife of a dead fighter, twenty-two-year-old Pyatimat Mutaliyeva," who attacked Yevkurov's motorcade, insisted Chechnya's chief policeman, Ruslan Alkhanov. Earlier, in March, the FSB had stormed Pyatimat's home and killed her husband, Magomed Bogatyryov, because authorities had information that the couple was plotting a suicide attack against President Yevkurov. But Pyatimat was found at home, alive and well, on the day of Yevkurov's attack. She had just taken a university psychology exam.

If it wasn't Pyatimat, then who was it? The FSB questioned her friends and began knocking on the doors of all recently widowed women. That a woman was involved seemed certain after crime scene investigators said they had found a clump of hair that seemed consistent with a female from the North Caucasus. But conclusive DNA tests proved otherwise.

On 5 September 2009 a Chechen woman detonated her suicide belt after a shootout with police resulting from a failed attempt to take her into custody. Police never released her name.

A week later police picked up twenty-one-year-old Sakinat Saidova in a cell phone store near the Sovetsky District police station in Makhachkala, Dagestan, and accused her of being a suicide bomber. A pistol, ammunition, and two grenades were found on her person. Sakinat's intention to blow herself up was revealed to the FSB in a letter asking the permission of Omar Sheikhulayev, the emir of Dagestani fighters, to carry out a suicide attack. A subsequent letter to her mother spelled out who was to get her belongings after the terror attack and asked her mother to raise her two children in strict Islam. Sakinat admits that Shamil Gasanov, a Jihadist leader in Dagestan, persuaded her to become a *shakhida*. Two of her brothers had been killed in spetz-operations, and her last husband, the well known emir of Dagestan, Ilgar Mollachiyev, had died in September 2008. She had been married two other times, both of them to fighters who had been killed in spetz-operations.

A few days after Sakinat's arrest, on the morning of 16 September, a middle-aged Chechen woman walked up to a traffic police car stopped at the intersection of Prospekt Putin and Mira Street in the Zavodsky District of Grozny and detonated her ten-kilogram bomb, killing two policemen and wounding three female and three male passersby. On 22 October two *shakhidas* were killed by raiding police in a house in the Oktyabrsky District of Grozny where homemade bombs were being assembled. On 6 January 2010 a male suicide bomber blew up his car outside a traffic police post in Makhachkala, Dagestan, killing six policemen.

I expect more suicide bombings in 2010. What will be different this year is that Moscow will likely be targeted again, but unlike in 2003–2004 the attackers will probably be both female and male and involve women from the neighboring republics of Ingushetia and Dagestan. It is becoming more difficult to recruit Chechen female suicide bombers.

"War will come to their cities," Wolves' leader and the emir of the Caucasus Emirate Doka Umarov promised on 10 February 2010. "If Russian's think that war is only on television, somewhere far away in the Caucasus and cannot touch them, then we are getting ready to show them that this war is returning to their homes."

I submitted the *Allah's Angels* manuscript to my publisher on 1 March 2010. Twenty-eight days later, two more of Umarov's *shakhidas,* neither Chechen, blew themselves up at two subway stations in Moscow during morning rush hour, killing forty people and wounding at least seventy. Maryam Sharipova, a twenty-eight-year-old schoolteacher and the wife of a Dagestani separatist leader, was the first to strike that morning—her target the Lubyanka subway station, located underneath the FSB's headquarters. Seventeen-year-old Dzhanet Abdurakhmanova (Abdulayeva), a separatist's widow, detonated her suicide belt some forty minutes later, at about 8:38 AM, at the busy Park Kulturiy station on the ring road.

Unless Doka Umarov is killed soon, Moscow should expect more bombings this year.

EIGHT

Rising from the Ashes

I contemplated suicide, but thanks to my children, I chose life.
Sovman Atgeriyeva, sister of Ichkerian vice premier
Turpal-Ali Atgeriyev

DOG-EATEN CORPSES and bodies stacked in piles; wailing children with missing limbs; the hungry and tortured; "invaders" with their big guns and Jihadists with their bombs; traitors, thieves, swindlers, and informers—all these are everywhere in wartime Chechnya. Some women go mad because of it all. Others join the Jihad. But for most who miraculously survive, life goes go on for the sake and preservation of the family.

The women labor against impossible odds. Data compiled by the "Women of the Don Region Union" NGO show that young Chechen women between 1994 and 2000 held out absolutely no hope of a better life. There wasn't much reason for optimism in 2001 either. The life of every ninth Chechen woman was endangered, nearly 70 percent had lost their homes, and 75 percent were unemployed. And to top it all off, thousands of women suffer from post-traumatic stress disorder, making it difficult or impossible for them to hold down a job, even if they could find one.

But the will and instinct of these women to stay alive and their strength, courage, and resourcefulness are nothing less than remarkable. Without even the basics of modern life—and whether they live in tents, train cars, apartments with only three walls, basements of bombed-out buildings, or with relatives and neighbors—the majority, many without husbands, refuse to surrender to hopelessness.

"Why search to survive if life doesn't want you?" Milana Terloeva writes in her book *Danser sur les ruines. Une jeunesse tchétchène.* "A girl's instinct for survival disappears," she continues, but then Milana remembers the words of her grandmother: "You must never give up on hope! It's necessary to survive at whatever cost."

"We really do have a special ability to survive in almost any situation," Elza Duguyeva, a Chechen wife and mother of three, told Czech journalist Petra Prochazkova in 2000.[1]

Most women don't run out and join a suicide battalion to end their desperation. Instead, they find ingenious ways to house, feed, and protect their families—and they search for the missing, march, protest, picket, negotiate ransoms for the release of loved ones or the dead, run house to house collecting ransom money, and do much, much more.

SWOLLEN WITH HUNGER

Khazimat Gambiyeva was a desperate woman. A nurse in the good days, she was at fifty-one years of age a sick old woman swollen with hunger, because she unselfishly gave all her food to her family of eleven children and grandchildren.[2] Chronic hunger, homelessness, poverty, and disease plagued Gambiyeva and just about everybody else in wartime Chechnya. The supply of food barely kept starvation at bay. People had learned from the first war. They had hoarded food in preparation for the second, but it was not enough. Families who farmed and could raise a crop and hide their animals from marauding thieves and from hungry Chechen fighters and Russian soldiers didn't starve to death. Just having a cow meant survival, because she fed the babies when mothers stop lactating. Dirty animals were sometimes hidden in camouflaged earthen dugouts alongside human beings. If families on the land did manage to raise a small crop of corn, something was kept back for the winter, and the rest was sold to whoever could buy it, to purchase other essentials.

Sometimes the Danish Refugee Council sent flour, but it too, along with whatever sugar, potatoes, and everything else there was, had to be hidden from all those who would steal or maliciously destroy it. The Russian Emergency Situations Ministry (MChS) also brought flour, but instead of delivering it to the needy, corrupt Chechen officials kept it for themselves and sold it at the market to line their own pockets. "We saw this," one MChS truck driver tells, "but we couldn't do anything about it. Our job was just to hand over the goods [to Chechen officials], and how they distributed them wasn't our concern." Corn fodder and hay, like houses, were at the mercy of Russian soldiers. Sometimes all were burned.

The situation was much worse in destroyed villages and settlements, flooded with refugees, and in cities where people who refused to leave had to make do with what they had stored up, what neighbors gave them, what those fleeing had left behind, or what they could scrounge, beg, steal, or catch. Sacks of potatoes left by the neighbors kept thirty-four-year-old Kheda Azhigova and her ten-year-old twins Rizvan and Zara alive in Grozny. Six-year-old Lida, who looked after her little brother and mother, who had gone mad, begged for food. She used to know an old woman across the hall in her apartment building who would give her something to eat, but she had died. Lida begged at the market and dug through street garbage to "come home with small pieces of bread for Mama."[3] Before they were married, Leila, Stas's wife, and her mother and fourteen-year-old brother ate wild pigeons they killed with a slingshot. Teenage girls "of other nationalities" sold sexual favors to Russian soldiers at the central market for a few cans of the Russian Army's stewed meat. "If hunger weakens us, we'll gnaw on roots," the Chechen national anthem goes. Some people did.

Everybody still in the cities lived in damp, cold basements without electricity, gas, or enough food. The children never stopped crying from hunger, the freezing cold, and the constant noise of exploding shells and shooting. People died in those pits of hell. Their bodies stank, but you didn't dare take them outside for fear of getting shot.

When there was a lull in the bombing and women weren't dodging bullets or Russian grenades thrown into their underground shelters, they went out and searched for food, water, and warmth. There had been huge breadlines in Grozny on 30 December 1994. A hot bowl of porridge for mothers and their children could sometimes be found at the mobile kitchen in front of the Leninsky District administration building. In 2000 ten thousand Grozny residents got daily bread rations. "I don't know what we would have done on our own," Taisa Batriyeva, says about the handout.[4] Sometimes the MChS serves meat stew—made from pigeon. But there are hardly any pigeons left.

In August 2000 Russian readers of the newspaper *Novaya gazeta* donated clothing, food (rice, raisins, oil), and medicine to a Grozny old folks' home.

"Now we'll survive the winter," Sister Zinaida Tagireyeva told Anna Polit-kovskaya. "We'll have the best dinners in Grozny."[5] Families who had any belongings left after the bombs and thieves claimed their share sell them off piece by piece—a set of earrings here, a bracelet or television set there—to buy food to survive one more day. When the money ran out and relatives had nothing more to give them, families turned to state handouts, if they could find them. A three-day ration of food in the Shalinsky District overrun with refugees consisted of three cans of evaporated milk and a can of processed meat for each person.

Women fought over these pathetic rations. "To tell me about the star-vation, Aishat [head of the regional migration services in the district center of Shali] has to shout over the howls of some women who are out of their minds with hunger and are cursing and ripping a three-day ration out of each other's hands," Anna Politkovskaya writes in *A Small Corner of Hell*.[6] "Old women tear each other's hair out. . . . And all on account of a bottle of oil, half a kilo of sugar and ten kilos of flour. A hungry horde is worse than a pack of wolves," Elza Duguyeva says.

Refugees in some shelters in Ingushetia had it better. They at least received a daily ration of two ladles of soup with meat, half a loaf of bread, and a cup of tea. Everybody had stomach aches, but in other camps there was no hot food at all. "We only get one hot meal a day. It is usually watery soup with almost raw potatoes and uncooked meat in it," Zelim Khan, a thirteen-year-old orphan living in a railway train camp in Ingushetia, complained.

Nearly 200,000 refugees fled to neighboring Ingushetia in the second war. Seventy percent of them lived with host families. The office of the United Nations High Commissioner for Refugees (UNHCR) program for host-family food assistance and the Swiss Disaster Relief /UNHCR's com-pensation programs help feed them. But other women lined the main street in Nazran begging, despite the taboo on begging in Chechen culture.

Even after the daily bombardment and the street-to-street fighting ended, the picture wasn't much prettier. Recovery was painfully slow. Thousands of displaced women, the elderly, the handicapped, and their families contin-ued to rely on international humanitarian help and state assistance for food and temporary shelter. The UNHCR provided "box tents" to some of the displaced. It also distributed food rations to families and schools in Chech-nya. Eighty-three thousand people received food rations in September 2006. Thirty-seven thousand out of 60,000 or so displaced were housed in temporary centers. In 2007, women could receive a World Food Program (WFP) food package in exchange for attending vocational training classes in sewing, hairdressing, or other work skills so they could learn to support themselves.

These food packages "helped us survive," Satsita Sadulayeva remembers—and "thanks to the classes, I can now share my pain with other women, and that has helped me enormously. Now I have the energy to work for my family's well-being." Widow Petimat Umakhanova, thirty-five, and her four children receive the equivalent of seventy-five dollars a month in state benefits and Red Cross help. She's going to school to become a beautician.

But seventy-two-year-old Khava Bumbarova, whose house was destroyed in 1999, is an old woman who can't work. She lives in a tiny room in a temporary housing center in Grozny with two iron beds, a small table, some shelves, a bowl for washing up in, and no toilet. The Russian federal migration service provides her with assistance, and UNICEF brings water. But the Ministry of Health wants the building back. Khava and the other 807 displaced people who live there will have to go elsewhere, probably to another center. But soon all of the centers housing 37,000 people will be closed down. What will Khava do then?

There are no state entitlements for widows and wives whose husbands have disappeared, either. Underage children with dead dads are entitled to compensation, but to get it the family must produce an official death certificate along with a government-issued "permanent address registration," something that is impossible for many families to do. Women who receive the 350,000 rubles compensation for their destroyed homes usually end up spending it on food and rent for shelter instead of building new houses or repairing their apartments. Few ever receive it anyway; corrupt and thieving Chechen officials see to that. Criminals bribe bureaucrats to file thousands of false claims, and corrupt officials see fit to charge a legitimate claimant up to half of the amount due to them. No more than 10 percent of legitimate claimants had received payments by the time the program was suspended at the end of 2004. It was reopened in 2008, but 75 percent of the claims filed that year turned out to be phony too.

FEEDING THE FAMILY

Work is a blessing. It brings sanity, purpose, and meaning to life in wartime. It's also needed by every Chechen woman to feed her family. Ignoring the dangers, and overcoming the stress and physical exhaustion, women in wartime who were capable of working and whose husbands were either dead, fighting, disabled, couldn't find work, or were hiding at home because they were too afraid to come out or their wives wouldn't let them somehow mustered the strength and courage to look for work. doing anything to earn a few rubles to buy food.

Not every husband at home in 2000 was allowed to work. "Most husbands sit at home. I am afraid to let mine out go into the street on his own. When he has no choice but to go, I prefer to accompany him. I protect him, not him me. . . . It's better for him to stay home," Elza Duguyeva said. There's good reason that Elza, not her husband, went out to procure the family's needs. Women could more easily come and go, negotiate and navigate the myriad of Russian checkpoints than Chechen men, who ran a high risk of being detained and maybe even disappearing.

There's hardly any work anyway. In 2003 40 percent of Chechens were living in poverty, while 32 percent had difficulty meeting even their most basic food needs. A 2006 United Nations World Food Programme (WFP) study shows that half of the population were living under the official poverty level of eighty-five rubles ($2.97) a day. With 318,000 unemployed in 2007, three-quarters of the working-age population were jobless.

How, then, did women feed their families? Some swept dirty Grozny streets and cleaned bus stops. Others dug trenches or moved bulky garbage cans. Before the wars it had been beneath a Chechen woman's dignity to do this kind of dirty work—Russian and Armenian women had done it.

Leila Adiyeva, a dishwasher and brick factory worker before 1994, stood out in the snow on the street corner in the first war and sold homemade buns she had made at home the night before. But she had to rely on food rations in the second war. Leila wanted to open a bakery in Grozny, but I don't know if she ever did. Other women collected bricks and other building material from bombed-out structures for sale or to repair or build new shelters. Still others made and sold homemade gasoline and kerosene. Elza Duguyeva and her children gathered scrap aluminum from trash heaps to sell to Russian soldiers, who resold it at home. Others stole copper electrical wiring and whatever other metal they could find or dismantle to sell to the illegal metal traders.

"And fools that we were, we took apart an enormous oil refinery and exchanged it for bread," Elza recalls. Every day Elza risked stepping on a land mine or setting off unexploded war ordnance just to make enough to survive on. "For a kilo of iron, I, along with both boys, get six rubles and that's a loaf of bread. For that, I labor for a whole day," she told Prochazkova. Elza's daily routine began at 5:30 AM. She rousted everyone out of bed, made breakfast, and got out on the street by the time martial law curfew was lifted at 8 AM. She returned home before dark, because the risk of getting shot as a *shakhida* was too great to stay out late. "I expect they [Russian soldiers and policemen] are just as frightened of me as I am of them, so they'd sooner shoot me than take the risk that I might be a kamikaze partisan [suicide bomber]," she explains. Elza and her family lived in a friend's dilapidated apartment, with a hole the size of a KamAZ truck in one side covered with tin. She carries hand-drawn water up five flights of stairs, because that chore is too degrading for her husband to do. "Our husbands aren't allowed to go for water. . . . Since time immemorial; it's been strictly a woman's job."

Elza Duguyeva is typical of the woman who refuses to give up. Like so many other women, she is much better at surviving than her husband is. "He is more distraught than I am," she says.

The Street Market Traders

While Elza collects scrap metal, most women work as Chechnya's street market traders. Since the early 1990s their numbers have soared, reaching the thousands today. A huge number of working women sell full- or part-time to support their families. Before the collapse of the Soviet Union, selling was beneath a woman's dignity; husbands wouldn't allow it. But since the collapse of the economy in the Dudayev years, women have been selling everything from sunflower seeds and homemade gasoline to humanitarian aid from abroad, as well as just about anything they can grow, bake, make, collect, or otherwise get their hands on.

Yakha Ugurchiyeva, sold guns at Grozny's vibrant weapons bizarre in the first war; a good Kalashnikov rifle would bring $550, and sometimes a couple of rifles could be traded for two pretty decent cars. Aliesha, the wife of the American *mujahideen* Aukai Collins, sold vegetables at a roadside stand in Kurchaloi in 1995. Raisa, Milana Terloeva's mother, sold at Grozny's central market goods she had bought in Moscow and Turkey. So did Nura Luluyeva and her cousins Raisa and Markha Gakayeva. Leila, Stas's wife, and her mother sold there, too.

While selling gives some women only a subsistence income or supplements her husband's income, others, like Ayshat Mizayeva, whose husband can't work, have become professionals at it. A librarian before the first war, Ayshat sells clothing she buys wholesale in Pyatigorsk, Russia, at Grozny's central market. "I've been selling in this market for about seven years [since 1997] now. At the beginning, I thought I wouldn't be able to stand it; especially since I lived with books all my life. But with the money I've earned here, I have managed to pay for my daughter's wedding and to send my son to university," she says.[7] Dubrovka terrorists Zareta Bairakova, Marina Bisultanova, and Aiman Khadzhiyeva sold there too. So did airliner bombers Satsita Dzhebirkhanova and Amnat Nagayeva. Beslan terrorists Rosa Nagayeva and Maryam Taburova were successful traders also. They shared a bombed-out apartment across the street from the market and sold children's clothing, school supplies, and toys they had bought wholesale in Baku. Margarita Ersenoyeva sold shoes at the market before she disappeared in October 2006.

But the market as a source of livelihood dried up for hundreds of women when on 14 July 2008 Grozny's city government closed portions of it for beautification and reconstruction. I don't know if Ayshat lost her "job," but forty-seven-year-old Maret did, and she wasn't happy about it. She protested, organizing a women's demonstration at President Kadyrov's country residence in Gudermes. "For many traders there, mainly women, their trading was the only income because Chechnya lacks workplaces, and the unemployment is enormous," Maret complains. "We don't know who to ask for help now. They threw us out of the market, we don't have another working place, but we need to feed our children," she pleads. She wants another location to sell in. A brand-new market, Berkat, just opened on the former grounds of the former Krasny molot factory, but the space there had already been snapped up by other sellers.

Five months later Grozny's mayor put more women out of work when he forcibly closed down the "spontaneous markets" littering the city. These were cars and makeshift roadside stands from which people sold food, clothing, building materials, and even illegal fireworks and alcohol. These "markets" cluttered practically every city street, creating an eyesore in a city being reborn.

The New Entrepreneurs

The more successful and ambitious sellers are now leaving the market and opening their own clothing boutiques, jewelry stores, beauty shops, cafés, and fancy restaurants like the Hollywood Restaurant in the Santa Barbara shopping center in downtown Grozny. The female entrepreneurial class in Chechnya is exploding.

Luisa Aftakhanova, a thirty-eight-year-old old unmarried woman who fled Grozny and lived in Ingushetia and Moscow during the war, returned in 2006 and now runs the Coral beauty shop there with two other beauticians, Rima Yukayeva and Lyuda Chubanova. "Women want to look pretty, despite the war," Aftakhanova says. The International Medical Corps may have helped Luiza get her start. The IMC has supported a beauty school since 2004, offering a three-month course to women from families facing severe economic hardship. By the end of 2004 the school had graduated nearly two hundred women. Twenty-seven-year-old Zarema, whose husband is disabled, finished the IMC course in April 2006. She dreams of opening her own salon someday but in the meantime works from home, cutting hair. "My childhood was good. I worked in a sewing shop making clothes. Then I worked for the Ingush national dance troupe. During the war, I went to Ingushetia. Praying five times a day has been the most important thing in my life. The second most important thing was learning how to style hair. I had half of the skills, and the teachers taught me the other half," she says.[8]

Beauty shops are popping up all over Grozny. Roza Zilbukharova, a new beautician, is a widow with children who lives in a rented apartment. Madina, another novice beautician, works in the Mikhail Lermontov State Dramatic Theater. Both beauticians were trained by CARE Canada's Center for Women. Roza even received a CARE Canada grant to buy equipment for her beauty salon. "We awarded her the grant because of her social conditions and the diligence she showed during the studies," Satsita Khaidukayeva, CARE's project manager says.

The IMC operates numerous business training programs in Chechnya. Thanks to them, in the spring of 2007 Petimat Berevyea became the proud manager of a brand-new grocery store in Achkoi-Martan. Kerry Woodham, IMC's Russian Federation program manager, says that the idea to open a store that would sell fresh meat, dairy, produce, and baked goods came from the community but that it was Petimat, a forty-year-old woman born with achondroplasia (the common cause of dwarfism), who championed the idea, studied accounting, financial and personnel management with an European Commission Humanitarian Aid Office (ECHO) grant, and is now running a thriving store.

The IMC helped forty-eight-year-old Zura Zaurbekova, a skilled seamstress before the first war, open her Belosheveika (seamstress) sewing shop in 2009. Zura's husband was working as a part-time driver and couldn't make enough money to feed their family. "We had no food for the children before the International Medical Corps found us," Zura says. So she put together a business plan for IMC's review and, like the other 190 entrepreneurs who got their start through IMC in 2009, opened her business. "I was so happy," Zura says.[9]

Banata Mustafimova received a grant too, from the Red Cross, to buy sewing machines. Now she runs a sewing shop and hires people to help her. In January 2007 the Red Cross made grants to over fifty people like Banata.

The Chechen government also has a program, called "From Survival to Prosperity," to support small-business development, but corrupt officials have stolen some of the four billion rubles allocated for it.

Rosselkhozbank's Chechen branch of the bank has put millions into small-business development since 2001. Zulai-Khan Tagirova is assistant director of the bank in Chechnya. "Over the past five years, the bank has provided loans to hundreds of enterprises," she says.

The Community Service Cadres

Women are heavily involved in community service work. There's a particularly rich cadre of them who do voluntary and paid community service work for international and local humanitarian organizations operating in the republic and in Ingushetia. Most are highly educated, some are doctors, and others possess professional and sorely needed technical skills. Seventy-five percent of the United Nations World Food Program's "cooperating partners" (NGOs) in Chechnya are staffed by women, who manage and distribute food directly to the needy. Some women who received aid and established early working relationships with foreign humanitarian organizations in the first war built on that experience to provide valuable help to other vulnerable women in the second.

Gistam Sakayeva, a former refugee and aid worker since the first war, when she was recruited by Doctors Without Borders from a refugee camp in Ingushetia in 1995, is one of them. After working for Handicap International, CARE Canada, and the Organization for Security and Cooperation in Europe (OSCE), she is now a board member of the Grozny-based NGO "Reliance," a grantee of the Open Society Institute (in the United States). In 2008 Gistam received the prestigious Women's Commission for Refugee Women and Children's "Voices of Courage" award for her work with the disabled, victims of domestic violence, and imprisoned perpetrators of honor killings. Gistam tells me that her organization helps single women, widows, "women-headed households," and the disabled to "create dignified, self-sufficient lives," by providing a variety of programs, including assistance to victims of gender-based violence, legal counseling, and health and hygiene classes—even income-generating courses such as pasta-making and bakery workshops. "Reliance," located at No. 6 Sherbakova Street in the Staropromyslovsky District of Grozny, has so far helped about five thousand women. It has four permanent staff and fifteen or more women who work part-time.

Besides Reliance, the only other local women's support and advocacy group in Chechnya is Women's Dignity, which is also based in Grozny. Despite many attempts, I was unable to get in touch with Lipkhan Bazayeva, an early organizer of the women's movement in Chechnya, who runs Women's Dignity.

Female doctors and pediatrician nurses today run the Doctors Without Borders' mother- and child-care programs in Chechnya discussed later in this chapter. Zina Batalova, a Grozny obstetrician and gynecologist, is the IMC team's medical programs manager in Chechnya and a medical brigade doctor.

Other women, like Zainap Gashayeva, Svetlana Umarova Aliyeva, and Mariam Yangiyeva, have organized the Chechen women's movement and human-rights NGOs like Ekho Voiny (Echo of War), the Women's Union of the Northern Caucasus, and others. They are discussed later.

The "Angel of Grozny"

Khadizhat Gatayeva cares for war-orphaned children to feed her "family." Khadizhat, who couldn't have children of her own because of a terrible automobile accident when she was thirty years old, and her husband Malik returned home from Siberia in February 1995, right in the middle of the first war. They opened a small café next to the central market, but in 1996 Khadizhat went to work as a nurse for Grozny's military commandant, Aslambek Ismailov, while Malik became one of his ambulance drivers. One day Ismailov asked her to look after seven war-orphaned children for the night. He hadn't been able to find a place for them to stay. Khadizhat didn't even have her own apartment—she and Malik were staying with friends—but she brought them home with her anyway.

"Children, this is your papa," Khadizhat told her wards as she introduced them to Malik. The next morning, she explained her living situation to Ismailov. She had had an idea! There were empty apartments all over Grozny; why couldn't he give her two of them—"for the children?"

"But they might be mined," Ismailov countered.

Khadizhat got her apartments, in a five-story building right across the street from the commandant's office, and within a month had twenty-six children to care for. Thus began the Rodnaya semya (Native Family) orphanage. But it takes money to feed and clothe all those kids. She got that too, from Chechnya's Ichkerian government and the OSCE. Native Family grew to over fifty children, housed in three apartments. She commandeered a third empty apartment. She got into hot water about that, but the OSCE bought the apartment and the other two for her and gave her a thousand dollars a month operating expenses for her orphanage.

In 1997 Khadizhat won the Ichkerian government's "Woman of the Year" award and became known throughout the city as the "Angel of Grozny." President Maskhadov was her biggest patron—"Maskhadov's children," people called Khadizhat's orphans.

"Uncle Basayev"—Shamil Basayev—was a patron too. In 1997 the orphanage celebrated its first wedding, when fifteen-year-old Milana married one of Shamil Basayev's bodyguards. Khadizhat fondly recalls that "the premier [Basayev] would often come to visit to see the children." He brought toys and dollar bills, once even a television set. All of the children studied in school, but in August 1999 their dreams of normal lives ended when Uncle Basayev invaded Dagestan and declared holy war on Russia. "We know how to shoot, but we'll never kill," one of Khadizhat's "sons" told her. But soon he and the other older boys ran off to join Basayev anyway.

"I'm a little bit like Mother Teresa. I always wanted to be like her," Khadizhat recalled in better days before the second war. But the second war inevitably came. When it did, Khadizhat and her children hid in a basement for an entire month before an escape could be arranged. Her brother in Ingushetia took eighteen of the children. Thirty-eight went with Khadizhat and

Malik to a sanatorium in Kharkov, Ukraine, and the rest, twenty-eight of them, were sent to Lithuania. Malik rented a small bus and drove the first twelve children to Kharkov. He had trouble getting across the Russian border, but, he says, says a $150 bribe to border guards did the trick. After that, Malik too went off to fight Russia.

Khadizhat soon returned to the North Caucasus; the German Cap Anamur charity bought four cottages and built a cafeteria, sport hall, and classrooms for her in Ingushetia. She kept the children there for a while. Then Cap Anamur purchased a large brick house in Grozny for her, and she moved Rodnaya semya back home. For a while, the "Angel of Grozny" glowed in the spotlight of international publicity. She and her orphans were featured in the 2004 documentary film *The 3 Rooms of Melancolia,* by Finnish film director Pirjo Honkasalo, and she is the main character in Asne Seierstad's wonderful book the *Angel of Grozny.*

But troubles began again in 2005. Khadizhat was running out of money, since Cap Anamur only funds projects for five years, and there was no help forthcoming from Russia or Chechnya's president. She had long since fallen out of favor with the pro-Moscow Chechen government, and Kadyrov had long wanted to close her down anyway. She had never officially registered her "orphanage," and it wasn't recognized by Chechnya's Labor and Social Development Ministry.

Since Malik was in exile in Lithuania, the Gatayev's in the summer of 2005 presented their situation to a conference at the Rudolf Steiner school in Vestfold, Norway. They subsequently met with Waldorf schoolteachers and students in Finland and were given 20,000 euros ($25,000) to begin the evacuation of children from Grozny, particularly those who were older and in danger of being drafted into the Russian Army or, worse yet, suspected of being militant fighters. Those in need of medical attention were evacuated first. Khadizhat moved them to Lithuania, where ten of the children evacuated in 2000 still lived in an apartment in the city of Kaunas. She moved fifteen more orphans there on 29 September 2005. In November 2005 the European Council for Steiner Waldorf Education, known as "Waldorf One World (or WOW) day," collected money for the renovation of the apartment.

In the meantime, WOW-day launched a campaign to buy Khadizhat a house. WOW put up 70,000 euros and the rest, 30,000 euros, was borrowed from a Finnish woman to purchase a house in Karmelava in the spring of

2006. The WOW-day 2008–2009 campaign aimed at raising money to pay the loan back and provide a thousand euros per month operating costs.

All was going well until the fall of 2008, when the Gatayevs abruptly fell from grace in Lithuania. On 15 October Lithuanian state security arrested both the "Angel of Grozny" and her husband on charges of extorting money from the teenage children in their care. They were accused of material deprivation of orphans and of "subjecting orphans to physical and psychological violence," "staging executions," and "imposing medieval traditions." The Gatayev's have been in and out of jail ever since.

Three teenagers at the home had accused them of attempted extortion, alleging that when they refused to pay the Gatayevs beat and threatened to kill them. The details of the case are secret and difficult to sort out. It's odd that Lithuanian state security became involved in what would normally be a criminal matter.

Khadizhat was in ill health when she was arrested. She reportedly suffers from heart problems; she fainted in court on 25 March 2009 and had to be rushed to the hospital. But she was well enough later to flee to Finland. Both her and Malik were arrested in Helsinki on 7 January 2010 at the request of Lithuania, after the Kaunassky Okrug court sentenced them to a year and a half in jail. The Lithuanian Department of Immigration has annulled their permission to live in Lithuania. They intend to apply for political asylum in Finland.

The Criminals

Other women turn to crime to feed their families or enrich themselves. The selling of babies to wealthy Chechen families is a profitable business in Chechnya. It's also illegal. You seldom hear about such things, but in April 2006 a scandalous case made headlines when five doctors, two of them women, were arrested for peddling unwanted children. Federal narcotics agents looking into the illegal sale of hospital drugs had stumbled across them.

Police arrested gynecologist Akhtayeva and charged her with selling a baby boy for three thousand dollars to an undercover agent. Since Akhtayeva has children of her own at home, she was released on a written promise not to leave Chechnya, but by 3 May she was back in jail, along with another woman, for trying to sell a second baby, this time for five thousand dollars. Two infant girls had already been sold, and a third baby was found in the apartment of one of the women. Another high-profile case came to light in

December, when a single woman, identified only as "Djuletta S——," tried to sell her nine-day-old child.

Children were sold in the first war too. "Ten years ago [1996] . . . I was riding in a taxi through the village of Assinovskaya in Chechnya. I saw six children standing in a line beside a wooden fence. When I wondered why they were standing there, the taxi driver answered, 'To be sold,'" Laila Bai-sultanova, a journalist recalls.

Mothers unable to take care of their children sold them to well-off people. "One girl has already been sold. She was nice and beautiful with fair hair. They bought her because she was very small. These ones are bigger and no one wants to buy them," the taxi driver told Laila.[10]

The birth of babies to single women (abortion is taboo in Chechnya), social stigmas, and economic desperation are fueling child trafficking in Chechnya. As in the case of rape a woman's life is finished if she gives birth out of wedlock. Elza P—— told me about one girl she knew of who had worn long gowns at home to hide her pregnancy; when she went to the hospital to have her baby, her parents disowned her. They never let her come home. Another girl simply took the baby and ran away with the child's father.

Maffina (Madina) Eldarova, deputy chief physician in Chechnya's maternity clinic explains, "Because of our traditional mentality, it is shameful for a single woman to give birth to a child. As a rule these [single] women deliver at home. Afterwards, so as not to reject the child officially, they secretly hand it over to someone else or abandon it like trash. They sometimes sell them too, which is even worse."[11] Elza P—— says that during the Dudayev years anyone finding a baby and wanting to adopt it could simply fill out the necessary paperwork and legally adopt it, with no difficulty.

Other women smuggle and sell drugs to make a living. After the collapse of the Soviet Union, Chechnya became a hub of narcotics distribution between the major producing regions of the Golden Crescent and the lucrative markets in Russia and Western Europe. The intricate web of smuggling routes used to bring foreign fighters and weapons into Chechnya was also used to smuggle drugs to the European market. Before Russian forces returned to Chechnya in 1999 drug production was on a full industrial footing. Kidnapped Russians and others were made slaves to cultivate poppy and hemp fields. Ten years later, with over 20,000 people dependent on illegal narcotics (including 10,000 heroin addicts), Chechnya has a serious and growing narcotics problem.

On 20 January 2006 police arrested a Chechen woman and her Tadjik partner for the sale of 23.6 kilograms of heroin to undercover state narcotics agents. While narcotics-related crime in Chechnya saw a slight decrease in 2008, the number of women prosecuted for selling drugs that year actually went up. At year's end, close to a hundred women were sitting in Chechen jails. One of those was a fifty-four-year-old Naursky District woman who was arrested on 5 July 2008 for selling a large quantity of heroin. Another was Fatima Bisultanova, who in September 2008 was given five years for peddling the prescription drug Tramal (Tramadol). She is a habitual offender and had been under investigation for a similar crime in the Shalinsky District at the time of her arrest. On 3 December 2008 charges were brought against a Gudermes woman and her companion, a corrupt senior police lieutenant, after they were caught red-handed with a large quantity of heroin in their car returning home from Khasavyurt, where they had purchased the drug.

Women are selling illegal narcotics more than ever before. It's a growing problem. "This was not the case a few years ago," a state narcotics control officer says. More women were caught, prosecuted, and put in Chechen jails in 2009 than in 2008. Many more are imprisoned at the Kizylurtovsky Women's Colony No. 8 in Dagestan. Of the 350 prisoners there in 2008, sixty were Chechen women—almost all serving time for the illegal manufacture and sale of psychotropic drugs. There are more this year, primarily because they are being taken from other prisons in Russia and moved closer to home.

Some women kidnap children for ransom. On 15 January 2007 two Chechen women and a policeman broke into an elderly woman's house in Ordzhonikidzevskaya, Ingushetia, stole her mobile telephone and television, and kidnapped her granddaughter for ransom. On 23 October 2008 police arrested a Grozny woman and several of her male friends for the kidnapping of three-year-old Royana Bagolova. They had broken into the family's residence in Nazran, Ingushetia, ransacked it for money, and when they couldn't find any kidnapped Royana and demanded 25,000 rubles ransom. Royana's case is identical to the 1998 kidnapping of three-year-old Lena Meshcheryakova.

Involvement in real estate fraud is common. On 9 August 2008 police arrested sixty-year-old Angelina Bakumeno for using forged documents to sell an apartment that didn't belong to her. Bakumeno had somehow gained access to government housing documents for apartments on Rosa Luxenburg Street in Grozny, prepared a fictitious purchase contract for one of them, registered it in her own name, then sold it to a third party for a million rubles. She had already served a five-year jail sentence for similar real estate fraud. There was an identical case in the spring of 2008 when Shovda Myagchiyeva used fake legal documents to sell a three-room Grozny apartment to a woman for 540,000 rubles. She was tried and sentenced to a little over three years for her crime.

On 5 September 2008 Saratovskaya Oblast and Groznensky District OVD police arrested an unidentified forty-nine-year-old woman from Petropavlovsky, Groznensky District, for grand theft. That same day, Chechen police detained two women with fake medical degrees. One was a twenty-eight-year-old who acquired a counterfeit degree in 2005 and had been working in Samashki's hospital ever since. The other was a twenty-year-old woman working at an outpatient clinic. Both were charged with forging counterfeit documents. On 7 October 2008 a forty-eight-year old Leninsky District woman was arrested on unspecified fraud charges.

Women can still make money by serving in noncombatant roles in the Jihad. The risk of getting caught is higher than ever now, but the money is good—at least, it was while Shamil Basayev was alive and finances were more plentiful. A woman could earn up to three hundred rubles for information on the location and movement of Russian military and police forces. Today money is tighter, and women risk being paid in counterfeit currency.

Female fighters during the active combat phases of the two wars were paid well too, but snipers received the best pay. A list of payouts on a piece of paper found in the pocket of a dead female sniper near the village of Bechik in the first war indicated that 170,000 rubles had been paid to a woman by the name of Fatima. Another, Oksana, received 150,000 rubles, and Lena got $30,000 for killing two spies. In the second war, female snipers were paid handsome signing-up fees of up to $10,000. Anya Klinkyevicha received a thousand dollars and a Zhigule car as a graduation present from sniper school. I said earlier that she was also promised between two and five hundred dollars for each Russian officer she killed. There was a time when Basayev paid as much as a thousand dollars for a dead Russian officer.

Suicide bombers still receive good compensation. At a thousand dollars, Zarema Muzhikhoyeva may have been the lowest paid. The families of many others who succeeded in killing themselves received thousands of dollars in addition to help in relocating to Azerbaijan or Turkey.

SO WOMEN WON'T HAVE TO CRY ANYMORE

There's a rebuilding frenzy going on in Chechnya today. The ruins of Grozny's city center are being magically transformed into a brand-new, modern European city. Schools there and across the republic have been rebuilt and are operating again, putting female teachers back to work and 213,000 children back in school (in 2009). Electricity is restored, ruined apartment blocks have been knocked down, and beautiful new ones are rising in their place. Shops, cafés, restaurants, and theaters are popping up like mushrooms, and a new mosque, the largest in Europe, capable of accommodating up to 10,000 people, has been constructed.

President Ramzan Kadyrov had promised to deliver a shiny new city center by the end of 2007, but according to Grozny's mayor, only 50 percent of the reconstruction was completed by then. Nevertheless, almost a thousand major projects had been done, including 847 buildings, twenty-three schools and thirteen kindergartens, two bridges, six mosques, twenty-five health facilities (including a children's hospital, a maternity hospital, and an adult rehabilitation center), fifty-two miles of roads, and a movie and performing arts theater. Five more kindergartens, eight middle schools, and 240 apartment buildings were under construction. There are construction materials at every building site in the city.

Before the last war the tallest building in Grozny was sixteen stories. Now, eighteen-, twenty-five-, and even forty-five-story apartment buildings, with underground parking and business centers, are being built. The elite "Grozny-City" development on Kadyrov Prospekt will sport a five-star hotel, a thirty-story business center, and even a helicopter landing pad on the roof.

Construction of a brand new women's prison in the Zavodsky District of Grozny, complete with a mother- and child-care center, also began in 2008. Female inmates in Chechnya have had to do their time in male prison colonies. Two women—Madina and Yasita—are among the 794 prisoners at Chernokozovo. There are between six hundred and a thousand Chechen women in Russian prisons outside Chechnya. Some of them will be brought back and housed in the new facility.

War-ravaged Gudermes, Chechnya's second most important city, is beautiful now. A new luxury hotel, the Kavkaz, and five new sixteen-story apartment building are going up. The city also sports a brand new aquapark, with separate pools for men and women, cafés, and restaurants. There's nothing physical left in Gudermes to remind the visitor that there was ever a war here.

There seems to be no end to the construction boom, which is creating new jobs. But not all is as rosy as it seems. There are still few legally binding employment contracts, and in 2007 construction workers' salaries were often weeks to months late, reduced by half, or not paid at all, prompting at least two mass demonstrations in June of that year. The economic crisis of 2009 has also postponed some projects and slowed completion of others.

How has the boom affected women's employment prospects? On the one hand, it is creating many new administrative jobs for women. In March 2007 there were nearly a thousand women employed in Grozny's apartment, communal services, and building organizations. And, of course, the new women's prison will employ a few hundred women. On the other hand, Chechnya still has the highest rate of unemployment in all of Russia—and there are still comparatively few jobs for women.

The overall unemployment situation is gradually being reduced, but not quickly enough. According to 2008 official statistics, there was a 35 percent drop in the number of unemployed men and women from 2007. But the 2009 figures were disappointing: there were still 300,000 unemployed, 45.5 percent of the working population. This came as a shock to Finance Minister Yeli Isayev, who said the number was almost certainly lower, given the tempo of the reconstruction.

In April 2009, the government announced that it would create 22,000 part-time jobs and six hundred new permanent ones. It's unclear how many of these went to the 24,000 higher-education graduates who flooded the labor market in 2009. It's also unclear how many joined the ranks of the Jihad as an alternative.

There is a sense of optimism now, a hope for a better economic future. Even Chechens I know who can never return home are impressed with the economic progress being made, despite the fact that it's being spoiled by the endless suicide bombings and militant attacks targeting police and civilians, a new epidemic of state kidnappings and disappearances, and a worsening security situation.

Kadyrov has promised to do much better by women. "You have suffered much, and as head of the republic I promise that the Chechen woman will no longer have to cry. To ensure that, I am doing everything possible and impossible," he told them at a city celebration in recognition of International Women's Day in March 2007. He apologized for the heavy work burden that Chechen women have to carry to support their families, and he promised that "in the near future everything will be put in its place and women will not have to work on the same level as men." But they still do.

THE MARCHING MOTHERS

When I asked Elza P——— how war has affected surviving women the most, she replied, "It's made them aggressive!" My first thought was that the Chechen family is in deep trouble, then, because aggressiveness in a female is a quality Chechen men do not like. But then Elza explained. This new "aggressiveness" has been manifested by hundreds, and sometimes thousands, of women taking to the streets and demonstrating against Russian military operations or for the return of missing family members, friends, and relatives. "We've had enough of being passive while we're being killed!" Mariam Arsanovkayeva, a protestor in the Grozny 2001 "peace march" asserted.

Strong-willed and angry Chechen women block roads, highways, bridges and railroad tracks; stop military and civilian traffic; picket government building and pro-Moscow Chechen officials to secure the release of detained persons; intervene in the detention of relatives, friends, fellow villagers, or even complete strangers; and negotiate the return of bodies. These actions by women are frequent, both spontaneous and organized by the Chechen women's movement.

These women are very good at what they do. "Many of us owed our lives to them," Dr. Baiev writes. "During the *zachistkas*, the women were always ready to mount a protest in an attempt to stop Russians from arresting or killing a man. They would press and press, try to overwhelm, hoping they wouldn't get shot, appealing to a man's natural instinct not to shoot women and children."[12] Both wars were replete with such examples of spontaneity. But Chechen women also organize large-scale rallies and demonstrations, with participants sometimes numbering into the thousands. Emotions run high, and the actions of these women are, understandably, not always orderly.

Thousands of determined women, young and old, first made their collective power known on 15 December 1994 when they blockaded the Moscow-to-Baku highway, briefly halting Russian military columns advancing toward Grozny. The women told General-Major Ivan Babichyev that his tanks would have to roll over their dead bodies if he wanted to get to Chechnya. "We didn't come here to kill innocent civilians. We'll find a way to settle this," he promised them. He never did, but the tanks didn't roll over the women, either.

The "Mothers' March for Life and Compassion," organized by the Committee of Soldiers' Mothers of Russia in the spring of 1995, is another example. This long "march," which left from the Kremlin for Grozny by foot and bus on 8 March, began with a few hundred people, rallied more women in Russian cities along the way, and was halted only by the blocking of the road to Achkoi-Martan and Russian artillery bombardment of Samashki. Russian forces loaded the exhausted and filthy women, who had knelt in the mud for hours outside Samashki, onto buses and sent them back to Ingushetia. That summer, on 5 July, angry women organized a march of 15,000 people through the center of Grozny to mark the funeral of a family of seven who had been murdered in their beds by unknown gunmen. Troops and Russian tanks halted the women at a bridge. One person was killed, but the marchers pushed and shoved their way past police lines anyway and went on to hold a defiant rally outside the ruins of the old Presidential Palace.

Two months later a Russian journalist wrote, "Outside the gates of the Russian military headquarters back in Grozny are a collection of women who come here every day for news of their missing husbands and sons. Yesterday, a list of prisoners at the Mozdok filtration camp was promised, and over a hundred women turned up, but the list never materialized. Today there are fewer, but one woman has been coming here every day for the last seven months."

The start of the new year in Grozny saw a week of marches for peace. And in midsummer 1996 hundreds of Chechen women participated in a huge peace rally at Grozny's Freedom Square. Chanting and flying banners that read, "Remove Russian troops from Chechnya," they made speeches and danced the traditional prayer dance. When the crowd started moving through the city, Chechen police blocked their path, but the women surged past them, dispersing only when they actually came face to face with gun barrels.

Spontaneous and organized demonstrations with some initial success became more frequent in the second war. During a March 2000 media tour of the Chernokozovo filtration camp a group of Chechen women surrounded a bus full of foreign journalists and shoved letters through open windows to them—letters accusing the Russian police of gross human rights violations at the facility. Five days later (on 8 March) several dozen women gathered in Grozny's Theater Square to demand the return of male relatives who had disappeared after being detained by federal forces.

Women were busy all year in 2001 because of the sweeping Russian cleansing operations taking place everywhere. On 28 February Alkhan-Kala residents gathered for an antiwar rally at the wood-processing plant and marched to the center of the settlement but were forced to disperse by soldiers firing warning shots over their heads. Then, on 2 March, a hundred women from the Chechen village of Dzhalka rallied in front of the federal administrative building in Gudermes, demanding the release of thirteen men who had been just been detained in a *zachistka*. Failing to get any satisfaction, they blocked the railroad tracks. On 8 March several dozen women again gathered on Teatralnaya Square demanding the return of their sons and husbands who had been recently taken by federal forces in cleansing operations.

A week later, women and residents of Argun rallied at the city offices of the military commandant concerning 170 people detained in the 11–14 March *zachistka* of Argun. All were released—minus four dead and seven disappeared.

Women participated in a mass rally in the village of Novogroznensky on 18 March over the attack on the village by federal troops three days earlier that had resulted in the deaths of a nineteen-year-old girl and a seventy-eight-year-old man. Three girls and a young woman had also been wounded when soldiers opened fire on houses and cars. Earlier that morning, Wolves had attacked a military convoy near the settlement, wounding nine servicemen. On 9 April the Grozny administration building was picketed by several dozen women demanding the release of Salman Abubakarov, a ninth-grader who had been arrested at home for possession of a grenade. The next day, residents of Dzhalka were picketing again, this time in front of the Chechen administration building, demanding the release of two shepherds detained the day before. The military commandant and other officials met with the demonstrators and assured them that relatives would be able to see the detainees and that the process of "filtering" them out would be accelerated. Most of the demonstrators went home around 2 PM, but about a hundred women who didn't believe that the officials would do what they had promised stayed behind.

But this was nothing compared to the ruckus caused by hardened female market traders the following month. While Grozny's central market is the lifeblood for many women, it has also been a haven for drug dealers, criminals, militant fighters, and terrorists, including female suicide bombers. That's why it's frequently raided. Two such raids *(zachistkas)* in late April and early May 2001 resulted in allegations of looting, beating, and detention of market staff and the death of three market guards, sparking the spontaneous action of angry female market traders.

After the first assault at 5 AM, on 29 April, a hundred women swooped down on the Zavodsky District police (MVD) station and demanded the release of the seven detained storeroom guards. All held valid passports and market work permits, and all were released that afternoon. When the second raid came, at ten o'clock in the morning on 1 May, the women pushed and shoved their way through the military cordon around the market, marched to the Zavodsky police station again, and demanded the release of thirty people who had been arrested. All but a few suspected thieves and drug dealers were freed.

But that night somebody murdered three market guards, which called for new and bolder tactics by the women. This time they pushed, pulled, and dragged burnt refrigerators, bombed-out car chassis, and other war junk to build a barricade blocking the busy intersection of Mira Street and Pobedy Prospekt in the center of Grozny. They halted military and civilian traffic for hours, demanding that the authorities find the murderers and stop cleansings of the market. They left only after Musa Gazimagomadov, the commander of Chechen OMON, showed up and promised to put the market under twenty-four-hour guard with twenty of his own men to prevent any such future incidents.

Two days later, on 4 May, several hundred Argun women blocked the bridge crossing the Argun River. They boldly demanded the release of a local female schoolteacher arrested the day before and got it. Their action caused huge traffic jams on the major highway connecting Grozny to Dagestan, but Russian soldiers at the bridge's checkpoint didn't interfere.

A week later the women returned to the bridge, this time demanding the bodies of three men who had been killed fighting Russian forces during a 7 May cleansing operation in Argun. After a Russian armored personnel carrier rolled over a demonstrator who was the sister of one of those killed in the cleansing operation, breaking her leg, infuriated women swarmed the commandant's office. They retrieved the bodies they wanted later that day.

On 2 May 2001 several hundred Chechens in Alkhan-Kala held a protest they had organized against Russian troops they accused of making arbitrary arrests. The protesters, many of whom were women and the elderly, urged the West to help stop the "genocide" of the Chechen people and demanded the release of thirty-six young men from the area who had been arrested by Russian troops. This inspired a third demonstration, on 14 May, at the ruins of the old drama theater in Grozny, where women demanded that Russia "stop executions" and "detentions without reason." Shouting "War is mothers' tears!" they demanded Russian military withdrawal from Chechnya. On 6 June more than a hundred people rallied near the central market in Argun to call for the release of people detained during more cleansing operations. On Saturday, 16 June, about a hundred women and children rallied in Grozny to again demand the withdrawal of Russian troops.

The rally, organized to coincide with a Russian-U.S. summit in Slovenia, was held in the city center and lasted ninety minutes. The protesters chanted "Withdraw the troops!" and carried posters reading "Bring our children back," "Stop genocide in Chechnya," "Occupiers out of Chechnya," "Stop killing civilians," and "Putin—murderer." On the morning of 21 June women blocked the Khasavyurt-to-Gudermes highway in protest against the taking of six young men from their beds at four in the morning by armed men in masks and camouflage uniforms. Representatives of the village administration were told in Gudermes that the men would be released in seventy-two hours if they were not guilty of anything. The demonstrators decided to stay on the highway until they were released. The villagers were soon joined by people from other settlements who began to shout radical political slogans, prompting the village demonstrators to disperse, so as not to jeopardize release of the detainees.

Eight days later dozens of women of Tsotsin-Yurt blocked the road passing through the village, where an earlier cleansing operation had resulted in the arrest of five people who were now being held at the Khankala military base. Protesters carried placards and signs reading "End the genocide of the Chechen people" and "Start negotiations with Maskhadov." Such displays did not weigh in favor of releasing the five prisoners. By evening, the Russian military had cleared the road, but this time the detainees were not released.

On 30 June several hundred people took part in another organized rally at Grozny's Teatralnaya Square, calling out slogans demanding an end to the war and the start of peace negotiations. Authorities made no attempt to break up the rally. Another rally, in front of the Grozny city administration building, on 1 July demanded the release of "citizens of Chechnya unlawfully detained by federal forces."

Police reaction to an anti-Russia "peace march" in Sleptsovskaya, Ingushetia, on 1 August was swift. The seventy-day scheduled march to Moscow had been organized by Aleksander Luboslavsky of the Russian magazine *Human Rights and Freedoms,* and it was supported by the Chechen National Salvation Committee, the Russian-Chechen Friendship Society, Ekho Voiny, the All-National Russian Committee for Ending War and Creating Peace in the Chechen Republic, the Moscow Helsinki Group, Human Rights Center "Memorial," the All-Russian Movement for Human Rights, Civil Assistance, and the Movement Against Violence. It was billed as the "Chechen version of the 1965 freedom march to Selma, Alabama."

The march was supposed to begin from the Sputnik Chechen refugee tent camp, where seventy women, elderly men, and children would march the first day of the thousand-mile trek. Two days before it was scheduled to begin, a meeting of thirty-four human rights organizations called it off because of security concerns. But Luboslavsky insisted that it go forward. Eighty-six marchers began, but police, having already surrounded the camp, halted them, arresting its organizers and some twelve protesters.

Two weeks later the representatives of "a relay peace march from Sleptsovsk" arrived in Georgia demanding that the "vandal aggressors . . . who are trying to destroy all living souls in Chechnya" must "get out of the North Caucasus," "stop their genocide of the Chechen people," "start negotiations with Chechen President Aslan Maskhadov," and initiate "a unilateral procedure for recognizing the independence of the Chechen Republic of Ichkeria which is trying to free itself from the colonial yoke." No wonder the FSB accused them of being Maskhadov propagandists.

Demonstrations continued into 2002. On 13 March an angry mob of nearly a thousand people from Stariye Atagi—a village that had been subjected to a harsh cleansing operation a few days earlier—descended on the main Chechen government administration complex in Grozny. Participants, mostly women and old people, brought with them the corpses of those killed during the cleansing operation, laid them in front of the complex, and insisted on meeting with government representatives. Not getting any satisfaction, nearly half the demonstrators broke down the fence and burst onto the grounds. The rest were cut off by security forces. Guards opened fire above the heads and at the feet of the demonstrators but were unable to disperse the demonstrators until evening. "It's better to die here from bullets than from torture during filtration. . . . We thought that you came to defend us from bandits, but you came to kill us. Monsters, butchers, go away!" the women shouted at the soldiers.

On 30 May 2002 the *Associated Press* reported that Chechen women from Stariye Atagi and Grozny were marching outside the offices of the Organization for Security and Cooperation in Europe (OSCE) in Znamenskoye. "Pinning portraits of relatives [of the missing] to the fence outside the OSCE offices. . . . Fifteen women carried signs written in both Russian and English reading 'Help us find our children seized by the Russian military' and 'We want our children back.'"

In mid-July one hundred women blocked the federal highway linking Grozny and Ingushetia. They demanded the release of five men arrested in federal operations in the village of Sernovodsk and the Wahhabi stronghold of Assinovskaya after Chechen fighters had shot and killed two Chechen policemen and wounded five others in Achkoi-Martan.

There were no less than seven mass demonstrations of women and their supporters in 2003, protesting the numerous cleansing operations in the republic and demanding the release of seized family members, friends, and relatives. The government's main administrative complex in Grozny was the focal point of most demonstrations. On 15 January people marched on the government complex but were prohibited from entering the grounds. Some women broke down the gate and got inside, where they were greeted by Movsar Khamidov, a government official, who began to tell them about all the "productive work" being done in the search for kidnapped persons. Despite his personal assurances that he would look into their cases, particularly the kidnapping of Anzhela Shakhmurazyeva, nothing happened.

At the end of May three hundred women and supporters from the villages of Mesker-Yurt and elsewhere boarded buses bound for Grozny to demand that the head of government, Akhmad Kadyrov, take immediate measurers to protect the inhabitants of Mesker-Yurt from the Russian cleansing operation going on there and lift the blockade of the village. The only result was that the water was turned back on.

Demonstrations continued into early June, when another hundred women, prompted by the disappearance of yet another teacher, Zara Bisayeva, descended on the Grozny administrative complex. This time, a bureaucrat appeared and accused the women of being paid by Chechen fighters to interfere with the work of the government, prompting the furious women to physically assault the offending bureaucrat. At the end of June, women protested that month's cleansing operations (three of them) in Gikalo, in which six people had been detained, demanding that they be freed or their bodies be returned to relatives. Protestors stood alongside the road holding up signs reading "Return our sons" and "The referendum has become hell for us." They blocked the road connecting Grozny with the foothills nearly all day.

On 13 August three male residents of the village of Mahkety were taken away by unknown armed men in camouflage clothing, prompting dozens of women from the villages of Tevzini and Makhety in the Vedensky District to rally at the Chechen administration building demanding their release. The women were met on the first day by the secretary of the Chechen Security Council, Rudnik Dudayev. The pickets continued for several more days until President Akhmad Kadyrov personally met with the demonstrators and told them that the men had been released.

A month later, on 15 September, a column of a hundred or so angry women, moved by rumors that somebody had seen an official list containing the names of thirty-two detainees being held at the Khankala military base, were back at the administrative building demanding to see the list, but no official could produce it. On 6 December six hundred Chechen women and their supporters blocked roads leading to the main administrative building, again demanding that their sons and relatives be found and released. This time, Chechnya's deputy prime minister, Movsar Khamidov, came out to tell the women that they should go to Gudermes to discuss their problems, but they were greeted there with warning shots over their heads and at their feet. Undaunted, they reorganized and twenty-one days later (27 December 2003) again blocked the entrance gate to the Chechen administrative complex.

The following year (2004) the Chechen administrative building and grounds once more became the scene of perpetual demonstrations that produced few satisfying results. On 3 March the NGO Council Information Center organized a mass protest of men and women, with their usual demands, blocking entrances to the grounds. Up to two hundred women were back on 2 June. A high-ranking MVD official ordered them to break up and, showing no emotion, commented, "I remember everyone, we'll look into it later." The women pelted him with rocks and anything else they could get their hands on, then managed to break through the security barriers and storm the building, but they were driven back by security forces firing over their heads.

Two weeks later, on 19 June, almost as many women from the villages of Assinovskaya and Sernovodsk blocked the Rostov-to-Baku highway, causing a huge traffic jam. They demanded that Chechen authorities release some thirty relatives detained by Russian forces during recent cleansing operations in the two villages. Politovskaya writes in her book *A Russian Diary*, "A meeting in the Chechen hill village of Sernovodskaya to demand the return of the latest group of men abducted by the federals has been dispersed with gunfire. Women from the neighboring village of Assinovskaya and from the district town of Akhchoi-Martan blocked the state highway with the same demand: stop these arbitrary abductions of their sons, husbands, and brothers."[13]

On 7 July 2004 relatives of kidnapped victims meet in Shali and resolved to block the Rostov-to-Baku highway, as well as the main roads linking district centers, and engage in other acts of civil disobedience if authorities didn't do more to investigate the disappearance of loved ones. The women said they were prepared to go on a hunger strike. "They [the Shali women] ask that European human rights campaigners and international organizations hear their cry of despair for a simplification of the procedure for according refugee status to Chechens. 'We have been driven out of Ingushetia, we are being murdered and our sons kidnapped in Chechnya, and in Russia we are second-class citizens.' Such is the resolution of the gathering," another Politovskaya entry reads.[14]

Demonstrations were less frequent in 2005 and 2006, almost nonexistent by 2007, perhaps because there were no more than nine abductions officially registered for the first six months of that year. And for the first time ever, a women's movement in support of Ramzan Kadyrov made its appearance. Interfax reported on 3 March 2005 that a conference entitled "Women for Peace and Stability in the Chechen Republic," organized by the Women's Dialog organization, published a resolution saying that the Russian government should not negotiate with Chechen separatists: "Russian and international public organizations should stop raising the issue of resuming talks with representatives of illegal armed groups and the so-called 'legitimate administration of Ichkeria.' Public and political organizations, movements, and parties should unite their efforts for the reconstruction and improvement of the humanitarian situation in the republic and step up their cooperation with the [pro-Moscow] Chechen leadership instead." The resolution further suggested "developing and adopting comprehensive programs for supporting family, maternity and childhood," creating a Mother and Child Social Rehabilitation Center in Grozny and providing for "the revival of a nationally oriented economy, creating jobs and developing national culture and folklore."

But women with other ideas were at it again on 1 July 2005, staging a rally in Grozny, demanding that the government do more to find and punish those responsible for allegedly abducting or killing their relatives. In recognition of "International Defense of Children Day," on 1 June 2006, a demonstration organized by the regional community organizations "Optimum," "Pravozhshchita" (In Defense of Rights), "Koalitsiya" (Coalition), and "Search for the Missing" formed a *zhivaya tsep* (living chain) at Neftuankov Square. Demonstrators, mostly women and the elderly, lined up on each side, carrying one or more portraits of missing relatives with slogans reading "Remove the mountainous burden from our shoulders," "Return our sons," "Ramzan, help return our sons."

On 30 August 2006 more than two hundred people, mostly women, carrying placards and photographs of relatives and friends marched all day long in Grozny. A girl, a medical college student and a resident of Shali, had been kidnapped in the Oktyabrsky District in the predawn hours the day before. Asmart, a fifty-seven-year-old Grozny resident, explained that "the primary goal of our action is to attract the attention of the government to the problem of missing people," adding, "More than 5,000 are missing in the republic. More than once we have conducted meetings, pickets and other actions of protest, demanding that the government find and return our sons, brothers, husbands, and fathers. But the government gives us only foggy promises. At one time it promised to create a special commission to look for missing people, but nothing has been done."

Women demonstrated for a different reason in the summer of 2007. On 5 June 100–150 men and women blocked the Rostov-to-Baku highway in the village of Chernorechye, Zavodsky District, because salaries due for their labor on construction sites had not been paid for months and they couldn't feed their families. The district head showed up with his security personnel. Arguments ensued, and shots were fired, wounding two women. A fraction of the salaries owed was finally paid on 10 June following a second demonstration.

Women had yet another reason to demonstrate outside the country home of President Ramzan Kadyrov in Gudermes on 23 July 2008, when another hundred women showed up to plead for his personal intervention in resolving their "unemployment situation" resulting from the closing of their selling stalls in Grozny's central market. OMON riot police firing rubber bullets dispersed the ladies and detained the ringleaders. The young women in the group were asked if they were married with husbands at home and, if so, why their husbands permitted them to carry on in such a despicable way.

On 18 December 2008 forty angry protesters, primarily family members and women from Materinskaya trevoga (Mothers' alarm), Laman az, Koalitsiya, and other organizations marched outside the office of Chechnya's human rights ombudsman demanding that the murderers of the three Ilayev brothers be tracked down and punished. On the night of 30 November Chechen police had broken into the Ilayev family home in Pervomayskoye and took Zalina Ilayeva, her pregnant sister-in-law Zarema, and Zalina's two younger brothers, Alvi and Akhdan, away for questioning. The women were freed within three hours, but the bodies of Alvi and Akhdan were found in the morgue on 3 December bearing evidence of torture. A third brother, Zurab, a policeman, was found on 10 December in a Grozny garbage dump. He had been beaten and strangled.

THE ORGANIZERS

The first war gave birth to the organized Chechen women's movement. Passionate activists formed a dozen or so organizations, most of them to protest Russian military operations in Chechnya, hunt for the disappeared, and monitor Russian human rights violations. Many become active internationally. Some have openly identified with Wolves and even collected money from abroad for the Chechen Jihad.

An observer to an organizing meeting of Chechen women on 24 August 1995 in the town of Sernovodsk noted, "Today I found myself in the middle of a national Women's Congress. About three hundred women from all over Chechnya have arrived in this border town to form a coalition of women's organizations and to plan a strategy for the next phase of their struggle. Women have been demonstrating every day in Grozny and in other towns, in some places putting barricades across the street to obstruct the movement of Russian tanks."[15]

Organizations like Ekho Voiny, Mothers of Chechnya, Women's Union of the North Caucasus, Beliy platok (White kerchief), Women's Dignity, Mothers' Pain, Mothers of Chechnya for Peace Association, Committee of Soldiers' Mothers of the Chechen Republic of Ichkeria, and many others were born at meetings like the one in Sernovodsk. These organizations and the women who run them have saved countless lives.

Zainap Gashayeva is one of the leading activists. She was a principal organizer of the Sernovodsk meeting and a cofounder of the Chechen women's movement. Born in Kazakhstan to Chechen parents, the mother of four children, a business school graduate, and former small-business owner in Moscow, she is a soft-spoken but relentless activist who, for the better part of a decade, was a tireless crusader for the Chechen Republic of Ichkeria and Chechnya's independence from Russia.

Irina Brenza, a journalist now living in Switzerland and an admirer, describes Zainap as "obsessed and driven. . . . She wakes up in the morning, makes up her hair, smoothes out her long skirt with her hands, paying no attention to her husband [Ramzan Gashayev, a former baker] who says that everything is in vain, that she should take care of her family, and that someday he will leave her because such a wife brings only misfortune to her husband." Gashayeva herself admits that "the war has become everything to me. . . . Neither my sister, nor my mother understand me." She told Anne Harrison in a May 1996 interview, "I'm so busy I even forgot my husband's birthday!" Zainap helped organize, and participated in, just about every early anti-Russian mass march and demonstration, including the 1995 peace march to Grozny.

She also cofounded two NGOs, including Ekho Voiny, an organization that described itself early on as a "social organization of the Chechen Republic of Ichkeria" and later as a "coalition of Chechen and Russian women" and an "interregional peacemaking society." She heads it today. She told a 2002 gathering at the Swiss Fund for the Defense of Freedom and Human Rights based in Bern, Switzerland, that Echo of war "works with Russian military commandants and communicates with representatives of the [Russian] president regarding human rights." But at home, she accuses Russia of falsifying information about the war, making it necessary for her organization to "monitor the conflict, collect facts and material about violation of human rights, theft and kidnapping of people, and summary executions." She says, "Our ultimate goal is to stop the war in Chechnya."

Echo of War women keep logs of military and police actions, indexes of victims, and video recordings of witnesses' statements. Its members document events, write down tank numbers and license numbers of other military vehicles participating in cleansing operations, record human rights violations, demand investigations by the procurator's office, and put intense pressure on both Russian and pro-Moscow Chechen authorities.

Gashayeva has made a career and a comfortable living, which has made her famous worldwide, out of painting Russia as the perpetrator of atrocities and genocide in Chechnya. A film has even been made about her exploits. The eighty-six-minute video entitled *COCA: The Dove from Chechnya— Europe in Denial of a War* premiered in Berlin in 2005. It won her organization the first International Human Rights Film Award at the sixth Gala of "Cinema for Peace" held in Berlin on 12 February 2007. COCA—"Coca" (dove) was Gashayeva's childhood nickname—has been screened in more than twenty international film festivals in New York, Amsterdam, Goteborg, Montreal, Talinn, Teheran, Warsaw, France, and Germany.

According to Brenza, President Dudayev implored Gashayeva to use her video camera as "a [propaganda] weapon" in the war against Russia. "She keeps her camera [hidden] under her skirt, and films bombed out villages, crying mothers who say the Russians have taken away their sons; cleansing operations, the 1999 Grozny market bombing, and just about everything else relating to operations conducted by Russian federal forces," Brenza says. Gasayeva probably has the largest collection of videos and photographs of the wars in Chechnya in existence.

She frequently travels to Western Europe and elsewhere to tell anyone who will listen and watch her videos that Russia is the sole cause of all the pain and suffering in Chechnya. She went on a speaking tour of Western Europe in June 1996. Three years later she was a delegate at the Hague Appeal for Peace Conference.

Testifying on behalf of the International Federation for Action of Christians for the Abolition of Torture, Gashayeva told the fifty-eighth session of the United Nations Commission of Human Rights in March 2002 that Russia was using Al-Qaeda's 9/11 attack on the United States as an excuse to commit further human rights violations in Chechnya, with "increased searches, arbitrary arrests, forced disappearance, rape, systematic torture and attacks." She called on Russia to invite the UN's rapporteur on extrajudicial executions, torture, and impunity to visit Chechnya, demanded an investigation into human rights violations in Chechnya and the prosecution of perpetrators, and proposed the establishment of an independent international commission of inquiry to look into human rights violations in the republic.

Brenza further describes Zainap as a woman who "seeks souls." Using subtle techniques to win converts, "she gathers soldiers to struggle against the war, soldiers without Kalashnikovs." Gashayeva herself proudly describes her own recruitment techniques: "The souls of strangers I manage to hook are close to me. I must touch them deeper, to drag them to the war using the gaff of our grief, but to act carefully, so that to gradually awake horror in them." Zainap Gashayeva and her organizations are well financed from abroad. She once told Viktor Popov of the Russian Information Analytical Center that she gets lots of help from Switzerland, Germany, France, and Turkey. In November 2002 she received a $6,500 cash award from Lotti Jacobi-Hartig, the president of the Swiss Fund for the Defense of Freedom and Human Rights based in Bern, Switzerland. This was followed by an annual award of $6,500 for "photo and video materials of the Chechen war," for "selfless help to the suffering of the homeless and women in war," and for "organized peaceful resistance to the violation of human rights in Chechnya." Gashayeva said she got the award for "fighting for the rights and freedom of the Chechen people." On 6 November 2005 she received the German Lev Kopelev Prize.

In 1995 Gashayeva, along with writer Svetlana Umarova Aliyeva and Mariam Yangiyeva, cofounded the Women's Union of the Northern Caucasus (WUNC) to document human rights violations by Russian troops in Chechnya. The women traveled the war zones, took photographs, and recorded more than two hundred videocassettes. They also participated in the antiwar movement in Russia and distributed small quantities of humanitarian aid donated by Oxfam and Saudi Arabia.

In 1997 the WUNC was funded by the Moscow-based Center for Peace and Community Development and the German Heinrich Boll Stiftung foundation. In November of that year it hosted an international women's conference to focus on "rebuilding societies ravaged by armed conflict." Maya Chovkhalova, a Grozny women whose husband was killed by shrapnel, now heads the WUNC, which participated in the October 2002 pro-Maskhadov Copenhagen World Chechen Congress.

Like those of Echo of War, most WUNC declarations are anti-Russian. The WUNC categorically accuses Russia of "shoving all Chechen boys who have reached the age of thirteen into filtration camps, where they are then beaten and raped."

In 2004 the WUNC was registered as a nonprofit organization in Moscow at No. 7 Godovikova Street, Apartment 2. Three members of the organization—Svetlana Umarova Aliyeva, Zainap Khamidovna Gashayeva, and Mariam Yangiyeva—are listed on their website, which states that its "spheres of interest" are "human rights, problems of soldiers' mothers, and the social empowerment of women."

Gashayeva's Echo of War, an organization she says is now engaged in humanitarian activities and help for homeless Chechen children and displaced parents, is located at the same Moscow address. Gashayeva, Echo of War, and the WUNC partnered with the Committee of Soldiers' Mothers of Russia to help many young Russian conscript deserters in the first war return home from Chechnya.

"We contacted Markha, a woman who lived in Alkhan Kala and who maintained contact with the Committee of Soldiers' Mothers in Moscow," Baiev writes in his book, when three young Russian conscripts came to his door and asked for help. The woman took a taxi to Nazran, Ingushetia, called their parents, and asked them to come and get the young men. The three escaped disguised as Chechen women, their heads covered with scarves.[16]

On 7 March 1995 the FSB arrested Zainap and her associate Adlan Betmirzayev for kidnapping Vyacheslav (Slava) Matveyev, a Russian deserter like those Baiev helped. Earlier, in December, Slava had run away from his unit near Samashki. Luba; an old Chechen lady had found him sick and hiding in the forest, took him home, and fed and hid him until he got well. In mid-February, she dressed him in women's clothing and took him through the Russian border guard post into Ingushetia, where she left him with the WUNC.

"When we saw this soldier we saw a boy made for life, for happiness, not for murder. We decided to fight for him," Zainap says. The WUNC hid him with an Ingush family, while the Mothers Committee back in Moscow tried to persuade his mother to fly to Nazran to pick him up. But she was scared. In the meantime, Slava had already been moved around between four families; then he disappeared. Gashayeva flew in from Moscow and, along with Betmirzayev, began to search for Slava. The next day she reported Slava missing to Ruslan, a policeman who had promised to help. Soon after that Gashayeva received a phone call saying that Slava's mother had finally arrived in Nazran. They met and went to the police station together the next day. It was then that Zainap and Adlan were arrested. Slava's mother had told the FSB that somebody in Chechnya had kidnapped her son. Zainap and Adlan were finally freed on 9 March, and Slava showed up the next day.

In the second war Zainap and Echo of War worked with the Russian organizations Women of the Don and Kindness Without Borders. Together with the Chechen Committee of National Salvation and the Society of Russian-Chechen Friendship, they helped organize the August 2001 peace march. She also monitored the 2003 Chechen presidential election, accusing the Chechen government of stuffing the ballot box.

There are many other women like Madina Magomadova, a tireless activist who founded one of the first human rights organizations in Chechnya, the well known Materi Chechni (Mothers of Chechnya), in May 1995. A biologist and lawyer before the first war, Madina was born on a collective farm in Kazakhstan, one of ten children. Her family later returned to Chechnya, living first in Shalazhi and then moving to back to the village of Yalkhoroi in the Galanchozhsky District, from where the family was deported during World War II.

Magomadova and her organization (which in 2007 had a hundred members and twenty-five active volunteers) search for the missing (Chechens and Russians) in Chechnya and are credited with negotiating the release of over several hundred Russian soldiers in the first war, some in exchange for Chechen prisoners. She has served on the OSCE's International Commission on Missing Persons, was a member of the Conciliatory Watchdog Committee on talks between Chechnya and Russia in the first war and of President Boris Yeltsin's Observation commission in 1995, and from 1996 to 1999 was vice president of the Observation commission.

She explained in a *Dosh* 2006 interview why she had taken up human rights work and founded the Mothers of Chechnya: "It was my personal grief . . . [m]y grief, my tears merged with the streams of grief and tears of other sisters, mothers, and wives. This is how my human rights activities began."[17] All this time she has been searching for her missing brother who disappeared in Grozny in January 1995.

The mission statement of the Mothers of Chechnya today says that it provides "social and legal help to families who have lost their breadwinners, to women, children and elderly people, and to refugees, internally displaced persons and other victims of the conflict who are in material need."Psychological rehabilitation of traumatized children and women is also provided. The group is located in Moscow at 26-54 Novopeschannaya Ulitsa. In 2007 Mothers of Chechnya received a $37,000 grant from the National Endowment for Democracy.

NINE

Saving Pompeii

It's a kind of revolution, the start of a matriarchy, which is threatening to destroy the nucleus of Chechen society—the family—and could ultimately be even more destructive than Stalin's deportations. The deportation killed us demographically, people died of cold and hunger. But this war is actually doing more damage by destroying Chechen traditional society and values.
Abdul Sultygov, Chechen sociologist

NEARLY TWO DECADES OF CHAOS, war, and the necessity of survival have transformed the Chechen woman into a stronger, more courageous, and self-reliant human being. It has also dramatically changed how she lives, her psyche, and her roles in the family and Chechen society. A reluctant participant, she has been forced to venture far beyond her traditional roles to assume new ones, many of which are inconsistent with harmony in the traditional family and are challenging Chechnya's strong patriarchal society. War has advanced her rights, but men are resentful, and a movement in the name of traditional Islam championed by President Kadyrov is rolling these rights back.

A GENERATION OF SOLITARY WOMEN

Nowhere is change more evident than in the numbers of unmarried women, a result of the depletion of the male population between the ages of fifteen and forty and of the lack of marriage prospects. The situation is so bad that young widows who, according to the ancestral Chechen tradition, should mourn for a year, are now strongly encouraged to remarry as soon as possible to have more children.

With the ratio of women to men about twenty to one, there are simply not enough males to go around, which is creating what Chechnya's deputy health minister, Sultan Alimkhadzhiyev, calls a "generation of solitary women." The fact that a lot of young men don't have incomes and can't afford weddings isn't helping either. Many women simply do not marry anymore. "An enormous number of women with no one to marry grow old on their own, dreaming of family and motherhood," Chechen university professor Aizan Tamarova says. "I am thirty-eight and I never married because of the war," says Luisa Aftakhanova, a Grozny hairstylist who moved back home with her parents in 2004 after fleeing Chechnya and living in Ingushetia and Moscow.

Many young women like Milana Terloeva have chosen to put off marrying and raising a family to focus on getting a university education instead. Milana was fourteen years old when the first war came along. She told me that war made her feel lonely, isolated, and hungry for knowledge of the outside world. Hidden in a neighbor's damp, mosquito-infested basement with thirty other people, she read by candlelight *Around the World in 80 Days* and other Jules Verne adventures. Reading became a kind of therapy, filling otherwise empty hours, giving her war-torn life hope, and helping her cope with the unknown.

Milana realized her dream of exploring the outside world. She studied at Grozny University and in 2003 was accepted into the Journalist Studies Without Borders fellowship program in Paris, completing a degree in journalism in 2006. After publishing her best-seller book, she returned to Grozny to set up a European cultural center. She was well on her way when I met her in 2007. I later heard from her friend that she had gone to work for the Human Rights Center "Memorial." I was told in early 2010 that she had had to flee Chechnya because of her work for "Memorial" and is now living in the United States.

If young women are having a hard time finding eligible men, it's almost impossible for a woman who has lost her husband and has children at home to find a new mate. Though illegal (by Russian law), polygamy is an option for unmarried and widowed women. The maternal instincts that Professor Tamorova spoke about, as well as material considerations, motivate some women to become the second, third, or even fourth wives in polygamous marriages. "I don't think about love anymore, or about having a stable family. Just one child would be good enough for me. It's easier for non-Muslims; they can have babies outside marriage, even by test-tube. But what can Chechen women do?" Laila, a forty-three-year-old teacher from Grozny, told the Institute of War and Peace Reporting in 2005.

During Soviet times there were few polygamous marriages, but they became "fashionable" in the first war, and their incidence significantly increased in the second. President Kadyrov encourages polygamous marriage. In 2006 he suggested that a Chechen man could have up to four wives, the maximum allowed by the Koran, if he could afford them. They're cheaper now. Money must still exchange hands as in a traditional marriage, but the cost now is only about two hundred dollars, compared to five hundred a few years ago.

"A man is a hero if he takes more than one wife," Said S—— told me. "Why?" I ask. "Because he's doing his duty," I'm told.

There are perfectly logical economic and demographic reasons for a Chechen woman to enter into a polygamous marriage. In a society where there are so many widows and so few social safeguards, it provides her a dignified way to survive and, at the same time, legitimately bear children to replenish a population diminished by war. It can also provide a young boy with a father, increasing his chances of growing up to become a "psychologically healthy man."

Polygamy is common among Chechens elites. Shamil Basayev had five wives, not all of them Chechen. He married twice in 2005. We'll never know what motivated Elina Ersenoyeva to marry him. Perhaps it was because Basayev was such a powerful man; maybe it was his charming ways. Or perhaps Elina was afraid he would kidnap her or harm her family if she refused. She must have known the marriage could end only in tragedy. One day, a woman, Abdulkhalima Sadullayeva, came to see Elina at work bearing a unique marriage proposal, saying she had a "great bridegroom" for her. Elina and Shamil were married in November 2005. A short while later, an elderly man appeared at Elina's house to tell her mother that Alikhan Abuyazidov was the name of Elina's husband, that he lived in Grozny, and that his family was from the Vedensky District (Basayev's home district). A woman introducing herself as Alikhan's mother dropped by bearing wedding presents. Elina understandably wanted to keep the true identity of her husband hidden from her family. It only became known after Basayev was killed by a truckload of explosives on 10 July 2006.

Ichkeria's President Aslan Maskhadov also had a second wife, a girl from the Nozhai-Yurtovsky District. Doka Umarov has at least two wives. Many Chechen fighters have multiple wives to facilitate their movement around cities and villages and to provide them support networks. For security reasons, the marriages are kept secret from one another. Polygamy is widespread in the Kremlin-backed Chechen government, where three-quarters of the ministers and high officials have at least two wives.

Nevertheless, Elza P—— tells me that polygamy is not accepted in mainstream Chechen society. "I can logically understand it, but my soul would protest," another woman, thirty, commented to the Union of Don Women research group.[1] Some wives have even committed suicide because their husband took a second wife. In June 2007 a forty-two-year-old mother of four in Michurin hanged herself because of it.

War has even compelled Chechen women to marry outside their ethnic group: "There are many cases of Chechen women marrying men from another ethic group, which used to be completely impossible in Chechen society," Selima Gapayeva, a "property agent" told the BBC's *Chechnya Forum* on 8 December 2004. Marriages to Ingush men, their ethnic kin, have always been acceptable. There are more of them now.

And despite the taboo, some women even marry foreigners (other than Russians). A Chechen girl from Serzhen-Yurt married Shamil Basayev's sidekick, Jordanian-born Khattab. She was his second wife; he had earlier married a Dagestani girl. Similarly, a Chechen woman married Jordanian-born Abu Khvas (alias Amzhet), who ran a terrorist training camp and in the second war organized terror attacks against Russia. Aukai Collins took a Chechen girl as his second wife. Collins met sixteen-year-old Ayeesha selling products in a roadside market stall in Kurchaloi. "She had fascinating light brown eyes, and her scarf only partially covered her auburn hair," he fondly recalls. He proposed on their second meeting. They were married a week later as Collins was about to have his leg amputated after being shot by a Russian soldier.

If war has compelled women to break traditional taboos to find husbands, it has also narrowed the field for some women loyal to the Chechen Jihad. Incredibly, there are those who believe that girls marrying and mothers raising babies have special obligations and critical roles in the Jihad. They believe women should marry only fighters, raising their male children and forming their character to be good Jihadists. Women are supposed to take their cue from Khava Barayeva, who implored women in her video to "marry only *Mujahideen* men because if not, your children will not grow to be pious men as they should be."

Larisa II (see chapter 4) also believed that women should marry only fighters so that "we will have little *mujahideen* who will have one goal and that is to get even for us." Collins' statement that "it was a big honor for a woman to marry a fighter in Chechnya" seems to support these kinds of calls for girls to marry only fighters. But Elza P—— disagrees. She says that normal mothers don't want their daughters marrying fighters, because there is a good chance the husband will be killed or become invalids. "Normal parents," she says, would object to such a marriage.

Wives have even divorced their husbands because they decided to fight Russia. When Said S——'s friend the Ichkerian minister of trade told his wife he was going off to fight, she threatened to divorce him and did. But he married another woman a week later.

Chechens say that the wars have increased bride stealing too. But Elza P—— says that war has had nothing to do it, that it has always been popular. Bride stealing seemed to have been more prevalent in the first war than in the second. Bersanova, herself a "stolen bride," shows in her research that society's attitudes toward it were less favorable after the first war, because of the epidemic of kidnappings for ransom in the interwar period, heightening the fear among parents that daughters might be kidnapped for ransom and not marriage.

EXTINCTION PREVENTED

While there are fewer marriages, married Chechen women are having more babies than ever. Chechen families are traditionally large, most having five members, but an exploding birthrate is jumbo-sizing some. "Indeed there are many reports (but no reliable statistics) indicating that despite the extreme hardship, fertility had risen in recent years, at least among the rural Chechens," Georgi M. Derluguian argues in his book *Bourdieu's Secret Admirer in the Caucasus*.[2] But it's not only in rural areas. Chechnya has the highest birthrate in Russia. In 2004 28,496 babies were born, and in 2005 there were five more births than deaths. By 2007 births had grown to 33,641 annually.

War is responsible. Birthrates have increased not to raise a new generation of fighters, as Khava Barayeva would have us believe, but to rebuild families weakened by war. Surviving parents are making conscious efforts to grow their families to save them from extinction and preserve their bloodlines.

There are other, less noble, but understandably human, reasons for the increase in the birthrate too. "Without electricity and very often nothing to do because husbands stayed in the house for safety reasons or because they had nowhere to go, more wives became pregnant," Said S—— told me.

Said S—— is convinced that the increased birthrate is beginning to off-set the twenty-women-to-one-man ratio and that the imbalance will quickly correct itself. Economic incentives help too. The Chechen government increased its stipend from seventy to one hundred rubles per child in 2008. Also, in early 2009 President Kadyrov gave a cash award of 50,000 rubles ($1,400) for each male child born on 8 March, the birthday of the Prophet Mohammed. There was only one catch—the babies had to be named after Mohammed.

PSYCHOLOGICAL INVALIDS

"We're all psychological invalids," a Chechen woman once told a Western journalist. "Many of us have lost our minds during these wars," Khadizhat Gatayeva told Asne Seierstad. It's easy to understand why. Over a decade and a half of perpetual violence, insecurity, and the stress of shouldering the burden of survival for her family have left the surviving Chechen woman exhausted, with deep emotional, mental, and physical scars. "I have aged twenty years, I was pretty, now I've turned into a monster. My sight is poor and I can't remember anything. .*. . I no longer resemble a human being," Elza Duguyeva says.

Elza's not alone. Chechen psychiatrist Kyuri Idrisov concludes that 86 percent of the population suffers from war related emotional and physical stress. A 2004 Doctors Without Borders study showed that 88.7 percent of people they surveyed experience psychological or psychosocial difficulties, or both; 87 percent said they have family members with mental disturbances, and almost 60 percent knew somebody with mental illness, while 10 percent knew someone who had attempted suicide.[3]

Suicide, once rare in Chechnya, is now more common, sometimes because of stress-related spousal abuse. Aslambek Shagayev, a thirty-nine-year-old police sergeant, was tried in October 2008 for driving his wife, the mother of three, to take her own life. For eight years of marriage he beat her.

She killed herself with his service pistol at home on 8 May 2008. On 2 June 2009, a nurse at a local hospital threatened to jump from a five-story building in the Oktyabrsky District of Grozny. Rescuers tried reasoning with her, but she just kept screaming that everything had "fallen apart" and that she would jump. Relatives finally talked her down, but "She refused psychological help," a police spokesman said. Tradition holds many women back from seeking help outside the family for their psychological trauma. In December 2009 a large group of Chechen refugees who seized a Polish train to protest poor living conditions in Poland threatened to commit suicide if their demands were not met. Domestic violence like that Gistam Sakayeva deals with is on the rise among the general population; it has always been high among the displaced.

How many women suffer from psychological disorders? Dr. Baiev says that "the whole [Chechen] nation is suffering from post-traumatic stress."[4] Mothers and children suffer the most. Mothers have difficulty lactating. According to Aida Ailarova, the UNICEF psychosocial recovery officer in Chechnya, every third child in 2008 showed pronounced symptoms of post-traumatic stress disorder (PTSD). Irritability, headaches, joint and body pain, antisocial and even violent behavior, insomnia, nightmares, stomach aches, dizziness, lack of interest in school or work activities, and difficulty in concentration and communication, as well as "shock" reactions to specific sounds, are common.

The ninety children, mainly girls, from the Shelkovsky District hospitalized on 25 September 2006 showed many of these and other symptoms. While there are those of us who believe the girls were subjected to a gas attack, psychiatrists at the prestigious Serbesky Psychiatric Institute in Moscow are convinced that they suffer from war related "psycho emotional stress." As to why this disorder "infected" mostly girls, Tatyana Dimitryeva, Russia's top psychiatrist and the institute's director, explains, "Girls have a high level of suggestibility. Thus, the sickness spreads from one to the other, from the mother to the daughter, and so on."

Idrisov agrees. "The psychological state of a child, especially a young child, depends not so much on what happens around him or her, as on the reaction and state of his parents. If the grown-ups (the mother first of all) experience emotional stress, it's immediately transmitted to the children," he told a World Health Organization conference in Moscow in 2002.

The consequences can be devastating. Abubakarova, a woman with four children, was sentenced by a Shalinsky court in the fall of 2008 for beating her five-year-old daughter and her other children with wooden sticks, while Olga Kostyukova was given eight months behind bars for neglecting and starving her one-year-old to death. In May 2009 a thirty-three-year-old Grozny woman went into a fit of rage and beat to death her nine-month-old stepson in the village of Geldagan, Kurchaloyevsky District. The baby had multiple broken bones, serious skull and brain injuries, contusions, and abrasions.

A Naursky District court sentenced Galina Nikiforova to 120 hours of community-service work for child neglect because she had been starving her invalid son and failing to give him his medication or to clothe him, making him live in filth, and "failing to provide for his psychological and physical development." In January 2010 the Staropromyslovsky District Court convicted Yakhta Tutayeva of child neglect and of the brutal October 2009 stick beating of her eight-year-old daughter for not doing her homework.

Traumatized children can display fits of violence. One day in a group therapy session Alisa D——, a little girl from Bamut living in the Sputnik internally displaced persons camp in Ingushetia, playing the role of "doctor," held a toy knife to the throat of her "patient."[5] Abuse was not responsible; repeatedly witnessing wartime killing was. Seven-year-old Madina Beksultanova used to wake up at night screaming from nightmares about how her father had died on New Year's Eve in 1994. Shrapnel had blown his head off when he threw himself on top of Madina to save her from an aerial bomb. Many children are unable to attend school because of such psychological trauma.

Kheda, a Chechen child psychologist, believes that the long hours women now spend at work are also having a detrimental effect on the psychological development of children. "The child's parents try to make up for time that was lost because of the war and put all their effort into earning money for the family. In pursuit of material goods, they deprive their children of simple parental attention. The kids don't get the motherly affection they need at that early age just as much as they need oxygen," she says.[6] Exhausted, women have little time for housework when they come home. Consequently, young girls in the family bear more and more of the burden of domestic work. Playtime is rare for some girls, while others are taken out of school to look after their younger brothers and sisters while their mothers are at work.

Yet mental health care in Chechnya is woefully inadequate to deal with all this trauma. The scarcity of resources is partly to blame. In 2006, there were only two hospitals providing psychiatric help, and many rural areas have no services at all. The World Health Organization estimates that there are no more than thirty psychologists in Chechnya, and an October 2007 ACCORD-UNHCR seminar in Vienna noted that treatment for PTSD is not available at all. UNICEF is helping with a network of psychosocial school programs and rehabilitation centers, nineteen of which were operational in 2008. The NGO Women's Dignity rehabilitation center in Grozny has one psychologist on duty.

With the help of the Open Society Institute (USA) and others Gistam and Reliance are working hard to build a women's community center in Chechnya that would provide a safe and nonthreatening environment for women to break the "culture of silence" and discuss taboo issues like gender-based violence. She says the center would be a place where women could openly share their feelings, receive emotional support, and gather information about coping techniques, develop social interaction and companionship, enjoy recreational activities, learn new skills and ways to take more control over their lives. I hope she gets the funding she has applied for.

Chechnya treats less than 2 percent of the nearly 42,000 invalid children and teenagers suffering from psychological and physical trauma. Only one rehabilitation center currently exists, and that is located in Argun. More help will become available when the new 220-bed Center for Medical-Psychological Rehabilitation for Children is opened in Grozny in 2010.

General health care is a bigger problem still. Forty percent of the people surveyed by Doctors Without Borders in the 2004 study had some form of physical, auditory, or visual disability, while more than half suffered from chronic physical illness. Life expectancy has dropped by seven years. Dr. Baiev calls Chechnya a "medical disaster area." Russian defoliants used on trees produce skin sores and intestinal disorders, while industrial and amateur oil refining has polluted the water and is responsible for increased rates of cancer, blood disease (such as leukemia), and mental illness. There are epidemics of hepatitis A, upper respiratory infection, and tuberculosis, while infections from whooping cough, mumps, and measles are common. Constant exposure to hazardous and radioactive materials from waste dumps—like Radon, near Tolstoy-Yurt, where the theft of radioactive materials began in 1997—make people sick, too, while women suffer from anemia and pregnancy complications.

The infant mortality rate in Chechnya is thirty for every one thousand born, twice the average for the Russian Federation, while 40 percent of children under one year of age who die do so at home without any medical treatment. Thirty-nine babies were born with congenital development abnormalities in 2005. In the first quarter of 2006 alone there were 185 stillbirths, 47 abnormal births, and 131 premature births, while 9 preemies died. Premature babies are increasingly common. Dr. Bela Nukayeva, head of the children's ward at the Central Maternity Hospital in Grozny, says that one and a half kilograms is a weight that no longer surprises doctors. One in three children is born with a birth defect. Schoolteachers report stunted growth and underweight children. A 2003 United Nations report listed food as the greatest need for children.

War left the health services infrastructure a mess. Two-thirds of the hospitals and clinics in Grozny were destroyed in the first war; many doctors fled, and stocks of medical supplies, anesthetics, antiseptics, and general medicines were exhausted. The outside world tried to help, but the epidemic of kidnappings and the killing of foreigners by Islamic Jihadists drove out organizations like the International Committee of the Red Cross (ICRC).

Hospitals in Grozny were only operating at 25–30 percent of their original capacities by the time the second war came along. The Russian government and Western humanitarian organizations are again trying to reconstruct the health care system, but rebuilding Grozny is taking priority, and the security risks for humanitarian organizations remain great.

Doctors Without Borders is still helping but by operating "remote-control projects" out of Moscow, with Chechen instead of expatriate staff on the ground supporting the neurosurgery and trauma departments, the intensive-care unit, and a reconstructive surgery project at Grozny's Hospital No. 9. It underwent extensive repairs and reconstruction and received new equipment in 2009.

Doctors Without Borders is also addressing mother and child care needs. There is a serious shortage of pediatricians in Chechnya. Mothers and their families have few places to go for care in rural areas, where there's no state health plan at all. Practitioner nurses operate less than two hundred dispensaries, which are understaffed and poorly equipped. In 2005 a Doctors Without Borders gynecologist, along with a pediatrician nurse, general practitioner, and a mental health counselor, began making trips to five locations an hour's drive outside Grozny, seeing seventy-five to eighty-five patients a day. That has since expanded.

Aiza (not her real name), a Doctors Without Borders doctor, sees lots of anemic women. Every second woman suffers from anemia, and 70–80 percent of pregnant mothers are anemic. More than half of all pregnant women are ill and have pregnancy complications.

"I . . . see lots of pregnant women. . . . I remind women about basic hygiene and tell them that they should try to buy cotton underwear to avoid infections, even if the synthetic stuff is much cheaper. I really work on persuading my pregnant women that the health of their child will depend on how they look after themselves during pregnancy, they need to rest and eat as well as possible," Aiza says.[7] Women's Dignity also has a gynecologist on staff at the rehabilitation center.

More help for veterans and invalids will be available in 2011 when a seven-story, 250-bed hospital will be completed in Grozny.

SAVING POMPEII

I asked Milana Terloeva her opinion of how war has changed the Chechen woman. "The loss of our men and being forced to assume the man's role in providing and protecting the family. Something women have become very good at," she answered.

Many women are the breadwinners in their family and in some families even wear the pants (figuratively speaking) as heads of family, budget managers, and bodyguards—and Chechen men resent it.

Elza Duguyeva's husband and thousands like him are bitter, resentful, and depressed, because they feel helpless and useless as a result of the shifted gender dynamics within the family. Before the wars, if a man couldn't feed his family he wasn't considered a man. Now he is humiliated by having a woman provide for him if he doesn't have a job, can't work, or is incapacitated. "He finds it terribly degrading and he's more and more desperate. My husband and I have lived together for thirteen years, and for the first time, we scarcely exchange a word. He was never one to lie down during the day, even for a moment. He now lies there for days on end with his eyes open, and says nothing," Duguyeva says.

Madina is another working wife and mother with a husband at home. "You know, the big problems in our family are because of that. Actually, all our problems have the same source—he doesn't know what to do with himself, and of course he gets angry with me. He's depressed because he's become a nobody."

This role reversal and the fact that many men, because of unemployment or disability, are still incapable of fulfilling their traditional family responsibilities are partly responsible for divorces and rising domestic violence. Zainap Gashayev's husband threatened to leave her, because "such a wife brings only misfortune to her husband." Gistam's husband wanted her to quit work and stay at home. When she refused, he beat her.

While Chechen women have ventured far beyond their traditional roles, Chechen men have stood still, frozen in time, desperately clinging to their strongly held belief that women are inferior, that they are the husband's property, and that the woman's proper place is in the kitchen. They're irritated by what they see as the "manly characteristics" (bossiness, loss of femininity) they say Chechen women have taken on, increasing disobedience to the husband and authority in general, the "scant" dress of young girls and even women into their thirties, wedding gowns that are way too revealing, and the threat that these women pose to sacred family life. Men are rising up against all this.

Men say that women have lost their true identity, that they should stick to their traditional roles and not "rise to the level of a man." They should dress conservatively, wear head scarves and dresses, and stop all this nonsense of trying to imitate Western women. "It's absolutely wrong for the wife to try to rise to the level of a man. If she does, she degrades her husband. She's a woman after all," Khozh-Akhmed Kadyrov preaches:

Women should take care of the cooking, and I say: women stay at home. Then your husband will do everything for you! The husband is the master of the house, and must provide food and security for the whole family. And women, why do you need to go outside? Regarding married life, the truth is that if a woman subjects herself to her husband's will, if she attends to his needs and doesn't quarrel or behave badly, she will go straight to Paradise.[8]

Men like Duguyeva's husband might sit at home and grumble to themselves about it, but more and more men are speaking out about how they feel. "The man should feed the family, and the woman should play the role of

mother and homemaker," one young man commented to the Union of Don
Women research surveyors.[9] A forty-five-year-old male holds the conviction
that "if a woman takes on this responsibility [of being the provider for the
family] and begins to feed the family, then the family will disintegrate."[10]

He's not alone in his belief. Most men agree that "violating the natural
order of the family, can only bring ruin to it." A twenty-one-year-old puts
it this way: "If a woman sells the whole day, how can she teach her children
to do anything else?"[11]

Despite the fact that there is no father in about every third or fourth
Chechen family, the man is still seen (by men) as vital to the psychological
well-being and development of male children. Men do not believe a woman
can properly educate a boy, since she customarily imparts societal values to
the daughter, whereas the father is responsible for the sons' manly development. "Today women have begun to educate the boy too," a twenty-year-
old complained to the Don women.[12] "They have this [crazy] idea to be like
the Western girl, like women in the West," a twenty-one-year-old says with
disdain.[13]

I have my own experience. I was discussing Terloeva's book with a
Chechen man, telling him how much she has accomplished in her young
life and what an independent and modern woman she is, when he politely
piped up and said, "Yes, but if she were around me she would know how to
properly behave!"

Some very powerful men see today's Chechen woman as a serious threat
to Chechen society. "Look at Pompeii," Khozh-Akhmed Kadyrov says.
"That was a punishment from God because people didn't behave properly.
The same is true here—two wars are enough. We don't need another one! If
you keep dressing that way, and if you don't listen to your husbands, there
will be another war!"[14]

Chechen sociologist Abdul Sultygov sees it as "a kind of revolution; the
start of a matriarchy, which is threatening to destroy the nucleus of Chechen
society—the family—and could ultimately be even more destructive than
Stalin's deportations [he says]. The deportation killed us demographically,
people died of cold and hunger. But this war is actually doing more damage
by destroying Chechen traditional society and values."

Ramzan Kadyrov has taken up the mantle of "saving Pompeii" and
Chechen society in his campaign for morality and revival of national traditions. He's convinced that the state needs to reeducate women on how to

properly behave, starting with how they dress. Kadyrov told his government ministers in September 2007, "In the history of our people, women have never dressed this way, with girls' stomachs and backs showing. If we go on like this, we'll loose our customs and announce that we are not Chechens and not Muslims. Our fathers would not have allowed this and we will not either." He considers short skirts and jeans or pants vulgar. Female students aren't allowed to attend university classes unless they're in dresses.

Low-cut, European-style wedding gowns are definitely out too. Brides are supposed to be "a symbol of modesty, but recently they've begun wearing dresses that are too revealing," Kadyrov says. Today a wedding dress must have long sleeves and a high neckline that will cover the collarbone. "After all, what husband would want other men looking down his wife's bosom during the wedding?" Little Stalin asks.

How, then, should women dress? "Just take a look at the girls from the Chechen department of the Chechen pension fund of Russia. They're pleasant to look at. They wear dresses sewn from one design, very beautiful costumes," Kadyrov suggests.

Head scarves are required dress. "Women without headgear are not allowed in this building," a sign outside Grozny's Youth Chamber reads. Signs like this cropped up everywhere in 2008. There's not a single government building now in which a woman is allowed to enter without wearing a head scarf. Violators complain that they're often grabbed by the hair and physically tossed out of public buildings.

They're evicted from their offices, too. On 12 December 2008 Chechnya's press minister threw Taisa Isayeva and her Office of the Information Center of the Union of Non-Governmental Organizations out of the House of the Press building in downtown Grozny because she refused to obey the security guard's order to put on a head scarf. After all, the building displays its own large black-and-white sign warning women without head scarves that they will not be admitted. After a few nasty incidents with "independent" women, the sign was changed to read: "Esteemed women should respect national traditions."

Natasha Estimirova lost her nomination to chair Chechnya's Council on Human Rights because she told a Russian REN-TV audience that she didn't believe the Chechen government should force women to wear head scarves.

Women are also fired from their jobs if they don't comply with the new "dress code." "I received a verbal warning that if I didn't wear a head scarf, I would lose my job. I had to wear it the next day so as not to bring trouble on myself," one woman who works in a regional administration says.

But the fuss isn't just about dresses and head scarves—they're mere symbols of the deeper backlash against women's rights and "the humiliation we have to cope with on a daily basis," a high-ranking government administrator recently told Svetlana Gannushkina, founder of Russia's Civil Assistance Committee: "My office can be stormed by armed young men just to check whether or not all the girls are wearing headscarves and becoming clothing. They lecture me as well as interfere with my work. Never before would strange men dare treat a woman, let alone their elder with a higher social rank, this way."[15]

"They [the men] have decided to seek revenge," Natasha Estimirova wrote in an article for the newspaper *Novaya gazeta* on 18 October 2007: "During the war and after the active military campaigns (when it was women who were hard at work and feeding the family) Chechen men understood that the role of the women in society had grown. But now they've decided to seek revenge, demanding a return to centuries old traditions," she wrote. A little over a year later she wrote: "At every public presentation Kadyrov himself accuses today's women of debauchery, of being flippant and 'Western' depravity. Listening to everybody around Kadyrov, you would think that all young Chechens are potentially Wahhabis (or the devil), that all young women are going into prostitution."

Kadyrov even came up with the bright idea of monitoring cell phone voice and text messages to "stop young married women from contacting their ex-boyfriends." And "Never in the past have Chechen women searched for a man by newspapers and acquaintances. We'll not have it," he vows. Little Stalin insists that women should know their place: "I have the right to criticize my wife. My wife does not have the right to criticize me, it's as simple as that. The Chechen wife is a housewife. . . . The woman should give her love to the man. . . . The woman is a property, while the man is the owner!" Kadyrov insisted in a 24 September 2009 interview with the newspaper *Komsomolskaya pravda*.

Polygamous marriages, bride stealing, honor killings, strict dress codes, demeaning language, expected blind obedience, unequal access to education, and even house arrest for some wives and forbidden access to money—is Chechnya returning to the Middle Ages?[16]

"Yes, we're a traditional, conservative society, with our own values, but the government has gone overboard, declaring unacceptable limits on women—that they should sit a home, they should obey their husbands. . . . As an individual, she has no rights even if her husband beats her, despite Russian laws to the contrary," Lipkhan Bazayeva says.

Women are humiliated. "After all, who bore the burden of feeding, sheltering, and protecting families; who searched for missing husbands, sons, and brothers, collected money and paid bribes; who protested and blocked the roads; who was victimized by both sides; and who found the way to tell the world about what was really going on in Chechnya?" Svetlana Gannushkina asks. "It's bad and it's getting worse," Gistam tells me.

Men are determined to keep control. "How do women live in Chechnya? They live as the men say," Taisiya, a twenty-year-old woman, declares. "What the president says is law," Gistam says. "No one dares to object to anything Kadyrov says or does, just as no one dared to object to Stalin's words or deeds in the former Soviet Union," Natasha Estimorova said in August 2008.

Some women have just given up. "A man can do many things, but a woman cannot; and for that reason you can't talk about equal rights," an eighteen-year-old tells the Union of Don Women.[17] " The man should be a bit higher," a nineteen-year-old asserts.[18] "She should always be weaker, even if she is not weak," a thirty-year-old female concludes.[19] " She may be a little stronger than men, but she should not show it," a forty-year-old woman warns.[20]

But other women aren't quitting so easily. "Earlier, I didn't participate even in elections. Now I believe that I should participate in everything that has to do with the formulation of society," one woman in her thirties told the Don women.[21] "I think every person should realize their full potential," one eighteen-year-old girl tells the Don women.[22] "I have a dream of being totally independent of anybody," another eighteen-year-old asserts.[23]

Gistam and Reliance intend to work hard to challenge and change perceptions of women in Chechen society, address gender equity issues, empower women, and protect their rights.

The new battle lines have been drawn!

Notes

PROLOGUE

1. For a complete biography of Shamil Basayev and the other cast of characters who led post-Soviet Chechnya down the road to chaos, political anarchy, economic ruin, and ultimately war and destruction, see *The The Wolves of Islam: Russia and the Faces of Chechen Terror* (Washington, D.C.: Brassey's, 2004).

2. The reader should note that I have used the term "Wolves" to describe those fighting Russia and the Kremlin-backed Chechen government. On 3 October 1998 the body of Akhmal Saidov, a Russian government official, was found near a checkpoint on the Chechen–Ingush border. Pinned to his coat was a bloody note signed "The Wolves of Islam." The terms "Wolves," "fighter," *"boyevik"* (fighter), and *"mujahideen"* are used interchangeably in the text.

CHAPTER ONE: *Mat Ogni*

1. Khassan Baiev with Ruth and Nicholas Daniloff, *The Oath: A Surgeon under Fire* (New York: Walker, 2003), p. 58.

2. This story is told in Asne Seierstad, *The Angel of Grozny* (New York: Basic Books, 2008), pp. 148–49.

3. Baiev, *Oath,* p. 84.

4. This case was reported by the Los Angeles–based International Medical Corps (IMC), which does work in Ingushetia and Chechnya. See Sergey Gagloev, "Kidnapped and Abused: Finding Help to Heal," International Medical Corps *2009 Archive,* 31 December 2009. Diana received IMC psychological counseling and has since left home and remarried.

5. The woman is cited by Petra Prochazkova in her article "The Aluminum Queen," *Prague Watchdog,* 6 April 2002.

6. The love story of Sasha and Gulya is based on a 2006 interview by Vadim Rechkalov and his subsequent article "Soldat i smertnitsa."

CHAPTER TWO: WELCOME TO HELL!

1. Arkady Babchenko, *One Soldier's War* (New York: Grove Press, 2006), p. 133.

2. Seierstad, *Angel of Grozny*, p. 26.

3. Babchenko, *One Soldier's War*, pp. 107–108.

4. As quoted in Baiev, *Oath*, p. 172.

5. Ruslan Khasbulatov, *Bolshaya Srategicheskaya Igra* (Moscow: Graal, 2003), pp. 204–205.

6. As quoted by Patrick E. Tyler, "Chechnya Caught in Unending Limbo of War and Peace," *New York Times*, 22 October 2000.

7. Ibid.

8. Aukai Collins, *My Jihad* (Guilford, Conn.: Lyons, 2002), p. 88.

9. Babchenko, *One Soldier's War*, pp. 145–46.

10. Akhmed Kelimatov, *Chechnya: v vogtyakh dyavola ili na puti k samounichtozheniyu* (Moscow: Yekoprint, 2003), pp. 476–77.

11. For the complete report see *By All Available Means: The Russian Federation Ministry of Internal Affairs Operation in the Village of Samashki: April 7–8, 1995*, Independent Research by the Observer Mission of Human Rights and Public Organizations in the Conflict Zone in Chechnya (Moscow: 1996).

12. Umalat Umalatov, *Chechnya glazami chechentsa* (Moscow: Edinstvo, 2001), p. 125.

13. See the O. G. Trusevich, comp., *Mass Violations of Human Rights during the Armed Conflict in the Chechen Republic: A Brief Review* (Moscow: Moscow Helsinki Watch), available at fsumonitor.com/MHG_99/Chechnya.shtml.

14. Her excerpted testimony can be found in Sergei Baimukhametov, "Kavkazskiy krovavy krug," *Chaika*, no. 16 (16–31 August 2007), pp. 22.

15. Gabrielle Giroday, "Russia's Black Widows: Have Female Suicide Bombers Become Terrorism's Political Pin-ups?" 1 May 2005, *Maisonneuve*, maisonneuve.org.

16. Andrew Meier, *Chechnya: To the Heart of the Conflict* (New York: W. W. Norton, 2004), p. 70.

17. Anna Politkovskaya, *A Small Corner of Hell: Dispatches from Chechnya* (Chicago: University of Chicago Press, 2003), p. 46.

18. Baiev, *Oath*, pp. 287–88.

19. Kelimatov, *Chechnya*, p. 429.

CHAPTER THREE: THE PAIN CONTINUES

1. For a complete discussion of this topic see Murphy, *The Wolves of Islam*, pp. 64–73, 76.

2. "Chechenskiye zhenshchiny i vooruzhenniy konflict: Izmeneniye plozheniya i roli v seme i v obshchestve, Otchet o rezultatakh sotsiologicheskovo issledovaniya Soyuz 'Zhenshchiny Dona,'" 2006, p. 8, available at www.donwomen.ru/files/Research _ChWomens-2.doc.

3. Kelimatov, *Chechnya*, p. 432.

4. As quoted in Trusevich, comp., *Mass Violations of Human Rights during the Armed Conflict in the Chechen Republic.*

5. Umalatov, *Chechnya glazami chechentsa*, pp. 239–40.

6. Politkovskaya, *Small Corner of Hell*, p. 42.

7. Valery Tishkov, *Understanding Violence for Post-Construction in Chechnya* (Geneva: Center for Applied Studies in International Negotiations [CASIN], January 2001), p. 29.

8. Yu. V. Nikolaev, *The Chechen Tragedy: Who is to Blame?* (New York: Nova Science, 1996), p. 101.

9. Ibid.

10. These executions and the events leading up to them are fully described in *The Wolves of Islam*, pp. 38–39, 248.

11. See "Terror Suspected in Toxic Poisoning of Children at Chechen School," *Russia-Eurasia Terror Watch*, www.retwa.com; see "News Archives" for 26 September 2005 and reporting through 2006.

12. Politkovskaya, *Small Corner of Hell*, p. 84.

CHAPTER FOUR: BAKING BREAD

1. As told to *Los Angeles Times* reporter Maura Reynolds in an interview. See "War Has No Rules for Russian Forces Fighting in Chechnya," 27 September 2000, available at articles.latimes.com/2000/sep/17/news/mn-22524.

2. See "Woman Claiming to Be Chechen Sniper Brutally Murdered after Party," *Russia-Eurasia Terror Watch*, www.retwa.com; see "News Archives" for 26 March 2006.

3. Kelimatov, *Chechnya*, p. 422.

4. Stanley Greene, *Open Wound: Chechnya 1994–2003* (London: Trolley, 2003), p. 208.

5. Ibid., pp. 160–61.

6. As quoted in L. Tsyvyana, "Svolochnaya voina. Perevod c frantsuzskovo," *Zvezda*, no. 2 (2001), available at www.magazines, russ.ru/zvezda/2001/2/niva.html.

7. For her complete story, see "What Your Children Do Will Touch You," *Human Rights Watch Report*, 2 July 2009, pp. 36–38.

8. As cited in the 29 September 2009 court testimony of defendant Oleg Petrovich Orlov in the (defamation) lawsuit against him brought by President Ramzan Kadyrov.

9. The statement made to a Grozny television audience on the program *Itogi* on 23 May 2009 is cited in ibid.

CHAPTER FIVE: THE SISTERHOOD

1. Other information says that Khava Barayeva was nineteen years of age; still other sources say twenty-two.

2. Other information says eighteen years of age, even twenty.

3. Yuliya Yuzik, *Nevesty Allakha* (Moscow: Ultra Kultura, 2003), p. 30.

4. Ibid., p. 70.

5. Tatyana Popova, *Nord-Ost-glazami zaloshnitsy* (Moscow: Vagrius, 2002), p. 168.

6. Ibid., p. 169.

7. According to her passport, Koku Vegetovna Khadzhiyeva was born on 9 April 1976, but Kalchuk lists her birthday as 15 December 1976.

8. Aset Vakhidovna Gishlurkayeva was born on 15 August 1973.

9. Zareta Dolkhayevna Bairakova was born on 30 April 1976.

10. Yuzik, *Nevesty Allakha*, p. 108.

11. Ibid.

12. See Eduard Topol, *O lubvi i terrore ili dvoye v dubrovke* [also *Roman o lubvi i terrore, ili Dvoye v "Nord Oste"*] (Moscow: ACT, 2003), p. 240.

13. Alla Illyichenko is quoted by Fred Weir in his "Chechen Women Join Terror's Ranks," *Christian Science Monitor,* 12 June 2003.

14. Popova, *Nord-Ost-glazami zaloshnitsy*, p. 17.

15. Topol, *O lubvi i terror ili dvoe v dubrovke*, p. 192.

16. Ibid., p. 202.

CHAPTER SIX: MOUNTAINS OF BODIES

1. There are two versions of Zara Mutazaliyeva's arrest. In the first, she was detained on 4 March in a routine police check. The second has it that police surveillance continued until 4 March 2004, when investigators received information that she was going to the Kometa police hotel on Vernadsky Prospekt. Police stopped her not far from the hotel and found two hundred grams of plastit-4 explosives inside her purse, but no detonator. She did not have an explanation for the explosives in her purse.

2. C. J. Chivers, "The School," *Esquire,* 14 March 2007.

CHAPTER SEVEN: I'M NOT WHO YOU THINK I AM

1. For a detailed description of the attack see *The Wolves of Islam*, pp. 234–36.

2. For news coverage of the attack, see, among other reporting, "Breaking News: Nalchik under Heavy Militant Attack, Many Deaths"; "1st Update: The Morning's Picture of Nalchik under Siege"; "2nd Update: How Many Terrorists Are There and Who Are They?"; "3rd Update: Nalchik This Afternoon & Evening"; and "Photo Essay of Terror in Nalchik," in *Russia-Eurasia Terror Watch,* www.retwa.com, "News Archives" for 13 October 2005.

3. See *The Wolves of Islam*, pp. 137–39, 177–78, 198–99, 254.

CHAPTER EIGHT: RISING FROM THE ASHES

1. Elza's story was first told by Petra Prochazkova in "Aluminum Queen." Prochazkova has since published a book about Elza and other women, *The Aluminum Queen: The Russian-Chechen War through the Eyes of Women* (Prague: Lidove noviny, 2002).

2. Politkovskaya, *Small Corner of Hell,* pp. 40–41.

3. As quoted in Seierstad, *Angel of Grozny,* pp. 91–92.

4. As cited in Patrick Tyler "Anguish at Every Turn in Ruined Chechen City," *New York Times,* 20 January 2001.

5. Anna Politkovskaya, *A Dirty War: A Russian Reporter in Chechnya* (London: Harvill, 2001), p. 254.

6. Politkovskaya, *Small Corner of Hell,* p. 42.

7. For the complete article about Ayshat see Ruslan Isayev, "The Chechen Woman and Her Role in the 'New' Society," *Prague Watchdog,* 21 June 2004.

8. Daniel J. Gerstle, "Beauty in Grozny," International Medical Corps *News,* 1 May 2006.

9. Simon Rasin, Maria Nazarenko, and Sergey Gagloev, "Stitching Broken Dreams," International Medical Corps *2009 Archive,* 31 December 2009.

10. Laila Baisultanova, "Chechnya: Children for Sale," CRS no. 72, *Institute for War and Peace, Reporting,* 4 January 2007, available at www.reliefweb.int/rw/rwb.nsf/db900sid /TKAE-6X62ZV?OpenDocument.

11. Ibid.

12. Baiev, *Oath,* 287–88.

13. Anna Politkovskaya, *A Russian Diary* (New York: Random House, 2007), p. 145.

14. Ibid.

15. Tim Wallis, *Peace News,* October 1995.

16. Baiev, *Oath,* p. 139.

17. Madina Magomadova, "Interview," *Dosh,* no. 3 (2006).

CHAPTER NINE: SAVING POMPEII

1. "Chechenskiye zhenshchiny i vooruzhenniy konflikt," p. 37.

2. Georgi M. Derluguian, *Bourdieu's Secret Admirer in the Caucasus* (Chicago: University of Chicago Press, 2005), pp. 44–45.

3. Kaz de Jong et al., *The Trauma of Ongoing War in Chechnya: Quantitative Assessment of Living Conditions, and Psychosocial and General Health Status among War Displaced in Chechnya and Ingushetia* (Amsterdam: Médecins Sans Frontières, August 2004), available at www.doctorswithoutborders.org/publications/reports/2004/chechnya_report_9-9-04.pdf.

4. See "Briefing on Chechnya with Khassan Baiev"(delivered to the United States Holocaust Memorial Museum, 7 October 2004).

5. As cited in Asiyat Vazayeva, "The Mental Scars of Chechnya's Children," CRS 165, *Institute for War and Peace Reporting,* 6 February 2003, www.iwpr.net.

6. As told to *Prague Watchdog* in June 2007.

7. MSF National Staff in Ingushetia and Chechnya, "Voices from the Field: Most Houses Are Either Destroyed or 'Wounded' by Years of War," *Médecins Sans Frontières,* 20 January 2006, www.doctorswithoutborders.org/news/article.cfm?id=1658&cat=voice -from-the-field.

8. Seierstad, *Angel of Grozny,* p. 104.

9. *Chechenskiye zhenshchiny i vooruzhenniy konflikt,* p. 37.

10. Ibid.

11. Ibid.

12. Ibid.

13. Ibid.

14. Seierstad, *Angel of Grozny,* p. 104.

15. Cited by Svetlana Gannushkina, "The Right to Be a Human," *Human Rights Center "Memorial" 2009 Chechnya Situation Report,* 6 April 2009, app. 4.

16. Women were further humiliated when only six females were included in the eighty-nine students selected to begin a new program of studies abroad in September 2008 as part of President Kadyrov's ten-year, $42 million program to develop high level skills needed by Chechnya. All six were sent to Germany; there were no girls in the United Kingdom study program.

17. *Chechenskiye zhenshchiny i vooruzhenniy konflikt,* p. 35.

18. Ibid.

19. Ibid., p. 38.

20. Ibid.

21. Ibid., p. 22.

22. Ibid., p. 35.

23. Ibid.

Index

Abakarova, Taisa, 39
Abdukarova, Zarema, 198
Abdulkadirova, Bucha, 74
Abdulkerimova, Desha, burned to death for
    spying for Russia, 89
Abdullaev, Nabi, 214
Achkoi-Martan, Chechnya, 37, 151, 167, 207,
    217, 228, 240, 245, 247
Achkoi-Martanovsky District, Chechnya, 19,
    44, 129, 154, 160, 203, 217
Adiyeva, Leila, describes how she survived in
    wartime, 225
Aduyeva, Taisa, 96
Aftakhanova, Luisa, 228, 257
Agayev, Islam, prosecuted for staging killing of
    suicide bomber, 75
Aibika, Dadi, 103
Aidamirova, Taisa, 38
Ailarova, Aida, comments on mental health of
    children, 262
airliner terror attacks (2004), 21, 187–91, 204
Akberdayeva, Zulai, 42
Akhayev, Umar-Ali, teenager murders Russian
    invalids, 88
Akhilgova, Roza and Zalpa, killed in acciden-
    tal shelling of home, 44
Akhmadov, Ilyas, xi

Akhmadov, Ramzan, 141
Akhmadov, Rezvan, 137
Akhmadov, Zelimkhan, 137, 148–49, 158
Akhmedova, Malika Zmayevna, 41
Alabayeva, Amina, dies in earthquake, 100
Aladamova, Madina, 199–200
Alayeva, Aminat, imprisoned in Mozdok fil-
    tration center, 85
Al-Bakar, Abu, 146
Albekov, Rizvan, executed in public square,
    2, 78–79
Albiyeva, Seda, killed by stray bullet during
    wedding party, 14
alcohol abuse by Russian soldiers, 30, 46,
    53, 97–98
Alenova, Anna, 97
Alikhanova, Lida, recounts life in bomb
    shelters, 38
Alisultanov, Aslanbek, 123
Aliyeva, Svetlana Umarova, helps organize
    women's movement, 230, 252–53
Alkhan-Kala, 9, 13, 38, 40, 47, 53, 60, 90,
    119–20, 141, 148, 190, 241, 243, 253
Alkhanov, Ruslan, 123, 209, 218
Alkhan-Yurt, 19, 38, 53–55, 66, 140
All-Russian Movement for Human Rights,
    244

Almazova, Roza, policewoman executed, 91
Al-Qaeda, 79, 210, 251
Altimirova, Khavra Gazaliyevna, *mujahideen* burn home of, 128
Amirova, Zaira, kidnapping and disappearance of, 77
amnesty, 79, 118, 130
Amtayeva, Raisa, 59
anti-war demonstrations, peace marches, 239–49
Archakova family (Aishat and Dugurkhan), killed and home burned, 55
Argun, Chechnya, 18, 98, 100, 111, 131–35, 200, 206, 241–42
Armavir, Russia, bombing of train station in, 138–39
arms trafficking/possession, 36, 46, 118, 134, 226
Arsanovkayeva, Mariam, participates in 2001 peace march, 239
Arsenikov, Musa, 19
Arsenikova, Dzhanet, honor killing victim, 19
Artamonov, Mikhail, 189
Arutyunov, Armen, sells illegal tickets to 2004 airline bombers, 188–89
Askhova, Zareta, 94
Assinovskaya, Chechnya, 86, 108, 154–55, 159–60, 176, 216, 234, 245, 247
Asukhanova, Lilia, 99
Asukhanova, Luiza and Sulikhan, wounded in bombing of Grozny central market, 36
Asuyev, Ruslan, stages the killing of suicide bomber, 75–76
Atabayeva, Madina, 41
Atakayeva, Aishat, kidnapping and disappearance of, 77
Atgeriyeva, Sovman, contemplates suicide, 220
Auduyeva, Madina, 77
Aushyev, Ruslan, 203
Avdarkhanov, Akhmed, torches policeman's family home, 127
Azhigova, Kheda, 222
Azhigova, Zara, 222

Babchenko, Arkady, 28, 34
Babichyev, Ivan, 240
Bagautdinova, Olga (Russian journalist), kidnapped for ransom, 124
Bagolova, Royana, three-year-old kidnapped for ransom, 235

Bagrov, Yuriy, 105
Baiev, Khassan, x, 8, 13, 53, 65, 120, 213, 239, 253; comments on psychological and physical health of population, 262, 264
Baisultanova, Laila, witnesses the sale of children, 234
Baisuyeva family (Maki and Medno), home torched, 128
Bakaeva, Milana. *See* Terloeva, Milana
Bakayeva, Aminat, 84
Bakayeva, Liana, honor killing victim, 19
Baku, Azerbaijan, 130, 147, 152, 154, 184, 191, 204, 227; terror training in, 184
Bakumeno, Angelina, jailed for forging real estate documents, 235
Balayeva, Milana, 98
Bapayeva, Luiza, imprisoned in illegal prison, 86
Barayev, Arbi, 60, 62, 65, 86, 132, 140–41, 143, 147, 158, 160
Barayev, Movsar, 136, 146, 161–63
Barzoyeva, Zara Magomedovna, killed in bombing of Mutayev family home, 37
Basayev, Shamil, 3, 4, 32, 34, 40, 48, 70, 71, 85, 93, 102, 105, 107–12, 123, 130, 132, 136, 142–43, 147, 152, 155, 157–58, 164, 166–69, 171–73, 182, 184, 196, 198, 205–7, 209, 210–12, 215, 231, 258–59
Basayeva, Khadichat, 38
Basayeva, Lipkhan, 202–3
Basayeva, Medina, 105
Basayeva, Zinada, 32
Bashayeva, Roza, 73
Batalova, Patimat, recounts artillery attack on refugee convoy, 39
Batalova, Zina, 34, 230
Batashyeva, A., 98
Batayev, Visit, 135
Batriyeva, Taisa, 222
battlefield: code of honor, 47–48; emotion, 46
Baymurodova, Aimani, 170
Baymurodova (Abalayeva), Shadhidat, mistakenly identified as suicide bomber, 170
Baysayev, Ousam, xi, 121
Baytukayeva, Khalimat, kidnapped and disappeared, 76
Bazayeva, Lipkhan: comments on women's rights, 271; helps organize women's movement, 230

beheading, of Russian soldiers, 47, 89, 116, 120

Bekeyeva, Aina Arslanovna, kills herself during spetz-operation, 208

Beksultanova, Madina, 263

Berevyea, Petimat, manages new store funded by International Medical Corps, 228

Bersanova, Zalpa, 8, 214

Beslan, North Ossetia, terror attack at school in, 74, 122, 124, 193–96, 204, 207–8, 210

Betergiriyeva, Luiza, killed at a Russian roadblock, 97

Betishyeva, Luiza, 63

birth: defects, 265; rates in Chechnya, 260–61

Bisayeva, Zara, disappearance prompts demonstrations, 246

Bisultanova, Fatima, convicted of narcotics trafficking, 235

Bitiyeva, Zura, 121; antiwar activist and family murdered, 84–85

Black Widows, 5, 137, 162–63, 166, 168–69, 181, 188, 193–95, 208, 214–15

blood vengeance, 8, 59, 82, 93, 137, 142–44, 146–49, 160, 161, 170–71, 174–76, 181, 183, 190, 204; as motive for suicide bombings, 213–14

Bogatyryov, Magomed, 218

Bolshaya Strategicheskaya Igra (book), 35

Booker, Sandy, dies in Dubrovka theater siege, 161

Borshchova, Antonina, 69

Brenza, Irina, praises work of Zainap Gashayeva, 250–51

bride stealing (kidnapping for marriage), 4, 11, 14–17, 69, 77, 110, 115, 120, 145, 151, 257–58, 260, 270

Budanov, Yuriy D., rapes and murders Elza Kungayeva, 54–55, 73, 107

Budennovsk, Russia, 48, 108–9, 112, 138, 211

Bumbarova, Khava, 224

Burayeva's, Zarema, provides safe house to fighters, 133

Burdenko Research Institute, 43

Bushuyev, Salambek, 62

Buzurkayeva, Taus, home of torched, 126

Cap Anamur charity, 232

CARE Canada, training programs of, 228–30

Carr, Camila, kidnapping and rape of, 69

castration of Russian soldiers and Chechen men, 47

Caucasus Islamic Institute, 117

Caucasus Wars (19th Century), 103–4

Center for Defense Information, 144

Center for Medical-Psychological Rehabilitation for Children, 264

Chabiyeva, Malika Mikailovna, 138–39, 209

Chadayeva, Aset, straps grenade to herself, 57–58, 144, 213

Chaikova, Nadezhda, kidnapping and execution of, 69

Chankayeva, Tamara, planes attack funeral procession of, 37

Chechen female administrators killed in 2002 administrative complex attack (Batmanova, Galina; Batyzheva, Zina; Doshukayeva, Lida; Dzhabrailova, Shukran; Ismailova, Malika; Khabzayeva, Muminat; Kozlova, Lidiya; Ludanova, Lidya; Murtayeva, Fatima; Murtayeva, Tamara; Pozdnyakova, Galina; Shevelyeva, Tatyana; and Svetovatchenko, Elena), 92

Chechen government administrative complex: 2002 terror attack on, 92, 166–68, 199; demonstrations at, 241, 244, 246; second planned attack, 207

Chechenpress, 31, 50

Chechensky Kapkan (film), 114

Chechen Society (newspaper), 70

Chechen State Teachers Institute (ChGPI), mortar attack on, 41

Chechen State University, 147, 151, 158, 202

Chechnya from the Ashes (film), 141

Chernokozovo filtration center, 83–85, 121, 241

children, 31–47, 52–54, 56–61, 85–87, 100–1, 161, 167–68, 223–26, 255, 264; child abuse/neglect, 263; infant mortality rate, 265; kidnapping for ransom and suicide missions, 68, 78, 235; mental health of, 255, 262–64; orphans, 38, 52; poisoning of, 93–96, 262; raising to become fighters, 120, 259–60; rape of, 100, 253; sale of, 233–34; taken as hostages, 193–96; wartime starvation of, 222

Chovkhalova, Maya, cofounds the Women's Union of the North Caucasus, 252

Chubanova, Lyuba, 228
cleansing operations. *See zachistka*
COCA: *The Dove from Chechnya—Europe in Denial of a War* (film), 251
code of military conduct, 48–50
collective punishment of fighters' families, 79, 125–29, 197
Collins, Aukai, American fighter in Chechnya, 46, 226, 259–60
community service, women in, 229–30
Conciliatory Watchdog Committee, 254
Coordinating Council of International Human Rights Organizations, 37
Copenhagen World Chechen Congress, 253
Coral beauty shop, 228
corruption/bribe taking, 72, 75–76, 85, 108, 188, 221–24, 229, 232–33
Council Information Center (NGO), 246
Council of Europe, 53, 56, 90,
Council of Human Rights (Grozny), 269
crime, 99; activities of women in, 233–36; against Russian civilians in Chechnya, 46, 87–88; committed by Russian soldiers, 47, 49–50, 55–56, 61–64, 97, 98
crucifixion, of Russian soldiers, xi, 47

Dadashyeva, Tamara, 93
Dadilov, Magomed, home torched, 128
Daduyeva, Ina, kidnapping and disappearance of, 70
Daduyeva, Tamara, 38
DAGAN International Charity Foundation, 114
Damayeva (Tsintsayeva), Maret Kutuzovna, mother and five children die in air strike, 43
Dambayeva, A.R., raped by Russian soldier, 61
Danish Refugee Council, 221
Dashayev, Ilyas, beheads woman for spying, 89
Daurbekova, Lola, interned in Chernokozovo filtration center, 85
Davidovicha, Nina, 69
Davletkayeva, Luba, 42
Davletkayeva, Zareta, 42
Debrishyeva, Esila, 37
Debriyeva, L., 37
decapitation of Russian soldiers, 46–48
Demilkhanova, Zulai, killed interfering with detention of Chechen man, 66

Deniyeva, Magomeda, voluntarily surrenders as fighter accomplice, 130
Derbishyeva, Alina, 37
Derluguian, Georgi M., 260
deserters (Russian soldiers), Chechen women hiding, 89–90, 253–54
Dimitryeva, Tatyana, comments on "psycho emotional stress" outbreak among children, 262
Dinamo Stadium (Grozny), 93, 186
divorce, 18, 25–26, 149, 211
djamaat, 89, 130, 149–50, 154, 180, 185, 192, 209, 215
Djokhar Dudayev Regiment, 105, 124, 139
Djokhar's Way terror unit, 138
Doctors Without Borders, 33–34, 229–30, 261, 264–66
domestic/gender based violence, 230, 261–62, 264, 267, 271
Dosh magazine, 94, 254
downing of Russian airliner (2004), 187–91
Duba-Yurt, Chechnya, 30, 39, 42, 59–60
Dubrovka female terrorists (by name): Aliyeva, Sekilat (Zara), 146–47, 149–50, 213; Bairakova, Zareta Dolkhayevna, 150–52, 227; Bakuyeva, Aishat (Luiza) Alavdinovna, 153, 160–61, 213; Bisultanova, Marina (Madina) Nebiyullayevna, 152–53, 215, 227; Bitsyeva, Zura Rezvanovna, 154, 159; Bityeva, Zaira Basirovna, 161; Dugayeva Madina, 156, 158, 159; Elmurzayeva, Seda Seitkhamzatovna, 161; Ganiyeva, Fatima, 151, 153; Ganiyeva, Khadchat (Milana) Sulumbekovna, 151, 154, 156, 159, 215; Gishlurkayeva, Aset Vakhidovna, 150–51, 163, 215; Isuyeva, Amnat, 153; Khadzhiyeva, Aiman Vagetovna, 150, 215, 227; Khadzhiyeva, Koku, 150, 215; Khadzhiyeva, Maryam Buvarisarovna, 146, 213; Khusenova, Liana Musayevna, 153; Khusenova, Luiza Alavdinova, 153; Kurbanova, Aimani, 154; Kurbanova, Raiman Khasanovna, 149–50, 154, 215; Marshugova, Maryam (Zura Arbi Barayev), 147–48, 213; Matayeva, Malizha, 151; Meferkhanova, Yakha Khamidovna, 161–62; Mutayeva, Malizha Daudovna, 159–60; Shakova, Fatimat Mukhamedovna, 161; Tushayeva, Aminat Khamzatgovna, 161; Vitaliyeva,

Malika (alias Yesira), 130, 147, 148, 151–53, 156–58; Yupayeva, Zaira Bashi-rovna, 153, 156, 158–59

Dubrovka theater siege, 70, 130, 136–37, 139–40, 146–66, 187, 197–98, 201–2, 208, 210, 214–15; changes in Basayev strategy as a consequence of, 166, 210

Dudayev, Dzhokar, x, 3, 9, 87, 88–89, 105, 109, 114, 139, 168, 202, 226, 234

Dudayev, Rudnik, 246

Dugayeva, Aminat Movsarovna, accused of terror conspiracy and disappears, 201

Duguyeva, Elza, 221, 223, 225–26, 261, 266–67

Durova, Nadezhda. *See* Molova, Taimaskha

Dyshne-Vedeno, 89, 128

Dzafarov, Zaur, 193

Dzagiyev, Kh. A., imprisoned for bride steal-ing, 15

Dzhabayev, Umar, 91

Dzhabayeva, Larisa, *mujahideen* rape and shot, 91

Dzhabrailov, Alik, 82

Dzhafarov, Vakha, 139

Dzhamaldayeva, Makka, 57

Dzhamburayeva, Asama, raped and shot by militants, 91

Dzhandarova Zalina, hostage says "Black Widows" blew themselves up at Beslan, 194

Dzhaubatryrova, A., 66

Dzhavatkhanova, Z. I., 62

economics of suicide terror, 209–10

Edisultanova, Malika, imprisoned in Mozdok filtration center, 86

Eldarova, Maffina (Madina), comments on sale of babies, 234

Elmurzayev, Ruslan, 152–53, 156, 164–65

Elza P——, x, 10, 11, 13, 16, 19–20, 22, 27, 32, 36–37, 51, 52, 234, 239, 259–60

Elzhurkayev, Kh., 66

Emergency Situations Ministry, 40, 60, 94, 221–22

employment/unemployment in Chechnya, 220, 224–39, 267

entrepreneurs, emergence of female class of, 228–30

Ersenoyeva, Elina, kidnapping and disappear-ance of, 70–71, 258

Ersenoyeva, Margarita, kidnapping and dis-appearance of, 70–71, 227

Estimirov family deaths (Hassan, Khass-Magomet, Khozh-Akhmed, Toita), 39

Estimirova, Natalya, kidnapping and murder of, 1–4, 18, 78–81, 129, 269–71

European Commission Humanitarian Aid Office (ECHO), 229

European Council for Steiner Waldorf Edu-cation, 232

European Court of Human Rights, 80, 84

expectant mother care, 265, 266

faith healers, killing of, 87, 91

family betrayal, selling of daughters and sis-ters for terror attacks, 154–56

Federalnoye Sluzhba Bezopasnosti (FSB), 23, 66, 75, 77–78, 91, 116, 122, 130, 132–34, 136, 138, 143, 146, 148, 151, 153, 156, 164, 169, 177–78, 184, 191–92, 197–206, 208, 244, 253

female fighters/snipers, 5, 30, 34, 39, 45, 47, 61, 74, 84–85, 102–35; Abukarova, Birlant Ananbekova, 121; Asya and Anya, 115–16; Basayeva, Medina, 105; Biluyeva, Lipa, 121; Birlant, 113; Cha-gayeva, Malkan, 123; Dadashyeva, Malikat, 123; Dundayeva, Raisa, 108–10; Filipova, Polina, 84, 121; Ibragi-mova, Yakhita 117, 118; Klinkyevicha, Anya (alias Antona Valyeva; Ruslana Ibragimova), 116–19, 236; Korzhikova, Svetlana, 108; Larisa I, 119, 125; Larisa II (sniper), 120, 260; Lolita (Elena P——), 111–13; Mansuyeva, Zama, 123, 236; Topchayeva, Tamara, 106, 108–10, 116–17, 124; Yunusova, Aina, 122; Zakiyeva, Raisa, 63, 122

female terrorists (other than Dubrovka): Abdurakhmanova (Abdulayeva), Dzhanet, 219; Abdurzakova, Zulai, 170; Alikhanova, Zarina, 92, 168–170, 215; Aliyeva, Zinaida (Marem Shari-pova), 174–76, 213; Barayeva, (Zhans-urkayeva) Khava, 9, 136, 140–41, 198, 214–15, 259–60; Bekeyeva, Aina Arsla-novna, 208–9; Dadashyeva, Aset, 138–39; Daurova, Z.A., 164–65; Dudayeva, Mareta, 142, 144; Dundayeva, Raisa,

108–10, 137–38; Dzhebirkhanova,
Satsita, 188–91, 204, 227; Gazuyeva,
Aizan, 58, 142–44, 213; Inarkayeva,
Zarema, 77, 144–45, 215; Isayeva,
Shukran Khasanova, 207; Katchiyeva,
Diana Saparovna, 208, 209; Khachu-
kayeva, Imana, 93, 181, 213; Khaldyk-
horoyeva, Lidya (Lida), 171–72, 179–80;
Magomedova, Luiza (Kheda), 140–41,
198; Mangeriyeva, Khedizhi ("Dirty
Shoes" bomber), 183, 213; Mitrayeva,
Madina Saidrakhmanova, 207–8; Musalayeva, Larisa, 170–71, 213; Muzhikhoyeva, Zarema, 155, 166, 171–74,
176–81, 215, 236; Nagayeva, Amnat,
21, 188–90, 204, 227; Nagayeva, Rosa,
188–90, 193–96, 204, 227; Osmayeva,
(Asmayeva) Luiza, 77, 172, 213, 215;
Sharipova, Maryam, 219; Taburova,
Maryam Yusupovna, 188, 189, 191, 193–
96, 204, 227; Taimashkhanova, Fatima,
138–39; Tumriyeva, Alina, 167–68,
215; Yelikhadzhiyeva, Zulikhan, 173–76,
215
Filipova, Irina, hostage comments on
Dubrovka terrorist Marsugova, 148
filtration points (prisons), 83–87, 121
financing of terrorism, 70, 131–33, 135, 166,
209–10, 249
food: hoarding and theft of 221–22; shortages
of/rations, 220–26. See also hunger

Gadayeva, Aimani, 56
Gadzhiyev, Geidar, 143–44
Gaeryekova, A., 97
Gaiberkova, Satsita, 34
Gaichayev, Ramzes, 88
Gairbekova, Satsita, serves as human shield for
Russian soldiers, 34
Gairekova, Isita, *mujahideen* bomb home of,
90
Gaitamirova, Elza Adiyevna, disappearace of,
199–200
Gakayeva, Elina, disappearance and return
of, 202
Gakayeva, Markha, detention and disappear-
ance of, 198, 226
Gakayeva, Raisa, detention and disappearance
of, 198, 226
Gambiyeva, Khazimat, 221

Gambulatova, Petimat Khumparovna, disap-
pearance of, 199
Ganiyev, Rustam, Chechen field commander
sells sisters for suicide mission, 155
Ganiyeva, Raisa, 155, 181
Gannushkina, Svetlana, cites enforcement of
headscarf law, 270–71
Gapayeva, Selima, 259
Garibekov, Shamil, 145
Gasanov, Shamil, Jihadist leader persuades
Sakinat Saidova to become *shakhida*, 218
gas attack (Shelkovsky District), 94–96, 262
Gashayev, Ramzan, 250
Gashayeva, Zainap, establishes Rodnaya
semya orphanage, 213, 230, 250–54,
267
Gatayev, Malik, 230–33
Gatayeva, Khadizhat, 38, 52; biography of,
230–33, 261
Gayribekova, Isita, home bombed by mili-
tants, 89–90
Geifman, Alla, kidnapping of, 68
Gekhayev, Akhmed, 61
Gekhayeva, Aishat, 35
Gekhayeva, Kurika Said-Khasanovna, accused
of conspiracy in Dubrovka siege and
disappears, 201
Gelayev, Ruslan, 102, 121, 125
Giriyeva, Dogman, 39
Giroday, Gabrielle, 58
Gishayev, Khingizhkan, 130
Gocharova, P., 87
Gochiyayev, Achemez, 192–93, 208
Goity, Chechnya, 42, 74, 100, 149
Goncharuk, Elena Vitalyevna, wounded by
soldiers firing into basement, 55
Gordaly, Chechnya, 123
Goryachenko, Elena, executed for practicing
faith healing, 91
Greene, Stanley, 115, 116,
Grigoryets, Elena, kidnapping of, 69
Groznensky District, Chechnya, 19, 20, 32,
43, 44, 123, 209, 236
Grozny, rebuilding of, 3–4, 78, 237–39
Grozny central market, 24, 36–37, 46, 72, 88,
98, 132, 151–52, 187, 190, 226–27, 242,
249, 251
Grozny Public Council for Assistance in
Ensuring the Rights and Freedoms of
Citizens, 80

Grozny theater-concert center, 2009 suicide bombing at, 129
Gubaryeva, Sasha, 13-year-old dies in Dubrovka theater, 161
Gubaryeva, Svetlana, Dubrovka hostage describes female terrorist, 161
Gudermes, Chechnya, 3, 45, 227, 241; rebuilding of, 237–38
Gudermessky District, Chechnya, 77, 91, 96, 127, 128, 216

Hague Appeal for Peace Conference, 251
Handicap International, 229
Harrison, Anne, 250
headscarf law, 80, 269
health, physical and mental health of Chechen population, 261–66
Heinrich Boll Stiftung foundation, 252
honor killing, 4, 17–20, 67, 230, 270
hospitals, 33, 34, 37, 39, 109, 111–12, 182, 236–37, 265
hostage taking, 108–15, 124, 136–37, 140–65, 193–96, 211
house burnings, 2, 4, 52, 55–56, 67, 99, 126–29, 154, 198, 206
human rights, 47, 67, 251–54
Human Rights Center "Memorial," x, xi, 2, 59, 74–75, 78–81, 127, 201–3, 213, 257
Human Rights Watch, x, 30, 38, 53–54, 138
human trafficking, 60, 67–69, 86, 132; selling of babies, 233–34
hunger, 5, 220–26, 265; of Russian soldiers in first war, 46, 221

Idrisov, Kyuri, comments on psychological health of population, 261–62
Ikhova, Tatyana, 205
Ilayeva, Zalina, 249
Ilayeva, Zarema, 249
Iliskhan-Yurt, Chechnya, 92, 169, 171
illegal prisons, 75, 86, 207
Ilyin, Vladimir, teen murders Russian invalids, 88
Imbir restaurant, Moscow, 177
Institute of War and Peace Reporting, 15, 258
intelligence collection, 5, 55–56, 119, 125, 132–33, 197, 202; HUMINT, 132, 208
International Committee of the Red Cross (ICRC) 96, 265; murder of nurses, 92
International Federation for Action of Christians for the Abolition of Torture, 251

International Helsinki Federation for Human Rights, 58, 206, 244
International Medical Corps (IMC), 205–6; training programs of, 228–29
Isayeva, Shukran Khasanovna, 207
Isayeva, Taisa, 269
Islambouli Brigades, 187–88, 192
Ismailov, Aslambek, helps establish orphanage, 231
Ismailov family (Akhmet, Fatima, Kheda, Zinaida), murder of, 60–61
Israilova, Khava, 64
Ivanova, A.A., Russian murdered in her home, 87
Izvestiya (newspaper), 155, 176, 178–80, 194

Jihad, 3, 5, 6, 9, 46, 120, 125, 133, 140, 186, 210, 215, 220, 236, 249, 259

Kadyrov, Akhmad, 12, 74, 92, 93, 168, 245; assassination of, 186; attempted assassination of, 169–71
Kadyrov, Khozh-Akhmed, 12, 18, 267–68
Kadyrov, Ramzan, 2, 4, 5, 6, 18, 20, 21, 42, 73–75, 80–82, 86, 98, 103, 125–26, 129, 170, 207, 211, 214, 227, 237–38, 245, 247, 249, 256, 258, 261, 268–71
Kadyrova, Shumist, kidnapped for a bride, 16
Kadyrovtsy, 74–75, 126, 127
Kagermanov family (Kheida, Lema Rashana, and Zhamilya) killed in bombing, 43
Kagirova, Malika, 41
Kalchuk, Viktor, 146–47, 151–53, 155, 157–59, 161, 165
Kamayeva, Satsita, detained as suspected suicide bomber, 204
KamAz truck, 93, 108, 140, 166, 168–69, 172, 181, 207, 226
Karabulak, Ingushetia, 131
Kasayeva, Elza, 54
Kasimova, Zarema, 85
Kasymova, Zaira, shot picking garlic in the forest, 64
Katchiyeva, Diana Saparovna, kills herself in spetz-operation, 208
Katsayeva, Luisa (Elza), kidnapped and disappears, 202
Kelimatov, Akhmed, 48, 65, 84, 108
Khabrailov, Arbi (alias Andrei), 178–79
Khachbarov, Rasul, 194
Khadayev, Khamid, 72

Khadzhimuradova, Khava, wounded by Russian sniper, 39
Khadzhinova, Liza, 34
Khadzhiyev-Aslambek, Abdul, 111
Khadzhiyeva, Kheda, 150
Khadzhiyeva, T., 98
Khadzhiyeva, Tamara, *mujahideen* executes, 90
Khalidov, Rustam, 88
Khalidov, Yusup, 96
Khalkayeva, Natalya (Kheda), noncombatant roles of, 132–33, 206
Khambiyev, Magomed, 74, 85–86
Khambiyev, Omar, 85–86
Khankala military base, 66, 83, 84, 97, 100, 121, 198, 243, 246
Khasavyurt, Dagestan, 133, 145, 147, 150–55, 243
Khasbulatov, Ruslan, 35,
Khasimova, Zarema, imprisoned in Mozdok filitration center, 85
Khasiyev, Anzor, 54
Khastayeva, Zarema, 41
Khasuyeva, Fatima, bombing of Grozny market claims leg of, 37
Khasuyeva, Zarema, caught smuggling counterfeit money, 131
Khattab (al-Khattab, also Samir bin Salekh al-Suweilem), 117, 259
Khibulina, Natasha, 90
Khodov, Vladimir (alias Abdullah), 195
Khuchiyev, Muslim, 80; Grozny's mayor threatens fighters' families, 127, 129
Khurikova, Seda, sister of Chechen field commander disappears, 199–200
Khvas, Abu (alias Amzhet), 259
kidnapping, 1–5, 11, 14–18, 27, 67–83, 86, 90, 100, 110, 115, 120, 132, 145, 151, 172, 198, 204, 212–13, 234–35, 245, 247–48, 251, 253–54, 258, 260, 265; statistics for war years, 67; for suicide missions, 76–77
Kikalide, Zurab, 94
Kitkeyev, Nikolai (alias Nikolai Samygin), 192–93
Kizlyar, Dagestan, 111–15, 135, 138
Kizlurtovsky Women's Colony No. 8, 235
Klebnikov, Paul, ix
Klimova, Olga V., 41
Kodzoyev, Magomed, organizes 2003 terror

attack on Akhmad Kadryov, 172
Koliyeva, Zura, *mujahideen* execute Alkhan-Kala district administrator, 90
Koman Sii (Honor of the Nation) medal, 109, 202–3
Kommersant Daily (newspaper), 164, 183
Komsomolskaya pravda (newspaper), 21, 190, 270
Komsomolskoye, Chechnya, 15, 20, 61, 91, 121, 156, 169
kontrakniki (contract soldiers), 34, 52
Korenkov, Nikolai, 189
Korgun, Aleksei, policeman mistakenly shoots women in forest as fighters, 64
Kornukayeva, Nabitsk, 53
Kostyukova, Olga, jailed for child abuse, 263
Kovalyev, Sergei, 17, 31, 50
Kozlova, Svetlana, interned at Chernokozovo filtration center, 84
Kozyreva, Natasha, 30
KrasAir Flight 2212, terror attack on, 191
Kruglikova, Nastya, hostage comments on Dubrovka terrorists, 162–63
Kulayev, Narpasha, 193–94
Kulikova, Annya, suicide bomber recruitment of, 185–86
Kumadova, Natasha, kidnapping and disappearance of, 75,
Kungayeva, Kheda (Elza) V., 73, 107; rape and murder of, 54–55
Kurchaloi, Chechnya, 19, 174, 259
Kurchaloyevsky District, Chechnya, 19, 93, 96, 126–27, 188
Kuzhiyeva, Larissa, 195
Kuznetsov, Sergei, 45
Kuznetsov, Vladimir, 40
Kuznetsova, Elena, 57

Labazanov, Anvar, 131
Labazanova, Malika, 57
Laipanov, Murat, 208
land mines, 40, 96–97
Lapin, Sergei, 72–73
Leninsky District, Grozny, Chechnya, 20, 40, 68, 76, 78, 95, 123, 129, 222, 236
Lenin State Library subway station, 165, 183
Lichtman, Laura, kidnapping of, 68
Linguistics University of Pyatigorsk, 186
living conditions (wartime), 220–27; poverty, 221, 225

looting, by Russian soldiers, xii, 47–50, 52–53, 55–56, 60, 198, 242

Lubyanka subway station (Moscow), terror attack at, 219

Luluyeva, Nura Said-Alviyevna, kidnapping and disappearance of, 198, 226

Luzhniki Stadium (Moscow), 150, 152

Magomedov, M. M., 61, 97

Magomadov, Ramzan and Malika, identify daughter as suicide bomber, 183

Magomedov brothers, Rizvan and Kharat, rape and dismember Elena Zemlyakova, 88

Magomedova, Khava, 198

Magomedova, Luiza, 12-year-old imprisoned at Chernokozovo, 85

Magomadova, Luiza, recruits Medi Musayeva for suicide mission, 204–5, 216

Magomadova, Madina, founds Mothers of Chechnya NGO, 254

Magomedova, Sara, 93

Magonov, Dmitry, tried for murder of Chechen civilians, 47, 60–61

Main Directorate of Operational Headquarters (MDOHQ) filtration center, 83

Makhachkala, Dagestan, 154, 159, 188, 218, 219

Makhauri, Kheda, 55

Makhmayeva, Kh., 98

Malgobek, Ingushetia, 15, 62–63

Malsogova, Zara, 32

Malsagova, Zulikhan, kidnapping and disappearance of, 209

Mamayeva, Keypa, witnesses wartime looting, 52

Mamitova, Larisa, 193

Mangeriyev, Ruslan, identifies daughter as suicide bomber, 183

marching mothers/pickets/demonstrations, 221, 239–49

marriage, 4, 7, 11–17, 69, 120, 145, 257–59, 270; djamaat-arranged, 149–51; to foreigners, 7, 21–26, 205, 259; polygamy 257–59, 270; of underage girls, 11–12

Martyrs' Brigade, 121, 122

Maskhadov, Aslan, xi, 28, 50, 74, 86, 107, 112, 115, 126, 143, 154, 157, 168, 171, 202, 231, 243–44, 259

Masyuk, Elena, kidnapping of, 69

Matayeva, Madina, 41

Maulatova, Tumisha, 42

Maulatova, Zarema, 42

McDonalds restaurants, terror threat against, 176–77, 180

Mdinaradze, Karen, 194

Medical Foundation for the Care of Victims of Torture, 54, 78, 85

Medov, Musa, attempted assassination of, 216–17

Medvedev, Dmitriy, 2, 79

Meier, Andrew, 58

Mekhidova, Lisa, recalls her wedding day, 13

Mekhkety, Chechnya, 41

Mekhstroy temporary refugee camp, Ingushetia, 138, 209

Melnikoff, Sergei, 120

men: behavior around women, 9; ratio to women, 257; role reversals with women, 266–71; traditional roles of, 226, 266–71; view of women, 4, 266–71

mental health, 150, 261; of children, 262–63

Meshcheryakova, Lena, kidnapping of, 68, 235

Mezhidova, Zalina, 61

Mezhiyev, Alikhan, 164–65

Migiyeva, Leila, looses left hand in bombing of Grozny market, 37

Mikahilov, Rezvan, 123

Mikhailov, Vladimir, 189

Mintsayeva, Yakha, kidnapped, 204

Mironov, Vyacheslav, 47

missing/disappeared people (Chechnya), 67, 69–72, 77–78, 86, 133, 198–204, 209, 240, 245–49, 252, 271

Mitrayeva, Madina Saidrakhmanovna, 207

Mizayeva, Ayshat, describes success as market trader, 227

Mollachiyev, Ilgar, 218

Molova, Taimaskha (Nadezhda Durova), 102–3

Moltenskoy, V., 49

Mon Kafé, 177–78

money: counterfeiting of, 125, 131; couriers of, 5, 125, 130–31; as personal motive for suicide terrorism, 139, 154, 156, 180, 215

Morozov, Aleksandr (Sasha), 22–23, 48

Morozova, Gulya, 22–23

Morozova, Kalimat, 22–23
Morozova, Yevgeniya, 21,
Moscow Directorate for Fighting Organized
    Crime Control (UBOP), 184
Moscow Times (newspaper), 16, 183
Moskovskaya pravda (newspaper), 109
Moskovsky Dvorets Molodyozhi (MDM)
    Theater, 158
Moskovsky komsomoletz (newspaper), 217
Mothers' March for Life and Compassion,
    240
mountain justice, Ramzan Kadyrov's version
    of, 5, 125–29
Movement Against Violence, 244
Mozdok, North Ossetia, 23, 39, 83; 2003 ter-
    ror attack in, 171, 179, 182; bus bomb-
    ing in, 217
Mozdok filtration center, 85, 240
Mudayeva, Khava, murdered for threatening
    to tell on cousin, 77–78
mujahideen, 46, 71, 105, 120, 128, 132, 150,
    171, 187, 226, 260
Mukadiyev, Rustam, suicide bomber kills
    policemen, 129
Murazaliyeva, Zara, convicted for recruitment
    of girls for suicide missions, 184–86
Murdalov, Aslan, 165
Murdalov, Astemir, 72
Murdalov, T.A., 59
Murdalov, Zelimkhan, 72
Murdalova, Rukiyat, 72
Murdalova, Zalina, 72
Murdashev, Vakhid, home burned, 126
murder: of pro-Moscow Chechen civil ser-
    vants, 89–90; of pro-Moscow Chechen
    policemen and families, 90; of Russian
    civilians and families, 46, 87–89
Musayeva, Liza Shitayevna, disappearance
    of, 199
Musayeva, Luiza Shitayevna, disappearance
    of, 199
Musayeva, Mayora, mutilated body of found,
    70
Musayeva, Medi (Medina), teenage suicide
    bomber triggers massive search, 204–5
Musayeva, Salmatu Shitayevna, disappear-
    ance of, 199
Muskeyeva, Mariyat, govt. official expresses
    positive view of bride stealing, 16
Muslim Society No. 3, 192

Mustafimova, Banata, receives Red Cross
    grant to buy sewing machines for new
    business, 229
Musuluyev, Zaur, 94
Mutakova, Khaldat, shot picking garlic in
    forest, 64
Mutakova, Zalpa, 64
Mutaliyeva, Pyatimat, falsely accused of being
    suicide bomber, 218
Mutayev family (Emina, Zara), killed in shell-
    ing of home, 37
Mutayeva, Luiza, disappearance of, 199–200
Mutayeva, Malizha, suspected suicide bomber
    disappears, 200
mutilation of bodies, 46, 47, 55, 87–89
Muzayeva, Imani, 35
Myagchiyeva, Shovda, jailed for forging real
    estate documents, 236

Nadterechny District, Chechnya, 93, 110,
    209; 2003 terror attack in, 169
Nagayeva, Amina, 190
Nagayeva, Bayan, 190
Nalchik, Kabardino-Balkaria, 68, 94; 2005
    terror attack on, 209
Nanayeva, Larisa, 41
narcotics/trafficking in, 52, 125, 214, 233;
    women's involvement in, 234–35
National Anti-Terror Committee (NAK),
    77, 209,
National Hotel (Moscow), 2003 terror attack
    at, 183
Naursky District, 71, 76, 83, 88, 156, 158,
    186, 263
Nazayeva, Khatimat, Russian soldier mur-
    ders, 98
Nazran (Ingushetia), 95, 151, 160, 178, 216,
    253; 2004 terror attack on, 121, 122
nerve gas attack, 93–95, 262
Nevesty Allakha (book), 143
Nevzorov, Aleksandr, 105
Nezavisimoye voyennoye obozreniye (newspa-
    per), 105
Nikiforova, Galina, convicted of child abuse,
    263
Nivat, Anne, x, 119–20, 213
non-government organizations (NGOs
    Chechnya): Beliy platok (NGO), 250;
    Center for Peace and Community
    Development, 252; Chechen Com-

mittee of National Salvation, 244, 254; Committee of Soldiers' Mothers of the Chechen Republic of Ichkeria, 250; Committee of Soldiers' Mothers of Russia, 106, 240, 253; Ekho Voiny (Echo of War), 213, 230, 244, 250–54; Koalitsiya, 249; Laman az, 249; Materinskaya trevoga (Mothers' alarm), 249; Mothers of Chechnya, 250, 254–55; Mothers of Chechnya for Peace Association (NGO), 250; Mothers' Pain (NGO), 250; Office of the Information Center of the Union of Non-Governmental Organizations, 269; Optimum, 248; Pravozhhchita, 248; Reliance (NGO), xi, 230, 264, 271; Search for the Missing, 248; Women's Dialog, 247; Women's Dignity, 230, 250, 264, 266; Women's Union of the North Caucasus (WUNC), 250, 252–53

Nord Ost: the book, 148; the play, 136

Novaya gazeta (newspaper), 202, 222, 270

Novikova, Masha, describes her wedding, 13

Noviy-Benoi, Chechnya, 96

Noviye Aldy, Chechnya, 53; cleansing operations in, 56–59, 213

Noviye Atagi, Chechnya, 70, 119, 123; murder of ICRC nurses in, 92

Novogrozny, Chechnya, 29, 30, 126

Nozhai-Yurtovsky District, Chechnya, 74, 89–90, 96, 128, 259

Nukayeva, Bela, 265

Nukhazhiyev, Nurdi, 20, 44, 94–95

Nutayev, Khusein, 94, 95

Observer Mission of Human Rights and Public Organizations in the Conflict Zone in Chechnya, 50, 52

Obshchaya Gazeta (newspaper), 69

Office of the Information Center of the Union of Non-Governmental Organizations, 269

Okhotny Ryad Shopping Center (Moscow), plot to attack, 185

Oktyabrsky District, Grozny, Chechnya, 39, 41, 70–72, 86, 109, 146–47, 204, 209, 248

Open Society Institute, 230, 264

Operation Fatima, 201–2

Operation Whirlwind, 168

Operational Investigations Bureau 2 (ORB–2), 73–74

Orbakaite, Kristina, 26

Organization for Security and Cooperation in Europe (OSCE), 230, 231, 245

Orlov, Oleg, 80, 81, 213

Osama bin Laden, financial contributions to Chechen Jihad, 210

OSCE International Commission on Missing People, 254

Ozdoyeva, Milana, detention and disappearance of suspected suicide bomber, 197, 203

Paiduyev, Rizvan, robs and rapes a 70-year-old woman, 98

Pankisi Gorge, Georgia, 199–200

Park Kulturiy subway station (Moscow), terror attack at, 219

Pashayeva, Maret, killed by grenade thrown into basement, 53

passport regime checks, 62

Patrushev, Nikolay, 77

Paveletskaya Metro (subway) station, 178

Perelevsky, Alexey, orders murder of Chechen civilians, 63

Pervomaiskoye, Chechnya, 89, 112–14, 133, 209, 249

Peterovna, Larisa, 88

Pikalyeva, L.I., 87

Pikalyeva, Z.A., 87

poisoning of school children in Shelkovsky District, 93–95, 262

police collaboration with jihadists, 76

Politovskaya, Anna, x, 2, 28, 59, 80, 167, 213, 223, 247

Popova, Tatyana, former hostage comments on Dubrovka terrorists, 147, 162

post traumatic stress disorder (PTSD), 220, 261–62, 264

Presidential Palace (Grozny), Russian bombing of, 115

Presidentsky kanal television, 114

Prochazkova, Petra, 21, 221

Prokhladny Air Force Base (North Ossetia), 171

Promedol, abuse Russian soldiers, 52

prosecution of Russian soldiers for crimes, 49, 50, 55, 61–63, 72, 75–76, 97–98

prostitution, 145, 222, 270
pseudo asthmatic syndrome, 94
psychological effects of terrorism, 211–12
psychological impact of war, 45, 95–96, 225, 226
psychological intimidation of population, 197
Pukhayeva, Zarina, survives Beslan school attack, 124
Putin, Vladimir, ix, 62, 154, 168, 212, 243
Pyatigorsk, Russia, bombing of train station in, 139

Radio Ekho Moskvy, 194
Radio Free Europe/Radio Liberty, xi, 80, 121, 214
Radon radioactive waste dump, 264
Raduyev, Said-Emi, jailed for bride stealing, 15
Raduyev, Salman, 102, 143, 111–14, 138
rape, 8, 17, 27, 51–54, 57–58, 61–62, 69, 73, 78, 85–86, 88, 91, 100, 106–7, 115, 142, 145, 172, 211, 212–15, 234, 253
Rashidov, Oleg, 189
Raspopova, I.M., murdered and body dismembered, 87
real estate fraud, 235–36
Rechkalov, Vadim, 155, 176–77, 179
refugees, 39, 40, 222–25, 262
Rezanova, V.N., disappearance of and apartment stolen, 87
Riyadus-Salikhin [Fields of Righteousness] Reconnaissance and Sabotage Battalion of Shakhids, 136, 157, 196, 210, 214, 216, 218
Rizhskaya Metro (subway) station (Moscow), 2004 terror attack on, 191–93
Rodnaya semya orphanage (Grozny), 231
Romashchenko, Anna, recalls Raduyev burning her policeman son in furnace, 112
Roshal, Leonid, 95
Rossiiskaya Gazeta (newspaper), 189
Rostovskaya Oblast, Russia, 21, 149–50, 189–90, 204–5
Rudolf Steiner school, 232
Russia Profile magazine, 5, 146, 209
Russian-Chechen Friendship Society, 98, 244
Russian Hell in the Year 2000 (film), 142

Saayev, Igor (alias Ruslan), 178, 180
Saayev, Sultan, 117

Saburayeva, Markha, kidnapping and disappearance of, 77
Sadayeva, Zula, 32
Sadullayeva, Abdulkhalima, delivers Basayev marriage proposal, 258
Sadullayeva, Khalimat, suspected of becoming a suicide bomber, 206
Sadulayeva, Satsita, 224
Sadulayeva, Taus, murder of, 99
Sadulayeva, Zarema, kidnapping and murder of, 82, 83
safe houses, 5, 125, 133–34
Said S———, x, 9, 11, 102, 111, 258, 260–61
Saidlayeva, Aishat, FSB questions as suicide bomber suspect, 202
Saidova, Sakinat, 218–19
Saidulayeva, Silva, Barayev's wife comments on Khava Barayeva, 141
Saidullayev, Khaji, 91, 128
Saidullayeva, Irina, held in illegal prison, 206–7
Saidullayeva, Taus, Wolves murder and torch her home, 91
Saigatova, Koka, shot for refusing to sell vodka, 97
Sakayeva, Gistam, xi, 229, 230, 262, 264, 267, 271
Samashki, Chechnya, 29, 31–32, 40, 50–52, 14, 158, 236, 240, 253
Samashki massacre, 1995 (women killed or wounded during bombardment and cleansing of): Akhmadova, Abi, 51; Akuyeva, Nurbika, 51; Alisultanova, Tamusa, 32; Aliyeva, Malika, 32, 51; Aliyeva, Petimat, 51; Amayeva, Raziat, 51; Atsayeva, Dagman, 52; Babayeva, Kulai, 32; Beksultanova, Yanist 52; Dazibayeva, Kalisa, 52; Gaitukayeva, Bata, 51; Gunashyeva, Khava, 51; Labazanova, Patimat, 32; Lyurmagomedova, Sanipat, 31, 51; Lyurmagomedova, Serizha, 51; Musayeva, Dzeki, 51; Masayeva, Raisa, 51; Musikhanova, Kulsum, 31, 51; Nosipova, Tamara Mugdanova, 31; Rasuyeva, Bata, 51; Rasuyeva, Kesirt, 51; Shuipova, Dagman, 52; Yamirzayeva, Zaluba, 51; Yurmagometova, Saripa, 31; Yurmagometova, Sarizha, 31; Zakiyeva, Aminat, 52; Zubairayeva, Louisa, 51

Satayeva, Aizan Abdulsalamovna, militant
  execution of, 89
Satterwhite, Jim, 65
Satuyeva, Khadichat, *Kadyrovtsky* kidnaps, 75
Saurin, Denis, 107, 108
Save the Generation (NGO), 82
Seierstad, Asne, x, 32, 261
Serbesky Psychiatric Institute, 94, 262
Sergen-Yurt, Chechnya, 42, 43, 44, 117
Sernovodsk, Chechnya, 207–8, 245, 247
Serzhen-Yurt, 63, 64, 259
Shabalkin, Ilya, 50, 133, 155–56
Shagayev, Aslambek, policeman jailed for
  wife's suicide, 261
Shaipova, Ruslana, mutilated body of found,
  70
Shakhazov, Eduard, 45
shakhid/shakhida, 65, 75, 140, 155, 161–65,
  169–70, 173–77, 182–87, 194–95, 198–
  209, 212–17, 219, 226. *See also* Black
  Widows, suicide bomber
Shakhguiriyeva, Masani, shot for refusing to
  give soldier vodka, 97
Shakhmurzayeva, Anzhela, 66, 245
Shakhtamirova, Zaira, 63
Shalbakin, Ilya, 51, 155–56
Shali, Chechnya, 30, 31, 41, 205, 247
Shalinsky District, Chechnya, 43, 48, 90, 101,
  135, 200, 223
Shamanov, Vladimir, 53, 107
Shankhullayeva, B. Kh., killed by Russian sol-
  diers robbing her house, 97
Shapirova, Elza, 9
Shatoi, Chechnya, 34, 40, 62, 121
Shatoisky District, Chechnya, 32, 39, 42, 44,
  128, 201
Sheikhulayev, Omar, 218
Shelchenko, Elena, 94
Shelkovsky District, Chechnya, 20, 22, 77,
  94, 98, 101, 135; poisoning of children
  in, 94–96, 262
Sheremetova airport (Moscow), 188
Shibekkhanov, Mairbek, 194
Shikhabov, Salambek, jailed for bride steal-
  ing, 15
Shkuratova, Mariya Grigoryevna, 30
Siber Airlines, 187–89
Sidgaliyeva, Aina, caught couriering money
  for fighters, 130
Sinyayeva, S.T., 87

Skoryatina, Elena, 107–8
Society of Russian-Chechen Friendship, 254
Soltukhanova, Markha, kidnapping and disappearance of, 70
Soslambekova, Aminat, 204
spetz-operations, 62–66, 76, 79, 81, 156, 160,
  198, 208, 218
spies, 87, 89, 119. *See also* intelligence
  collection
Stariye Aldy, Chechnya, 158
Stariye Atagi, Chechnya, 19, 37, 43, 65, 70,
  123, 199, 244–45
Staropromyslovsky District, Chechnya, 37,
  52, 55–56, 74, 100, 129, 132, 202, 208
Staroshchedrinskaya, Chechnya, 77; nerve gas
  attack at school in, 93
State Duma, 81, 126, 183–84, 206
sterilization of Chechen girls, 95
Steshin, Dmitriy, 190
Stolypin wagons (filtration point), 83
street market traders, 132, 187–91, 226–28
Studies Without Borders (journalism) program (Paris), 257
Studner, Peter, 180
suicide (not terrorism), 17, 99, 103, 208, 212,
  220, 259, 261–62
suicide belt, 75, 136, 163, 165, 180–81, 189,
  193, 195, 208, 218–19
suicide bomber, 4, 5, 9, 11, 17, 21, 46, 65, 70,
  75–79, 83, 91–93, 128, 133, 140–46,
  155, 166, 169–74, 184, 186, 191, 201–2,
  205, 208, 210–12, 216–17, 226, 242;
  pay of, 236; profile of, 201, 203, 213–
  16; training of, 140, 172, 184, 198, 202,
  205–8, 259. *See also shakhid/shakhidas*
suicide terrorism: personal motives for,
  137–42, 160–61, 180–81, 209, 212–16;
  spontaneous acts of, 213; as war fighting
  tactic, 210–12
Sukhanov, Alexei, tried for murder of
  Chechen civilians, 60–61
Suleimanova, Aishat, shot for refusing to give
  Russian soldiers beer, 98
Suleimanova, Aset, 42
Suleimanova, Malkan, killed during bombardment of Shatoi, 33
Suleimanova, Zareta, loses eye and part of
  skull in missile strike on her house, 43
Sultygov, Abdul, 256, 268
Sunzhensky District, Chechnya, 76, 95, 129

Surguyev, Isa, 73–74
Swiss Fund for Defense of Freedom and
   Human Rights, 250

Tagireyeva, Zinaida, 223
Taimashkhanova, Lida, found shot and
   stabbed with son in home, 54
Takayev, Apti, 215
Talalayeva, N.D., 97–98
Tamarova, Aizan, discusses plight of single
   women, 257
Tarintsyeva, V.I., 87
Tatashyeva, A. Sh., 99
Tatayeva, Yakhta, jailed for child abuse, 263
Tazabayev, Kh., 206
Techiyev, Uvais, 123
teipes, 9, 25, 156
Temirsultanova, Deti, 53
Temirsultanova, Eliza, interned in Chernoko-
   zovo filtration center, 85
Temirsultanova, Malika, recounts attack on
   refugee convoy, 31
Temirsultanova, Sordat, 53
Temirsultanova, Thaus, 34
Tepsurkayeva, Dagman, 37
Terloeva, Milana (Milana Bakaeva), xi, 221,
   226, 257, 266–68
Terror in Moscow (film), 163
Three Comrades (documentary film), 13, 16
Timirsultanova, Eliza, imprisoned in Cherno-
   kozovo filter, 84–85
Tkachyev, Igor, 113, 120
Tlisova, Fatima, comments on Estimorova's
   murder, 2
Tolshyeva, Zula, 41
Tolstopaltsyevo, Russia, 178, 180
Tolstoy-Yurt, Chechnya, 70, 264
Tonkonogova, Larisa Pavlovna, 41
Topol, Eduard, 137
Topol, Sergei, 109
Torshin, Aleksandr, xi, 4, 78, 194
Torchin, Kazik, 193
torture, 18, 67, 73–74, 78, 84–86, 212, 220,
   233, 249, 252
training/training camps for terrorists, 117–18,
   140, 172, 184, 198
Trampe, Tamara, 121
truck and car bombings, 92–93, 140–42, 166–
   69, 172, 197, 181–82, 207, 216–19
Tsagarayev, Magomed, 74, 142, 200

Tsagarayeva, Seda, executed by means of
   explosives, 74
Tskayeva, Fatima, 195
Tsuyev, Yusha, 90
Tumriyev, Gelani, 166–68
Tumriyeva, Alina, 166–68
Tumriyeva, Raisa Abdulkadyrovna, identified
   as possible suicide bomber, 217–18
Tunayeva, A., murdered by Russian service-
   man, 61, 97
Turchayev, Yunadi, commands Grozny *muja-
   hideen*, 132, 206
Turlayeva, Leila, *Kadyrovtsky* burn home of,
   126
Turlayeva, Mandat, *Kadyrovtsky* burn home
   of, 126
Turpulkhanov, Wakhid, 117
Tushino airfield, Moscow, 2003 terror attack
   at, 173–76, 178–79, 184
Tutayeva, Yakhta, court convicts for child
   abuse, 263

Udogov, Movladi, 141–42, 210
Ugurchiyeva, Yakha, 46, sells arms in Gro-
   zny, 226
Ulman, Eduard, murders Chechen civilians,
   62–63
Umakhanova, Petimat, 224
Umalatov, Umalat, 52, 85
Umarkhayeva, Zara, killed when shell landed
   on roof of yard shed, 38
Umarov, Doka, 75–76, 134, 218–19, 259
Umarov, Ilyas, 17
Umarova, Khazman (Raisa), 113, 114
Umazhayeva, Malika, district administrator
   executed, 90
UNICEF, 69, 70, 96, 224, 262, 264
United Nations Commission on Human
   Rights, 251,
United Nations High Commissioner for Ref-
   ugees (UNHCR), 223
Urus-Martan, Chechnya, 63, 74, 84, 85,
   95–96, 130, 142, 143, 200
Urus-Martanovsky District, 42, 44, 54, 64,
   95–96, 143, 152, 200, 204
Uspanova, Aset Mustapayevna, 41
Uzdinov, Khapani, 208
Uzumkhadzhiyeva, Tamara, 151
Uzuyeva, Zura, 41

Vachagayev, Mairbek, 115
Vazayeva, Asiyat, 15
Vecherny Chelyabinsk (newspaper), 124
Vedensky District, Chechnya, 35, 40, 43, 44,
    76, 86, 89, 127, 129–30, 134–35, 151,
    188, 190, 202, 246, 258
Verbitsky, Aleksandr, 54–55
Verne, Jules, 257
Vladkino subway station (Moscow), 118
Vnukovo Airport, Moscow, 178
Volgo-Aviaexpress airlines, 187, 189
Volodina, Maria, 167
Voronova, Darya (Dasha), attempted recruit-
    ment for suicide bombing, 185–86
Vorozhdeniye (newspaper), 29, 69
Vremya novostei (newspaper), 43

Wahhabi/Wahhabism, 4, 10, 19, 49, 91, 110,
    117, 125, 130, 140–42, 143, 146–55,
    158–59, 167–69, 186, 191, 192, 201,
    203–5, 215–16, 245, 270
wartime casualty statistics, 27, 31
wedding (traditional), 14, 257, 267–68
White Ravens: Nightmare in Chechnya, (film),
    121
Women: character and survival instincts of,
    220–39; as family providers, 220–39;
    266–67, 270–71; hiding Russian sol-
    diers, 88–89; involvement in kid-
    napping of children, 69, 235; in
    noncombatant roles, 5, 46, 119, 125–35,
    236; in prisons, 235, 237; role in rescu-
    ing Chechen men, 66, 239; traditional
    roles of, 4–20, 25–26, 267–71
Women for Peace and Stability in the
    Chechen Republic conference, 247
Women of the Don Region Union NGO, 71,
    220, 254, 259, 268
Women's Commission for Refugee Women
    and Children, 230
women's movement, 230, 239–55
women's rights, xi, 4, 266–71
work skills training, 228–30, 263
World Food Program, 224–25, 229
World Health Organization, 262, 264
www.amina.com, 113, 114,
www.Kavkazcenter.com, ix, 182, 210
www.Kavkaz.memo.ru, 83
www.KavkazWeb.net, xi

www.MVDinform.ru, 123
www.NEWSru.com, 164, 194
www.retwa.com, ix
www.ruscourier.ru, 25

Yakyayev, A., 30, 59, 60
Yamadayev, Baudi, 98
Yamadayev, Sulim, 98
Yandarbiyev, Zelimkhan, 105
Yandarova, Malika, shot and killed by stray
    bullet while playing, 99
Yangiyeva, Mariam, helps organize women's
    movement, 230, 252, 253
Yangulbayeva, Madina, *mujahideen* carjack
    vehicle, 64
Yedelyev, Arkadiy, 72, 76
Yefimova, Nina, kidnapping and execution
    of, 69
Yegorov, Aleksandr, 54–55
Yegorov, Aleksei, 192
Yelbuzdukayev, Uvais, 37
Yelistanzhi, Chechnya (women killed in the
    7 October 1999 missile strike on): Art-
    suyeva, Shamsa, 35; Artsuyeva, Taisa,
    35; Durdisva, Zina, 35; Gabayeva,
    Madina, 35, Gekhayeva, Khizhan, 35;
    Gekhayeva, Yepsa, 35; Mukhmadova,
    Malkan, 35; Peterova, Satsita, 35;
    Saitova, Aset, 35
Yelki-Palki restaurant, Moscow, 176
Yeltsin, Boris, 17, 37, 254
Yeltsova, A.V., Russian soldier accidentally
    shoots, 97
Yeshilkhatoi, Chechnya, 134
Yesilayev, Vakha, 94
Yesmurzayeva, Elza (Aizan), fortune teller
    executed by *mujahideen*, 91
Yessentuki, 2003 train bombing in, 182, 184,
    203
Yevkurov, Yunus-Bek, attempted assassina-
    tion of, 218
Yevseyev, Mikhail, 197, 203
Yokhina, Valintina, 69
Yukayeva, Rima, 228
Yukhinov, Apti, 62
Yunusova, Madina: abduction and murder of,
    79; home of burned, 129
Yusupov, Khasan, 43
Yusopov, Yakha, 43

Yusopova, Aimani, 43
Yusopova, Elina, wounded in bombardment
    of Stariye-Atagi, 44
Yusupova, Kamila, 43
Yusupova, Kheida, 40
Yusopova, Lida, 201
Yuzik, Yulia, x, 143–45, 148–50, 154–55,
    157–58, 160

zachistka (cleansing operations), 45–60, 66,
    151, 176, 198, 213, 239, 241–44, 245,
    251
Zahigova, Kheda, comments on danger of
    "safety corridors," 30

Zakayev, Akhmed, 164, 212
Zakriyeva, Berlant, killed by suicide bomber
    while out for a walk, 93
Zaurbekova, Zura, opens sewing shop, 229
Zavodsky District, Chechnya, 56, 59, 71, 83,
    98–99, 170, 219, 237, 242, 248
Zemlyakova, Elena, criminals rape and dis-
    member body of, 88
Znamenskoye, Chechnya, 89, 93, 169, 171–
    72, 206
Zubayev family (Alina, Larisa, Luiza Malika,
    Mariat, Ruslan, Said-Magomet Zeinap),
    found shot and bodies burned in family
    home, 56

About the Author

Professor Paul J. Murphy, PhD, is a former U.S. senior counter-terrorism official who lived, worked, and traveled extensively in Russia and Central Asia between 1994 and 2004. He studied in the former Soviet Union; has taught at universities in the United States, Australia, and Russia; and appears as a commentator on American, Australian, and Russian television and radio programs. He is currently director of the Russia-Eurasia Terror Watch (www.retwa.org) and teaches politics.

The **Naval Institute Press** is the book-publishing arm of the U.S. Naval Institute, a private, nonprofit, membership society for sea service professionals and others who share an interest in naval and maritime affairs. Established in 1873 at the U.S. Naval Academy in Annapolis, Maryland, where its offices remain today, the Naval Institute has members worldwide.

Members of the Naval Institute support the education programs of the society and receive the influential monthly magazine *Proceedings* or the colorful bimonthly magazine *Naval History* and discounts on fine nautical prints and on ship and aircraft photos. They also have access to the transcripts of the Institute's Oral History Program and get discounted admission to any of the Institute-sponsored seminars offered around the country.

The Naval Institute's book-publishing program, begun in 1898 with basic guides to naval practices, has broadened its scope to include books of more general interest. Now the Naval Institute Press publishes about seventy titles each year, ranging from how-to books on boating and navigation to battle histories, biographies, ship and aircraft guides, and novels. Institute members receive significant discounts on the Press's more than eight hundred books in print.

Full-time students are eligible for special half-price membership rates. Life memberships are also available.

For a free catalog describing Naval Institute Press books currently available, and for further information about joining the U.S. Naval Institute, please write to:

Member Services
U.S. Naval Institute
291 Wood Road
Annapolis, MD 21402-5034
Telephone: (800) 233-8764
Fax: (410) 571-1703
Web address: www.usni.org